AF412120

Third Way Reforms

Social Democracy after the Golden Age

This book examines the transformation of contemporary social democracy through the concept of "third way" reforms. It proposes a set of theories about the possibility for continuing social democratic ideological adaptation, for ideologies to overcome institutional constraints in triggering pathbreaking innovations, and for social democracy to bridge the insider–outsider divide. Empirically, the book utilizes these theories to account for social democratic welfare state and labor market reforms in nine advanced industrialized countries after the end of the Golden Age.

Based on the logic of "public evils," the book proposes that the ideologically contested nature of institutions provides incentives for institutional innovation. Social democratic ideology shapes the fundamental characteristics and content of the third way policy paradigm, and the paradigm's practical implementation continues to be path dependent on historical institutional settings.

Jingjing Huo earned his Ph.D. from the University of North Carolina at Chapel Hill and currently teaches at the University of Waterloo in Ontario, Canada. His primary research interest is comparative political economy and institutions, and his work appears in *Comparative Political Studies*, the *Canadian Journal of Political Science*, and the *Journal of European Social Policy*.

Third Way Reforms

Social Democracy after the Golden Age

JINGJING HUO
University of Waterloo

CAMBRIDGE UNIVERSITY PRESS
Cambridge, New York, Melbourne, Madrid, Cape Town, Singapore, São Paulo, Delhi

Cambridge University Press
32 Avenue of the Americas, New York, NY 10013–2473, USA

www.cambridge.org
Information on this title: www.cambridge.org/9780521518437

First published 2009

Printed in the United States of America

A catalog record for this publication is available from the British Library.

Library of Congress Cataloging in Publication data
Huo, Jingjing, 1977–
    Third way reforms : social democratic welfare states after the golden age /
    Jingjing Huo.
        p.   cm.
    Includes bibliographical references and index.
    ISBN 978-0-521-51843-7 (hardback)
    1. Welfare state – OECD countries.   2. Labor policy – OECD countries.
    3. OECD countries – Social policy.   4. Socialism.   I. Title.
HN16.H86 2009
330.12′6–dc22   2008037007

ISBN 978-0-521-51843-7 hardback

To Helen

Contents

Tables and Figures   *page* ix
Acknowledgments   xv

1   Introduction   1

2   Theorizing the Third Way   7
    1. A Theory of Third Way Ideology   7
    2. A Theory of Positive Externalities of Organization   21
    3. A Theory of Institutional Innovation   26
    4. The Methodology of the Book   49

3   Constraints on Action: Institutions and Ideas   51
    1. Institutional Settings for Third Way Reforms   51
    2. The Ideological Basis for Third Way Reforms   65

4   Prelude to the Third Way: The Unemployment Problem
    and Earlier Responses   84

5   Expansion in Active Protection   101
    1. Active Labor Market Policies   102
    2. In-Work Incentives   155
    3. Flexicurity   175
    4. Analysis of Active Protection   191

6   Restructuring Passive Protection   198
    1. Reactionary Compensation   199
    2. Anticipatory Compensation   243
    3. Analysis of Passive Protection   264

7   Economic and Corporatist Contexts for the Third Way   268

8   Conclusion: Theories of Possibilities   314

References   324
Index   351

Tables and Figures

TABLES

2.1 Three Ways to Social Justice   *page* 21
2.2 Organizational Integration of Women and the
      Unemployed 1998/2002   26
2.3 Rival Hypotheses on Third Way Reforms   47
2.4 Power Shifts Between Left and Right   49
3.1 Key Features of Institutional Background   52
3.2 Key Features of Third Way Ideological Transformation   66
4.1 Key Developments in the Economy Before Third
      Way Reforms   87
5.1 Key ALMP Developments   104
5.2 Key In-Work Incentive Developments   156
5.3 Key Flexicurity Developments   177
5.4 Prais-Winsten Estimates of ALMP Expenditure,
      Employment Protection, and Social Security/Payroll Taxes   196
6.1 Key Reforms in Reactionary Income Compensation   201
6.2 Key Reforms in Anticipatory Income Compensation   245
7.1 Key Developments in Economic and Corporatist Contexts   271

FIGURES

2.1 The Third Way Policy Paradigm   42
4.1 Standardized Unemployment Rate in Nine Countries
      1960–1995   85

4.2 Unemployment of One Year and Over as Percentage of Total
Unemployment in Low-Level Countries 1984–1994   85

4.3 Unemployment of One Year and Over as Percentage
of Total Unemployment in High-Level Countries
1984–1994   86

5.1 Overall Organization for Chapter 5   102

5.2 Expenditure on Labor Market Training as Percentage of
GDP in Denmark 1982–2003   107

5.3 Expenditure on Training for the Disabled as Percentage
of GDP in Denmark 1982–2003   109

5.4 Unemployment with Duration of One Year and
Over as Percentage of All Unemployed in Denmark
1990–2004   110

5.5 Relationship Between Unemployment and Inflation
in Denmark 1982–2004   111

5.6 Active Labor Market Expenditure in Sweden as
Percentage of GDP 1982–1994   114

5.7 Labor Market Training Expenditure as Percentage of
GDP in Sweden 1991–2003   115

5.8 Unemployment with Duration of One Year and Over as
Percentage of All Unemployed in Sweden 1991–2004   116

5.9 Labor Market Training Expenditure as Percentage of
GDP in Norway 1990–2003   119

5.10 Labor Market Measures for the Young as Percentage of
GDP in Norway 1990–2003   120

5.11 Relationship Between Unemployment and Active Labor
Market Spending in Norway 1986–2003   122

5.12 Active Labor Market Expenditure as Percentage of
GDP in the Netherlands 1980–2002   124

5.13 Labor Market Measures for the Young as Percentage of
GDP in the Netherlands 1980–1999   125

5.14 Unemployment with Duration of One Year and
Over as Percentage of All Unemployed in the Netherlands
1983–2004   126

5.15 Labor Market Measures for the Young as Percentage of
GDP in France 1990–2003   130

5.16 Active Labor Market Expenditure as Percentage of
GDP in France 1990–2002   132

5.17 Total Unemployment and the Share of Long-Term
Unemployment in France 1990–2002   132

5.18   Training and Youth Employment Programs Expenditure
       as Percentage of GDP in Germany 1993–2003   135
5.19   Total Active Labor Market Measures as Percentage of
       GDP in Germany 1993–2003   138
5.20   Total Unemployment and the Share of Long-Term
       Unemployment in Germany 1993–2003   140
5.21   Labor Market Programs (Total and for Youths) as
       Percentage of GDP in the UK 1993–2003   140
5.22   Total Unemployment and the Share of Long-Term
       Unemployment in the UK 1994–2004   142
5.23   Labor Market Training as Percentage of GDP in the
       UK, France, and Germany 1993–2003   144
5.24   Labor Market Programs (Total and Training) as
       Percentage of GDP in Australia 1985–2003   146
5.25   Total Unemployment and the Share of Long-Term
       Unemployment in Australia 1990–2000   148
5.26   Employment Subsidies as Percentage of GDP, Australia
       and Scandinavia Compared 1990–2003   149
5.27   Active Labor Market Expenditure as Percentage of
       GDP in New Zealand 1985–2003   151
5.28   Tax Wedge for Average Production Worker (APW) in the
       Netherlands 1981–2004   157
5.29   Total Weeks of Parental and Child-Care Leave Schemes
       in the Netherlands 1980–1999   159
5.30   Tax Wedge for Average Production Worker (APW) in
       Germany 1979–2004   161
5.31   Public Transfers on Assisting Families with Children as
       Percentage of GDP in Germany 1996–2003   162
5.32   Labor Force Participation for Females 15–24 Years of
       Age in Germany 1983–2003   164
5.33   In-Cash and In-Kind Incentives for Work in the
       UK 1993–2003   166
5.34   Public Expenditure on Parental Leave as Percentage of
       GDP in the UK 1993–2003   167
5.35   In-Cash and In-Kind Incentives for Work in
       Australia 1980–1996   170
5.36   Unemployment Rate for Females 15–24 Years of Age in
       Australia 1980–1996   171
5.37   Part-Time Employment as Percentage of Total
       Employment in the Netherlands 1983–2003   181

5.38 Protection for Regular Employment in France
1985–2003   184

5.39 Employment Protection in Germany 1985–2004   185

6.1 Overall Organization for Chapter 6   199

6.2 Unemployment Benefits Replacement Rate and
Duration in Denmark 1980–2002   202

6.3 Employment Service Expenditure as Percentage of
GDP in Denmark 1983–2003   205

6.4 Change in Unemployment Rate and Replacement in
Sweden 1991–2001   208

6.5 Passive and Active Benefits in Sweden 1991–2002   211

6.6 Passive and Active Benefits in Norway 1990–2000   214

6.7 Passive Benefits Replacement Rates in the Netherlands
1980–2002   219

6.8 Unemployment Benefit Duration and Qualifying
Conditions in the Netherlands 1980–2002   219

6.9 Passive Benefits Replacement Rates in France 1988–2002   221

6.10 Active Labor Market Expenditure as Percentage of
GDP in France 1988–2002   221

6.11 Percentage of Labor Force Covered by Unemployment
Insurance 1982–2002   227

6.12 Unemployment and Sickness Insurance in Germany
1992–2002   229

6.13 Poverty (50% Median) Rates in the UK 1979–1999   230

6.14 Social Expenditure as Percentage of GDP under the ALP   232

6.15 Poverty (50% Median) Rates in Australia 1981–2001   232

6.16 Unemployment Benefit Replacement Rate in
Australia 1982–2002   234

6.17 Passive Benefits Replacement Rates in New Zealand
1980–2002   236

6.18 Total Social Expenditure as Percentage of GDP in
New Zealand 1980–1998   237

6.19 Share of Total Unemployment for 60–64 Years of Age
in Denmark 1983–2001   249

6.20 Expenditure on Employment Measures for the Disabled as
Percentage of GDP in Norway 1990–2003   252

6.21 Sickness Insurance Replacement Rate in the
Netherlands 1980–2002   253

6.22 Employment Measures for the Disabled as Percentage
of GDP in the Netherlands 1980–2002   255

6.23 Share of Total Employment for 60–64 Years of Age
in the Netherlands 1980–2002   258

6.24 Share of Total Unemployment for 60–64 Years of Age
in France and Germany 1990–2002   260

7.1 Budget Balance and Inflation in Denmark 1988–2001   272

7.2 Wage Coordination and Wage Moderation in Denmark
1982–2000   275

7.3 Budget Balance and Inflation in Sweden 1990–2001   277

7.4 Wage Coordination and Wage Moderation in Sweden
1980–2000   279

7.5 Wage Coordination and Wage Moderation in Norway
1982–2000   282

7.6 Budget Balance and Inflation in the Netherlands
1980–2001   284

7.7 Wage Coordination and Wage Moderation in the
Netherlands 1980–2001   285

7.8 Budget Balance and Inflation in France 1980–2001   289

7.9 Kenworthy's Wage Coordination Score, France in
Comparison 1980–2001   292

7.10 Inflation in Germany and the EU Compared 1994–2004   294

7.11 Wage Moderation in Germany and the EU Compared
1994–2004   294

7.12 Budget Balance and Inflation in the UK 1991–2001   297

7.13 Total Social Expenditure as Percentage of GDP in the UK
1991–2003   299

7.14 Effective Tax Rate on the Average Production Worker
(APW) in the UK 1993–2004   299

7.15 Wage Coordination and Wage Moderation in Australia
1980–2000   303

7.16 Effective Tax Rate on the Average Production Worker
(APW) in New Zealand 1994–2004   304

7.17 Wage Coordination and Wage Moderation in New Zealand
1980–2003   307

Acknowledgments

The origin of this book was a Ph.D. dissertation on labor market and welfare state reforms completed in 2005 at the Department of Political Science, University of North Carolina at Chapel Hill. My appreciation goes first and foremost to my mentor John D. Stephens. John opened my eyes to the possibilities in developing theories from third way reforms. From separate dissertation chapters to the final version of the book, he has read the entire manuscript word by word numerous times. He spent hours going through each chapter with me, called up country experts to discuss my treatment of cases, and offered me kind encouragement at moments when my confidence in the project fluctuated. It is a great privilege to have him as my mentor. His deep knowledge, disciplined approach, and total devotion to his students made the book possible. Similarly, I would like to thank the other members of my committee: Evelyne Huber, Liesbet Hooghe, Gary Marks, and Donald Searing. The book covers a relatively large set of themes, theories, and cases. The deep insight of these scholars combined to offset my own seriously limited abilities to traverse across and make sense of these highly dispersed topics. Even more importantly, just like John, they were always eager to find for me reasons for optimism and confidence as I struggled with the project. My gratitude also goes to Herbert Kitschelt and John Myles, who carefully reviewed parts of the manuscript, respectively, in its dissertation and final book stage. I would also like to thank Moira Nelson at Bremen International Graduate School of Social Sciences for her help in our joint econometric analysis (together with John D. Stephens), which appears in this book.

In total, three readers for Cambridge University Press left me with fifteen pages of dense, sharp, and thought-provoking comments. Their vision of theoretical innovation opened up possibilities for improving the book that I could not have imagined on my own. Just as I felt my own efforts at generating a theory were running into diminishing returns, the three readers pushed my productivity frontier further outward and helped me build newer theories.

In between the original dissertation and the book, the project has undergone a total transformation. Most of this work in revision was completed while at the Department of Political Science, University of Waterloo in Canada. I would like to thank my colleagues in the department who not only provided an encouraging and friendly research environment but also offered generous help and suggestions whenever I needed them. At Cambridge University Press, I would like to thank Eric Crahan, who oversaw the project's progress through its various phases with patience and generous encouragement. I would also like to thank Ernie Haim, Emily Spangler, and the painstaking and meticulous copyediting work of Phyllis Berk.

Finally, I would like to thank my wife Helen Hui Feng. For seven years Helen had to endure extended geographical separation as we studied and then worked in different countries on the diametrical opposites of the North American continent. Helen's tenderness and perseverance turn big difficulties into small ones and transform brief moments of joy into long-lasting memories. This book is an appreciation of the endless possibilities of life Helen has brought me.

I

Introduction

Since the start of the New Labor government under Tony Blair, the phrase "third way" has come to symbolize the transformation of contemporary social democracy. The Blair revolution played an indispensable role in stimulating today's third way literature. Chronologically, it ushered in a new era in comparative research: No third way studies predated New Labour. Cross-sectionally, its impact reached many countries. The only two social democratic governments openly self-identifying as the "third way" were the Tony Blair and Gerhard Schröder administrations, but this notion has been utilized to evaluate center-left reforms across the industrialized world. This situation, however, creates some analytic dilemma. If the concept only describes governments that are Blair's contemporaries, the analysis suffers from post hoc theorization. What caused such a qualitative change in contemporary social democracy since 1997? After all, the timing of New Labour's rise was arbitrary. If the concept is extended backwards to describe center-left reforms well before New Labour, then does it really imply anything distinctly new? There had long existed a rich literature on social democratic transformation (Stephens 1979; Esping-Andersen 1980; Korpi 1983; Przeworski and Sprague 1986; Kitschelt 1994). Third way theories will become trivial if they are simply a new way of referring to well-known arguments about social democratic reforms.

By examining welfare and labor market reforms in nine countries, this book shows that not only can the third way account for social democratic transformation through a longer historical framework, but it also brings new insights to contemporary social democracy. Beyond the topic of social democracy, this book has a broader theoretical pursuit, to explore the mechanisms of institutional innovation, and it is on this bigger theme that the entire book's arguments evolve. In the process of making these arguments, I also propose a theory about the externalities of organizations. Now, I outline each of the major issues at stake in this book.

IS THE THIRD WAY A RETREAT FROM SOCIAL DEMOCRACY?

In the comparative literature, there are conflicting opinions about the prospect of social democracy. The more pessimistic perspective is that social democracy is gradually but increasingly becoming indistinguishable from the center Right (Thomson 2000; Moschonas 2002), and the more optimistic account suggests that it continues to make some fundamental difference (Scharpf 1991; Garrett 1998). To the extent that both arguments examine the correlation between social democracy and policy outcomes, it is difficult to draw a firm conclusion because they utilize different data, evidence, and method. In any case, as P. Hedsötrm and R. Swedberg (1998) point out, correlation alone does not establish causality because it does not show the "social mechanism" behind the correlation. The mechanisms identified so far have largely supported the pessimistic view. Electorally, the mechanism is the need to appeal to nonworking-class allies, and economically, it is the current era of budget austerity (Przeworski and Sprague 1986; Kitschelt 1994; P. Pierson 2001b). Both mechanisms increase the pressure for social democracy to make ideological concessions. On this basis, the third way becomes merely "between the Left and Right": less social democratic, but not yet completely neoliberal. On this basis, the third way will be a truly sterile concept because it adds nothing new to what the existing literature has to offer.

I propose a different argument in this book. Cross-class appeals do not have to involve serious ideological compromises. In fact, one key concession made by social democracy to the allies has been to prioritize "enabling to work" over "passive help." This tactic enabled two of the most important social democratic principles, solidarity and egalitarianism, to survive. The soaring unemployment since the 1970s further increased the value of this work-oriented strategy. In other words, electoral heterogeneity and increasing unemployment provided the necessary conditions for ideological adaptation: Solidarity became increasingly productivist and egalitarianism increasingly prioritarian, focusing on protecting the worst-off. Meanwhile, neither solidarity nor egalitarianism was abandoned as a fundamental principle. This is why there was no retreat from social democracy in the ideological revision. This substantiates the originality of the third way notion: Rather than just another way of measuring "de-social democratization," the third way indeed refers to a new type of social democracy.

The third way ideology can be reflected in a policy paradigm that centers on labor market activation. This paradigm includes expansion of active social protection (especially enabling to work), restructuring of passive benefits, and retrenchment of early exit pathways, all situated in a macroeconomic context of prudence and corporatist wage moderation. In the book, I show that this policy paradigm is distinctively associated with social democratic incumbency, which lends support to the power resources theory of the welfare state, challenging the dominant path-dependency literature.

HOW DO INSTITUTIONS INNOVATE?

To the extent that power resources has greater explanatory leverage than path dependency in accounting for third way reforms, it brings new insights to theories of institutional evolution. So far, path dependency has been a fundamental thesis of this literature: Options for changing rules of the game are limited by preexisting rules (Skocpol 1992; P. Pierson 2004). The third way paradigm requires changes to many institutions of many types: social security, employment policy, and industrial relations, to name a few. The range of possible changes that can be implemented on each such institution will be narrowed by factors associated with the rule's initial creation. A major contribution in the path-dependency literature is to reveal the social mechanism behind such pattern: Earlier institutions self-reinforce because of positive feedbacks; time accumulation increases the information and sunk cost of devising new rules (Olson 1982; Mahoney 2000). Institutional innovations, in other words, are costly changes.

In the real world there are clearly pathbreaking changes. Sometimes actors do not merely change the rules but also get rid of them totally, installing new rules that contradict all the earlier principles, for example, when passive welfare was turned into active social protection. These changes are often characterized by frequent reversals, as actors replace one another in their contest to control the institutional agenda. The "politics matters" thesis in comparative political economy literature has offered strong evidence for such patterns (Boix 1998; Korpi and Palme 2003). However, the social mechanism behind such changes remains unclearly specified. What, in particular, is the source of incentives for actors to absorb the cost of institutional innovation? On this issue, Kathleen Thelen (2004) broke new ground, arguing that when existing rules generate negative feedbacks for peripheral actors without the power of rule making, these rules create incentives for capturing the institutional agenda, and in turn, for innovation. In this book, I explore in detail such mechanism of institutional innovation. Why do institutions generate positive feedbacks in some cases but negative ones in others? Path-dependency theories have made clear the nature of positive returns, but what is the source of negative ones? At what point do institutions' negative externalities overcome their positive ones, so that costly changes are no longer regarded as costly?

To answer these questions, I propose a "logic of public evils," and argue that ideological beliefs are the fundamental source of negative returns from institutions. The premise for the logic is that both institutions and ideologies are constraints on individual action but that they operate through opposite mechanisms. Institutions constrain all actors and two mutually contradictory institutions cannot coexist stably. By contrast, ideologies mutually conflict, and each only binds some individuals but not others. In other words, people live with one common set of rules on which they agree to disagree. For those who disagree, the rules become "public evils": The impossibility of exit and the conflict with their own beliefs create incentives for making costly changes to institutions. Are these incentives strong enough to even out the costs? The more intense the ideological preferences, the greater this possibility. To demonstrate this contingent relationship, I compare policy paradigms with policy implementation in various dimensions of third way reforms. To the extent that policy implementation is more ideologically indifferent than fundamental policy paradigms, I show implementation to be heavily path dependent, while different paradigms are strongly associated with different partisan ideologies.

IS IT STILL IMPORTANT TO GET ORGANIZED?

The emphasis on work over passive welfare has been an effective social democratic strategy in preserving solidarity across classes, but this solidarity is under new threat, as vulnerable groups are continuously created by socioeconomic changes. New social risk groups not only receive less social protection than the core blue-collar constituencies but also have little organizational influence within the labor movement (Taylor-Gooby 2004; Armingeon and Bonoli 2006). To what extent does this reduce the incentives for social democratic parties to extend solidarity to these vulnerable groups? Do the weakly organized have to suffer as a consequence of the strongly organized? If yes, is it still important for the labor movement to get organized?

In the book, I propose a theory about the positive externalities of organization: Those who cannot organize can enjoy the benefits of organization, to the extent that their preferences overlap with those who can organize. Where women are organizationally integrated in the labor movement, there is greater public provision of welfare services and less rigid labor markets, and these benefits spill over to new risk groups, such as single-parent families and part-time workers (male and female). Similarly, where the unemployed are strongly unionized, labor market activation prioritizes training over cutting benefits, and this indirectly provides help for marginal groups, such as the young or those with low skills. Organization is important for another reason. Institutions affect a large number of actors, and in cases where the cost of institutional change is widely diffused, collective action failure can perpetuate preexisting institutions. Because this institutional constraint operates through cross-sectional cost diffusion rather than time accumulation, I treat it as an important contributing factor to path dependency, rather than equating it with path dependency. Organizational integration and coordination provide the necessary communication and monitoring channels for preventing free riding and collective action failure. In this book, corporatist coordination is often important in making radical policy changes possible, by securing cooperation from both unions and employers.

THE ORGANIZATION OF THE BOOK

In Chapter 2, I set out in detail the main theoretical propositions. As said earlier, the primary focus of the book is to compare how ideologies and institutions constrain individual actions differently and explain the circumstances where ideologies lead to pathbreaking institutional innovation. Chapter 3 sets the empirical scene for this comparison, by outlining the nature of third way ideology and traditional institutional settings for each of the nine countries covered. To put the third way reforms in context, Chapter 4 outlines the socioeconomic problems and government responses before the start of third way reforms, focusing especially on the increase in unemployment, which played a crucial role in stimulating labor market activation. Chapters 5 through 7 examine in detail the third way reforms, respectively, for active protection, passive protection, and the macroeconomic and corporatist contexts. Evidence for institutional innovation was especially strong for active protection, where third way ideology most intensely self-differentiates from other partisan philosophies. The ability of ideology to constrain government policy declines as one moves into passive protection and external economic contexts. In concluding, Chapter 8 emphasizes that the book's theories describe contingent possibilities rather than certainties of outcome. Throughout, I present some conditions under which institutional innovations can happen, social democracy can adapt while remaining genuine, and the insider–outsider divide can be bridged. Clearly, the extent to which these outcomes eventuate depends on the extent to which these conditions are fulfilled.

Throughout the book, I utilize quantitative indicators for policies and socioeconomic outcomes to aid the case narratives. Since left–right policy contrasts are the primary mechanism in my examination of ideological influence on policy changes, in most cases the quantitative indicators capture changes across time, under different partisan governments. For specific countries and policy dimensions, the time frame varies, depending on different data availability and the timing of social democratic incumbency. Expenditure on active labor market measures will likely increase/ decrease as an automatic consequence of rising/falling unemployment. In order to isolate partisan effects on these policies, unless otherwise noted I control for unemployment for all labor market expenditure figures, dividing them by the standardized unemployment rate. Expenditure is thus "share of GDP per unemployment percentage." In addition to comparative historical research, in Chapter 5 I also use pooled time series analysis to highlight the fundamental association between social democracy and activation. This econometric analysis is taken from my collaborative work with Moira Nelson and John D. Stephens of the University of North Carolina at Chapel Hill, published in 2008 in the *Journal of European Social Policy* (vol. 18) as "De-commodification and Activation in Social Democracy: Resolving the Paradox."

Theorizing the Third Way

1. A THEORY OF THIRD WAY IDEOLOGY

1.1. The Social Democratic Ideology

In order to properly evaluate the third way, I first examine the ideology of social democracy in general and then explain how its adaptation through time leads to the third way. There are some recurring key themes in social democratic ideology and discourse, such as social justice, fairness, solidarity, and egalitarianism. To serve as defining properties of social democracy, these concepts must have sufficient discriminating power to differentiate between social democracy and alternative values. On its own, neither social justice nor fairness satisfies this requirement. Clearly, no parties or interest groups advocate injustice or unfairness. By comparison, both solidarity and egalitarianism have more limited constituencies, and the varying importance accorded to these values is often crucial in determining what is socially just or fair for one party rather than another. Therefore, I will focus on them as two key philosophical principles that define social democracy and its adaptation through time.

By examining eight countries over a century, Steinar Stjernø (2005) identified solidarity as a principle shared but interpreted differently by social and Christian democracy. He traced the origin of solidarity as a value-laden discourse to French classic social theory, especially Auguste Comte's ([1852] 1973) idea of debt to past generations and Émile Durkheim's ([1893] 1984) mechanical and organic variants of solidarity. While Durkheim's mechanic solidarity is premised on homogeneity and common consciousness in closed primitive societies, the growing division of labor and specialization in modern societies leads to organic solidarity, based on interdependence between complementary skills. The organic version of Durkheim later went on to become crucial in the social democratic incorporation of solidarity as a fundamental value. However, Durkheimian solidarity itself is prepolitical, and it is Karl Marx and his revisionists, such as Karl Kautsky and Eduard Bernstein in Germany and Ernst Wigforss in Sweden, who introduced solidarity as a rallying principle for the labor movement and their political ambitions. Marxist (and its more restricted Leninist) solidarity is internal to the working class and against capitalists, and despite its utopian outlook, it relies on a strong assumption of class-based self-interest. This concept is echoed in Max Weber's ([1922] 1978) theory of solidarity, which, unlike Comte or Durkheim, is based on social relationship and class.

The irreconcilability of different class interests behind Marxist solidarity implies that conflicts, revolutions, and dictatorships are inevitable on the path toward working-class emancipation. Unconvinced by the enormity of these social costs, the social democrats split with Marxism. Despite its less utopian outlook, social democratic solidarity went beyond (but still retained) self-interest and incorporated morality, ethics, and emotions as the basis for solidarity. For this reason, the concept is surprisingly flexible (Stjernø 2005). It, for example, is not necessarily in conflict with either Protestant values (such as in the Norwegian Labour Party) or Catholic teachings (which, for instance, retained significant influence on the Australian labor movement). This concept is the basis for a decades-long process of forging alliances across classes to harmonize common interests. Social democratic solidarity, in other words, is of the wage earners, rather than just the working class.

The immediate question is, then, about the difference between social and Christian democratic solidarity. While both rely on empathy and compassion, in Christian democracy such feelings are taken directly from humans as God's image (and, hence, the dignity and value of each human being before God). To exercise such solidarity, collective mobilization through the state is subsidiary to the role of more natural constituencies of God, such as the family, church, and other similarly organic communities. This principle of subsidiarity was cemented through encyclicals, such as the *Rerum Novarum* of Pope Leo XII in 1891 and *Quadragesimo Anno* of Pope Pius XI in 1931. It is clearly incorrect to infer from this that Christian democracy is against state welfare, given the generous transfer-based Bismarckian welfare states. Instead, the primary difference is the greater willingness by Christian Democrats to balance subsidiarity against the state in welfare provision (van Kersbergen 1995; Stjernø 2005), a principle that went on to have major policy legacies in welfare state services.

A second defining component of social democratic social justice is egalitarianism. Unlike solidarity, egalitarianism's ideological constituency is more confined to the center Left. From the secular Right, libertarians such as Robert Nozick (1974) have trenchant criticisms against egalitarianism, and Christian Democrats are also ready to accept inequality as the natural order of society. These arguments cannot be taken to their extremes, and the "paradox of redistribution" clearly shows that there is also significant redistribution in Christian democratic welfare states (Korpi and Palme 1998). Nevertheless, the force of the paradox thesis is in comparing against policy consequences of market-based welfare, which is only marginal in social democratic welfare states. Therefore, it is still important to highlight the greater importance of egalitarianism in social democratic than Christian democratic ideology.

When it comes to social democratic egalitarianism, typical welfare redistribution and wage compression programs immediately come to mind. However, beyond these policies, it is important to ask how much genuine connection can be established with egalitarianism as a philosophical principle, which is itself exceedingly complex. One key question is whether social democratic egalitarianism is a means or end, because radical egalitarians like Larry S. Temkin (1993) made clear that they should value equality intrinsically rather than instrumentally (Holtug and Lippert-Rasmussen 2007b: 2; Shapiro 2007: 17). For example, Social Democrats who believe in income redistribution *as crucial for improving the welfare of the less fortunate* are not strictly egalitarians, but those who believe in it because it is intrinsically socially just probably are. This question of income redistribution has limited discriminating power because redistribution as a means does not necessarily conflict with redistribution as an end, as far as social democracy is concerned.

To clarify the position of social democracy, I turn to a scenario where means do not serve the ends. A key criticism against egalitarianism has been the "Leveling Down Objection" (Parfit 1991). In other words, to believe in equality as intrinsically good, one *has to* accept that, at least in some aspect, it is good to reduce welfare of the better-off without improving the welfare of anyone. Destruction of equipment, properties, and wealth belonging to capitalists, as an extreme example of Leveling Down, is intrinsically egalitarian. Not infrequently, such practice was seen in the process of communist revolutions, but social democracy has by and large shunned it completely. In other words, it is important to highlight the instrumentalism in social democratic egalitarianism, where the end is often simply to show solidarity toward the worse-off by improving their lot. The pragmatism here opens a bridge with prioritarians such as Derek Parfit

(1984) and John Rawls (1971), and, as will be explained later, this proves to be a crucial component of the social democratic ideological adaptation.

1.2. Setting the Stage: Solidarity with the Poor, not Charity

The third way transformation is closely intertwined with the gradual evolution in solidarity and egalitarianism as two key components of social democratic justice. Across countries, much of the third way policy package came into a coherent being after the 1980s, as did many of the contemporary thinkers and discourses associated with the third way, such as Anthony Giddens and Amitai Etzioni. But more of this later. The ideological momentum behind such thinking can be traced back to several decades earlier.

A key part of the split between communism and social democracy was the latter's redefinition of solidarity. Fraternity internal to the working class was extended across the class divide to become one for the wage earners. On a practical level, this became necessary because after the split, social democrats had to rely on the electoral dimension and their simply nonexistent working-class numerical majority (Przeworski and Sprague 1986). On an intellectual dimension, this presented a more complex problem. The rejected Marxist and Leninist solidarity was based on class self-interest, but not so clearly on rational calculation. Mancur Olson (1965), among others, made it clear that one does not have to be self-interested to be rational, or the other way around. The refusal by communist revolutionaries to defect when the alternative is execution cannot easily be explained as being "strategic" or "incentive compatible," especially when some simply died thinking it was the moral thing to do. Unlike norms or conventions, morality is largely reliant on self-censorship, rather than on the potential threat of third-party monitoring or punishment (Mantzavinos 2001). It is not difficult to account for the extraordinary strength of such solidarity because it was genuinely solidarity among the equals, based on a high level of homogeneity in experience and background (of extreme suffering and exploitation). This bears similarity to the mechanical version of Durkheim's concept, based on shared feelings and common consciousness.

When social democrats extended solidarity beyond the working class, it became more heterogeneous. Rather than *within* the working class, now it is *with* the working class (for farmers, and later white-collar workers). Solidarity across conflicting interests and unequal statuses has less "shared feelings or common consciousness" to rely on, and instead must rely on mutual needs. This is reflected in Durkheim's own gradual transformation from mechanical to organic solidarity, the latter based on complementarity between different skills as a result of increasing division of labor. As mentioned earlier, social democracy adopted this organic interpretation for its own solidarity discourse, relying heavily on the urging of ethics and compassion. If anything, such emphasis on the emotional aspects reflected precisely the fear that the inevitably more instrumental nature of heterogeneous and unequal solidarity can undermine its strength. Fundamentally, if solidarity among the poor becomes solidarity between the poor and rich, how is this different from charity? Without some reciprocity from those helped, it is difficult to make the distinction. One sees an early hint of communitarian notions of rights and responsibilities, which later came to constitute an important component of third way discourse in many countries.

Here, it is important to emphasize the contingent nature in the relationship between electoral needs and inclusive solidarity. Heterogeneity in electoral composition necessitates the broadening of solidarity as an ideology, but to what extent and how fast the corresponding ideological adaptation can take place depends on other factors. Very often, the ideological responses lag considerably behind, and when this happens, the heterogeneous social democratic electorate operates more as a trade-off between conflicting constituencies than solidarity across them. This electoral dilemma makes it very difficult for social democratic parties to present a coherent ideology attractive to both workers and their electoral allies. When social democrats make appeals to other constituencies, they inevitably dilute the class consciousness on which their core constituency rests. This problem is especially serious where the labor movement is itself weakly organized, where there is strong communist competition, or where other partisan forces appeal to workers on cross-cutting social cleavages, such as ethnicity, religion, and language. When this happens, a heterogeneous social democratic electorate indicates as much electoral failure as success because it often means that a large number of core working-class voters are lost as a trade-off. For example, the French Socialists historically made major inroads into the farmers' constituency due to the highly differentiated social structure and radically divided politics of rural areas. However, at the same time, the Socialists had a very weak hold on their core constituency due to competition from both communists and the center Right (Bartolini 2000: 484–485; Knutsen 2006: 47–94; Przeworski and Sprague 1986: 147–167).

It is in Scandinavia where such trade-off is least steep. Not only is the labor movement strongly organized and centralized, but these societies are also most homogenous on ethnic, religious, and other cultural grounds. Historically, the social democratic parties in these countries were the first to establish a coherent ideology of broader solidarity among workers and other constituencies. The ability of such ideology to appeal to different sectors rests on its strongly productivist and developmentalist orientation (Stjernø 2005). Here, the fundamental purpose of solidarity is to help the worse-off *so that they can produce more and better*. The premise, in other words, is on work, and better work.

The Rehn-Meidner model in Sweden is an explicit representation of this logic. Through its solidaristic wage arrangement, more productive workers show solidarity with less productive ones so that the latter *increase their productivity*, rather than just getting a wage increase. If the less productive lose their jobs, they are helped with active labor market training so that they can rejoin in more productive employment. The policy effect from such ideological transformation is especially strong in Sweden (and Norway, to a lesser extent), given the social democratic political dominance in these two countries. This discussion provides a philosophical basis for the uniquely pioneering role in emphasizing labor market activation of Swedish and Norwegian social democracy. They are the ideological prototype for today's third way transformation. Outside Scandinavia, the social democratic electoral dilemma of trade-off was more serious by comparison, due to stronger competition from other cleavages (such as religion in continental Europe and Australia) and the relative political weakness of the Left (such as in Anglo-Saxon countries). As Chapter 3 shows, a fully coherent ideology of productive and inclusive solidarity did not come to fruition until after the early 1980s.

Despite the timing differences across countries, at a fundamental level the adaptation of solidarity followed a similar internal logic: The inclusion of more heterogeneous and unequal interests reduced the importance of shared consciousness and increased the need to differentiate solidarity from charity. This led to greater reliance on reciprocity and a productivist outlook, and this is the key to the third way focus on enabling to work. The heterogeneity of the social democratic electorate is an important factor behind the broadening and productivist orientation of its ideology. However, clearly there are also more idiosyncratic factors that affect the nature of social democratic ideology in particular countries in distinct ways. In both Australia and the UK, for example, the historical influence of Fabianism led to a pragmatic and reformist orientation in social democratic thinking, with an early focus on production and wages. In France, by contrast, the strong historical legacy of orthodox Marxism has presented additional barriers toward reaching out to other classes on an ideological level.

Besides increasing electoral fragmentation, another systematic and related factor in the creation of work-centered ideology is the presence of unemployment. As unemployment becomes more serious, it is easier for productivism to compete for ideological attention with other noneconomic issues, such as ethnicity and religion. There is greater need for work-oriented beliefs also because the growing size of the nonworking population directly compromises the integrity of solidarity based on reciprocity and mutual contribution. By contrast, where unemployment is virtually negligible, it is difficult for a discourse on labor market activation to resonate with the public. In the Antipodes, for example, the heavily protected manufacturing industries and the scarcity of labor meant that there was little substantive meaning to either productivism or combating unemployment. As detailed in Chapter 3, the primary social democratic focus in Australia and New Zealand had instead been on wage arbitration, and the issue of enabling to work or human capital upgrading did not become important until liberalization forced the protected sectors to compete internationally, in the process unleashing a rapid increase in unemployment.

Another major dimension of social democratic ideology is egalitarianism, which, as said earlier, is instrumental rather than for its own sake. The purpose, in other words, is to show solidarity with the less fortunate, rather than leveling down. This is reflected in the ideological belief in wage compression when there is work and in highly de-commodifying wage replacement when work is lost. A key question here is "equality of what?" Ronald Dworkin (1981a, b) made the hugely influential distinction between misfortune due to "bad brute luck" or "bad option luck," and he suggested that egalitarianism should not be extended beyond those who fell on hard times due to factors out of their control. The preference for equality of resources over equality of welfare is endorsed by most contemporary egalitarians, such as Richard Arneson (1989), John Roemer (1996), G. A. Cohen (1989), and Peter Vallentyne (2002). However, this debate about the "currency of egalitarian justice" did not fully begin until the end of the capitalist Golden Age, and before then, neither wage compression nor wage replacement was under threat as fundamental principles. When this debate took place in due course, the changing conceptualizations of egalitarianism and solidarity joined hands to influence the third way ideological adaptation.

1.3. Fully Third Way: Prioritarian Egalitarianism and Productivist Solidarity

Compared with the times of Bernstein and Wigforss, after the Golden Age there was even greater ideological pressure to broaden solidarity in response to the growing fragmentation of traditional electorates. Among other things, demographic changes, the transition to a service economy, expansion of the female labor force, and the rise of individualism, plus a serious slowdown in economic growth, all meant that solidarity with the working class as a social justice principle now has to accommodate even more heterogeneous and fragmented interests. In addition to being productivist and reciprocal through employment, solidarity now also needs to be gender egalitarian and relevant to new types of social risks. These latter requirements, in particular, turned out to be difficult, and they duly presented further electoral and policy dilemmas for some social democratic governments. I will discuss this implication later. For now, I focus on a key development since the 1970s that forced social democracy to further revise both solidarity and egalitarianism: the unemployment problem.

A major consequence from the folding of *les trente glorieuses* was a rapid increase in unemployment to levels not seen in the postwar period. In addition, the nature of such unemployment (as well as the remaining jobs) also became very different. In Chapter Four, I will provide more empirical details about the rise of unemployment for specific countries. Here, it suffices to highlight the ubiquity of this issue: It deeply affected each country covered in the book. Fundamentally, the source of such an unemployment problem was the secular structural shift in the economy, from manufacturing to service industries, as well as demographic changes leading to increasing labor market exclusion for vulnerable groups, such as single mothers and the young. Strict employment protection and the consequent insider–outsider divide directly contributed to this worsening labor market exclusion problem (Rueda 2005, 2007). During the 1980s, these structural problems were confounded with a series of policy mistakes by governments in their attempt to deal with changes in the international economy, especially the rapid deregulation of credit markets followed by insufficient restraint in aggregate demand. At the same time, for national governments, traditional economic stimulants such as devaluation, interest rate manipulation, or deficit spending became infeasible due to increasing capital mobility. Wage compression and replacement are two key representations of traditional social democratic egalitarianism. Now, this crisis of work threatened the legitimacy of both.

Wage compression, as the Rehn-Meidner model demonstrated, worked very well with a manufacturing-dominated economy, where low productivity sectors, in order to stay competitive with their rising wages, are encouraged to rapidly increase their productivity. As the economy shifts further to services, however, wage compression becomes a problem. By observing the process of performing chamber music, William Baumol (1967) formulated the well-known thesis of the "cost disease of handcraft industries." Because of the much lower capacity to rapidly increase productivity in service industries, their productivity will become progressively lower relative to the rest of the economy. Their wages, however, are affected by the overall wage rate in the economy, especially when there is significant wage compression. Consequently, over time, the cost of labor in service industries will become progressively higher than the rest of the economy, pricing them out of the market and contributing to job losses. In turn, the consequently rising unemployment and newly emerging social risks significantly increase the pressure on the social security system, stretching its capability to sustain income parity between those in and out of work. In addition to their shrinking revenue base, a further problem for unemployment benefits is the potential work disincentives they create.

These employment problems forced social democrats to reevaluate wage compression and wage replacement on a policy level, but the direction of change also manifested itself on a broader intellectual level, amid the ongoing debates between libertarians and their opponents. The consequentialist libertarians advocate individual liberty for its welfare-maximizing potential, and they are deeply grounded in the economics discipline (for example, Friedrich Hayek, Milton Friedman, and James Buchanan, all Nobel laureates). Their thoughts constituted the fundamental basis for neoliberal doctrines and policies. Friedman, for example, deeply influenced the economic policies of conservative governments in the United States and UK. By contrast, social and political theorists such as Robert Nozick and Isaiah Berlin questioned egalitarianism by directly focusing on the right to liberty as natural rights. Berlin (1969) is well known for making a clear distinction between positive and negative liberty, and emphasizing the asymmetry between them. In other words, negative liberty (freedom from interference on individual actions) has clear priority over positive liberty (the opportunity to fulfill one's own potential). In this light, there is little justification for collective resource mobilization by the government to safeguard social rights (such as welfare state transfer programs).

Dworkin (1985) criticized this asymmetry proposition, arguing that without some basic level of social resources (and hence the guaranteeing of positive liberty), it is difficult for an individual to exercise negative liberty. For example, without adequate food, clothing, and basic education, there is little substance in the freedom to participate in democratic deliberations. Therefore, positive and negative liberties should be symmetric, and egalitarian distribution of social resources can be justifiable. This relates directly to the "equality of what" question, another key contribution from Dworkin, who argued that individuals should be held fully responsible for their own choices (option rather than brute bad luck). Therefore, equality of resources is preferable to that of welfare, and along similar lines, Arneson (1989) promoted "equality of opportunity for welfare." On a policy level, this more stringent definition of equality provides a philosophical basis for shifting attention away from straightforward income/wage parity to the goals of creating more opportunities for the excluded to return to employment.

These "opportunity rather than outcome" theories of egalitarianism, however, treat "desert" as a key criterion for resource redistribution. In other words, there will be those who, all things considered, are responsible for their own misfortune. The implication for welfare state policy is that for some people, benefits should ultimately be reduced or withdrawn, even if they are, in terms of outcomes, the worst-off. Rawls (1971), on the other hand, denies that questions of desert can be used to defend inequality. He argues that those who behaved more responsibly do not necessarily deserve better because they do not deserve the causes leading to their more responsible behavior, such as more disciplined upbringing or frugal parents (Holtug and Lippert-Rasmussen 2007b: 19–20). Instead, inequality should only be justifiable when it improves the welfare of the worst-off, as Rawls argues in his now classic Second Principle of Justice.

Rawls's theories prevented a possible degeneration of desert-affirming egalitarianism into a theoretical justification for harsh workfare principles premised on cutting benefits "for the scoundrels." His arguments also provided a *prioritarian* logic for shifting the attention of social protection from equality per se to protecting the worst-off. As said earlier, social democratic egalitarianism is more pragmatic (as a means) than radical (as an end for itself). It shares key common principles with prioritarianism (Parfit 1984, 1991), as both are opposed to "Leveling Down" and both believe in the social purpose of equality. However, a distinction for prioritarians such as Parfit and Rawls is that they also believe it is socially just to improve the situation for the worst–off, even if this does not affect the gap between the worse- and better-off. On a policy level, the crisis of unemployment demanded the relaxation of traditional egalitarian mechanisms, such as wage compression and replacement. Prioritarianism provided the intellectual justification for the corresponding policy reforms, such as shifting from wage parity to protecting the really worst-off: those who work in poverty or are simply excluded from work.

In short, the crisis of unemployment forced a rethinking over traditional social democratic egalitarianism. The response, by shifting resources away from wage compression and replacement toward employment (making work pay and enabling to work), reflected an increasingly prioritarian orientation in social democratic egalitarianism. For the "equality of what" question, the new emphasis on enabling to work also suggests that it is equality of resources rather than of welfare. The increase in unemployment also affected the nature of solidarity, the other key social democratic ideological principle. As economic and social changes further fragmented traditional social structures, "inclusive solidarity" became even more heterogeneous in its composition and reliant on reciprocity. If more and more people stop working, the sustainability of such solidarity will come under serious threat. Therefore, it became urgent to prioritize and highlight the productivist purpose of solidarity. This direction of change, with its growing emphasis on active participation, found some intellectual support from communitarians.

Communitarians question the emphasis on individuality in liberalism. Michael Sandel (1982, 1996), for example, criticized Rawls's theory of justice for its thought experiment about the "veil of ignorance" as a mechanism for determining justice. He suggested instead that people are not "unencumbered selves" and that the interconnection between them makes it impossible to hypothesize a veil of ignorance about each other. Some key principles of communitarianism include shared responsibility, reciprocity, and participation (Shapiro 2007: 30–31), all friendly to the concept of productivist solidarity. Some communitarians, such as Sandel, Alasdair MacIntyre (1981), and Michael Walzer (1983), focus on the ontological and epistemological aspects of communities and therefore engage directly with their libertarian counterparts, such as Nozick. Other communitarians, such as Amitai Etzioni (1993) and William Galston (1991), are more consequentialist, focusing on the policy implications of their communitarian principles, and for this reason they had more direct influence on government thinking. Etzioni, for example, was a senior advisor to the White House under the Carter administration and served in an unofficial advisory role on communitarian issues for both Bill Clinton and Tony Blair. In his book, Etzioni (2000) openly praised and identified the policies of the Blair government as a good representation of his communitarian principles and called New Labour the "third way."

Despite the common emphasis on participation and responsibility, there is one key difference between communitarianism and social democratic solidarity. Communitarians prioritize civil society over the state as the key player in cementing mutual responsibility and providing help, and there is closer affinity with Christian democratic solidarity on this issue of subsidiarity. By contrast, collective resource mobilization through the government remains central to social democratic thinking. From a different perspective based on themes of postmodernity and deliberation, Anthony Giddens (2000), as another key advisor to Blair on third way policies, also emphasized the importance of reciprocal and inclusive solidarity. However, he was skeptical about the role of traditional social communities in sustaining solidarity.

The preceding discussion has offered a theory about the ideological adaptation of social democracy leading to the third way. The purpose of the ideological changes was pragmatic, a combination of electoral needs and changes in economic circumstances. As solidarity became more inclusive to account for the growing heterogeneity of traditional constituencies, it also became more dependent on reciprocity, work, and productivity. Therefore, when rising unemployment after the Golden Age threatened its foundation, enabling to work became the core of social democratic solidarity. The unemployment crisis also transformed the concept of egalitarianism, which became more prioritarian, focusing increasingly on protecting the worst-off. The policy impacts from changing egalitarianism and changing solidarity converge: Enabling to work and eliminating poverty in work are increasingly prioritized over wage compression and replacement.

Diverse country and historical contexts have left their own imprint on social democracy, leading to varying policy traditions and strategies. French social democracy, for example, has a particularly strong self-image of socialism through state ownership. Australian and New Zealand social democrats have relied particularly heavily on wage arbitration to deliver social justice. More broadly, labor market activation and female employment is more strongly encouraged in Nordic countries than in continental Europe. By contrast, redistribution through the manipulation of means testing is more frequent in Anglo-Saxon countries than elsewhere (Pontusson 2005). Nevertheless, this book shows that despite all these variations, social justice focused on enabling to work and making work pay occupies a central place in contemporary social democratic ideology and policy. With its philosophical origins explained in some detail, I now discuss why this new way toward social justice can be referred to as the third way.

1.4. More Than Three Ways to Social Justice

Out of its context, the label "third" conveys little information about the substantive content of the ideology, beyond saying that some traditional notions of "left" and "right" are transcended. Instead, it primarily serves as an analytic and rhetorical construct in public discourse. For this reason, over the past century various third ways appeared, which in content had little to do with the social democratic transformation examined in this book. For example, during the interwar period, both fascists and the antifascist Italian social liberals resorted to a "third option" rhetoric, and today the Greens also regard their philosophies as beyond the traditional Left and Right (Bastow and Martin 2003). To appreciate the "thirdness," it is important to examine the first and second ways, which are themselves specific to historical and political contexts.

Based on the third way discourse from various social democratic parties (outlined in greater detail in Chapter 3), the Right and Left in question are typically neoliberal doctrines and traditional social democracy (for argument's sake, respectively the second and first way). Earlier, I discussed in detail traditional social democracy and its evolution toward the third way under the pressure of soaring unemployment. Here, as a contrast, I briefly outline the parallel responses from secular Right and Christian democratic parties to these economic problems.

As I showed earlier, neoliberals combine the beliefs from the economics discipline and the natural right to individual liberty. Their key verdict over the collapse of the Golden Age was that the state became too large and interfering. Therefore, the main logic for reform was cost cutting and the retreat of the state. In Anglo-Saxon countries, the neoliberal doctrine led to large scale privatization and the drastic reduction of welfare state benefits. For the Christian Democrats, responding to the crisis was more difficult because their social and religious origin shaped their attitude toward welfare and family relative to work. Historically, in Catholic strongholds, large swaths of concentrated land ownership employing massive cheap farm labor often constituted the de facto continuation of a typical feudalist economy, characterized by noncommodified mutual obligation and patronage between lords and peasants. Politically, this was the fertile ground for upper-class conservatives. They were anticapitalist, against class division, and simultaneously paternalistic with a belief in the idea of *noblesse oblige*. The Bismarckian welfare states served to re-create the precommodified feudalist arrangement (Esping-Andersen 1990). To preserve hierarchy and prevent social mobility, the rural and Catholic conservatives strongly encouraged loyalty and attachment to the existing social status, through the accumulation of a long and stable employment career. This uninterrupted career history was made possible by very strict employment protection and was strengthened with generous contribution-linked welfare benefits. In addition, the religious importance of natural organic communities reduced the possibility of mobilizing the substantial untapped female labor force. Faced with economic crisis, the social democrats increased the emphasis on enabling to work, while the secular Right focused on downsizing. By comparison, the Christian Democrats were heavily constrained by their own social and religious legacies from following either option. To counter unemployment, they resorted to encouraging an early exit from the labor market.

Neoliberals directly question the legitimacy of solidarity and egalitarianism, and this is where they differ from the third way. For traditional social democracy, egalitarianism relied on wage compression/replacement, and solidarity had little work emphasis; this is where *it* differs from the third way. Christian democracy has a more complicated relationship with third way social democracy. Both oppose the individualism advocated by libertarians and accept the communitarians' notion of mutual help. Both, in addition, welcome the infusion of Christian values into morality, compassion, and ethics. However, whereas the state is subsidiary under Christian democracy, collective resource pooling through the state remains fundamental for social democracy. Furthermore, while neither embraces equality for its own sake, social democrats are much less tolerant of inequality than their Christian democratic counterparts and are more ready to redress the situation through redistribution. Finally, on (especially female) employment, Christian democracy is more passive.

It is important to examine more than specific third way labels used in public discourse, which, while often reflecting values and principles, are also affected by other political considerations. In fact, other than New Labour, the label "third" has very limited currency within contemporary social democracy. Even its adaptation to the German Social Democratic Party (SPD) as the *Neue Mitte* was accepted with little enthusiasm. In France, Lionel Jospin publicly distanced the Socialists from the "third way" characterization. However, empirical analysis in the next few chapters shows that in values and policies, these parties do share many similarities. Therefore, the third way should be defined by productivist solidarity and prioritarian egalitarianism, rather than whether a party made explicit reference to some notion of "thirdness" in public discourse (and in most cases, there was no such reference at all). Table 2.1 outlines key components of the third way ideology and its policy implications, in contrast with Christian democratic, neoliberal, and traditional social democratic approaches to social justice.

TABLE 2.1. *Three Ways to Social Justice*

	First Way (Social Democracy)	Third Way (Social Democracy)	Second Way (Neoliberal)	Christian Democracy
Philosophy of social justice	Solidarity	*Productivist* solidarity	Individual liberty (natural right, economically efficient)	Solidarity within natural communities
	Egalitarianism	*Prioritarian* egalitarianism		Hierarchy is natural
Policy principle	Wage compression	Eliminating poverty in work	Retrenchment and privatization	Early exit
	Wage replacement	Enabling to work		

2. A THEORY OF POSITIVE EXTERNALITIES OF ORGANIZATION

Historically, a key difficulty in broadening social democratic solidarity had been winning over better-off groups as allies, for instance, farmers and the rising middle class. When solidarity was no longer based on shared experiences and common consciousness, the instrumentality of its purpose increased, especially for those who came from a relative position of strength. While it might not be very easy to convince the worse-off about the need for a common bond with the better-off, this convincing is even more difficult for the better-off. It is clear what benefits the worse-off can get from being helped, but what actual benefits the better-off get in return is not immediately clear. For a long time, the core blue-collar workers remained a worst-off segment of this cross-class electoral alliance. However, changes in socioeconomic circumstances over the past three decades have shifted the relative social position of the blue-collar constituency. For the first time, as a major group they are no longer the worst-off. Therefore, there is less ground for supporting a notion of solidarity that continues to prioritize those (others) who are worst-off. Potential resistance from the historical core constituency of social democracy hence poses an increasingly serious problem for inclusive solidarity as a key component of the third way.

The newly emerging worst-off segment of society includes single mothers, youth with inadequate skills or education, and part-time workers, among others. They are worst-off not only because they economically are poorer than the unionized male core workforce but also because they and their families face new social risks that the core do not have to contemplate, especially social problems associated with persistent exclusion from the labor market due to their less advantageous position in the job market. The social problems are more than long-term unemployment. They extend to the neglect of children when females cannot combine work and family, and extreme poverty even if they do work (especially for the young unskilled, whose entry level is now relegated from manufacturing to the bottom rung of service industries) (Taylor-Gooby 2004; Armingeon and Bonoli 2006). These social risks are new because either their constituencies used to be negligible (such as women intending to participate in the labor force), or the nature of their problems used to be less damaging (such as the unskilled). Electorally, the ability of these new groups to organize and mobilize is often very weak, and by contrast, the unionized blue-collar core constituency is not only better protected socioeconomically but also much stronger in its political strength. Rather than more inclusive solidarity, social democracy in this context leads to a widening divide between the well-protected insiders and the rest, who become outsiders (Rueda 2005, 2007).

This problem challenges the third way ideology. So far as it is focused on prioritarian egalitarianism and productivist solidarity, the implementation of both will be more difficult given the electoral dilemma of the insider–outsider divide. Unionized core workers now have to prioritize these new risk groups in their egalitarianism principles and show solidarity by helping these people back to more stable and worthwhile employment. The incentives to do so, however, are not necessarily strong because the political resources of the new groups are negligible. There is no doubt that this electoral problem makes the practical implementation of third way ideology more difficult. However, while D. Rueda interprets this as a problem intrinsic to social democracy, my argument is the opposite: A stronger labor movement, especially in its organizational capacity, makes the insider–outsider divide a less serious problem. This argument builds on a theory of the positive externalities of organization.

It is indeed clear that much of the new social risk constituency is weakly organized politically. This is the fundamental reason behind the thesis that, policy wise and ideologically, they become outsiders unrepresented by social democracy. However, if their interests *partially* overlap with constituencies that are organizationally more established within social democracy, these interests will be represented, simply by association with the politically more powerful. In other words, a strong political organization has positive externalities that flow to the politically weak when their preferences overlap. Among the various new social risks, two interrelated primary categories are risks related to the inability to maintain typical work patterns and the lack of sufficient human capital. I will now examine each category in detail. In both cases, it is clear that when the necessary organizational capacity within the labor movement exists, the benefits spill over into even weakly organized groups, and hence reduce the problem of their exclusion as outsiders.

People unable to maintain typical work patterns are diverse in their circumstances, including part-time workers, females balancing family and work, and individuals with frequent disruptions in their careers. Among them, females have the greatest potential for political influence within social democracy, not only due to their large numbers but also to intellectual support from feminist thinkers. In many cases, women have made only limited headway in gaining political influence inside social democracy, but in Nordic countries they are relatively successful. As noted earlier, Scandinavian social democracy benefited from friendly socioeconomic cleavage conditions and quickly extended its support base into constituencies often considered hostile in other countries. In addition, the lack of Catholic doctrine about the traditional role of women in the family also reduced the barrier between females and the working class. As an indication of the significant female integration into the core blue-collar constituency, Nordic women are close to parity to men in union membership and are actually more likely to join the union than men today. Therefore, a distinctive feature of the Scandinavian labor movement is that male andfemale workers are equally integrated organizationally, whereas in most continental European countries, more men than women are organized (Ebbinghaus 2006: 137–138).

Olson (1965) offered two related arguments about the benefit of being organized. Firstly, the hierarchical nature of organization, and its ability to assert authority, simply force people to put aside some of the differences in their interests and act in concert. In other words, for the same number of individuals with conflicting interests, collective action is more likely when they are constrained by a common organization than if they remain as floating individuals. Secondly, and this is the more widely utilized part of Olson's arguments, organization reduces the cost of information for its members. It provides channels for communication, and mutual monitoring, and it acts as a shortcut for strategic information about how other individuals are likely to act. By reducing uncertainty and strengthening communication, again organization makes collective action more likely.

For these two reasons, core unionized male workers accept gender-egalitarian normative principles and policies more easily when women are organizationally integrated into the labor movement, as in Scandinavia. For example, in Sweden, the Swedish Trade Union Confederation (LO) started to demand the expansion of public child care beginning in the 1960s. With women's federations supporting day care from within the social democratic party, Olof Palme linked gender egalitarianism to labor market policies as early as the 1972 party congress (Daguerre 2006: 216–217). The goods delivered by such an advocacy coalition (extensive welfare state services, large public sector, relatively flexible labor markets) flow much farther beyond women, reaching other politically more vulnerable groups with overlapping interests. These groups include part-time workers, fixed-contract workers, people with disrupted careers, and in general anyone suffering from the bias of the labor market toward stable careers in core manufacturing industries. The benefits from organization are not only policies but also stronger preferences among core workers for continued expansion of these very policies. This latter type of benefit is also important because it is the conflicting preferences between insiders and outsiders that result in the divide in policy outcomes. Rueda (2007) argues that a key factor that reduces the conflict in preferences is the absence of strict employment protection, and for similar purposes K. Armingeon (2006) highlights the size of public sector employment. These two favorable conditions, of course, are more likely to be present the more fully women are integrated into the labor movement, which in itself speaks of the greater strength of social democracy.

I now illustrate this logic of the positive externalities of organization for the other major type of new social risk, inadequate skills or education. Like part-time workers, the unskilled are weakly organized inside the labor movement across countries, even in Scandinavia. If anything, the unskilled are least underrepresented in unions in the UK and Ireland, given the dominance of general unions in these countries. On this basis alone, social democratic parties have little electoral incentive for taking their interests on board. By contrast, as a group, the unemployed have greater political clout, again especially in Scandinavia, and the Ghent system of worker-managed unemployment benefits (in Denmark and Sweden) provides further incentives for the unemployed to remain organizationally integrated despite losing their jobs. However, in continental Europe, due to weak union representation, the unemployed are sometimes forced to organize their own protest groups outside the labor movement, such as in France (Ebbinghaus 2006: 135–137). The organizational integration of the working and nonworking within one movement makes collective action easier. Insiders are stronger in their preference for policies that primarily benefit the unemployed, such as active labor market policies premised on training and education, as well as some flexibility in the labor market. Especially significant are the training and education opportunities bundled into active labor market policies. These human capital investment measures serve many purposes, such as maintaining contact with the labor market, smoothing disruptions in career patterns, and up-skilling. All unemployed, rather than just the unskilled or least educated, can benefit from them. This is where the interests overlap, between groups that are politically stronger (unemployed) and weaker (unskilled), and the weaker receives positive externalities from the better organization of the stronger.

Outside Scandinavia, there is mostly weaker organizational capacity for integrating either women or the unemployed (often both), and social democratic governments face a greater electoral dilemma when core constituencies resist third way policies that primarily benefit new social risk groups. This is especially so when the countries in question already have a strict employment protection system. This theoretical perspective provides a helpful interpretation of the difficulties, documented frequently in the empirical chapters, for social democrats in securing union consent for their active labor market measures or labor market flexibility measures.

In this section, I offered a theory of the positive externalities of organization. It modifies the Rueda thesis that social democracy leads to the insider–outsider divide and an electoral dilemma in covering new social risks. It really is the political weakness of social democracy that leads to these problems. When the labor movement is strong enough, at least some outsiders are in, and once they are in, it is much easier to integrate than to exclude their interests; this kick starts the mechanism of positive externalities. Clearly, this theory is contingent rather than deterministic. The positive externalities of organization offer the *possibilities* for including outsiders, but to what extent this can happen is an empirical question, depending on the actual organizational capacity in the labor movement specific to each country. Table 2.2 is taken from Ebbinghaus (2006: 128), based on calculations from International Social Survey Program data for 1998/2002. While all countries with both strong female and unemployed unionization are in Northern Europe and all with the opposite properties are in continental Europe, there are clearly some intermediate cases. In France, for example, integration is strong for women but weak for the unemployed, and the similar is the case for Norway. The impact of these intermediate patterns of organizational integration is reflected in policy outcomes. For example, Norwegian employment measures for social assistance recipients are heavily

TABLE 2.2. *Organizational Integration of Women and the Unemployed 1998/2002*

	Employed Density	Unemployed Density	Ratio U/E	Men Density	Women Density	Ratio W/M
Denmark	85.7	79.5	0.93	87	89	1.02
Finland	-	-	-	75	83	1.11
Norway	64.9	17.7	0.27	55	60	1.09
Sweden	84.9	71.7	0.84	79	85	1.08
UK	34.3	15.8	0.46	30	29	0.97
Ireland	42.6	15.4	0.36	40	46	1.14
Austria	41.4	36	0.87	55	33	0.61
Belgium	-	-	-	59	49	0.83
Germany (W)	25.3	11.1	0.44	37	21	0.56
Netherlands	32.4	17.4	0.54	31	20	0.65
Switzerland	34.1	17.7	0.52	38	29	0.77
France	18.5	2	0.11	19	18	0.91
Italy	36.3	5.7	0.16	36	37	1.05
Portugal	21.3	7.7	0.36	23	19	0.83
Spain	18.6	7.9	0.42	21	13	0.63

Source: Ebbinghaus (2006): 128.

coercive rather than enabling, by Scandinavian standards, and French public child care is more generous than other continental European cases. In addition, while unionization is important, political influence within the parliamentary party is an alternative route serving the same purpose of organizational integration. Where feminists had strong influence within the social democratic cabinet (such as in the Netherlands and the UK), social policies also became more gender friendly. I will discuss these policy details more fully in the empirical chapters.

3. A THEORY OF INSTITUTIONAL INNOVATION

3.1. The Existing Literature: New Politics of the Welfare State

In this book, I not only examine the ideology of the third way but also its projection onto real policy changes in third way reforms. A key question here is whether these changes faithfully reflect the ideological principles or are constrained from doing so by prior institutional legacies. In short, what incentives can ideologies offer for actors to carry out costly institutional innovation? To set the scene for this broader theoretical discussion, I now outline how the contemporary welfare literature has approached the impact of institutional constraints.

In contrast with discussions of welfare state expansion up to the 1970s, the current literature has offered markedly different explanations for welfare retrenchment, aptly characterized as the "new politics of the welfare state" (NPWS) (P. Pierson 2001a; Huber and Stephens 2001; Scharpf and Schmidt 2000; Green-Pedersen 2002). Compared with the old politics of welfare state development, a distinctive feature of the retrenchment literature is that partisan government matters much less for policy changes. In the literature on welfare expansion during *les trente glorieuses*, the power resources theory was the dominant theory. It argues that welfare state development is a result of political organization by wage earners, through both unions and social democratic parties. Incumbency of left parties is the most important predictor for welfare state expansion (Stephens 1979; Esping-Andersen 1980; Korpi 1983). On this basis, several theoretical extensions have been developed. Incumbency hegemony from the Right, for example, is a major impediment to welfare state development (Castles 1982; Hicks and Swank 1984), and in the absence of strong social democratic parties, electorally dominant centrist parties can take over the role of welfare activism (Hicks 1999). On the whole, the power resources thesis offers a clear argument that ideological differences matter in welfare state development.

However, this line of argument has suffered a clear setback in the NPWS literature. This literature addresses a different macrocontext from the 1950s and 1960s. Today's welfare states face a set of complex but common challenges. Domestically, these challenges include persistent unemployment, escalating budget deficits, and an increasing burden on social security. Internationally, capital has become increasingly mobile, and the growing possibility for businesses to move abroad threatens traditional economic stimulants, such as lower interest rates, devaluation, or deficit spending. Most European countries are now under the additional constraint of the Stability and Growth Pact and the tight monetary policy of the European Central Bank. Domestic or international, these common changes are not reversible in the immediate future. They have created a macrocontext for today's welfare state development, which P. Pierson (2001b) aptly characterizes as "permanent austerity." Faced with this common pressure, different countries have responded in different ways. For each country, its strategies are heavily path dependent on, and constrained by, prior institutional contexts. On a macro level, these institutional settings encompass both welfare state and labor market regimes. On a micro level, they constrain the preference distributions and policy assumptions of government officials, employers, and employees (Hall and Soskice 2001; Swank 2002). In NPWS, the interaction between path dependency and permanent austerity has led to "diverse responses to common challenges" (Scharpf and Schmidt 2000), and the dominant welfare reform pattern is "refracted divergence" (Myles and Quadagno 2002: 51).

In this theoretical framework, there is no uniform welfare retrenchment across the advanced industrialized countries. According to Pierson (2001b), the retrenchment pattern is a combination of cost control and recommodification in liberal welfare regimes, cost control and rationalization of existing social programs in social democratic welfare regimes, and cost control and updating of existing social programs in continental welfare regimes. Along a similar line, D. Swank (2002) suggests that international capital mobility is either neutral or even positive for welfare state development in countries with a strong institutional basis for social interest representation, such as social corporatism and universally available benefit programs. By contrast, there is much greater pressure for retrenchment where welfare interest representation is fragmented and social programs characterized by narrower constituencies.

The role of partisan government has been clearly overshadowed by this dominant path-dependent thesis of welfare retrenchment. In NPWS, the programmatic objectives of parties are significantly diminished. Social democrats are constrained from delivering comprehensive social protection, while the secular Right is constrained from drastically reducing government involvement in social protection. Welfare retrenchment is limited, regardless of partisan color. Where politics still plays a role in NPWS, it is now largely nonideological, based instead on the balancing between vote or office maximization (Kitschelt 2001; Green-Pedersen 2002). Rather than spurts of new thoughts coming out randomly, ideological adaptations have always occurred as practical responses to changes in realities (Freeden 1996). The need to maintain a broad electoral alliance has always been an important factor in the evolution of a more inclusive concept of solidarity. However, the NPWS literature has expanded this logic significantly further. In policy changes where electoral needs conflict with ideological principles, rather than adjusting the latter to accommodate the former, parties all but abandon the latter, leaving policies to be largely dictated by median voter needs. In other words, left parties are unwilling to expand social security and the secular Right unwilling to cut, but in neither case has the policy decision been accurately reflective of their ideological beliefs. Instead, the motive has been to hold onto votes, which can be lost either due to an economic crisis or unpopular cuts in benefits.

The power resources theory was developed during the Golden Age to refute the Marxist accusation that social democracy has achieved little for the working class. Now, NPWS implies that, short of a past legacy in generous welfare, there is little further potential for social democracy to cater to wage earners. The pragmatic orientation within social democracy has more or less made its programmatic orientation irrelevant, and social democratic parties are no longer seriously constrained by ideologies. This book makes a different argument. In the following sections, I will compare the mechanisms through which institutions and ideologies limit options for individual action, and explain how the intrinsic properties of political ideologies provide the potential for radical policy changes against institutional constraints.

3.2. Defining Institutions

The institutional economics literature has offered rigorous and internally consistent definitions of institutions (North 1990; Aoki 2001; Mantzavinos 2001). These conceptualizations significantly enriched theories not only within economics, such as financing, technological innovation, and the firm, but also within institutional comparative political economy, ranging from comparative welfare states to the varieties of capitalism. In short, institutions are rules of the game. They are humanly devised constraints that limit options for behavior. The ability of institutions to constrain behavior relies on enforcements. Institutions enforced through state and legal sanctions are formal institutions, such as laws (including policies enacted from legislation) and contracts. Informal institutions, including norms and conventions (such as corporatism), rely for enforcement on mutual or third-party (non-state) monitoring and sanctions (North 1990). Through enforcement of various kinds, institutions prevent actors from taking certain actions and reward them for taking others. For example, in contribution-based continental welfare states, income transfer payments are generous (often enough for the whole family), but not available without a stable and uninterrupted working record. Constrained by this formal rule of the game, male workers all but abandon family duties to their wives, and they agree to have a portion of their wages deducted, for future benefits. Meanwhile, the option of sharing family duties between couples and working part time is automatically closed by the rewards and sanctions of continental welfare institutions. This illustrates the power of institutions in limiting options for individual action.

Formal organizations, such as parties, unions, and business chambers, are not institutions in the definition of D. C. North (1990), M. Aoki (2001), or C. Mantzavinos (2001). Instead, these organizations are makers and players of the institutional rules. Third way reforms are primarily attempts to change formal institutions: welfare state and labor market policies. Compared with informal ones, formal institutions are easier to make and unmake because the power to devise formal rules is more narrowly concentrated in one actor, the government. Such power is enormous, given the small number of rule makers relative to the large number of population to be affected by the rules. Meanwhile, this power for rule making is also highly uncertain, disappearing instantaneously with the change of government. As will be noted later, the contested as well as power-laden nature of formal institutional design is a key reason why political agents are willing to absorb the (sometimes enormous) cost of abandoning old institutions and devising new ones, in this process triggering institutional innovation rather than just reproduction.

In order to discuss how ideologies overcome institutional barriers, it is important to first examine how these barriers function. Two ostensibly obvious properties of institutions are (1) history: they persist (for at least a reasonable period of time), and (2) large numbers: they intend to affect all players of the relevant game. Because of history and large numbers, institutions increase the difficulty of change through both dynamic and cross-sectional mechanisms, that is, path dependency and collective action failure. Clearly, in their role as institutional constraints, these two mechanisms are inseparably intertwined. The path-dependent cost of change accumulated through time is often intensified as a result of the inability among actors to cooperate. However, conceptually, it probably is more accurate to regard collective action failure *as one contributing factor* to path dependency, rather than simply equating it with path dependency, because on its own the logic of collective action operates not through time but through large numbers (of players). Throughout the book's analysis of path dependency, where collective action failure is a contributing factor, its role in path dependency will be highlighted. Now, I examine these two mechanisms in some detail.

3.3. The Constraint of Time: Path Dependency

Earlier, through the example of contribution-based benefits in continental welfare states, I illustrated the capacity of institutions to discourage acts that break the existing rules of the game. On its own, this is still different from path dependency because here, the severe costs of choosing closed rather than open options are directly part of the institutional rules. If the rules do not prescribe them, there will be no such costs. However, as institutions persist through time, they lead to additional costs of switching to closed options. These costs are not part of the original institutional rules. Instead, they are simply generated by, and increase with, the accumulation of history (P. Pierson 2004).

These time-related costs are the defining characteristics of path dependency: Given enough history, early rules of the game, even if imposed by random, become increasingly costly to reverse. Time, in other words, provides a major exogenous source of institutional self-reinforcement. As institutions persist, players become better players over time due to iterative learning-by-doing and information accumulation about existing rules of the game. Two highly distinctive characteristics of information are its indivisibility and non-exhaustibility. In other words, information will not diminish either by more people using it or by repeated usage over time. The capacity for the same information to be utilized with more intensity and variety constitutes, respectively, the economy of scale and economy of scope. Such benefits are often conceptualized as the externalities of (information) networks (Chandler 1990; Foray 2004). Actors can therefore avoid having to reinvent the wheel, and they can progressively reduce the costs of obtaining the necessary information to evaluate each next decision to be made.

By comparison, the information cost of designing entirely new institutions is enormous due to the absence of history (hence, no economy of scale or scope) for these new rules. For example, for continental European governments planning to increase in-work incentives, the information cost (such as trial and error, policy debacles, and the inefficiency of policymaking under uncertainty) of devising new negative income taxes will be significantly greater than simply lowering existing social security contributions. The information cost of unmaking old rules is ex post, occurring after the old rules are abandoned. There might also be ex ante cost of innovation, occurring and growing steadily even before new rules are adopted. Actors sometimes make unrecoverable investments in accommodating existing rules of the game, and once the rules are changed, these unrecoverable investments become sunk costs. An important reason behind the difficulty in retrenching continental social security is the fact that workers give up a portion of their wages as deductions into contributions. These unrecoverable investments become the sunk costs of abandoning existing rules, and they steadily accumulate with the passage of time.

Because of information and sunk costs, institutional changes are highly path dependent. For the same reform, different starting points will lead

to increasingly diverse trajectories of change over time. This is the fundamental logic behind the "refracted divergence" observation in the NPWS
literature. However, this "divergence in change" argument leads to more
fundamental questions: Where did the changes come from in the first place,
and how did these changes overcome their own information and sunk costs
to get started?

3.4. The Logic of "Public Evils"

Institutions as rules of the game are not the only form of constraint on
options for action. Another major constraint on individual action is ideology,
a coherent belief set that serves as an information shortcut for evaluating
policy issues and making strategic decisions (Downs 1957; Aldrich 1995).
Just like institutions, values and ideologies are option-limiting devices, constraining individuals from taking certain actions while encouraging them
to take others. With some accumulation of time as a certain ideology is
implemented through policy, the consistent selection of some policy options
over others leads to an increasingly distinct set of policy patterns. When
power reverses to other partisan groups, a different ideological constraint
sets in, leading to different policy patterns. This is the fundamental logic
behind the power resources thesis that partisan color matters in welfare
state changes. Now, both institutions and ideologies are essentially option-
limiting devices, but why does one reinforce path dependency while the
other triggers institutional breakthrough?

Both institutions and ideologies constrain individual action, but there
is some fundamental difference between them. Institutions, as North said,
are rules of the game. They intend to affect all agents in the relevant game.
It is appropriate to emphasize "intend" here because there is the possibility
for shirking and not playing by the rules, such as free riding or even breaking the laws. But at least these rules are meant to bind everyone, and to
make these rules meaningful, the number of shirkers has to be trivial relative to nonshirkers. Institutions, in other words, are in effect public goods.
Secondly and related to the first point, no mutually conflicting institutions
can stably coexist. Ideologies have the opposite set of properties. Each ideology constrains only some people but not others, and for ideologies to be
a useful device for differentiation and identification, conflicting ideologies
must coexist stably. In other words, people agree to disagree. Therefore,
due to differing beliefs, people have conflicting preferences for rules of the
game, and meanwhile they have to abide by the same uniform set of rules.
The potential for conflicting preferences is especially great when the rules

in question are formal institutions, such as government policies. This is because, unlike informal institutions (such as conventions or norms), only some individuals get to make the formal rules, and everyone else has no choice but to play by the rules, despite their different preferences. For those unhappy with the rules, should they absorb the information and sunk costs to change the rules?

Albert Hirschman (1970) observed responses to the decline of product quality in consumer markets and extended the logic to product decline in political markets. Hirschman's "exit, voice, and loyalty" arguments provide a fundamental logic for the reason people do sometimes choose to make costly changes to existing situations. There are two distinctive characteristics of consumer markets that typically do not exist in political markets. Firstly, when product quality declines, there is unlikely to be more than a trivial difference among individual consumers' evaluation of the situation. Regardless of the nature of their belief sets, few consumers will interpret malfunctioning batteries or deteriorating tastes of food as *improvement* in product quality. Fundamentally, ideological beliefs are irrelevant in consumer markets, and people typically do not agree to disagree. Secondly, when a certain product declines, consumers can typically exit and switch easily to comparable substitutes. They can switch to a different brand of battery with negligible personal cost. In this way, they escape the negative consequences of product decline without having to assume the cost of improving the product in question.

On both these dimensions, political markets have the opposite characteristics. Firstly, when the product in question is a government policy, people often do disagree in their opinion on the policy. Because ideologies serve as filters for assessing policy issues, conflicting ideological preferences lead to conflicting assessments of the same political product. When budget austerity leads to drastic increase in unemployment, those from the Left believe this to be utter failure, while neoliberals regard it as the early sign of success in exercising economic discipline. In political markets, therefore, people agree to disagree, and often many remain unhappy with what is on offer. Secondly, unlike consumer markets, individuals typically cannot exit from the political market, especially if the goods in question are public goods, such as policies. Hirschman made the insightful observation that for the unhappy many, the public goods become "public evils." The term "public" is important, as it indicates the nonexcludable nature of these goods: Even if the consumers do not make or agree with the rules, they live with their consequences. Even for welfare policies that ostensibly target a minority of the population, such as means-tested benefits, everyone is affected, either by being excluded from the benefits or paying for them through income taxes.

Hirschman pointed out that if the low-cost option of exit is closed, the only other response to product decline is the more costly strategy of voice. The public evil nature of institutional rules and the political contestability of rule-making power are important incentives that can potentially offset the information or sunk costs of pathbreaking institutional changes. I emphasize the qualifier "potentially" due to the contingent nature of this argument. Public evils provide incentives for assuming the costs of institutional change, but whether the incentives are actually strong enough to overcome the costs depends on the situation. The more intensively people disagree, the more objectionable the policy in question for the unhappy, and the greater the incentive for change relative to its information and sunk costs. This is what Thelen (2004) refers to as the "political contestability" of institutions. Under what circumstances do people have relatively strong conflicting preferences, and when do they remain more indifferent? To answer this question, it is helpful to more closely compare the role of policy paradigms versus policy implementation.

As the key behavioral manifestation of ideological principles, policy paradigms should include some fundamental policy objectives plus a *summary representation* (Aoki 2001)[1] of the policy tools that can attain these objectives. I use the term "summary representation" to emphasize the highly parsimonious nature of paradigms: They set out a small number of defining attributes of all relevant policy tools that can lead to the same objective. Among the various policy tools that fit the summary representation, which particular tool to pick out is a question of implementation. The fundamental third way policy objective, for example, is enabling to work. A summary representation of policy tools that serve this purpose can include active labor market measures, in-work incentives, labor market flexibility measures, and so on. From the in-work incentive toolkit, whether one chooses negative income taxes, reductions in social security contributions, or expansion of public child care becomes a question of implementation. To the extent that these different policy tools all serve the same policy objective, actors are indifferent about which particular one to choose, and the absence of conflicting preferences lowers the political contestability of policy implementation,

---

[1] The term "summary representation" can be traced to Aoki, but he utilized it in a much broader theoretical framework of defining institutions and conceptualizing firms as nexus of contracts.

relative to policy paradigms. In the last paragraph, the logic of "public evils" suggested that more (less) politically contested institutions provide greater (smaller) incentives for absorbing the costs of creating new rules that accommodate ideological preferences. Therefore, policy paradigms are more likely to be guided by the partisan color of government, while policy implementation within each paradigm is more likely to be path dependent. In other words, the third way reform policy paradigm of enabling to work should be distinctively associated with social democratic incumbency, and meanwhile, the implementation of activation strategies should still be path dependent, reflecting diverse historical legacies of different welfare and labor market regimes.

3.5. The Constraint of Large Numbers: A Contributing Factor to Path Dependency

Institutions typically affect a very large number of players, and this creates some additional difficulty for change, in terms of how each individual actor evaluates his or her own contribution to changing the rules, relative to the community of actors as a whole. Hirschman's argument that goods in the political market are often public evils has important implications because it connects us directly to Olson's (1965) well-known thesis about public goods and the logic of collective action. Good or evil, products that are public share the common characteristic of nonexcludability: No individual can be excluded from their positive (or negative) externalities, regardless of whether he or she has contributed to the products. For public goods of this kind, the possibility for collective action failure increases with the number of beneficiaries. The larger the group, the smaller the weight of each individual's contribution to the delivery of the goods and the greater the individual incentive to shirk, by avoiding the cost of contribution while still deriving positive utilities from the goods.

From public goods, the logic of collective action can be extended to public evils, which are just the mirror image of public goods: Everyone derives positive utilities from the goods' absence. For social democratic governments to transform passive welfare states to active ones, it is often necessary to obtain from the labor movement the consent to, for example, reduce existing welfare benefits. To do so, each union has to absorb the enormous communication and other costs in persuading its own members. However, with many unions all having to do this, the contribution to doing so from any single union becomes trivial, and the individual cost of persuading its own members also becomes not worthwhile. As R. Tuck (2008) stressed, the problem of individual causal inefficacy is the root of collective action failure. With its own contribution now insignificant, it is rational for the individual union to simply shirk, relying on other unions to purchase the consent of their own members, which can generate sufficient grassroots support for the party to go ahead with its reforms. Of course, as Olson pointed out, when each union shirks on this basis, the public goods cannot be generated. The party gets no support from the movement, and the reform stalls. Technically, the party can still move ahead with the reform without grassroots support. The Dutch social democratic party (PvdA) did so in reforming social security benefits, and New Zealand Labour did so in economic reform in 1984. But then, the political cost will be steep. The serious electoral setback suffered by the PvdA in 1994 was openly attributed to its involvement in the nonconsensual social security reforms, and in New Zealand both major parties learned the same lesson.

As said earlier, it is clearly impossible to entirely separate this process from path dependency. In the collective action game, the personal cost being contemplated by each individual is itself often the result of past institutional constraints; the size of the cost will increase with time, and when changes fail to occur, past institutions are reinforced. Nevertheless, here the cost deters action through its cross-sectional diffusion across the players, rather than through the accumulation of time. This is why the collective action problem is better treated as a contributing factor to path dependency than just as path dependency itself.

Given a situation of large numbers, Olson offered some suggestions about how collective action failure can be avoided. By being organizationally integrated rather than remain free floating, actors have access to more direct channels for communication and monitoring of each other's action. The hierarchical nature of organization and its ability to assert authority also reduces the opportunities for shirking. I already utilized this argument in Section 2 of this chapter, where I discussed the importance of organizational integration for reducing the insider–outsider divide. To carry the argument further, the more centralized and better coordinated the organization, the more likely collective action, again for the same reason of better communication and monitoring. This highlights the importance of corporatism in dismantling the collective action barrier to third way reforms. Corporatist institutions are themselves an example of informal rules of the game. Through the peak authorities for both unions and employers, corporatist institutions generate centralized interest representation and highly coordinated negotiation patterns. In the book's empirical chapters on the third way reform experience, the presence or lack of strong corporatist institutions is often crucial in whether third way reforms are stalled due to resistance from social partners, on issues ranging from reforming passive benefits to relaxing employment protection. When these reforms fail to occur and traditional institutions reinforce themselves, it is undoubtedly correct to identify the process as path dependent. However, it is theoretically important to highlight the non-time-related factor behind such path dependency: collective action failure.

3.6. The Third Way Policy Paradigm

After having discussed in detail the theories of institutions and ideologies in constraining individual action, now I outline the third way paradigm in detail. This paves the way for later empirical comparison of how ideology affects policy paradigms versus policy implementation. The third way ideology focuses on enabling to work and making work pay. On this basis, social democratic solidarity is productivist, and egalitarianism is prioritarian. Strategies of social protection can be active or passive, and the third way ideology leads to distinct strategies for these two types of protection.

3.6.1. *Active and Passive Social Protection: Key Third Way Strategies*

Active social protection primarily operates by facilitating entry into the labor market, whereas passive protection facilitates exclusion from the labor market. The most important component of active protection belongs to active labor market policies (ALMPs). Diverse in design, different ALMPs share the common characteristic of making an offer to the unemployed, either in the form of job placement or training and education. The act of making an offer is significant because, different from any other social and labor market policy instrument, ALMPs move the labor market to the unemployed. In other words, ALMPs are the primary strategy that brings the labor market to the door of the unemployed by offering direct interaction between the two parties. Compared with other policies, the extent of state intervention and resource commitment involved in the making of an activation offer is innovative. In active social protection, ALMPs can be supplemented by two other types of measures. Unlike ALMPs, they do not offer the unemployed any direct interaction with the labor market. Instead, they indirectly increase the possibility for such interaction, by adjusting the structure of the labor market so that it becomes more accessible to people who cannot work with normal schedules or conditions for family or health reasons. At the same time, job security for atypical workers and social security for those temporarily excluded from the labor market are also enhanced. Therefore, these strategies are called "flexicurity" measures (Wilthagen 1998), a combination of flexibility and security. In the event that interaction with the labor market does occur, there are further measures that increase the financial return or reduce the family-related cost of working. Such measures are called in-work incentives.

While active protection is in the labor market, passive protection belongs to the formal social security system. Whereas active protection helps individuals regain income, passive protection compensates for income loss by replacing income with welfare benefits. Passive income compensation can be reactionary or anticipatory. Reactionary compensation targets persons already outside the labor market, and anticipatory compensation targets those still inside the labor market. The former is reactionary in the sense that compensation occurs after loss of income, and the most typical example is unemployment benefits. The latter is anticipatory because compensation actually triggers exit from work. Anticipatory compensation includes a wide range of labor market-clearing measures, which serve the purpose of reducing the labor force. Also known as early exit pathways, these measures can be age related, health related, or in the form of leave schemes. In the former two cases, exit from the labor market is permanent, whereas in the third one it is temporary. While reactionary compensation such as unemployment benefits reduces the incentive for returning to work, anticipatory compensation goes one step further, by removing people from work. In other words, the early exit pathways are ALMPs in reverse.

For these reasons, in third way reforms, active protection would expand significantly, but passive protection will more likely go through either restructuring or retrenchment. For reactionary compensation such as unemployment benefits, there is no clear ideological reason for blanket cuts. These benefits can create disincentives to enter the labor market, but they also provide a vital source of income for those who really can't work. The prioritarian principle of egalitarianism implies that while there might be selective cuts to remove the welfare trap, at the same time the cuts should be limited. More importantly, these cuts should be balanced by some redistribution toward the most needy, for example, through changes to the taxation system or to welfare financing patterns. While such restructuring strategies are suitable for reactionary compensation, there can be more straightforward cutbacks on anticipatory compensation because of the "activation in reverse" nature of these early exit pathways. By turning people with earning power into those without earning power, these pathways conflict with both the principles of productivist solidarity and prioritarian egalitarianism.

In general, in order to effectively activate the labor market, the primary policy focus would be on expansion in active protection. Adjustment to passive protection is a useful supplement, but this alone will not be sufficient to increase labor market activation. Active protection, especially ALMPs, is the primary medium through which direct interaction between the unemployed and the labor market is established. This is also where significant further growth for the future is possible, as for most countries active protection started from scratch only since the mid-1980s. By comparison, the long-term potential for adjustments in passive protection is more limited. Passive protection, intrinsically, does not directly create any opportunity for interaction between the individual and the labor market. Instead, adjustments to passive protection can only reduce the potential for work disincentives. What is more, reforming social security often involves taking away the existing financial or administrative privileges of social partners, especially unions, who have developed a proprietary interest in the benefits. This problem is especially serious in insurance-based continental welfare regimes, where changes to unemployment insurance benefits, pensions, or existing work regulations are often fiercely opposed by unions and consequently aborted.

Blanket dismantling of social security without corresponding expansion in active measures is *not* the way to labor market activation. On an ideological level, reactionary compensation serves the social justice purpose of protecting the most vulnerable. On a more concrete policy level, adequate out-of-work benefits, as long as they are combined with appropriate targeting and limited duration, can potentially encourage people to more effectively search for jobs fitting their skills. Combining expansion in active measures with rollback in passive measures is more likely to be effective in employment promotion than relying only on cutting passive measures. In this book I make a clear distinction between expansion of active protection and the restructuring of passive protection, but it is important to keep in mind that in actual third way reforms, active and passive strategies always occur simultaneously. Expansion of active measures inevitably involves corresponding changes in passive measures, and tightening passive benefits are often part of an ALMP strategy. Changes to unemployment benefits, for example, often imply strengthening the obligation to accept activation offers, and the jobs offered in ALMPs are often paid as benefits in social security. Nevertheless, although changes to active and passive sides of protection happen simultaneously and interactively, they do follow distinct logics and strategies.

3.6.2. *Macroeconomy and Corporatism: Key Third Way Contexts*

Jobs, and well-paid jobs, are the core practical purpose for the third way ideology of social justice. This ideology addresses the post-oil-shock context where Keynesian demand management is no longer as effective. For this reason, third way policies, active or passive, focus more on facilitating labor market entry than on directly expanding the size of the labor market through economic stimulants. This also brings a potential problem of its own. When the labor market shrinks, opportunities for labor market entry also decline. The main third way strategies are largely powerless in reversing this situation. Besides some direct job creation schemes, most activation measures aim to bring existing jobs and the unemployed together, and they cannot significantly affect the actual size of the labor market. Activation in the context of shrinking labor markets cannot lead to major improvements in employment opportunities for those excluded.

Job creation, of course, is technically not a labor market or social policy issue. Instead, the creation of investment, growth, and employment is more directly influenced by monetary and fiscal policies on a macro level. Therefore, for the core strategies of third way reform to be effective in the long run, a larger macroeconomic context of growth and competitiveness is necessary in order to keep the labor market growing. The options for fueling economic growth, however, have been greatly narrowed in the last two decades. Internationalization of finance, hard currency, and the Stability and Growth Pact have all ruled out some traditional economic stimulants, such as competitive devaluation, public sector borrowing, or lowering interest rates. The remaining viable option for stimulating growth is to pursue wage restraint and maintain a cautious anti-inflationary principle. In other words, core activation strategies of the third way require a job-growth economic context characterized by prudence and wage moderation.

Compared with wage moderation, a prudent approach to the economy appears to be easier to enforce because the domain of economic policy is precisely where changes in the external context (the Stability and Growth Pact and the internationalization of finance, for example), as well as in the domestic context (secular shift toward the service economy), are occurring. Being directly implicated by these changes, the pressure to adapt is relatively strong, and the potential for resistance for institutional reasons relatively weak. On this front, governments are forced to make serious efforts in enforcing a policy of economic prudence. They prefer supply- to demand-side measures and cut social security contributions to reduce labor costs. Where third way reforms start from a basis of strong regulation or protection, governments have to follow up with comprehensive deregulation and privatization, including not only the loosening of credit or interest rate control but also the transfer of industrial assistance from uncompetitive to competitive industries.

Ideologically, economic prudence is probably not an end in itself. It is, instead, merely a macroeconomic context, creating the necessary conditions for sustained economic and job growth, which helps labor market activation policies. This instrumental feature of social democratic economic prudence is worth highlighting, because where a prolonged period of austerity was already excessive enough to actually hurt employment, such as in New Zealand, Germany, and France in the late 1990s, the government responded with some expansionary measures rather than further austerity (more details in the empirical chapters). In addition, economic prudence also serves social purposes. Revenues saved as a result of economic efficiency can be channeled into increased public expenditure (such as spending on combating social exclusion), rather than into blanket tax cuts.

Compared with economic prudence, wage moderation as the other part of the economic context is more difficult to achieve because incomes policy is where social partners have historically come into conflict to a great extent. A voluntary incomes policy in the framework of corporatist concertation is often crucial for wage moderation. For this reason, next to the macroeconomy, corporatism should also be part of the third way policy paradigm, serving as another important context for core activation strategies. Essentially, corporatism is important in this book for two reasons: Theoretically, as discussed in Section 3.5, it is an important mechanism for ensuring collective action. Empirically, it happens also to be a major component of the third way policy paradigm, through its connection to wage moderation and economic prudence as the contexts for core third way strategies.

3.6.3. *The Paradigm and Its Contingent Relationship to Theories*

Overall, on a policy level, the third way ideology manifests itself in adjustments to both active and passive social protection. Adjustment strategies

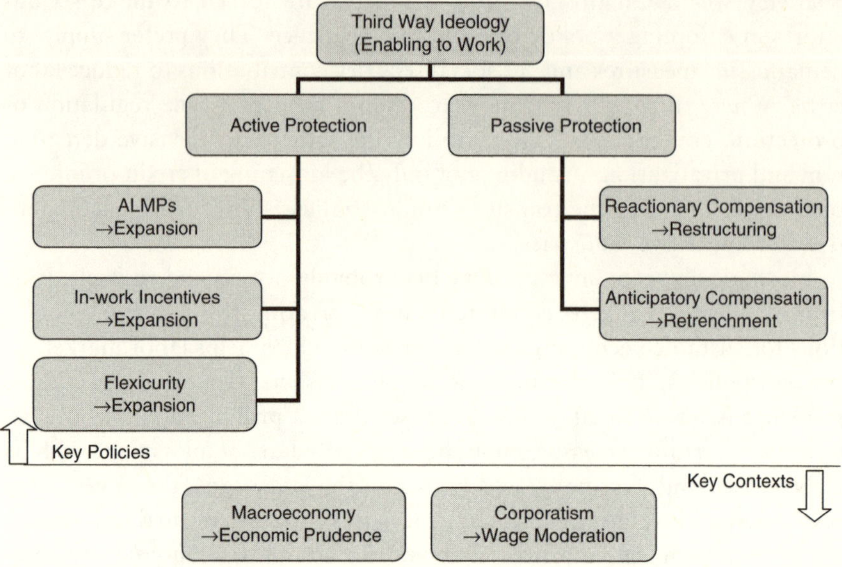

FIGURE 2.1. The Third Way Policy Paradigm

are diverse, including expansion, restructuring, or retrenchment, and the adoption of specific strategies depends on the actual policy area in question. The third way policy paradigm cuts across the social security system and labor market, and it also involves changes in the macroeconomy and in industrial relations. Figure 2.1 outlines the key components and structure of this third way paradigm.

In Sections 3.3 through 3.5, I provided a set of theories about the institutional barriers to ideologically motivated policy changes, as well as the circumstances under which it is possible for ideologies to overcome these barriers. Path-dependency theorists argue that accumulation of time leads to information and sunk costs in unmaking old institutional rules. In response, the theory of public evils suggests that the impossibility of exit and the conflicting ideological preferences over public policies offer incentives to incur these costs for making institutional changes. It is important to reemphasize the contingent nature of this theory. It merely suggests the possibilities for ideologies to trigger pathbreaking institutional changes. Whether such possibilities are sufficient is a question of a more empirical nature, depending on the circumstances for each specific case. In between policy paradigm, on the one hand, and policy implementation within a given paradigm, on the other, the former is more likely to be determined by partisan ideology. The latter, by contrast, is more likely to display patterns of path dependency. As a further indication of the contingent nature of this theory, path dependency can also be broken simply through mechanisms unrelated to the framework of public evils. For example, the economic situation of permanent austerity led to a radical but bipartisan turn toward monetarism in macroeconomic policy across the advanced industrialized countries.

Reflecting the same logic, while corporatist institutions generally help reduce collective action failure and path dependency, there is nothing deterministic about this process. Institutions affect all actors, but not necessarily all actors *pay a cost* in changing institutions, especially when cost is understood as some decline of personal utility or welfare. In fact, in some instances of rule changing, such as the introduction of monetary rewards for working, most individuals derive benefits rather than costs. In such cases, strong corporatism is less important to the outcomes of reforms. Similarly, in reforming unemployment benefits, corporatist breakdown is more likely to be a stumbling issue in countries with Ghent and insurance-based systems (such as Sweden) than non Ghent (such as in Norway) or tax-based (such as in Denmark) systems. In other words, collective action (and by association corporatism) is not a relevant mechanism in all policy changes and all contexts. This is different from the information cost for policymakers, which is more or less ubiquitous with any attempt to replace old rules with new ones. Another reason why the corporatist explanation should be nondeterministic is what J. Mahoney and G. Goertz (2006) call "equalfinality": Many other factors can also prevent (or facilitate) reforms taking place. In New Zealand, for example, the government pushed forward highly radical reforms without corporatist cooperation, and in the Netherlands, some reforms can occur only through the *removal* of old corporatist institutions.

These instances will be discussed in greater detail in the empirical chapters, but the general argument here is that unlike path dependency, corporatism (as a contributing factor to path dependency) does not affect the institutional constraint on third way reforms in all cases. In addition, there are other exogenous factors that do not even relate to path dependency (for example, permanent austerity in the macroeconomy), which can further affect both the reform process and its outcome. Now, it is possible to connect these theoretical arguments to the one ideologically contested paradigm examined throughout this book: the third way.

3.7. Power Resources in the Third Way Paradigm

In Sections 1.2 through 1.4 of this chapter, I explained in detail the fundamental difference between the third way ideology and its center-right alternatives. A key task for the book's empirical chapters is to demonstrate, on this basis, that social democratic incumbency indeed uniquely leads to the third way policy paradigm highlighted in Figure 2.1, while governments of other partisan colors offer distinctively different policy packages. The NPWS literature, by contrast, argues that partisan differences have by now diminished significantly. In other words, the conventional retrenchment literature and this book offer rival hypotheses about the extent of partisan differentiation in contemporary policy reform paradigms.

Since the third way ideology is premised on enabling to work, the left–right differentiation in incumbent policies should be greatest in active social protection. The core of active social protection is ALMPs. These measures have significant potential for growth, and they also require substantial state spending. By means of these policies, the state takes a proactive role in social protection by bringing together the labor market and the unemployed. They are the essential means for increasing labor market participation. For these reasons, social democrats would significantly expand active social protection, including not only ALMPs but also in-work incentives and flexicurity measures where necessary. For precisely these characteristics of active protection, both Christian Democrats and the secular Right would be much less enthusiastic about expansion. The former are skeptical about activation per se, while the latter are opposed to increased state involvement. Especially for the secular Right, the concern with cost saving can drive the government to roll back some existing ALMPs. In contrast, the NPWS hypothesis will suggest a different outcome. Active social protection is where the potential for expansion is greatest. However, with the exception of Sweden (and partially Norway), a historical institutional legacy of passive welfare states would create enormous costs in switching to active protection across all these countries. On top of this path-dependency barrier, the external context of permanent austerity in the economy further limits the center-left ability to increase state spending. Therefore, based on NPWS, both social democratic and center-right incumbency should refrain from expansion in active protection.

In comparison with active protection, partisan differentiation should be less notable in passive protection. For reactionary compensation such as unemployment benefits, parties from both the Left and Right want to remove work disincentives. For anticipatory compensation, all governments want to limit these early exit pathways. However, there should still be some reflection of ideological difference between the third way and center-right alternatives. In reforming unemployment benefits, which can potentially sustain the status of loss in earning power through income replacement, social democrats should emphasize restructuring rather than drastic retrenchment. The purpose of restructuring is to reduce work disincentives by putting some limit on benefit eligibility, while intensifying benefits for the worst-off. In contrast to such prioritarian egalitarianism, the secular Right would favor significant cuts in benefit levels to save cost, while Christian Democrats would be more hesitant about both drastic cuts and removing work disincentives. In other words, their main reaction would be inaction.

The similar is true for anticipatory compensation. These early exit pathways create the status of loss in earning power through income replacement. While all governments want to restrict such measures, the social democratic focus would be on encouraging labor market retention or reentry, by enabling measures targeted at early leavers. By contrast, the secular Right would emphasize cutting benefits for cost reduction. Christian democracy, again, would be reluctant to remove these labor market–clearing measures. Nevertheless, as NPWS has shown, in reality the center Right is often constrained from drastically retrenching social security due to the unpopularity of cutting benefits. Therefore, on the whole, the rival hypotheses on passive protection offered by this book and the retrenchment literature will be more similar, as both predict limited reform in social security, featuring more restructuring than drastic cuts.

Finally, partisan differentiation would be most limited beyond the key strategies of active and passive protection, especially in the macroeconomic context for the third way. The economic arena is where permanent austerity is most directly reflected. Traditional policy options for stimulating economic and job growth are now limited due to capital mobility. To the extent that economic austerity does not hurt employment growth, social democrats would converge toward the center-right position on the macroeconomy, especially in their efforts to control inflation and a budget deficit. This is where the competing hypotheses from the conventional literature and this book are essentially the same, because both arguments acknowledge the need to adjust economic policy to permanent austerity. Nevertheless, here it should still be possible to observe some limited partisan difference between social democracy and the center Right, especially with regard to whether economic prudence should be continued when it evidently deflates the economy, and whether revenues from prudence should be reinvested in public spending in the long run.

The core of the third way is active protection, and here there would be significant difference in policy paradigms between social democracy and center-right governments. Across countries, the initiation of social democratic incumbency would involve a shift of policy paradigm toward enabling to work and making work pay. *Such significant association between incumbent ideology and policy paradigm strongly suggests a power resources theory of third way reforms: They depend heavily on the Left coming into government.* In other words, contrary to the conventional understanding that partisan government matters less in the era of welfare retrenchment, *in third way reforms partisan government still determines the fundamental nature of reform paradigms.* Table 2.3 outlines the main competing hypotheses between NPSW and this book's power resources thesis. In the table, cells with darker shades indicate more limited partisan differentiation and smaller contrast between rival hypotheses. It is evident that the difference between power resources and NPWS is greatest for the most crucial component of the third way and least so for the external context of the third way.

3.8. Path Dependency in Third Way Implementation

The earlier theoretical discussions made clear that while partisan ideologies tend to dominate in policy paradigms, within a given paradigm its implementation tends to be path dependent. It is abundantly clear that the book's purpose is not to dispute the presence or importance of path dependency in welfare reform patterns, which is the core argument underlying NPWS. In fact, the book's empirical chapters show many examples of how, for the same third way reform, different institutional legacies across countries lead to divergent patterns of implementation over time. Instead, the primary challenge for the book is to highlight what NPWS perhaps overlooked: the coexistence of path dependency and path departure for the same set of reforms, and the relationship between these two patterns of institutional evolution. In other words, while institutional legacy does dominate the practical implementation of a given policy paradigm, it is partisan ideologies that actually differentiate one paradigm from the other. The essential argument for the book is that *path-dependent institutionalism in third way reforms can be regarded as a midrange causal variable, nested within political agency and ideologically motivated policy innovations.* This is why in Table 2.3, the rival hypotheses focus on the extent of partisan differentiation, rather than whether there is

TABLE 2.3. *Rival Hypotheses on Third Way Reforms: Power Resources versus the New Politics of the Welfare State*

	Rival Hypotheses ⇨		Power Resources	New Politics of the Welfare State
Third way reforms ⇩	Active protection		Left incumbency→expansion Right incumbency→less expansion, sometimes rollback	Limited expansion for left and right
	Passive protection	Reactionary	Left incumbency→restructuring Right incumbency→retrenchment or inaction	Both left and right restrain from radical retrenchment
		Anticipatory	Left incumbency→retrenchment Right incumbency→retrenchment or inaction	
	Macroeconomic context		Left incumbency→prudence for social purposes Right incumbency→prudence as an end	Left converge to right in economic prudence

Note: Cells with darker shades indicate more limited differentiation between partisan governments and between rival hypotheses.

path dependency. For the presence of path dependency in policy implementation, the book offers confirming, rather than rival, hypotheses to NPSW.

In active protection, the most important element is ALMPs. Here, there are differing ways of combining the right and obligation to activation. Greater emphasis on the obligation to work leads to greater tolerance for push measures premised on cutting benefits. Greater emphasis on the right to activation leads to more pull strategies premised on human capital investment. Therefore, under the common paradigm shift toward ALMP expansion, different social democratic governments will move forward in different ways. In Scandinavia, because of traditionally strong attention to human development and job training, activation will emphasize the right more than the obligation to work, especially compared with Anglo-Saxon countries. When it comes to increasing in-work incentive measures, the actual type of incentives adopted will again reflect different welfare regime settings. Where payroll taxes traditionally play an important role, such as in continental Europe, reduction in social security contributions naturally emerges as a cost-efficient way of increasing financial incentives for working. By contrast, negative income taxes (essentially means-tested benefits) lend themselves especially well to Anglo-Saxon countries, where benefits already rely heavily on means testing. For Scandinavian welfare regimes, a tradition of public child care already serves as a highly effective form of in-work incentive, especially for females.

In passive protection, both reactionary and anticipatory compensation reflect path dependency on existing institutional contexts. For reactionary compensation such as unemployment benefits, changes to existing arrangements will be difficult in continental European countries dominated by social insurance schemes, where people make contributions over time and regard benefits as deferred wages. With the social insurance component almost intact, these countries' main achievements have been limited to installing a tax-funded minimum tier, targeted at the worst-off, which meanwhile further segments the protection for insiders versus outsiders. For Anglo-Saxon welfare states, a further tightening of prevalent means-testing schemes would be a more suitable strategy. By contrast, in Scandinavia, the historical attention to labor market activation and human capital development suggests that there would be intensified efforts to tie benefit eligibility to training or other job-placement offers. For anticipatory compensation that takes people out of the labor market, all social democratic governments want to roll them back, but with very different outcomes. In continental Europe, where both unions and employers have historically benefited massively from using early exit pathways as labor market–clearing channels, there would be strong efforts to thwart such reforms. Finally, in the macroeconomic context, neither institutional legacies nor ideologies can exert a

TABLE 2.4. *Power Shifts Between Left and Right*

	Social Democrats out of Government	Social Democrats in Government
Denmark	1982–1993	1993–2001
Sweden	1991–1994	1994–2006
Norway	1982–1985	1986–1989, 1990–1997
Netherlands	1981–1989	1989–2002
France	1993–1997	1988–1993, 1997–2002
Germany	1983–1998	1998–2005
United Kingdom	1979–1997	1997–
Australia	1996–2007	1983–1996
New Zealand	1990–1999	1984–1990, 1999–2008

strong influence on reform strategies: The pressure of permanent austerity will lead to convergence toward economic prudence and wage moderation, as long as these two objectives can help employment growth. Compared with the era of Keynesian demand management, this is a pathbreaking and yet largely bipartisan change in economic policy.

4. THE METHODOLOGY OF THE BOOK

The book's macrocausal analysis (Ragin 1987; Przeworski and Tenue 1970) covers three country cases for each of G. Esping-Andersen's (1990) three main types of welfare regimes: social democratic (Sweden, Denmark, and Norway), continental (the Netherlands, France, and Germany), and liberal (United Kingdom, Australia, and New Zealand). These three institutional traditions are the primary basis for the path-dependency thesis in NPWS, and furthermore, there are also country-specific institutional legacies (such as statism in France and arbitration in Australia) that can further constrain institutional changes. As Table 2.4 shows, all these nine countries also have relatively clear alternations between periods when social democracy was in and out of government, making it possible to track changes in welfare reform patterns in association with changes in the partisan color of government.

The primary empirical focus of this book is third way policies. As third way reforms took place against the background of the Golden Age that has ended, the overall time frame for the empirical analysis is the period since the early 1980s. Within this general time frame, periods of analytical emphasis vary among the nine country cases, focusing on periods of significant third way reforms to flesh out sufficient details and complexities in core third way strategies. To avoid choosing on the dependent variable, while the analytical focus is on periods of third way reforms during social democratic incumbency, contrasting policy paradigms under center-right incumbency are also briefly discussed, which helps highlight the association between social democracy and the third way paradigm. Based on process tracing, this comparison utilizes the method of agreement: Across nine different cases, the similarity in the third way policy paradigm is traced back to the similarity in the partisan color of incumbency (social democratic). Meanwhile, I also use the method of difference: Differences in third way implementation among nine cases of social democratic reforms are traced back to different institutional legacies in each welfare state regime.

Besides narratives, the two key approaches in macrocausal analysis are nominal and ordinal strategies (Mahoney 1999). Nominal comparison directly implements the method of agreement, the method of difference, or Boolean algebra. Here, variables have mutually exclusive categories, and causality is established by eliminating alternative variables. Key works of this methodological tradition include J. Goldstone (1991) and T. Wickham-Crowley (1992). In my book, process tracing from third way paradigm (present or absent) to social democratic incumbency (in or out of power) is an example of nominal comparison; so is process tracing from policy implementation patterns to institutional legacies (differences in kind rather than in degree).

J. Mahoney (1999) argues that while this approach has the advantage of significant parsimony, it suffers from excessive determinism. In other words, one negative case out of nine invalidates the entire causal relationship. For this reason, I supplement the nominal strategies with ordinal analysis. Ordinal comparison can still utilize the logic from the method of difference or agreement, but variables have ordinal rather than exclusive categories. Rueschemeyer, Stephens, and Stephens (1992) is a good representation of this approach. In my book, for example, I use the more ideologically contested nature of policy paradigms to explain why they are more influenced by the partisan color of government than policy implementation. Similarly, I use the weaker coordination capacity of social partners in some countries (such as Germany) than others (such as the Dutch Wassenaar) as one factor to explain less successful flexicurity reforms in the former. While the ordinal strategy is less deterministic in its causal relationship, it is also less parsimonious because it cannot eliminate alternative causes. Not unexpectedly, the best approach for balancing the strengths and weaknesses of nominal and ordinal strategies is to combine them, and this book adopts what Mahoney (1999) calls the "triple combination": narratives, nominal comparisons, and ordinal comparisons. Well-known examples of this approach include T. Skocpol (1979), B. M. Downing (1992), and A. S. Orloff (1993).

3

Constraints on Action

Institutions and Ideas

On a broader theoretical level, the primary focus of this book is to compare how institutions and ideologies constrain agents' options for action, and in turn when ideological beliefs provide enough incentives for undertaking costly changes to existing rules of the game. On an empirical level, this question is examined in the context of how third way ideologies lead to activation-based welfare state changes, which depart fundamentally from historical policy institutions. In this first empirical chapter, I outline the main institutional settings and evolution of third way ideology for each of the nine countries covered in the book. The chapter shows that there is indeed a genuine transformation in social democracy on an intellectual level, and the institutional rules of the game outlined here reassert themselves frequently in later empirical chapters on core third way reform strategies.

1. INSTITUTIONAL SETTINGS FOR THIRD WAY REFORMS

While fundamentally premised on social policy traditions, the institutional constraints on third way reforms also cover characteristics of labor markets, production regimes, industrial relations, and the economy. Many such characteristics are on a system level in terms of "regime types," but there are also important institutional settings that are more country specific. As a roadmap, Table 3.1 outlines some key institutional features that later played a relevant role in third way reforms.

Denmark

Historically, the typically small and medium-size Danish firms demanded a relatively high level of labor market flexibility and job mobility, a characteristic that makes Denmark distinct not only from Coordinated Market

TABLE 3.1. *Key Features of Institutional Background*

Countries in order of appearance in the chapter	Institutional Background ⇨	Welfare State Typology	Other Important Institutional Features
	Denmark	Social democratic welfare state	• High labor market mobility • Welfare state used to be highly passive
	Sweden		• Strong tradition of labor market activation since Rehn-Meidner
	Norway		• High job mobility • Strong regional policy based on active state intervention helped employment
	Netherlands	Christian democratic welfare state	• Wassenaar revitalized corporatist arrangement • Disability benefits are used to externalize employment pressure
	France		• Strong tradition of *dirigisme* • Lack of strong corporatist institutions
	Germany		• Industry-level bargaining dominated by IG Metall • Heavy reliance on early retirement to reduce labor force
	United Kingdom	Liberal welfare state	• Flat-rate benefits funded not through tax but through contribution • Industrial relations voluntary and adversarial
	Australia		• Arbitration delivers wage earners' welfare state • Domestic industries heavily protected
	New Zealand		• Welfare state veering toward universalism by the mid-1970s • Arbitration not very effective in delivering wage testraint

Economies on the European continent but also neighboring Sweden. Overall, regulation of the Danish labor market has been characterized by a high degree of consensus as well as collective self-regulation, a pattern consolidated in terms agreed upon in the "September compromise" of 1899. In this agreement, social partners recognized each other as legitimate negotiating partners for legally binding collective bargaining, and rules for resolving industrial disputes were hammered out. In the September compromise, rules were also negotiated for industrial peace and for freedom of association for employers and employees, and the discretion for hiring and firing decisions was reserved for employers. Over time, the welfare state and the labor market in Denmark have evolved into a partnership model with a relatively high level of autonomy. Many of the issues regulated by legislation in other countries, such as working time or holiday entitlements, are worked out through collective agreements and developed by regional policy committees in the Danish context (Larsen and Bredgaard 2004: 11–12; Benner and Vad 2000: 410; C. Larsen 2004: 4–6, 17).

Unemployment insurance, in particular, is negotiated according to the Ghent model (seen also in Sweden and Finland), which is characterized by voluntary membership in unemployment funds tied to unions as well as solidarity in professionally limited areas, and by insurance funds that are heavily subsidized by the state. Unions, therefore, maintain a strong influence over unemployment benefits management, but in a larger context of corporatist rather than adversarial working relations with employers (Dahl et al. 2002: 9). Relatively high levels of minimum wages negotiated in a collective manner also made it easier to offer reasonably paid jobs, the core principle of action in later third way reforms.

While labor market policies presented a relatively auspicious backdrop for future reforms based on activation, the Danish welfare state did register a few distinctive characteristics of passivity by the late 1980s. On the one hand, a historically well-developed public service sector, plus systems of education and training, encouraged labor market participation for women as well as men, an advantage absent in most continental European countries except France. On the other hand, social security benefits characterized by a very high level of replacement rates and long duration posed clear work disincentives. At the height of its generosity, for example, the duration of unemployment benefits could be up to nine years, while replacement rates could exceed 90% of a normal job wage for many low-skilled groups. Historically, within the circle of Scandinavian welfare states, the Danish system had been comparatively passive (Madsen 1999: 78; Hespanha and Møller 2001: 57). The passivity in the social security system was further aggravated by the general lack during the 1980s of active labor market policies, apart from vocational training programs and general mobility-enhancing measures. During the Golden Age, promotion of high employment relied heavily on demand management for expanding the public sector and, in effect, expanding the overall size of the labor market, while incentives for labor market entry were not emphasized and labor market measures played a minor role. However, simple demand-side job creation had gradually proven less effective in sustaining high employment since the late 1970s.

Sweden

As a typical example of social democratic welfare regimes, the Swedish welfare state is characterized by generous levels of benefits, universal structure of distribution, and a high level of state spending commitment to social services. After a period of polarized competition across party ideological lines, the successful passage in 1959 of the supplementary earnings-related pension (ATP) reforms not only consolidated the earnings-related and high replacement principle of Swedish social benefits but also secured the subsequent support of centrist and liberal parties for continuous welfare expansion during the Golden Age. The emphasis on work-related benefits and replacement rates means that, in cash transfers, the Swedish arrangement is not very different from the typical setup in continental welfare regimes, whereas the tax-funded social services component, on the other hand, is much more developed by comparison. Meanwhile, administration of social transfers remains centralized, while that of social services has devolved to the regional level (Hort 2002: 135; Benner and Vad 2000: 404–405; Huber and Stephens 2001: 124–125). The major exception to this pattern is unemployment insurance, which till today remains decentralized. Like in Denmark, unions are closely involved in the administration of unemployment insurance benefits through the Ghent system, based on voluntary participation and state subsidies. Unions have put up consistent resistance against attempts by the state to make unemployment benefits compulsory or state run (Hort 2002: 133).

There has also been a long tradition of corporatist relationship between unions and employers, consolidated over time through institutions such as the National Labor Market Board (AMS), where both sides of the social partnership work out policies in the labor market. This high level of coordination among social partners is also facilitated by a significant level of organizational centralization for both employers and employees. By the end of the 1960s, union density had reached 80% for blue-collar workers and 60% for white collar workers, whereas the employers' organization, SAF, covered companies involving 90% of the total workforce in the private sector (Benner and Vad 2000: 403). The Swedish corporatist framework, however, suffered a gradual decline after the mid-1980s, as SAF withdrew from centralized bargaining and then from the AMS itself as well. The subsequent decline of coordination in wage bargaining contributed to a bout of wage drifts during the 1980s, which in turn contributed to a sharp rise in unemployment in the 1990s, but the situation for wage moderation started to improve again in the 1990s. The gradual decline of the corporatist framework reduced the potential room for negotiation and trade-offs, and as unions cautiously guarded their control over benefits through the Ghent system, later third way reforms in unemployment insurance in Sweden proved difficult. However, for much of the Golden Age, passivity in Swedish social security in the form of potential work disincentives had not significantly contributed to unemployment, because active measures targeted at the labor market were deployed simultaneously.

In Sweden, formal employment protection is relatively strict, but a greater level of labor market flexibility exists on the ground as unions and employers come to individually negotiated agreements inside the firm over this issue.[1] During the Golden Age, Sweden, and to a lesser extent Norway, were the only two cases where active labor market measures were widely used as a crucial strategy to promote employment. The use of ALMPs in Sweden, in particular, had a long tradition. Swedish labor market activation can be traced back to the key policy framework guiding postwar economic policy development, the Rehn-Meidner model. Designed during the 1950s for a domestic economy dominated by high-productivity manufacturing industries and massive oligopolistic firms trying to remain competitive in the international market, the Rehn-Meidner model uses solidaristic wage polices to price low-productivity labour-intensive industries out of the market. Then, through the AMS, active labor market measures kicked in to move the displaced labor into higher productivity sectors (Huber and Stephens 2001: 127–128). Structural unemployment, therefore, was kept low and the Swedish economy remained on a highly competitive growth path.

On top of ALMPs, further expansion in the public employment sector since the 1960s has offered not only more job opportunities but also child-care

---

[1] Interview by John D. Stephens with the chief economist of the Swedish Confederation of Professional Employees in June 1999.

places for women, contributing to an internationally high level of female participation in the labor market. The Rehn-Meidner logic of eliminating low-productivity industries using low wage dispersion, however, started to backfire as secular shifts from manufacturing to low-productivity service sectors gathered pace after the end of the Golden Age. As the whole productivity base of the economy declined further, wage compression under Rehn-Meidner started to harm instead of help employment. In this process, the expansion of the public service sector increasingly took on the burden of sustaining job growth.

Norway

Similar to those in Sweden, welfare benefits in Norway are generous in level and universal in distribution, and social transfers are usually insurance based, a funding pattern also seen in continental welfare regimes. However, compared with other Scandinavian cases, Norwegian public provision of child care and other policies facilitative of female employment are considerably less extensive. In industrial relations, the Norwegian institutions are characterized by regular centralized bargaining and a strongly corporatist working relationship between employers and unions, consolidated as a central policy objective in an agreement between LO and the main employers' organization, NAF/NHO, in 1966. With an internationally high level of centralization in wage bargaining, collective agreements are legally binding for the negotiating parties, and the National Wage Board, comprising representatives from the state and social partners, is an important institutional basis for consensus in wage negotiations. In addition, as a result of the Basic Agreement, work councils were also established as a platform for workplace participation, where plant management and shop stewards can cooperate on productivity issues. In Sweden bargaining was considerably decentralized after the late 1980s as employers' organization gradually withdrew from the relevant institutions; by contrast, in Norway centralized bargaining not only remained but further strengthened. Employees enjoy a relatively high level of job security, but overall labor market rigidity is not high. This is due not only to the prevalence of flexible working-time arrangements but also to significant labor market mobility as a result of the large share of small firms in the Norwegian economy (Dolvik et al. 1997: 70–71; Huber and Stephens 2001: 258).

Although trade union density in Norway is high internationally (around 56% to 57% since the 1980s), it is considerably lower than other Scandinavian cases (Dolvik et al. 1997: 82). Compared with Sweden, both unions in the core export-oriented industries and Norwegian capital are relatively weak. The lower union density in Norway is related to the fact that unemployment insurance, unlike in Sweden or Denmark, is administered by the state rather than through the Ghent system whereby unions can have a significant influence based on affiliation with insurance funds. The weakness of large manufacturing industries is also due to the relative strength of small work units based on primary economies in the country's periphery, such as fishing. The relative dominance of the periphery in the Norwegian economy has shaped the economic policy profile of the state. Unlike the Rehn-Meidner method of pricing low-productivity industries out of existence, highly supportive regional policy to combat employment based on intense state intervention is the more typical strategy in Norway. The state has played a significant role not only in reaching tripartite agreements in industrial relations but also in an active industrial policy through low interest rates and in a credit policy favorable to industries. The historical weakness of Norwegian capital means that employers reconcile with, rather than strongly resist, the government's active intervention, such as through regional policy. Besides Sweden, Norway is another country that adopted a work line of labor market activation well before the ending of the Golden Age, but activation took a less prominent position in the overall policy framework than in Sweden. This is partly because active state intervention, through demand-side job creation in declining areas, had substituted for the role in Sweden of ALMPs (Huber and Stephens 2001: 131–134).

The Netherlands

The Dutch social security system, especially its disability benefit component which ran into a serious crisis by the mid-1990s, represents many typical problems faced by continental welfare states for the past three decades. On the one hand, unemployment in continental Europe increased due to a combination of labor market rigidities, insufficient wage restraint or dispersion, and a shift in the economy to lower-productivity service sectors. On the other hand, the insurance-based social security system was heavily reliant on social contributions for funding. As a result, collusions between employers and employees, made easier by the generally close relationship between the two sides in Coordinated Market Economies, led to the shedding of unproductive labor through a series of labor market exit schemes. The short-term costs of economic adjustment inside the firm were externalized onto the social security system.

Whereas in Germany early retirement was the typical tool used in cost externalization, in the Netherlands disability and sickness benefits took center stage. Dutch employers and unions dominated corporatist institutions responsible for the administration of the two benefits, and criteria used in granting disability benefits were especially lax. These benefits offered protection on the basis of social risk (incapacity due to personal reasons), not professional risk (incapacity in the course of work). Through collective agreements, both sickness and disability benefits were often topped up to 100% of previous earnings, and those on full-time disability pensions were not required to be available for work. At its height, between 30% to 50% of disability beneficiaries were really full- or part-time unemployed instead of being disabled. Similar to early exit schemes used in other continental welfare regimes, the disability and sickness benefits became serious welfare traps and contributed to a high level of passivity in Dutch social security (Wilthagen 2004: 23–26; van der Veen and Trommel 1999: 291; Hemerijck and Visser 2000: 239).

For this reason, retrenchment in disability benefits was a particularly important component of later Dutch third way reforms. Meanwhile, the problem of passivity in Dutch social security was further complicated by a narrow focus on the size of, instead of entry into, the labor market during employment policymaking in the Golden Age. ALMPs were absent, and employment promotion policies during the 1970s relied mainly on demand-side job creation in labor-intensive sectors, such as construction and public infrastructure. Throughout much of the 1970s and 1980s, unemployment was tackled through the use of subsidized labor to compensate for shortfalls in demand (de Schampheleire and van Berkel 2001: 45; Visser and Hemerijck 1997: 159).

Other features of Dutch welfare and labor market institutions also influenced future third way reforms. Divisions along religious lines among unions and employers' organizations, on top of a steady decline in union density, made voluntary and centralized bargaining increasingly difficult, and consequently, state intervention became increasingly frequent in reaching wage agreements. The problems of malfunctioning voluntary incomes policy and growing wage drift were gradually overcome only after unions signed up for the corporatist framework of the Wassenaar agreement in the early 1980s. The central logic of Wassneaar was a trade-off between wage restraint plus public expenditure cuts, on the one hand, and business commitment to employment creation, on the other. The decline of union strength relative to employers played an important role in unions' quick acceptance of the corporatist agreement.

The strong Christian democratic influence on Dutch welfare state development created clear passivity problems for later third way reforms, for at least two reasons. First of all, the Christian democratic emphasis on generous social transfers, often further intensified as a result of interaction with a social democratic coalition partner, led to the most generous social security benefits among continental welfare regimes (van Kersbergen 1995). Potential work disincentives in these benefits, however, were not balanced with pro-employment measures in the service side of the welfare state, unlike the Scandinavian cases. The emphasis on the principle of subsidiarity and the breadwinner family model led not only to underdevelopment of public services, especially child care, but also to bias against female employment in income tax assessment (for example, in the unit of calculation in the household). For this reason, in addition to disability reforms, expansion in employment for women became another important development in later third way reforms.

France

A highly distinctive institutional legacy in France is the statist emphasis in public policy. Historically, the French political system was strongly influenced by polarized ideological battles through repeated contestations over the republican versus monarchist visions of the nation, and the republican ideology has cast a long shadow over French social policy today. This is seen in the emphasis on the authority and responsibility of the state to tackle poverty and social exclusion as collective, rather than individual, issues. Since the 1983 U-turn, such *dirigisme* has diminished in economic policy, but emphasis on state responsibility continues to frame the development of French social and labor market policy. In addition, as I will discuss later in this chapter, such statist orientation has also directly affected the ideological beliefs of the Socialists.

French unions and employers' organizations are typically weak in strength and particularistic in organizational pattern, and the inability to coordinate agreements on either side has led to an adversarial incomes policy ineffective in securing wage restraint. Intense conflict between weak interest groups in French policymaking means that there is a long tradition of state intervention in industrial relations, and union resistance became an important obstacle toward government attempts to reduce rigidity in the labor market (Vail 1999: 314; Palier 2002: 2–3; Hantrais 1996: 52).

The same problem also affected the process of reforming French social security. Instead of a typical continental welfare regime, the French welfare state has been known as a hybrid system in which Bismarckian and Beveridgean principles coexist (Théret and Barbier 2002: 5). As in other continental welfare states, most cash benefits in France are contributory and earnings related, and there is a highly visible linkage between payment and entitlement, making it difficult to directly cut the level of benefits. As the deficit in the social security system started to grow after the mid-1970s with the gradual rise in unemployment, the government's typical response was to further increase revenue by raising social security contributions, instead of reducing benefits. Social security contributions stood at 44.4% of payroll in 1992, compared with 17.2% in 1970. Frequent increases in social contributions also made "the social treatment of unemployment" an attractive option, whereby retirement ages are lowered and workers removed from the labor market through early exit. Another example of a Bismarckian feature in the French welfare state is the breadwinner family model used in benefit design and distribution. In this model, social transfers to children and women come as an extension of benefits for the male employees (Palier 2000: 116–120; Clegg 2002: 209).

These Bismarckian characteristics in the French welfare state presented the potential for passivity typical of continental welfare states, but the republican emphasis on solidarity and the social responsibility of the state also put in place employment-friendly measures, in the service component of the French welfare state. This is seen especially in the historically extensive provision of public child-care places, which reduced the costs for women to enter employment. Emphasis on republican solidarity also contributed to the Beveridgean features of French social security, especially the push toward universal access through expansion of existing schemes, as well as the creation of new supplementary schemes, within the overall framework of social insurance (Théret and Barbier 2002: 5–8). This hybridized nature of social security benefits proved useful for later French expansion of ALMPs, as social contributions were combined with tax revenues into a universal contribution, used by the Socialists to pay for the government's main active labor market measures.

Germany

In principle, there is a low level of state autonomy in German industrial relations, and social partners not only take center stage in negotiating incomes policies but also become closely involved in the administration of social security benefits. In the German income policies arena, the principle of *Tarifautonomie* is reflected in coordinated industry-level bargaining free from state intervention, which usually follows the lead of the metals union. However, the organizational strength of German unions in general, and the dominance by the giant IG Metall in particular, means that piecemeal efforts to pursue wage restraint or implement regulatory reforms (such as increasing flexibility in the labor market) are often impossible without in effect winning over the whole labor movement. For example, the strong attachment of IG Metall to the early retirement schemes since the 1980s has made later attempts by the Red-Green coalition to reverse this practice very difficult. For this reason, corporatism in the German context is primarily symbolic and does not have substantial economic impact in reality, and "corporatism without state" in Germany is characterized by a lack of central concertation (Hemerijck and Manow 2001: 227; Manow and Seils 2000a: 140; Lehmbruch 2003: 153–154). The reluctance to abandon existing labor market practices is not limited to the unions. There is a high level of collusion between employers and employees in shedding workers through the social security system in order to reduce the labor force in periods of demand slack. The long-term costs involved in this process, in turn, are paid for by successive increases in social security contributions. Therefore, despite their public rhetoric to the contrary, in practice German employers can be as reluctant to dismantle the existing welfare state arrangement as unions.

This problem of social partnership collusion in externalizing the cost of economic adjustment is present in all continental welfare regimes, where insurance-based social benefits are funded by contributions and where Coordinated Market Economies premised on niche products suffer from sectoral transitions to the low-productivity service sector. However, this problem is especially serious in the German context as several contributing factors have fed on one another in a vicious circle. On the one hand, the share of the low wage sector in service employment is particularly small in Germany; on the other hand, the dominance of IG Metall in core industries means that general downward wage flexibility is particularly difficult to achieve. Therefore, large ranks of low-skilled workers are continuously dismissed from the core industries due to wage as well as non-wage labor costs. Once they are out of the labor market, these workers are often unable to find low wage–low productivity jobs. Instead, they move into long-term unemployment, encouraged by labor market exit schemes paid for by social security contribution increases. Further rises in social security contributions, meanwhile, further add to non-wage labour costs (Manow and Seils 2000a: 156).

Therefore, outflow from the German labor market was particularly serious, a problem further perpetuated by the dominance of the Christian Democratic Union (CDU) in government throughout most of the 1980s and 1990s. Over an extended period of sixteen years, the Christian democratic bias toward massive use of social transfers to reduce the labor force worsened the passive nature of German welfare state institutions. This situation means that reduction in social security contributions, as well as a crackdown on labor market exit schemes, inevitably became the centerpiece of later active labor market reforms. The potential for passivity in the German welfare state is not limited to the use of payroll taxes to stimulate labor market exit. As is typical of continental welfare regimes, female employment is low as a result of the breadwinner model of benefit calculation, on the one hand, and severe underdevelopment of public services, on the other hand, especially child-care places.

United Kingdom

A unitary system of administration in Britain and single-party governments based on the first-past-the-post system, plus a weak upper house, means that governments can typically carry out policies without major compromises with the opposition. On the one hand, this smoothed the way for third way reforms under New Labour; on the other hand, this also facilitated an extended period of radical neoliberal strategy involving cost control, austerity, and welfare retrenchment under the previous Conservative government. The negative employment and social exclusion consequences of the Thatcherite reforms went on to become a crucial premise for the third way reforms under New Labour. As an example of liberal welfare regimes, means-tested minimum-level benefits have constituted an important component of social transfers in the British welfare state. At the same time, the tax-funded service side of the British welfare state has maintained a level of commitment to the Beveridgean ideal of universalism based on citizenship. This is seen especially in the National Health Service, which is one of the few main welfare institutions that escaped a frontal assault during the Thatcher period.

To some extent, Beveridgean universalism is also reflected in flat-rate benefits paid to all claimants from the compulsory National Insurance, which covers not only retirement pensions and unemployment but also sickness, maternity, and accident compensation. Although National Insurance is based on contributions, it has over time become a form of general taxation in practice. Unlike insurance-based social transfers in continental welfare states, in the British National Insurance there is no clear linkage between the amount of contributions and the amount of benefits paid back, and this characteristic has allowed governments to raise contribution rates instead of direct taxes to pay for increases in public spending. National Insurance in effect becomes a stealth tax. In fact, it is precisely tax increases disguised as National Insurance contributions that provided an important financial resource for third way active labor market measures under New Labour. Furthermore, since entitlements to National Insurance benefits depend on contributions, means-tested social assistance becomes an important backup for those excluded from the bulk of the social security system.

Unlike the cases of continental and social democratic welfare states, unions in Britain are detached from the social insurance system. This has prevented the emergence of "social wage" (Rhodes 2000a: 24–27), which is an important tool for achieving nominal wage restraint. This social wage mechanism operates by offering full employment as well as expansion in social benefits and services, in exchange for union agreement to give up nominal wage claims. Both unions and employers in Britain remain fragmented in organization, and industrial relations in the British context are traditionally voluntarist as well as adversarial. A low level of coordination for multiple bargaining units and government's inability to directly intervene with legislation further contributed to a general state of persistent wage inflation in the British economy, until well into the Thatcher period.

Australia and New Zealand

The distinctive characteristics of Antipodean welfare states set down important institutional parameters for later third way reforms. Within G. Esping-Andersen's (1990) liberal welfare regimes, Australia and New Zealand have often been grouped together in a unique category known as the wage earners' welfare states. The key strategic principle of the wage earners' welfare arrangement is to deliver the bulk of social protection through full employment and high living wages determined by means of the arbitration process. In addition, arbitration also delivers various other social benefits, such as sick pay or workers' compensation. In Australia, this "basic wage" concept of social protection was solidified after the Australian Court of Arbitration passed down the Harvester Judgment in 1907 to establish the first Twage-fixing system in Australia and set a weekly minimum wage determined by the cost of living. Meanwhile, in order to sustain full employment and a good living wage for the Australian core industries, massive protection for domestic industries, in the form of high tariffs as well as an overtly racist white Australia immigration policy, was carried on by governments left and right well into the late 1970s. The informal and occupational side of the Australian welfare state has occupied a significant place in Australian social policy (Castles 1988; Castles and Pierson 1996: 237–238).

The Australian labor movement and its political representatives made an important contribution to the development of the wage earners' welfare state. The settler country context contributed to a working-class radicalism particularly characterized by egalitarianism. While the formal welfare state for a long time exhibited basic liberal welfare characteristics, such as means-tested benefits and the minimum provision of social services, means-testing is distinctively applied from the top instead of bottom margin, and implemented in a purposely unstigmatizing way (Castles 1994). Before the establishment of Superannuation in the late 1980s, the Australian welfare state was basically noncontributory. On the one hand, there was no stigmatizing separation between social insurance and means testing; on the other hand, a high proportion of the population received means-tested benefits (M. Jones 2002: 25–26; Castles and Pierson 1996: 237–238). These historical and institutional legacies clearly left their mark on later third way reforms during the 1980s and 1990s. Changes in social security, for example, involved further intensification of means testing for middle-income earners, while the worst-off benefited. In addition, the iterative process of arbitration in delivering wages and benefits familiarized the Australian labor movement with the concept and practice of "social wage." This went on to become the fundamental basis for the Australian Accord, through which the Australian Labor Party (ALP) successfully secured union cooperation in wage moderation for most of the 1980s and 1990s.

As another example of the wage earners' welfare state, New Zealand's informal social security based on a basic living wage and full employment had historically played an important role in delivering the bulk of social protection. Different from the Australian Court of Arbitration, the New Zealand arbitration panels also included one representative from both employers and employees, who over time had come to exert dominant control over the panels and impaired their impartiality. In addition, compared with their Australian counterparts, the arbitration panels had a lower coverage of the labor market. With this combination of institutional weaknesses, arbitration in New Zealand had generally been less successful in enforcing discipline among social partners and in pursuing wage restraint in times of economic pressure (Schwartz 2000: 78). During both the 1960s and 1970s, there were frequent upward drifts in wage claims, wildly beyond the target set by arbitration through a series of General Wage Orders.

There are some serious problems inherent in the wage earners' welfare state design, especially with regard to the large scale of protection offered to domestic industries in order to secure full employment and living wages. Together with Canada, the development of the Antipodean political economy fits within the framework of the staples thesis (Innis 1940). The development of the domestic economy in these settler countries on the periphery took place primarily during the process of exploiting raw materials for more industrially advanced core countries. For this reason, the domestic manufacturing industries are intrinsically less competitive and efficient than the core countries in continental Europe. The arrangement of wage earners' welfare leads to a situation whereby wages and costs in low-productivity sheltered sectors are deliberately inflated through arbitration, and in the process squeeze rents out of exposed sectors based on staples production. As a result, while the productivity gap between exposed and sheltered sectors widened, the long-term ability of exposed sectors to export profitably also declined (Schwartz 2000: 82–83). These underlying structural problems became critical when decline in exporting sectors accelerated, due to gradual loss of the European agricultural market after the mid-1970s, especially after the British entry into the European Economic Community (EEC).

2. THE IDEOLOGICAL BASIS FOR THIRD WAY REFORMS

While the institutional characteristics outlined in the previous sections shaped the policy process, each case of social democratic incumbency was also constrained by the party's ideological beliefs. Across all the nine countries, there was a process of intellectual adaptation within social democracy, with growing focus on work as the fundamental premise of social justice. However, the timing differed significantly across countries, due to the conditions for cementing cross-class solidarity specific to each country. The German SPD, for example, was fifty years behind its Swedish counterpart in adopting the third way philosophy. Also varying significantly across cases are the mechanisms and intellectual sources of the ideological transformation. In some countries it occurred in the debate on citizenship, in others on communitarian values, in yet others on social exclusion. Unions, social liberals, and feminists all contributed to the change, depending on the country. Nevertheless, in general, the productivist emphasis suffered a decline in the prosperous 1960s, indicating again the vital importance of rising unemployment as a necessary condition for the third way ideology. In Table 3.2 I outline the key third way ideological developments in each country.

TABLE 3.2. *Key Features of Third Way Ideological Transformation*

Countries in order of appearance in the chapter	Evolution of Third Way Ideology	
⬇	Denmark	• LO proposed the concept of "developmental work" since 1991.
	Sweden	• Wigforss and Myrdal pioneered the work line in the 1910s to 1930s.
	Norway	• Labor already adopted productivism in 1939, renewed as the *arbeidslinje* in 1992.
	Netherlands	• Discourse on citizenship in the 1990s; Joke Smit set scene for gender-friendly policies
	France	• Strong influence of orthodox Marxism • Statist emphasis on social exclusion
	Germany	• Productivist logic pioneered in the 1989 Berlin program
	United Kingdom	• Communitarian influence from Amitai Etzioni • Postmodern influence from Anthony Giddens
	Australia	• Origin in social liberalism • White Paper on Employment and Growth in 1994
	New Zealand	• Neoliberal hijack by Roger Douglas • "Workforce 2010" refocused on activation

Denmark

During the 1980s, while the bourgeois government stuck with the passive emphasis on welfare, in opposition the social democrats underwent an intellectual transformation, which has extended well into their government tenure since 1993. The further increase in unemployment threatened the electoral sustainability of solidarity among wage earners, because increasing numbers of them stopped working and slipped into the questionable status of pure charity receivers. Therefore, in value and discourse, the labor movement sharply increased the emphasis on the productivist and developmentalist purpose of social protection. In 1991, the LO put out a publication fittingly titled "Developmental Work," followed in 1995 by another document, "Work and Development." In these publications, the unions suggested that a shift of focus in welfare policy should take place, from the market to production. "Market" here referred to the *redistribution* of wealth allocated by the mechanism of the labor market, while "production" referred to the *creation* of additional wealth. This document crystallized the concept of "developmental work," the key intellectual justification for the social democratic reforms during the 1990s. Reflecting the common internal logic behind such ideological transformation, during the same period the Swedish LO also introduced precisely the same developmental work concept, arguing that a more comprehensive solidaristic work policy should replace the traditional solidaristic wage policy. In this new normative principle, the emphasis on enabling self-fulfillment strongly anticipated the concept of "reflexive welfare" in postmodern societies with growing individualism, for which Anthony Giddens, as the principal third way spokesman for New Labour, is best known (Hvid 1999: 48).

The change of heart for Danish unions was also due to a growing recognition of the structural nature of unemployment problems plaguing the country since the late 1970s. Because of the growing mismatch between the growth in wages and productivity, the two main options for employment promotion were either lower wages and unemployment benefits or stronger incentives to work (Goul Andersen 2002a: 66–67). Finding the first option ideologically unpalatable, the Danish labor movement avoided lower minimum wages or unemployment benefits by accepting stronger incentives, either negative (obligations) or positive (rights), to work. The productivist and developmental logic is strongly reflected in the emphasis on improving skills and qualifications, so that differences in employability can be reduced to a level compatible with the traditionally small wage dispersion delivered through Danish incomes policy. This tight focus on skill upgrading is also related to the small and open nature of the Danish economy, dominated by medium and small businesses. For these businesses, the upgrading of skills and qualifications is particularly important for surviving external competition (Torfing 1999: 17–19).

In addition to unions, there were also signs of change within the social democratic party. For much of the postwar period, the dominant discourse on economic and social policy was Keynesian consensus and class compromise, endorsed by most mainstream parties. After the late 1970s, this dominance was challenged from all quarters. The Radical Liberal Party, by frequently holding the balance of power in the Folketing, tried to push forward a more radical alternative based on a universal citizens' income, culminating in the formalization of this concept in the party's conference in 1994 (Loftager and Madsen 1997: 136). However, the social democrats remained apathetic toward this idea and went on to develop their own thematic discourse based on workfare, which highlighted the values of individual responsibility, help received in return for contribution, and inclusion of the marginalized. This trend was confirmed by the analysis of S. P. Jespersen and S. L. Rasmussen (1998), who detected a clear increase in communitarian references in public discourse on activation. However, despite the stronger emphasis on individual responsibility, this stance was still substantially different from the rhetoric articulated by the center Right. The social democrats drew a clear line between themselves and the increasingly neoliberal discourse focused on increasing wage dispersion, cutting the minimum wage, and cutbacks to unemployment benefits, which was endorsed primarily by center-right parties and the business community. Furthermore, the social democrats also emphasized the social responsibility of the firm in taking care of its employees (Møller 1999).

Sweden

For the Swedish Social Democratic Party, the normative emphasis on employment and productivity can be traced back to the party's early history. Already in 1910, Ernst Wigforss, in parallel to his German revisionist counterpart Eduard Bernstein, developed some ideas about broadening working-class solidarity, which were reflected in the early establishment of an electoral alliance with the peasants, and later with white-collar workers. In 1934, Gunnar Myrdal, one of the most notable economists in the social democrats' history (who went on to share the Nobel Prize with Hayek forty years later), was already arguing for a "productivist" social policy. Because of favorable circumstances, such as the marginal influence of a large rural class and weak Catholicism, all three Nordic countries had a distinctively early process for broadening the social democratic electoral alliance. In parallel, there was early conceptualization of a productivist ideology focused on the common interest between workers and employers in better employment. In fact, if anything, the formal introduction of productivism into party platforms was earlier in both Denmark (1934) and Norway (1939) than in Sweden (1944) (Stjernø 2005: 109–121; Hort 2005: 150). However, because of its much greater electoral strength and dominance in government, it was Swedish social democracy that managed to thoroughly implement such productivity-centered ideology, by means of an actual policy paradigm focused on better employment, especially the solidaristic wage concept in the Rehn-Meidner model. This was the key reason why there is a long tradition of activation in Swedish (and Norwegian, to a lesser extent) welfare states. For this reason, it is fitting to describe changes since the late 1970s as intensification, rather than fundamental transformation, of the existing paradigm.

Under the influence of key party intellectuals such as Tag Erlander and Olof Palme, the party program of 1960 reduced the emphasis on productivity and highlighted instead more abstract concepts, such as individual freedom, democracy, and common bonds with Third World countries (Stjernø 2005: 121). Secure in the peak of Golden Age economic growth, this slight departure from an employment focus did not present a serious problem for the sustainability of the solidarity principle. However, when this period of growth was over and it became apparent that unemployment could not return to the low levels of the early postwar period, the labor movement renewed and further strengthened the focus on activation in its discourse. The Swedish unions made clear their belief that a workfare state can primarily serve to increase welfare. In 1985, the congress of the Swedish Metal Union put forward a report called "The Good Work," whose content foreshadowed the launch of the "developmental work" concept by the LO in 1990 (followed a year later by the Danish LO as well). As was discussed earlier in the Danish context, the vision of a productivist welfare system focused on enabling individuals bears a strong similarity to the third way doctrines developed by Giddens for the reformist Labour Party a decade later (Hvid 1999: 47–48).

In the mid-1980s, officials in the Ministry of Finance under the leadership of Kjell-Olof Feldt Thnd those in the Bank of Sweden under Bengt Dennis established close, mutual intellectual support. Consequently, the government became increasingly receptive toward a norm-based monetary policy (Ryner 2002). This was a crucial component of the so-called third road economic policy, which, despite its familiar title, is a narrower concept than the third way ideology examined in this book. The neoclassical economic principles in the "third road" approach were strictly limited to economic policy. In social and labor market policy, although the Bank attempted to impose its ideological weight through a commission report headed by Assar Lindbeck (former Social Democrat, chairman of the Nobel selection committee), the party and unions responded negatively. LO's Social Justice Commission (which recruited, among others, both Walter Korpi and Esping-Andersen) defended the normative value of the welfare state against the libertarian right theorists, criticizing in particular the asymmetry between positive and negative liberty advocated by Isaiah Berlin. There was similar discourse in the Palme Welfare Balance Commission, established by the social democratic government in 1999. In this latter report, there was also evidence for the growing prioritarian emphasis in social democratic thinking on egalitarianism as an ideological principle. While equality remained a key focus of investigation, the commission gradually acknowledged helping the most disadvantaged and fighting poverty as the overall objectives of social protection (Hort 2005).

Norway

In the party program of 1939, the Norwegian Labor Party for the first time adopted a productivist outlook in its ideology, highlighting the importance of employment and productivity. According to this discourse, the bond between workers and employers is based on their shared interest in increasing production. By the time of the 1945 party program, the productivist flavor had further strengthened, in what is now directly referred to as *economic* solidarity among all individuals engaged in work. Soon after this, in a process parallel to that in Sweden, the social democratic discourse became more abstract, radical, and generalistic, advocating a common stand with Third World countries in the 1953 program and openly pledging shared beliefs with Christian values in the congresses of 1959 and 1979. There was also reference to the vague concept of common bonds with the society in general. At the same time, the pragmatic focus on employment and production diminished, in the context of rapid economic growth and high employment during the Golden Age (Stjernø 2005: 118–126).

Into the early 1990s, however, the government rapidly refocused its attention on the work approach, as unemployment started to become a serious problem. In 1992, Labor formulated a distinct "work line" (*arbeidslinje*) in its ideological discourse, which stipulates that waged work should be the first choice for all persons who are able to support themselves (Halvorsen 2002: 175; Kildal 1999: 353). The work-line doctrine largely renewed the traditionally strong emphasis on labor market activation in Norwegian social democratic ideology. However, an innovation in the work line is its much stronger communitarian emphasis on individual incentives, responsibility, and mutual obligation. The social democrats justified the normative value of the work line on the following grounds: (1) It contributes to increasing productivity; (2) it facilitates the integration of the socially marginalized; (3) it develops human competence (in both moral value and human capital); (4) it reinforces self-respect; and most crucially, (5) there should be reciprocity between duties and benefits. Despite the growing emphasis on the obligation to work over the right to welfare, there are still clear differences between the ideological discourse of Labor and the center Right. While Labor prefers resources for enabling to work, the Christian Democrats stuck to early exit and the secular Right wanted to cut costs.

Through interviews with party officials across the ideological spectrum, Anders Nordlund (2005) found that Labor representatives were very enthusiastic about the new emphasis on labor market activation, and they placed the opportunities for training side by side with the requirements for job search at the top of their priority list. The Christian democratic representatives, by contrast, showed their ideological difficulty with the concept of activation, especially where work potentially encroaches upon the organic role of the family. They argued that activation of the elderly by reforming the early retirement programs was a step too far. On the other hand, conservative party officials were open about their belief in cost cutting and privatization, suggesting that too much of the economy was handled by the public sector. They expressed a desire for a "system change" whereby there should be a "restricted state" and individuals would be given the liberty to choose, through a tax reduction.

The Netherlands

As the Dutch problem of labor market exclusion (especially early exit through disability benefits) worsened into the late 1980s, ideological discourse across the partisan spectrum increased the emphasis on participation and inclusion. The debate on participation took place primarily with a revival in Dutch political discourse of the citizenship concept, given its close connection to the communitarian notions of responsibility and reciprocity. The think tank Scientific Council for Government Policy played an important role in the resurgence of the citizenship discussion, with its 1990 publication devoted to labor market policies and a 1992 publication on the meaning of citizenship. The 1990 report, titled "A Working Perspective," proved crucial as it explicitly highlighted the need to increase labor market activation. A major departure from previous discourse on citizenship was that this time, there was an explicit recognition in the equality of men and women in participation (Plantenga 1998: 57).

All the main parties interpreted the citizenship concept from a strongly communitarian perspective, but with different flavors. For the Christian Democrats, what this means is the search for a "caring society," where the primary deliverers of care remain women in the family as well as church and neighborhood organizations. Therefore, the Christian democratic notion of communitarian participation was based not on employment but on civil society (Voet 1998: 18–19). For the Liberal Party, on the other hand, citizenship was premised on the libertarian notion of a "bourgeois citizen," regardless of gender, who has the natural temptation to free ride on collective welfare, and should therefore not expect benefits without contribution. Meanwhile, state intervention, according to the Liberals, was already excessive (Bussemaker 1998a: 339–340). The Dutch communitarian discourse on participation addressed citizens of various social categories, but, in the context of Dutch labor market reforms, especially important was the debate over citizenship for women. It was precisely on this issue that the Dutch third way (flexicurity) reform was a well-known and unusual success, as compared to other continental European countries. The considerable increase in Dutch employment was based largely on the creation of part-time jobs, mostly for women. Therefore, it is helpful to highlight in particular the ideological transformation over this issue, especially the feminist contributions to the citizenship debate and their close ideological affinity with the PvdA.

While the Liberal and Christian democratic parties focused respectively on civil society and on restoring the individual, the PvdA citizenship discourse focused on both social rights and labor market participation for women. The gender egalitarian nature of the discourse was distinctive, given the dominant Christian democratic institutional context of Dutch social security. An important figure of influence behind the social democratic gender discourse was Joke Smit, feminist and member of the PvdA. Her article "The Discomfort of Women" (published in *De Gids* in 1967), about the plight of women in unequal social relationships, provoked enormous intellectual reaction in the country and had a deep impact on the PvdA government. In 1975, the Labor government under Joop den Uyl established the Emancipation Commission and two years later published the memorandum on women's equality "Emancipation: Process of Change and Growth." Reflecting the strong political influence of women inside the PvdA, the social democratic minister responsible for welfare and employment policy took over the policy portfolio for women in 1994 (Outshoorn 1998: 111; Bussemaker 1998b: 339–341; Plantenga 1998: 57).

France

Like its other southern European counterparts, the early formation of the French labor movement was heavily affected by orthodox Marxism and anarcho-syndicalism. Not only was the ideology of the French Socialists directly influenced by this Marxist legacy, but it was further hardened in the persistent electoral competition between the Socialists and their communist counterparts. In addition, the electoral weakness of the party and, for much of the early postwar period, its remoteness from the prospect of power, all contributed to the radicalizing of its ideology. For these reasons, the broadening of the electoral alliance beyond the working class was slower than in other social democratic cases, as was the creation of a productivist and employment-centered concept of solidarity. It was not until after the early 1980s under the Mitterand presidency that the party paid renewed attention to this idea (Stjernø 2005: 193–196). On the one hand, unemployment and social exclusion were increasing; on the other hand, the presidential and two-ballot system put unusually strong pressure on the Socialists to construct a broad alliance covering the left and right spectrum. The creation of more employment, in other words, became the unifying objective that appealed to the whole country (Thomson 2000: 74).

For the Socialist governments of both Michel Rocard and Lionel Jospin, discourse on the normative value of employment and participation focused on the issue of social exclusion in particular. The patterns of French social segmentation overlap heavily with the geographic isolation of stagnant pockets in the suburbs, and the effect of exclusion spilled over directly into highly salient issues, such as youth crime and public disorder. The ideological discourse on social exclusion not only reinforced the importance of citizenship and solidarity through social participation but also paved way for the further transformation of socialist egalitarianism as a key principle. The concept of exclusion highlights the horizontal nature of the problem: a segmentation between those who are "in" and "out," more than a vertical problem of income inequality between those who are "up" and "down." This serves as a crucial ideological justification for intensifying the prioritarian nature of socialist egalitarianism. Echoing the "equality of what" debate among egalitarian thinkers such as Ronald Dworkin and Richard Arneson, the Socialists increased the emphasis on the notion of "*équité*" and downplayed the importance of "*égalité*." Equality of opportunity, in other words, was prioritized over equality of outcome, and this justified a shift from methodological income redistribution to protecting the worst-off and preventing long-term unemployment. These principles were directly reflected in two of the most innovative labor market measures under French social democracy: the introduction of Minimum Income of Insertion (RMI) and the substitution of income tax for payroll tax by means of the General Social Contribution (Béland 2007; Clift 2003: 126–127).

Another important aspect in evaluating French partisan ideologies on social justice is the prominent role of the state. Through various revolutions and restorations, the concept of the republic came to represent and symbolize the fundamental values of social justice and equality in the French nation, in what is known as *service publique*. This deeply influenced the ideological theorization of the Socialists (and all other parties). Jean Jaurés, a key early figure in the French Section of the Workers' International (SFIO), suggested that the French Revolution of 1789 had to be continued by the Socialists, in order to translate political equality before the law to social equality through social rights. This, plus the stronger influence of Marxism, led to a doctrinaire preference for state intervention by the Socialists (Clift 2003: 124–125). As Chapter 5 explains, such statist preference led to problems in the actual implementation of active labor market measures because of the weak standards it imposed on the obligation for benefit recipients.

Germany

The Bad Godesberg program of 1959 represents one of the most important ideological changes for the German SPD. With this program, the party departed from the socialist objective of industry nationalization, and embraced the market economy. However, on this occasion there was still no attempt, unlike in Scandinavia, to promote a developmental concept of common interest between workers and other classes in increasing productivity at work. In Bad Godesberg, the foundation for social democratic solidarity was instead workers' common interests in fighting *against* employers. Rather than becoming more pragmatic over time, these ideas soon became further removed from the issues of growth and employment.

This was a process mirrored in many other countries in the 1960s, as economic prosperity and social protests combined to push social democracy away from production-oriented interests and focus instead on abstract and social issues. In the SPD program in 1975, social democratic solidarity came to take on a heavily universalistic notion that now embraced every human being and all countries.

This euphoric outlook had disappeared by the time of another major ideological revision, in the 1989 Berlin program. There were now significantly higher levels of unemployment than in the Golden Age (to increase rapidly after reunification) and significantly lower rates of economic growth. Chaired by Jochen Vogel and Oscar Lafontaine, the commission for the Berlin program made history by, for the first time, introducing a productivist logic into social democratic solidarity, whose purpose was not to struggle but to work for increasing growth and prosperity. The program called on workers to show solidarity by cutting working time (a six-hour working day and a thirty-hour working week) and wages so that more jobs would become available. It was only after a determined confrontation by Lafontaine with strong union resistance that this principle was included in the program. Fifty-five years after the Danish social democrats first introduced a work-centered perspective on social justice, the German SPD now followed suit. The lateness was directly related to the slower success in establishing a broader electoral basis beyond the working class, which in turn was due to the more hostile social cleavage structure common to most continental European countries (Stjernø 2005: 103–109; Roder 2003: 122).

Under the leadership of Gerhard Schröder, the focus on employment further intensified in SPD ideological thinking, accompanied by a growing willingness to reform the welfare state to achieve this purpose, especially tighter conditioning of benefits. While Lafontaine stood on the side of the reformers over working-time reduction, on this issue of benefit restriction he thought the party went too far. His resignation in 1999, and the growing dominance by Schröder within the SPD (for example, with Wolfgang Clement taking over as minister for economics and labor), demonstrated the great distance the party had traveled on the normative value of work. The emphasis on benefit conditioning first appeared in the party's 1997/1998 election manifestos, and it intensified further by the time of the 2001/2002 manifestos. While the Scandinavian (especially Danish) model on activation was frequently referred to during the first Red-Green government, over time the UK model became dominant in party discourse, with a growing communitarian emphasis on individual responsibility. In 2003, Olaf Scholz

(General Secretary of the SPD and a key ideological ally of Schöder) put forward the idea that social justice should be less about redistribution and more about access to the labor market for those excluded, in essence giving a strong prioritarian interpretation for traditional social democratic egalitarianism (Roder 2003: 162–194; Meyer 2005: 79; Seeleib-Kaiser and Fleckenstein 2007: 440).

While the SPD increasingly highlighted notions of individual responsibility and obligation to work, there was still a fundamental difference from the neoliberal discourse on taking away benefits and removing work disincentives. Rather than relying on sanctions, in SPD language there had been a consistent emphasis on training, reskilling, and education, ever since its election manifesto in 1983. Enriching human capital steadily replaced demand management as the key strategy for increasing employment. As chairman of the SPD, Lafontaine in 1998 made clear that supply-side labor market policies should not be used to cut labor costs, and should instead enable the state to fund research and development (R&D), schools, and training opportunities. This human capital outlook was also formally included in the party's 1998 election manifesto. Compared with the late 1990s, the emphasis on public sector initiatives in enabling to work further strengthened in the 2001/2002 election manifestos (Roder 2003: 156–157).

United Kingdom

The 1945 and 1950 programs of the British Labour Party had a strongly productivist orientation. Alongside expansion of the welfare state, Labour also emphasized the importance of continuously producing and exporting more. This pragmatism in Labour ideology can be explained by a combination of historical factors, such as the dominance of English liberalism in the trade unions, the influence of Fabianism, and the Christian socialists, whose philosophy influenced New Labour's third way ideology. Even in its early period, Labour programs lacked the radical and Marxist interpretation of political objectives that characterized much of European social democracy during the same historical period (Stjernø 2005: 132–135). By the late 1970s, however, the situation was different. The party was returned to opposition after a few years of rancorous relationship with unions and the failure in economic policy. This, together with the neoliberal reforms under Margaret Thatcher, resulted in a period of radicalization in Labour ideology, symbolized by the strongly socialist 1983 election manifesto under the leadership of Michael Foot. The moderation of Labour ideology, which led ultimately to New Labour and Blair's third way discourse, started right after Foot's replacement by Neil Kinnock. Although the pace of reform slowed down temporarily during John Smith's short rule, it intensified significantly after Blair took over as leader in 1994 (T. Jones 1996: 132–135).

In a larger context of economic failure, increasing unemployment and its social consequences, there was growing emphasis on employment and active citizenship in Labour ideology. This was reflected in (1) the work by the Commission of Social Justice and supported by the Labour think tank, the Institute for Public Policy Research; (2) the Rowntree Foundation Inquiry into Income and Wealth; as well as (3) the Dahrendorf Report initiated by the Liberal Democrats. In all these works and as a result of Labour's own public discourse, increasing attention was given to the concept of social inclusion through paid employment. By contrast, inequality reduction was given less emphasis, and where it was mentioned it was in a context of increasing economic efficiency and social cohesion (Levitas 1998: 29–48; Jordan 1998). R. H. Tawney, as one of the most notable intellectuals in Labour's history, argued for greater equality of outcome because inequality directly threatens individual liberty. He also strongly believed in direct redistribution of income as a crucial strategy toward achieving equality. This belief in equality of outcome was more or less maintained by other Labour thinkers, such as Anthony Crosland and Roy Hattersley.

However, by the time of New Labour, commitment to equality of outcome was already replaced in party discourse with "equality of opportunity and fairness of outcome," as well as "progressive universalism." The latter new concept, for example, was used by Chancellor Gordon Brown to justify the new tax and benefit system in the 2003 budget, which provided some level of benefits for most people while focusing in particular on the most needy. This kind of prioritarian orientation in egalitarianism should not be regarded as a New Labour invention. If anything, other than George Bernard Shaw and the Marxists within Labour during the early 1920s and 1930s, the party never advocated radical egalitarianism, which includes "Leveling Down," as an end to itself. Nevertheless, the shift of attention from income redistribution to helping the worst-off was clear, reflecting a significant intensification of prioritarian beliefs associated with John Rawls or Derek Parfit (Beech 2006: 154–176).

Blair's work-centered third way ideology utilized two distinctive schools of thoughts: communitarianism and theories of postmodernity, the latter by Giddens, who himself became closely identified with Blair's third way project by serving as his advisor. As noted in the theoretical discussion in Chapter 2, compared with social theorist communitarians, such as Alasdair MacIntyre and Michael Sandel, it was the consequentialists (who espouse communitarianism for its purportedly beneficial economic and social consequences), such as Amitai Etzioni, Philip Selznick, Henry Tam, and William Galston, who had more direct influence on partisan ideological transformation, primarily for the Clinton Democrats in the United States, but also for New Labour under Blair. In addition, Blair also cited the Scottish Christian socialist John Macmurray as a crucial source of intellectual support, which demonstrates the continuing historical influence of Christian socialism in the British labor movement. Macmurray was not identified as a communitarian in his time, but the emphasis he gave to the notion of community heavily influenced Blair, who claimed to have read his works intensively while a student at Oxford.

The common feature from all these variants of communitarian thoughts is a relatively strong prescriptive emphasis. While both this and Giddens's postmodernity arguments lamented a culture of dependency, the former blamed it on excessive individualism and lack of personal discipline, while the latter defended growing individualism (Hale 2004: 87; Goes 2004). Prescriptive communitarianism, therefore, paved the way for the growing emphasis on the obligation to work and for greater tolerance of compulsion (especially for the young unemployed) in New Labour's third way activation principles. Partly due to the resistance of unions, the attempt by British Labour to establish a broad electoral alliance with the middle class had been largely unsuccessful, and on this basis a notion of inclusive solidarity was historically not a centerpiece of the party's ideology. The concept of a community, premised on active participation in paid employment, now provides some approximation to such ideology.

Key to Giddens's theories are concepts of reflexivity, de-traditionalization, and self-construction, all meant to highlight the increasing levels of personal autonomy in late modern societies. On this basis, he criticized both traditional Taylorist production methods and passive welfare states for their repressive nature and the individual dependency they created. Drawing inspiration from the highly human-capital-enriching production organization on the Japanese shop floor, he argued that productivism, a concept historically associated with the British Labour Party, should be updated as "productivity," to signify the transformation from compulsive work to proactive participation and self-realization in work. Similarly, he suggested that the traditional passive welfare state should be replaced by a "positive/generative" welfare state, so that the focus of welfare moves away from individual control to self-development and the enabling of individual growth (McCullen and Harris 2004). Blair picked up the themes of compulsion, personal responsibility, and morality from the communitarians, many of whom are themselves ambiguous about the continuing relevance of egalitarianism and the state in delivering social justice. Giddens provided a crucial balance to this perspective, in highlighting the priority of enabling to work over coercion, and in defending the welfare state by giving it a new, activation-centered purpose.

Australia

Because of its British origin, Australia inherited liberalism as a key component of political thought. Ideas of liberalism came to structure the normative values and public discourse of all major parties, including the ALP. This gives a distinctively local flavor to the ideological contests in Australia, where the key dividing line between the Left and Right is drawn not against liberalism but within it, and neoliberal reforms are typically referred to as rationalist. The two major variants of liberalism are economic and social liberalism. The former represents classic laissez-faire belief in the natural right to individual liberty and the economic efficiency of the free market. Its revival under the secular-right Liberal Party, especially since John Howard replaced Andrew Peacock as party leader in 1990, was the core of neoliberal reforms in Australia. Social liberalism, on the other hand, came to influence the ALP heavily. The social liberals, inspired by thinkers such as Tawney and J. A. Hobson, argued that poverty deprives citizens of the opportunity to develop their full potential, and that this is a welfare loss to the society as a whole. For this reason, the state has an obligation to eliminate the social obstacles toward human capital development. Coupled with this, there was also the reformist influence from Fabianism, especially its pragmatic belief in productivity and education (Smyth 2002: 427; Beilharz, Considine, and Watts 1992: 15–22).

Another distinctively local flavor to the Australian ideological debate on welfare and work (shared to some extent with New Zealand) was an ambiguous relationship between "fair wage" and "redistribution" as two competing ideals about social justice (Smyth 2002: 427). The Antipodean history of white colonies again proved an important context, where the abundance of land and the scarcity of labor meant that full employment was often literally a reality. Henry Higgins, attorney-general in the first federal Labor government and himself a key representation of radical social liberalism, formalized the priority of adequate wages through the Harvester Judgment on arbitration in 1907. By means of arbitration, employers were prevented from paying unacceptably low wages, and "fair wage" came to be the cornerstone in the ALP discourse on social justice, while redistribution through social security was equated with minimum provision. Despite its premise on good wages, employment was only a latent component of political thinking in the ALP. The virtual existence of full employment and the heavily protected (and hence unproductive) nature of these jobs during the 1960s meant that labor market activation through training and education as an objective was largely irrelevant. The productivist concept of social democratic solidarity in Scandinavia focused on securing more jobs and better productivity. However, its Australian equivalent (often dressed up in a discourse about citizenship rather than solidarity per se) was not clearly productivist, as it focused almost entirely on good wages through protectionism. The goals of increasing labor market participation and human capital endowments did not become important in ALP thinking until the Antipodean economies lost their former exporting advantage in primary resources and unemployment became a reality after the late 1970s.

For the new attention to labor market activation in its political thinking, Labor drew inspiration from the "active society" concept proposed by the Organization for Economic Co-operation and Development (OECD). This concept itself was a response to international increases in unemployment since the 1970s. The new values of active society and enabling to work received growing attention from two key publications by the ALP, first the report from the Australian Social Security Review in 1988 and later the White Paper on Employment and Growth (Working Nation) in 1994. Labor argued that unemployment assistance should be reformed to become an integrated component of labor market activation, and especially in the Working Nation document stressed the importance of working in return for benefits. The Keating government's discourse on activation altered the Australian concept of citizenship, giving it a more communitarian emphasis, where inclusion in the community was based more on participation than T. H. Marshall's ideal about natural social rights as citizens (Shaver and Saunders 1995; Shaver 2002). Despite this growing emphasis on the individual obligation to work, Labor discourse was highly distinctive from its Liberal counterpart, with its emphasis on training and education, rather than on cutting benefits, as the primary basis for labor market activation, a logic further strengthened in the Working Nation publication.

During the economically difficult period of the 1980s, the neoliberals who gained ground in the Liberal Party advocated cost-cutting strategies adopted by their American counterparts, but the ALP went in the opposite direction, arguing for a greater involvement of the public sector in social investment. Labor thinkers, including Ralph Willis, John Langmore, and

Neil Blewett (who all worked for employment or social security portfolios under the Hawke or Keating governments) all rejected the "fight inflation first" doctrine of the economic liberals and argued for a greater role of the state in both guaranteeing equality and preventing social misery for the most needy (Smyth 2002: 431–432).

New Zealand

For some period of time, the response of the New Zealand Labour Party to the economic problems of the 1980s was significantly different from that of social democratic parties in other countries. When the fourth Labour government under David Lange began in 1984, there was indeed a radical ideological departure from the previous center-right National administration. However, rather than toward productivist social justice premised on public investment in enabling to work, Labour veered rightward, adopting a neoliberal ideology and policy program focused on a minimalist state. This does clearly demonstrate the power of political ideology in overcoming path-dependent institutional constraints, but its attempt at radical privatization and cost cutting in the economy had little resemblance to the third way.

There are two related reasons for why, in this case, New Zealand's main party of the Left wanted so much to introduce the free market at the expense of the state. Firstly, as the next chapter will discuss in greater detail, state intervention had probably already reached its physical limit by the time Labour came to power in 1984. Labour had to deal with consequences of the paternalistic social and rural policies of the Muldoon government, plus a series of public sector investments in natural resources known as the "Think Big" projects. On top of the unemployment problems seen in other countries, there were in New Zealand unprecedented levels of public expenditures and national debt, as well as currency speculation as soon as Labour came to power. This leads to the second reason for Labour's right turn: These unusually serious economic problems of Keynesian intervention provided legitimacy to thinkers inside the Treasury and the Reserve Bank. Steeped in the laissez-faire liberalism of Hayek and Friedman, these economist intellectuals promoted a radical neoliberal ideology. Referred to as the "Troika," Roger Douglas, Richard Prebble, and David Caygill advocated a project of structural reform that foreshadowed the Washington Consensus proposed by John Williamson of the Institute for International Economics, which later came to be particularly associated with liberalization schemes imposed on Latin American countries by the International Monetary Fund (IMF) and the World Bank (Peters and Marshall 1996: 1–18; Harris 1999: 20–33).

Despite his substantive control over government policy direction, from the very beginning Douglas, as minister of finance, met strong resistance within the Labour Party to his neoliberal ideas. In 1985, the party's regional conferences rejected the market-oriented reform plans, and by the 1987 conference the Broad Left faction, which opposed the Treasury, had achieved a majority, largely boosted by trade union votes (Kelsey 1995: 37). There was accusation that the Douglas team kept ignoring Labour's election manifestos. The most publicized attack came from former party president Jim Anderton, who went on to resign from Labour in 1989 and formed NewLabour (one word), which took away more than 5% of the Labour votes in the 1990 election. Lange himself as prime minister became disillusioned with Douglas's radical experiments, and the tension culminated in the firing of both Douglas and Prebble from the cabinet in 1988. Over the decade of the 1990s under the National government, the neoliberal reforms further intensified, fundamentally transforming the employment relations system and deeply affecting the social security system. The drastic extent of the reforms, along with citizens' open discontent with them (shown in the referendum over the Mixed Member Proportional electoral system in 1993), paved the way for another ideological transformation within Labour.

When the fifth Labour government came to power under Helen Clark in 1999, on an intellectual level it had all but abandoned the Douglas doctrine completely. Instead, it renewed its defense of the role of the state. Given the unemployment problems besetting the country since the 1970s, both Labour and its neoliberal predecessors emphasized the importance of work. However, this time Labour rejected the approach narrowly based on monetarist management of the economy. In response to the major disruptions to the labor market and employment system brought on by the Nationals' reforms, Labour put forward a social policy-centered publication, "Workforce 2010." The document's emphasis on participation and employment was set in an explicit human capability framework, outlined this time not by the Treasury but by the Department of Labour (Lunt, Spoonley, and Mataira 2002: 352). Within Labour, the most important advocate of this work-oriented third way ideology was Steve Maharey, who commented favorably on Blair's third way projects in his contributions to a weekly column. Although the fifth Labour government lacked a distinctive set of ideological discourses in the fashion of its British counterpart,

Maharey argued strongly for a coherent ideological core as the guideline for the party. He himself held the highly relevant portfolio of social development and employment, and he identified one of the key tasks for the party as creating a developmental focus for social policy (Eichbaum and Shaw 2006).

4

Prelude to the Third Way

The Unemployment Problem and Earlier Responses

To provide a historical context for third way reforms, this chapter outlines
the developments in key economic and social problems being increasingly
confronted by the nine countries after the Golden Age, and how pre-third
way governments attempted to respond to these difficulties. Amid all these
interconnected problems of economic and social policies, rapidly increasing
unemployment was especially relevant for third way reforms. As Figure 4.1
indicates, this is a universal and clear-cut trend across all the nine cases
covered in the book. The unemployment problem not only directly shaped
strategies of active and passive protection but also required corresponding
adjustments in macroeconomic and incomes policies. For the third way ideology, unemployment posed one especially serious threat, in labor market
and social exclusion due to long-term unemployment. The exclusion of the
worst-off contradicts the principles of both solidarity and prioritarianism
(protecting the weakest).

Unfortunately, historical data are relatively scarce for long-term unemployment, only sufficient for a decade span of nine-country comparison.
To better discern the pattern of long-term unemployment, I have graphed
the nine countries in two separate groups. In the low group (Figure 4.2),
the share of unemployment one year or longer out of total unemployment
ranges from 14% to 29%. In the high group (Figure 4.3), it ranges from 40%
to 50%. Clearly, for the high group, long-term unemployment remained
about as high at the end as the beginning. For the low group, it increased
consistently through time, drawing these countries closer to the high group.
In short, persistent labor market exclusion became a problem common to
all countries by the eve of third way reforms.

There are some systematic factors that account for this general rise
in unemployment, such as the growing entry of females into the labor

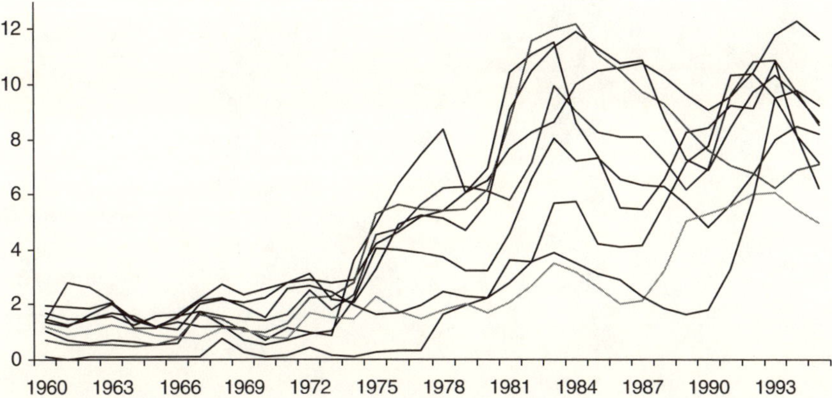

FIGURE 4.1. Standardized Unemployment Rate in Nine Countries 1960–1995 (*Data source:* OECD 2007a).

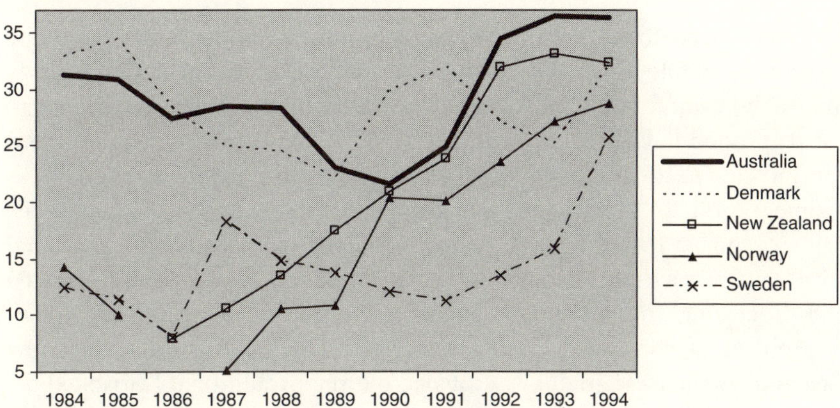

FIGURE 4.2. Unemployment of One Year and Over as Percentage of Total Unemployment in Low-Level Countries 1984–1994 (*Data source:* OECD 2007a).

force. This, to a large extent, invalidates the conventional "jobless growth" interpretation of unemployment. Jobs are growing, but the labor force is simply growing faster. The inability of Christian democratic governments to increase female employment either through large wage dispersion in the private-service sector or large expenditure in the public-service sector is a crucial cause behind the high level of unemployment in continental Europe (Iversen and Wren 1998). In Nordic countries, macroeconomic policy mistakes, such as credit market deregulation followed by hard currencies, constrained job growth. The hard currency principle also forced members of the

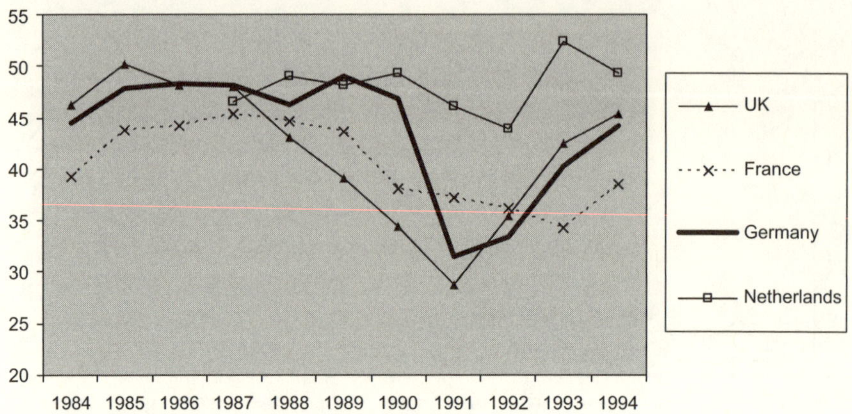

FIGURE 4.3. Unemployment of One Year and Over as Percentage of Total Unemployment in High-Level Countries 1984–1994 (*Data source:* OECD 2007a; data for the Netherlands start from 1987).

Economic Monetary Union (EMU) to maintain high interest rates despite growing unemployment. Globalization, to the extent that it significantly intensified capital mobility, reduced the ability of small open economies to use regulation to channel inward investment. There are also more context-specific causes for the unemployment problem. For example, the USSR's disintegration took markets away from Northern Europe. Although the primary impact fell on Finland (whose economy was affected on a national level), Norway's most northern region also had to adapt, especially for the cod processing and shipbuilding industries (Stokke and Tunander 1994). A problem of somewhat similar nature confronted Australia and New Zealand, as the EEC gradually crowded out their traditional British export markets. Finally, reunification in Germany also contributed to its own rising unemployment (more details later). For each country, Table 4.1 provides a road map of key developments related to the unemployment problem.

Denmark

At the time of the first major upset for the Danish party system in 1973, the unemployment rate was only 0.9%. However, by the early 1990s, there was a dramatically increased crisis of labor market exclusion in the form of an unemployment rate peaking above 10% in 1993. Among Nordic welfare states, Denmark had an unemployment crisis of the longest duration (Huber and Stephens 2001: 262; Ploug 2000: 4). Overall, after the late

TABLE 4.1. *Key Developments in the Economy Before Third Way Reforms*

Countries in order of appearance in the chapter	The Growing Employment Problem
Denmark	• Bourgeois government failed to halt rising unemployment
Sweden	• By the early 1990s, worst recession since the 1930s
Norway	• Sharp increase in unemployment peaking at 8%
Netherlands	• Serious outflow of labor force into disability programs • Unemployment reached 12%. • Centre-right coalition targeted inflation
France	• Center Right intensified privatization and cuts in social security • Center Right left office with 12% unemployment in 1997
Germany	• Christian democrats externalized unemployment onto the social security system. • Unemployment reached 11.6% in 1998
United Kingdom	• Radical neoliberal experiment under Conservative government • Male economic inactivity reached 3 million.
Australia	• Unemployment doubled under center-right coalition government. • Unemployment duration longest since the 1930s
New Zealand	• Severe economic downturn due to oil shock • Unemployment increased fivefold under the Nationals • Debt and deficit reached crisis level

1970s, the country had suffered a persistent unemployment problem and the consequent pressure on the existing social security system. The bourgeois parties presided over much of this period of unemployment increase. They placed less emphasis on the actual goal of reducing unemployment and more emphasis on shoring up competitiveness and minimizing costs in the economy. However, the bourgeois government made only limited attempts to reduce public expenditure. The cuts in benefits under the center Right were dictated by short-term budgetary considerations and constrained by possible electoral backlashes, and on the whole the government managed to slow down only the speed of the increase in welfare state spending instead of a rollback (Goul Andersen 2000: 72–73).

At the same time, demand-side measures to promote employment through job creation or the enlargement of the labor market were gradually abandoned. After the 1970s, an important cause of the unemployment problems in Denmark had been the relatively low productivity of its manufacturing industries, which were traditionally characterized by small firms and an orientation toward the mass instead of niche markets. Throughout the 1970s, while the technological component of Danish manufacturing industries was less dense than that of their Swedish counterparts, wages (in level as well as rate of increase) were higher, subjecting Danish industries only to more intense competitive problems in open markets. As unemployment problems persisted and then worsened during the 1980s, the bourgeois government's main solution to the problem of low productivity was to further lower wages (instead of raising the level of job qualifications seen under the social democrats since 1994) (Lind 1999: 195; Benner and Vad 2000: 434–435).

Although the bourgeois prescription for reducing unemployment attempted to highlight the inadequate consolidation of public expenditure, in actual policy terms the Danish state had gradually turned to fiscal consolidation to sustain competitive economic growth after the mid-1970s. The tax base was broadened and rates were lowered through a series of tax reforms. The adoption of a hard-currency approach in the 1970s and the pegging of the krone to the deutsch mark in 1982 made wage restraint all the more important for sustaining employment. After a wage drift in the 1970s, as well as between 1983 and 1986, wage growth was contained to a level below that of both Sweden and Germany by the late 1980s (Benner and Vad 2000: 457). In other words, the tight economic policy adopted and further tightened after the late 1970s by the Danish governments, while certainly important, would not have been sufficient alone to bring on the Danish job miracle since 1994, which wrestled unemployment back to less than 5% in five years. The important missing piece was the introduction of active labor market measures, which started with the third way reforms after 1994.

Sweden

By the early 1980s, the Swedish social democrats had already adopted a "third road" to economic growth, which departed from both traditional demand-side Keynesian economic stimulation and monetarist policies in the neoliberal direction. Instead of the Rehn-Meidner emphasis on low-wage dispersion, the third road opted for wage restraint and reductions in public spending, and the government made efforts to limit the growth of social expenditure. However, while opting for increasing economic prudence, the third road also attempted to use two significant devaluations of the krona (by 10% in 1981 and then by 16% a year later) to increase competitiveness and stimulate the economy. This strategy started to unravel after the mid-1980s, when a combination of wage drift and low productivity wiped out the effect of the two devaluations. In addition, rapid deregulation of the capital market piloted since 1986 by the Finance Ministry led to a chain of events that further increased unemployment. As deregulation deepened, the government continued with tax deduction for interest payments. The economy started to overheat, and there was a huge spike in real estate prices and a boom in the construction and retail markets. When the real estate bubble burst, consumer retrenchment followed, with sharp increase in interest rates. These developments coincided with a shift to hard currency. The krona was pegged to the European Currency Unit (ECU) in 1990 and was in floatation by 1992. The hard-currency approach ruled out further devaluations to stimulate the economy. During the 1980s, Sweden escaped the chronic unemployment problems besetting Denmark, but by early 1990s the country had witnessed its worst economic recession since the 1930s. Between 1990 and 1992, the employment ratio dropped from 80% to 70%, whereas unemployment shot up fourfold (Eitrheim and Kuhnle 2000: 48; Huber and Stephens 2001: 242; Benner and Vad 2000: 420–423).

The bourgeois parties in government oversaw this period of dramatically deepening recession, and similar to their Danish counterparts, the center Right made some limited attempts to reduce the size of public spending, but the generous welfare state was left largely intact due to its popularity and wide constituency. With the start of the bourgeois incumbency, supply-side measures took on growing importance in the economic policy package, and new overall targets for macroeconomic policymaking were set at price stability and low inflation. There was comparatively less emphasis on active labor market measures, and ALMPs requiring significant expenditure were specifically scrapped for cost reasons (Hort 2002: 140). As in Denmark, this growing crisis of unemployment set the scene for a later refocus on activation, as the social democrats renewed their third way tradition after returning to power in 1994.

Norway

In Norway, the strong regional policy based on active state intervention prevented a decline of employment in the short term. Meanwhile, the persistent shoring up of low-competitiveness industries in the periphery of the country had over time contributed to relatively high costs of labor. However, on the whole, this potential for structural unemployment had only limited impact on employment levels because of the relative success in continuous pursuit of wage restraint. During the 1980s, both Norway and Sweden resorted to devaluations to stimulate the economy. The Swedish strategy was later increasingly neutralized by the inability to maintain voluntary wage restraint in the framework of the third road macroeconomic approach, but the higher degree of bargaining centralization in Norway helped sustain wage restraint and industrial competitiveness. A high level of employment up to the late 1980s was also maintained by the increasingly profitable, and prominent, position of the oil industry in the Norwegian economy. Continuous state revenues from the oil sector helped retain a budget surplus, and the Norwegian welfare state was under less pressure for retrenchment than its Swedish or Danish counterparts (Ploug 1999: 99; Eitrheim and Kuhnle 2000: 53).

However, oil prices started to fall after the mid-1980s. Coinciding with an international recession triggered by a hard-currency squeeze on an overheated credit market, unemployment increased sharply, reaching a peak of 8% (Dolvik et al. 1997: 55). On the one hand, this unemployment crisis was more temporary and less structural in nature than other Scandinavian cases because of more successful wage restraints in Norway. On the other hand, in the context of four decades of government policy more or less successfully targeted at full employment, this sudden crisis in unemployment was unexpected. This has provided the backdrop for the efforts by the Labor Party to renew the Norwegian active labor market measures since the early 1990s.

The Netherlands

In the Netherlands, the clearest representation of its labor market exclusion crisis was an explosion in the number of disability benefit recipients, which approached 900,000 by 1990, a volume all the more perverse given the fact that, at the time of its creation in 1967, the disability benefit scheme was designed for a maximum capacity of a fourth of that volume (200,000 beneficiaries) (Hemerijck, Manow, and van Kersbergen 2000: 220).

In addition to escalating enrollments in sickness and disability schemes, the labor market exclusion crisis as the backdrop for later third way reforms also manifested itself in a straightforward rise in unemployment after the late 1970s, peaking in 1984 at 12% based on OECD and International Labor Organization (ILO) calculations. An important contributor to this loss of jobs was the discovery of North Sea gas, which led to overvaluation of the guilder and a declining competitiveness of the exporting industries (Huber and Stephens 2001: 169). Two Lubbers administrations, based on a coalition between the Christian Democrats and the Liberals, presided over much of this period of growing unemployment. Faced with the economic decline, the center-right coalition highlighted excessive expenditures and the deficit as important causes. In an effort to downsize the state and rekindle the economy on a competitive growth path, the Lubbers "no nonsense" administrations took the initiative by presenting the unions with the no-alternative choice of the Wassenaar agreement. Soon to follow were freezes in minimum wages, public sector wages, and the pegging of the guilder to the deutsch mark in 1983. The effect of these austerity measures in fiscal consolidation was actually quite swift, as inflation was reduced to near zero by the mid-1980s and public-sector deficit reduced by 3% in three years. In the process of these changes, employment objectives were given less emphasis, and, in fact, the deficit reduction between 1983 and 1986 was precisely achieved through a further drop in public employment (and salaries as well) (Hemerijck, Manow, and van Kersbergen 2000: 216–217).

The coalition's growing concern with cost saving also influenced the reforms of the Dutch social security system during the mid-1980s, which also marked the first major initiative by the Dutch state to address the disability crisis. A "price policy" was adopted for these reforms, focused on lowering benefits and shortening durations. In 1985, benefits of all insurance schemes, ranging from unemployment and disability to sickness, were uniformly reduced from 80% to 70% of previous earnings (Hassel and Ebbinghaus 2000: 76–77; van Oorschot 1998: 9). The conspicuous failure of such a "price" approach to reduce the number of beneficiaries paved the way for the later turn to a third way "volume policy" in the 1990s. With a focus on the ratio between net participation in the labor market and the whole population, the "volume" approach was in close alignment with the social democratic objective of labor market activation.

France

Upon entering office in 1981, the Socialists embarked on large-scale nationalizations and demand-side subsidies in an attempt to stimulate economic growth and jobs. Minimum wage as well as social transfers were also increased. The ensuing escalating budget and trade deficits put significant pressure on the franc. In order to avoid a sharp devaluation and to remain in the European Monetary System, the government was forced to abruptly reverse its interventionist and demand-side measures implemented during the first two years in office. Premised on the *franc fort* principle, the government not only pegged the franc to the deutsch mark but also reduced industry assistance, abolished planning targets, and decreased capital grants and subsidies. Although the bulk of the U-turn took place primarily on the economic and industrial policy front, its impact soon spread into the labor market and the welfare state, characterized by increasing unemployment and labor market exclusion. As rapid economic austerity and liberalization reforms immediately followed equally rapid demand-side stimulation, inflation was reduced from 9.6% to 2.7% between 1983 and 1986, but unemployment shot up to 10.4%. Average unemployment for the next ten years was 10.8%, compared with an average of 3.5% before the U-turn (OECD 2007a; Levy 2000: 324–325).

In response to this crisis of unemployment, the Socialists introduced the Minimum Income of Insertion (RMI) in 1988. This put in place a substantial expansion in French active labor market measures and set the Socialist policy strategy in a third way direction. However, this early development was cut short by the return of the Gaullists to power in 1986. As one relatively early example of social democrats forced to choose labor market activation for combating unemployment, the first few years of reforms under Socialist Prime Minister Michel Rocard were marred by contradictions. Despite expansion in active protection, early retirement schemes financed by increasing social contributions continued to further aggravate labor market exclusion well into the early 1990s. In addition, by 1993, the Socialists were returned to opposition, and the following five years under the center-right government saw growing policy emphasis given to deficit reduction.

In economic policy, both the Édouard Balladur (1993–1995) and Alain Juppé (1995–1997) administrations were marked by further deepening in the process of economic liberalization. Privatization of the state sector continued, and a wide range of regressive taxes were introduced. In social and labor market policy, changes were increasingly dictated by short-term concern with cost and deficit reduction. Instead of increasing state expenditures to finance active labor market measures, Balladur adopted a typical strategy of low-wage compulsion into employment, by proposing an "insertion wage" for youths, set at 80% of the minimum wage. Employers at the same time were relieved of any responsibility for qualifications and training. Massive protests forced the withdrawal of this measure, but the pattern of welfare state downsizing limited by the vehemence of popular protests, characterized by J. Levy (2000: 332–333) as "negotiation between the state and the streets," persisted under the Juppé government.

After the center Right came to power, they started to downgrade the traditional strategy of raising social contributions to finance welfare state expansion. In a reversal of direction, direct cuts in benefits followed. At the same time, however, massive early retirement continued to be encouraged in order to alleviate costs to the firms. The transfer of power to Juppé in 1995 intensified the attempt to downsize the social security system, and the government's social security reform proposal extended the target of benefit cuts into the civil service. The lack of consultation, on top of the radical nature of retrenchment proposals, led to public anger in the streets and later at the polls in 1997. However, five years of policymaking in an effort to restrain public expenditure had not made a clear impact on economic performance. As the center-right parties were ejected from office in 1997, unemployment was at 12%, crowning a decade of unemployment above 10% (OECD 2007a).

Germany

Unemployment problems in Germany first started to surface after the oil shocks of 1973. During the period between 1971 and 1974, not only was the deutsch mark floated against the dollar, but the Bundesbank also formally subscribed to a monetarist policy, by targeting the growth in the volume of money and maintaining a tight anti-inflationary principle. Throughout the 1980s and 1990s, a substantial revaluation in the deutsch mark followed. On top of the international recessions triggered by the oil crisis, these changes on the monetary front contributed to losses in German industrial competitiveness and to economic decline. Whereas unemployment was below 1% before 1973, two years later it climbed to 4%, and by the early 1980s it had reached 8% (Huber and Stephens 2001: 265).

However, with the Bundesbank now determined to enforce a tight monetary policy, Keynesian demand-side stimulants were practically ruled out in Germany by the mid-1970s, earlier than most other OECD countries. After the German federal budget turned into a surplus by the end of the 1980s, there was clearly limited competitive leverage in further monetarist belt tightening. Without the immediate pressure of cost control, the Christian democratic government did not roll back the welfare state, despite its rhetoric of radical change when entering office in coalition with the Free Democrats (FDP) in 1982. Instead, their response to the persistent unemployment problems focused on passive removal of the denominator: The labor force was continuously diminished by labor market exit schemes. Among these schemes, the removal of older workers through early retirement played a key role, especially after German reunification brought the East German industries to near total collapse. A special early retirement scheme for workers over 55 years of age was created for East Germany, and between 1989 and 1997, old age insurance contributions rose from 18.7% to 20.3% of payroll (Bleses and Seeleib-Kaiser 2004: 72–73).

As a whole, the process of reunification contributed significantly to the unemployment problems by generating a "regional transfer economy" within the German economy. Effective demand in the new *Länder* was significantly higher than the region's GDP, overshooting by around 66% in 1991. Even ten years later, this demand excess remained at about 40%. This regional trade deficit was financed by annual net transfers from the west half of the country amounting to 70–75 billion euros, or 4% of GDP in the West. Not only did such enormous outflow of state revenues contribute to growing budget deficits and tie the government's hand in fiscal stimulation under the Stability and Growth Pact, but these investments also had unsatisfactory returns. Capital formation and technological innovation remained slow in the East, with labor productivity only two-thirds of the West, even a decade after reunification. In the process of reunification, West Germany's welfare state structure was directly installed in the new *Länder*, and unemployment in the East triggered a severe increase in overall social expenditure (topping 32% of the GDP by 1996) and social security contributions (Hübner 2004: 117–19; Seeleib-Kaiser 2004: 125–6).

Just as the passive side of the German social and labor policy apparatus was emphasized by the Kohl government after the 1990s, its active side was sidelined during this process, because both sides were financed from the same funds. Unlike the practice in Scandinavian countries, where ALMPs are funded by taxation, labor market measures in Germany draw resources from the same social security contributions as unemployment insurance. As massive inflows from East Germany into the social security system took place, the initial burst of training and active job creation measures intended to increase East German employment was rapidly scaled back (Manow and Seils 2000b: 282–293). As a result of the reunification bailout, the increasing tax and social security contribution burdens, as well as the total government expenditure, alarmed the Bundesbank, which subsequently reacted by raising interest rates and sending Germany into a recession in 1993. By the time the Red-Green coalition came to power in 1998, unemployment had climbed above 10%. This crisis of labor market exclusion, which had progressively worsened over the previous two decades, formed the context for later active labor market reforms.

United Kingdom

While there was continuous failure to pursue wage restraint, the British economy was also slow in productivity and technological upgrading. This was due to low spending on R&D and inadequacy in training, in a Liberal Market Economy production regime oriented toward competition on price and reluctant to provide supply-side public goods. In addition, the economy was particularly vulnerable to financial pressure from changes in the international economy, and persistent current account deficits translated into downward pressure on the pound. In response, a series of stop–go policies followed throughout the 1950s and 1960s, further disrupting economic growth and expansion of the welfare state.

The confounding problems in incomes and economic policies came to a head after the oil hikes of 1973 induced a deep recession. The contraction of the economy coincided with a period of current account deficit between 1973 and 1977, as well as the chronic inability of the Wilson and Callaghan Labour governments to control wage and price explosions. Meanwhile, there were escalating industrial conflicts over wages well into 1979, when the Conservatives returned to power under Thatcher. For stagflation problems of the late 1970s, the policy response from the Conservatives was one of the most faithful representations of the neoliberal prescription, focused on cost control and minimizing the state in order to achieve economic competitiveness. In public discourse, many center-right governments have emphasized the importance of cost reduction in reversing economic decline since the early 1980s. However, in actual policy implementation, the neoliberal strategy of drastic downsizing was implemented only in the most auspicious circumstances, where there were minimum veto points in political institutions and narrow constituencies in welfare state benefits: Britain, as well as New Zealand (to be discussed later).

Under the British Conservatives, a project of radical deregulation in the labor market and de-legitimization of unions was begun. The Trade Union Act of 1984 and the Trade Union Reform and Employment Rights Act of 1993 abolished the closed shop, introduced secret balloting, severely limited the rights to industrial action, and also made unions liable for the costs of industrial action. Trade unions were required to give seven days' notice for strikes, and injunctions against unlawful industrial actions were allowed. The effect of these changes was significant. Between 1979 and 1994, trade union membership declined from thirteen million to eight million, and most restrictions on working hours, dismissals, and wage standards were nonexistent by the end of the Conservative period (Millar 2002a: 161–162). The basically flattened field of labor relations by 1997 means that, in the third way reforms under New Labour, securing the macroeconomic context of wage restraint was relatively easier, and the introduction of further labor market flexibility less important, than many other third way reform cases.

The destruction of the union-based potential for wage explosion did help in addressing the root causes of British stagflation during the 1970s and 1980s. However, other components of the Conservative economic projects were less effective in resuscitating economic competitiveness. In particular, Conservative measures were unambiguously negative with regard to their impact on employment as well as social exclusion. Parallel with deregulation in the labor market was significant privatization in the public sector and radical liberalization in the macroeconomy, premised on a tight monetarist policy stance. Between 1979 and 1995, employment in the public sector fell from 7.5 million to 5.2 million. The high-profile privatization of housing started in 1981, and by the end of the Conservative period, the public share of the British housing sector had been reduced to 19% (Millar 2002a: 162–163; Page 2002: 172–173).

A new medium-term monetary policy was adopted, with a focus on the supply of broad money, which includes cash, credit, and public-sector borrowing. In addition, the banking and credit market was liberalized, and the rapid increase in consumption taxes went hand in hand with cuts in income taxes. The reforms aimed at reducing state expenditure also spilled into social security and left a deep impact, despite the lack of clear evidence that welfare state expenditure was contributing to the competitiveness problems in the British economy. The Beveridgean universal side of the British welfare state was severely scaled back and the means-tested residual side expanded. While the number of people dependent on social assistance doubled from four to eight million under the Conservatives, entitlement to National Insurance was simultaneously restricted. Quasi markets replaced public delivery in social services, and the government actively encouraged individual private pensions, whose coverage in population grew from 1.5 to 14 million over the course of the 1980s. Despite all the welfare retrenchment, contraction in state expenditures, and a tight monetarist policy, productivity in Britain remained the lowest among the Group of 7 (G7) at the end of the Conservative period, and the British economy had not emerged from a low-cost low-wage trap. Meanwhile, the labor market and social consequences of the reforms were negative. Whereas unemployment stood at 5% in 1979, the average unemployment for the 1980s was 10%, and 9% between 1990 and 1997. Forty percent of the unemployed in 1997 were long-term unemployed, and male economic inactivity stood at three million. These labor market exclusion problems contributed further to rising poverty and inequality by the end of the Conservative period (Millar 2002a: 149; Rhodes 2000b: 51; OECD 2007a).

Australia

In Australia, the center-right coalition presided over the initial stage in the unraveling of the Golden Age. During this period, the typical response of the shell-shocked governments across the OECD world was to continue pump priming and further expansion of resources in the last round of attempts to revitalize the economy through Keynesian demand stimulation. For this reason, austerity measures adopted by the Fraser coalition government were limited in scope. Officially, the center-right government pursued an "anti-inflation" strategy until mid-1982. In this process, public expenditure was cut during the first few years and the welfare state scaled back, seen especially in the abolition of Medibank. However, the Liberal Party was quick to reverse its direction when unemployment picked up as an early result of these austerity measures, and the government also relaxed its initial stance of anti-inflation (Cass and Whiteford 1989: 280–284; K. Davis 1989: 70–71). More fundamentally, the center Right made little attempt to address two root problems behind the economic decline: excessive protection of domestic industries and growing pressure for wage inflation hidden in the arbitration system. In fact, the coalition government publicly condemned the attempts by the previous Whitlam Labor government to lower tariffs, and committed itself to reversing what it called the "free trade" policies under Whitlam. In 1980, the Liberals conceded to wage awards for public-sector unions well above the arbitration target. By December 1982, the government was forced to impose a wage freeze (Schwartz 2000: 108; Davis 1989: 71; Bennett and Cole 1989: 163). The task of fundamental overhaul in the economic structure, including full liberalization of the credit and banking sectors plus the dismantling of domestic protection, was left to the ALP governments in the early 1980s.

Meanwhile, the labor market and social consequences of the indecisive Fraser administration had manifested themselves fully by the time of power transfer to the Left in 1983. Throughout the coalition government period, unemployment was on a path of monotonic and rapid increase, from 4.8% in 1975 to 10% in 1983. Both the collapse of a resource boom and a wage explosion contributed during the early 1980s to this sharp rise in unemployment. In the Australian context of occupational welfare premised on full employment, an unemployment rate of 10% looked especially alarming, when compared with an average unemployment of less than 2% during the late 1960s and early 1970s. The average duration of unemployment, meanwhile, was also longer than any period since the Great Depression of the 1930s, and there were increasing numbers of people withdrawing from active job searches (that is, people in joblessness). Another trend taking off during this period was an increase in labor market exit before the pension age, and the bulk of these early withdrawals from the labor market were actually involuntary. These labor market exclusion problems further contributed to an increase in welfare dependency, as more people of working age were transferred from the wage earners' welfare state to the means-tested and minimum formal welfare state. Therefore, despite the belt-tightening rhetoric of the Fraser government, social expenditure kept climbing through the 1970s and early 1980s. During the 1970s, the social expenditure hikes were primarily a result of new programs and real increases in benefit levels. However, by the early 1980s, the rising social expenditure was simply due to substantial increases in unemployment. Poverty, meanwhile, also increased for all categories, especially for families with children, and for families where one or both parents were excluded from the labor market (Cass and Whiteford 1989: 275–284; M. Jones 2002: 12–16).

New Zealand

After a brief period of three years out of office, the center-right parties in Australia and New Zealand returned to power during the same year (1975). They did so against the backdrop of ineffective and inflationary attempts by the previous social democratic governments to wrestle with the first signs of stagflation. The coalition under Malcolm Fraser in Australia subscribed to an anti-inflationary policy, reduced public investment as well as public deficit, and removed the most significant universal component of the Australian welfare state (Medibank). By contrast, the National government under Robert Muldoon went in the completely opposite direction. Until 1975, the formal side of the New Zealand welfare state had retained the typical characteristics of a liberal welfare regime, such as flat-rate means-tested minimum benefits and meager social services. However, soon after the Nationals returned to power, a tax-funded and universal superannuation scheme was introduced. Available to everyone with twenty years' residency at the age of 65, the Superannuation was far more generous than Labour's two-tier pension schemes, which it replaced (McClure 1998: 191–192; Bassett 1998: 344–345). By the time the Nationals left office, Superannuation had become by far the largest component of government social expenditure.

In the economic sphere, the center Right significantly expanded credit assistance, not only to manufacturing but also increasingly to the primary sector, which was feeling the pressure from the slack in European demands. A Supplementary Minimum Price was introduced in 1978 in order to maintain price stability for farmers, and the price assistance was paid significantly far above likely market returns. Meanwhile, the government continued with credit to the Dairy Board at a 1% interest rate (Bassett 1998: 352–353). What took the government's experiments in state expansion to new heights was the Nationals' plan to stimulate economic growth by using New Zealand's natural resources to attract energy-intensive industries. The government started to pump significant public expenditure into the exploration of natural gas and oil, not only in tax write-offs and grants but also in direct investment in the construction of large-scale power stations and processing plants across the country. By the time of the 1981 election campaign, these changes, in addition to the prospect of further gas exploration on South Island, had crystallized into a series of "Think Big" projects under the Nationals. They promised that these projects would create up to 410,000 new jobs during the 1980s. Government outlays, ranging from superannuation and industrial and agricultural assistance to state building in the energy sector, were continuously paid through public-sector borrowing, and the Nationals stuck to textbook Keynesian demand stimulation well into the early 1980s (J. Gould 1982: 156; Bassett 1998: 365–366).

On the whole, the large-scale intervention had not been effective in reviving the New Zealand economy. The Think Big projects rested on the incorrect assumption that oil prices in the international market would continue to ride on the momentum of the OPEC hikes in 1979. As oil prices started to decline during the early 1980s, the crash in the resources economy triggered a deep economic downturn in New Zealand as well as Australia. While unemployment was practically nonexistent (0.08%) the year before the entry of the Nationals into government, by 1984 it had climbed to 5.7%. Overseas debt, meanwhile, shot up from 1.4 to 12.4 billion between 1976 and 1983, and during a similar period, the proportion of government expenditure used to service the debt rose from 6.5% to 17%. Finally, when the Nationals were replaced by the fourth Labour government in 1984, public expenditure as a percentage of total GDP stood at 41%, a level not seen outside the Scandinavian countries. This scale of statism, combined with the economic crisis, made the neoliberal case easier for the incoming Treasury under Roger Douglas, who purposely stayed away from new expenditure commitments in the labor market. And, as a final parting shot, the Nationals refused to hand over power immediately after their election defeat, obstructing Labour's attempt to devaluate the dollar and triggering massive speculation. The field was now open for the monetarist alternatives from the fourth Labour government (Kelsey 1995: 27; Bassett 1998: 365–366; OECD 2007a).

5

Expansion in Active Protection

This chapter focuses on the active dimension of social protection. As its name suggests, active social protection operates primarily by facilitating entry into the labor market for the unemployed and those out of the labor force. Fiscally, implementation of active labor market programs requires very large increases in public spending. Intellectually, active social protection requires a clear ideological transformation, toward a more productivist notion of solidarity and prioritarian orientation in social democratic egalitarianism. The active dimension of social protection is where the difference between social democrats and their center-right counterparts is clearest in policy paradigms.

Across the nine countries examined here, the transfer of power to social democracy almost always initiated the clear expansion of various measures in active social protection. By contrast, center-right incumbency demonstrated much less enthusiasm in increasing the active measures. Instead, there was either little action or, in some cases, much enthusiasm for rolling back existing active schemes. Such consistent policy contrast between left and right incumbencies across diverse country settings clearly reflects a power resources pattern of welfare state changes. While there are strong policy paradigm contrasts for different partisan governments, within the same type of partisan government there are also enormous diversities across countries in policy implementation. Here, institutional constraints provide the key explanation.

On a theoretical level, the nine country cases in this chapter illustrate the combination between a power-resources explanation of policy paradigms and a path-dependent explanation of policy implementation. On a thematic level, the chapter breaks down active protection into three distinct aspects: active labor market programs (ALMPs), in-work incentives, and measures to combine labor market flexibility and security (flexicurity measures). Because of the large spending involved, plus the innovative strategy of bringing the labor market to the unemployed, ALMPs are the core of active social protection. In-work incentives and flexicurity serve as supplements, subordinate to the overall objective of ALMPs. As a road map for the analysis cutting across theoretical, thematic, and empirical dimensions, this chapter is organized around the three policy themes. For each theme, empirical case analysis reflects the combination between power resources and path dependency on a theoretical level. Figure 5.1 illustrates the organizational framework for the chapter.

1. ACTIVE LABOR MARKET POLICIES

The social democrats have expanded active social protection primarily through the introduction of new ALMPs and increases in the volume, scope, and financial resources for these programs. Although diverse in design,

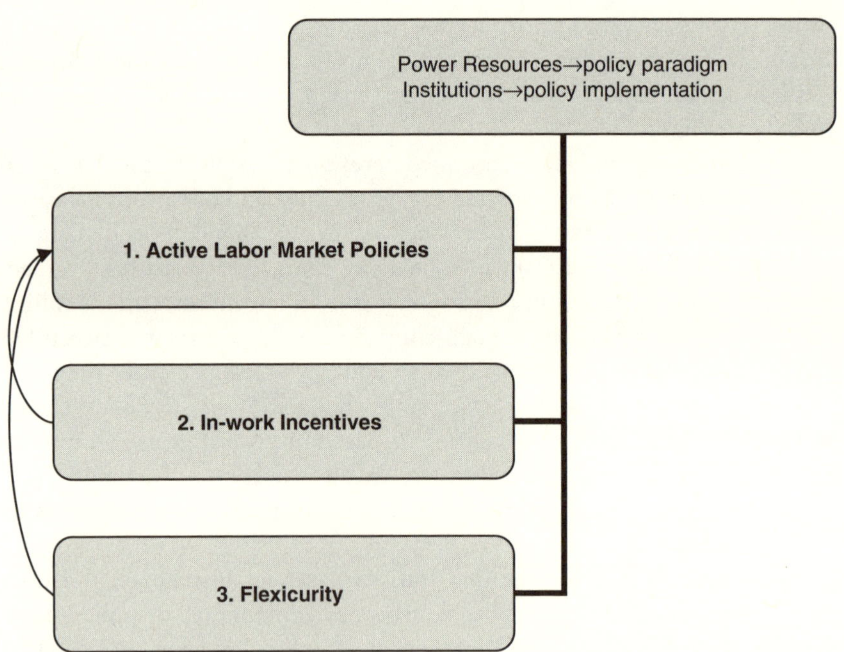

FIGURE 5.1. Overall Organization for Chapter 5

mechanism, and target population, ALMPs do share the common characteristic of making an offer to the unemployed. This offer could range from a temporary training scheme, education opportunity, or job apprenticeship to direct placement in new jobs created in the public sector or subsidized in the private sector. In addition, all ALMPs, to different extents, combine the offer of activation with an obligation by the unemployed to respond actively. Such obligation ranges from showing up for interviews with labor market officers or demonstrating job-searching activities to compulsory acceptance of job or training placements.

Although active and passive measures are treated separately in the book for a clearer focus, it is important to emphasize that social democratic expansion of active protection, especially ALMPs, is intrinsically linked to corresponding changes in passive protection. Very often, an offer of ALMP to the unemployed remunerates the participants in the form of increased welfare benefits; meanwhile, benefit entitlement is increasingly conditional on participation in activation offers.

Among the various components of active protection, ALMPs are, unsurprisingly, the most dominant one in terms of financial commitment, and most innovative in terms of activation strategies. This is not only because ALMPs often involve direct increases in public expenditure as the source of financing, but also because they directly offer a passage into the labor market. The ALMPs bring the labor market to the door of the unemployed, saving them the often impossibly difficult task of reaching out on their own in search of work. In addition, the making of an activation offer by the state creates the first substantial opportunity for policymakers to explicitly combine rights and duties to work and to fine-tune the balance between the two, not only in actual policy implementation but also in deeper programmatic philosophy. Therefore, it is usually in the evolutionary process of ALMPs that social democrats demonstrate the clearest evidence of ideological transformation, from income replacement to income regain, and from traditional egalitarianism to making work pay.

ALMPs are where paradigm shifts, were they to occur, are most likely to be in evidence. In almost all country cases, key policy changes in ALMPs reflect the difference between social democratic expansion and much less activism by center-right parties (with occasional rollback). Within social democratic expansion, meanwhile, diverse implementation patterns and outcomes reflect path dependency on existing institutions. Table 5.1 provides the key developments in ALMPs for each country and their theoretical implications.

TABLE 5.1. *Key ALMP Developments, by Country and Theoretical Implications*

Key policies in order of appearance in the chapter	Theoretical Implications ⇨	Power Resources	Path Dependency
	Denmark	1994 Labor Market Reform	Nordic→ emphasis on human capital, training, marginal labor force, and the right to activation
	Sweden	Strong ALMP tradition since Rehn-Meidner	
	Norway	Solidarity 2000	
	Netherlands	Jobseekers' Employment Act 1998	Continental→ reforms more timid (especially France and Germany); unable to activate marginalized labor force
	France	Minimum Income of Insertion	
	Germany	Job-AQTIV 2002	
	United Kingdom	Six New Deals	Anglo-Saxon→ strong emphasis on obligation to activation; coercion rather than human capital investment; limited fiscal commitment to ALMPs
	Australia	Working Nation 1994	
	New Zealand	Limited expansion in ALMPs	

Denmark

The very first tentative attempt in Denmark to formally link rights and duties to labor market activation can be traced back to 1990, when the then-bourgeois government introduced a Youth Allowances Scheme. Primarily targeted at those unemployed younger than 24 years of age, this scheme required social assistance recipients to participate in activation in order to be eligible for benefits (Rosdahl and Weise 2001: 160). However, this measure was very much the exception rather than the norm, and labor market policy in Denmark continued to be dominated by labor-force-reducing and other passive measures, until the labor market reform of 1994.

With the 1994 reform, for the unemployed individual there was now both a very explicit obligation to participate in ALMPs and the right to do so, in an individualized plan drawn up between the unemployed and the local labor market office. Until the early 1990s, the traditional Danish social security system offered members of the unemployment funds the privilege of receiving benefits as a right when unemployed, with the sole condition that they be available to the labor market on "normal conditions." There was a very narrow interpretation of labor market mobility with regard to both skills and geography, and normal conditions in this context referred to "the same conditions which apply for every one else on the labor market" (Hespanha and Møller 2001: 58; Loftager 1998: 14). Since 1994, the unemployed individual has had to accept ALMP offers not on normal conditions but on conditions decided by the labor market authority, which can potentially imply not only lower wages but also limits to rights previously available in a normal working contract, such as the right to wage negotiations, holidays, unemployment insurance, or membership in a trade union. In addition to enforcing the obligation on the unemployed, the new activation line emphasized the responsibility of both the state and private enterprises to provide sufficient ALMP job opportunities for the unemployed (Ploug 1999: 96–98; Rosdahl and Weise 2001: 160; Loftager 1998: 14).

During the 1994 reform, the social democrats severed the connection between job training and the unemployment benefit system, so that participation in ALMPs would no longer give entitlement to unemployment benefits if the individual were to come out of the training period still unemployed. This move finally reversed a long trend started under the social democrats themselves in 1979, when they introduced a Job-Offer-Scheme. With the Job-Offer-Scheme, a job of at least seven months was guaranteed to all long-term unemployed. However, because of insufficient job demand in both public and private sectors, people who were offered a temporary job were rushed out of it right after seven months, in order to make way for the next eligible long-term unemployed. By the 1980s, this recycling trend had intensified, as the unemployed in general were entitled to unemployment benefits for three years, including six months of participation in a job-training program, which in turn led to entitlement for another three years of benefits. Now, the government's reform in 1994 once and for all ended this practice of recycling the unemployed between the benefit system and ALMPs (Kvist 2000: 21; Kildal 2001: 7; Abrahamson and van Oorschot 2002: 8).

Under the social democrats, the duration of the unemployment benefit was split into one passive period followed by one active period. During the passive period, the state was to offer individualized counseling to the unemployed to help them draw up an individual action plan about participation in ALMPs and reintegration into the labor market. During this phase, the unemployed were to have much discretion in choosing a preferred activation method from the available options. One crucial stated objective of these plans was to achieve an appropriate balance between the wishes of the individuals and the local market demands. During the active period to follow, the state was to be obliged to make ALMP offers based on the action plan drawn up during the passive period, and correspondingly the unemployed individuals were obliged to accept these offers. The ALMP offers from the state could encompass a very wide range of activities, including specialized individual job training, pool jobs, job rotation, and leave schemes, as well as training or education in the formal academic system (Bjorklund 2000: 155–156; Etherington 1998: 153–154; Dahl et al. 2002: 21).

Just as the total duration of unemployment benefits was being reduced, the passive component of benefit duration was also gradually crowded out by the active component. In 1995 the active period kicked in after four years of benefits, but by 1996 the lag was reduced to only two years, and by 1999 to one, and the active period had to involve activation for at least 75% of the time. The reduction in the passive period was extremely steep for the young, already down to six months by 1996. For social assistance recipients, on the other hand, after January 1994 they were required to be activated after only one year on social assistance.

With these measures for the unemployed, both rights and obligations to activation were significantly strengthened. In terms of obligations, the act severed the link between ALMPs and the right to unemployment benefits, and social assistance would now be significantly reduced if the unemployed were to refuse a reasonable ALMP offer. In terms of rights, for low-skilled people unable to compete in the normal labor market, the social democrats tried to create an intermediate labor market with relatively low wages, by passing in 1994 a law on wage-subsidized home service. As a whole, with their labor market reforms throughout the 1990s, the social democrats formally specified and conferred both rights and obligations on the unemployed, without at the same time bringing any changes to the level of benefits (Torfing 1998: 252–253; Kosonen 2001: 166; Goul Andersen 2002b: 155). The overall development trend for Danish ALMPs is that, increasingly, activation measures are utilized for more people, in more situations, and for longer periods, whereas the activation period kicks in increasingly earlier in the unemployment spell, and the scope of activation measures also continues to grow (Kvist 2000: 25–26).

In addition to intensifying the enforcement of both rights and duties to activation for the unemployed, the social democratic blueprint for ALMPs was also characterized by a very conspicuous human capital emphasis. Figure 5.2 shows a clear expansion of public resources devoted to training

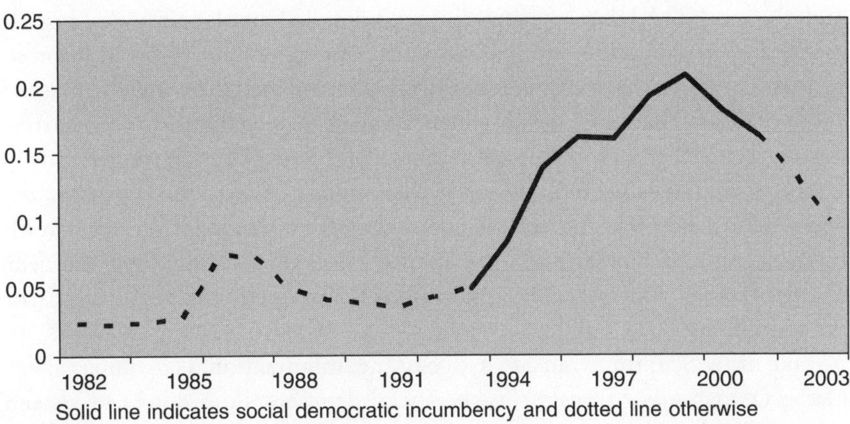

FIGURE 5.2. Expenditure on Labor Market Training as Percentage of GDP in Denmark 1982–2003 (*Source:* OECD 2006a).

measures under social democracy, in contrast with the preceding and succeeding bourgeois governments. The government used unemployment benefits of up to 100% to support the participation of unemployed adults in the general education system, and after 2001 the government also introduced an apprenticeship for adults (Dingeldey and Linke-Sonderegger 2004: 15). As a result of the labor market reforms, all unemployed, regardless of whether they were entitled to social insurance, had the right to receive an ALMP offer of either education or job training. On the one hand, full-time ALMP participation through education or job training was made compulsory after a certain period of unemployment, to reflect the general principle of the 1994 reform in emphasizing the obligation to accept activation. On the other hand, the government also emphasized the right to ALMPs, by making the measures flexible and adjustable to the needs of both the unemployed and to prevailing conditions in the labor market (Torfing 2001: 302–303; Bjorklund 2000: 155; Loftager and Madsen 1997: 124–125).

To this end, the government decentralized policy implementation to the regional level in order to facilitate the adjustment of local ALMP design to individual needs. The most important component of this devolution process was a considerable strengthening of the power for the fourteen regional labor market councils. Meanwhile, the government also introduced a system of planning guidelines and targets to ensure that regional policies comply with the national goals for labor market measures. On the whole, while overall ALMP policy goals continued to be set by the Ministry of Labor and the national labor market council, detailed implementation instruments and specifications were devolved to the regional level. In addition to decentralization, the social democrats also introduced growing elements of customization in public employment services responsible for administering the ALMP offers. The customization reforms were characterized by a strong emphasis on employer services, employers' satisfaction, and the active recruiting of employers as customers of employment services. With these organizational reforms, the Danish labor market underwent a clear change from a rule-based benefit system to one oriented to the needs of individuals.

Like other Scandinavian cases, due to the organizational encompassment of the Danish labor movement, the social democrats did not have a steep electoral trade-off in conflicting preferences between insiders and outsiders. In both the second and third phases of the labor market reform in 1996 and 1999, there was growing attention to the vulnerable new social risk groups such as the long-term unemployed, low-skilled, disabled, and other individuals with reduced capacity to work (Jensen 1999: 1). Correspondingly, the concept of "encompassing labor market" took center stage in the government's activation policies. This constitutes a clear contrast with the practice of the bourgeois parties. During the 1980s, the center-right parties did not make any significant effort to activate these marginalized segments of the labor market. The bourgeois government's strategy was in alignment with its principle in other areas of social policy, including the reduction in cash assistance and the imposition of a waiting period for sickness benefits (Benner and Vad 2000: 448–449). By contrast, the encompassing-labor-market notion under the social democrats clearly stipulated that, on the one hand, persons with reduced capacity to work should keep a job, and on the other hand, measures should be taken by the firm at the workplace to preserve the employee's full capacity to work during his or her whole working life. Figure 5.3 shows that social democratic incumbency featured much stronger expansion in employment measures for the disabled than did the bourgeois administrations.

With the encompassing-labor-market logic in mind, the government created flex jobs based on permanent wage subsidies for persons with permanently reduced capacity to work. The Ministry of Social Affairs launched the campaign "It Concerns Us All" to raise awareness and exchange information on the social responsibilities of enterprises for marginally excluded people. In 1995, the government recommended that the social partners include "social chapters" in their next round of collective agreements. These social chapters were bargained at the local level, and they

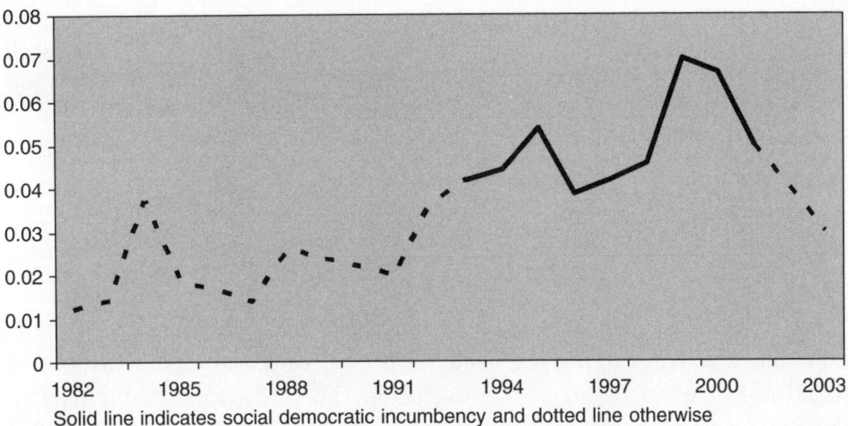

FIGURE 5.3. Expenditure on Training for the Disabled as Percentage of GDP in Denmark 1982–2003 (*Source:* OECD 2006a).

served to encourage unions and employers to work together in facilitating ALMP and employment opportunities for individuals with reduced working capacity, health problems, or long-term exclusion from the labor market. Based on the social chapter, new types of jobs were to be created on a local level, whose wages and working conditions were suitable for people with reduced capacity (Lind 1999: 198; Madsen 2003: 105). This creation of a transitional or intermediate labor market is one of the most important instruments used by the social democrats to integrate the marginalized unemployed. In addition, the government also combined assistance to the long-term unemployed with individualized ALMP action plans, to accommodate the needs of both the unemployed and the local labor market. For the more difficult group of low-skilled young unemployed, the government introduced special youth measures in 1996. With this scheme, individuals in this target group have a right and duty to ALMPs on highly reduced benefits after six months of unemployment. The offers of ALMPs include both education and training and can last for at least eighteen months (Goul Andersen and Jensen 2002b: 69; Madsen 1999: 76; Kildal 2001: 8).

The social democrats' measures combating new social risks appeared to have delivered some dramatic results. Five years after the labor market reform began, there had been a 61% decrease in long-term unemployment and a 67% decrease in youth unemployment (Jensen 1999: 11). Since 1993, the social democrats in government expanded child care by some 130,000 places. Half-time day-care places had largely been converted into full-time places maintaining good quality care. This policy resulted in one of the highest employment rates of women with children among the advanced industrialized countries (Dingeldey and Linke-Sonderegger 2004: 17; Benner and Vad 2000: 458).

On a broader level, it is clear that the ALMPs made some impact. Unemployment decreased over the whole decade after the start of the reforms. There were increases in both labor market participation and employment, which then stabilized at a high level, and after 1995 hidden unemployment also started to fall. As Figure 5.4 shows, the social democrats oversaw a persistent drop in long-term unemployment, an important step toward bridging the insider–outsider divide and combating new social risks due to labor market exclusion. The most remarkable part of the achievement, however, is seen in Figure 5.5: The over 60% reduction in unemployment occurred without any serious inflationary consequences. Since the labor market reforms began, a dramatic shift in the Phillips curve had taken place as it became almost horizontal, which indicates a genuine reduction in structural unemployment. If there is a country with a record comparable to the Dutch miracle in dealing with unemployment, this would be Denmark (Benner and Vad 2000: 451; Becker 2000: 231; Madsen 2003: 98–100). In addition, welfare dependency also lessened, as the proportion dependent on public support decreased from 29% to 26% of all working ages between 1994 and 1998, although some of this decrease might be accounted for by early retirement (Abrahamson and van Oorschot 2002: 14).

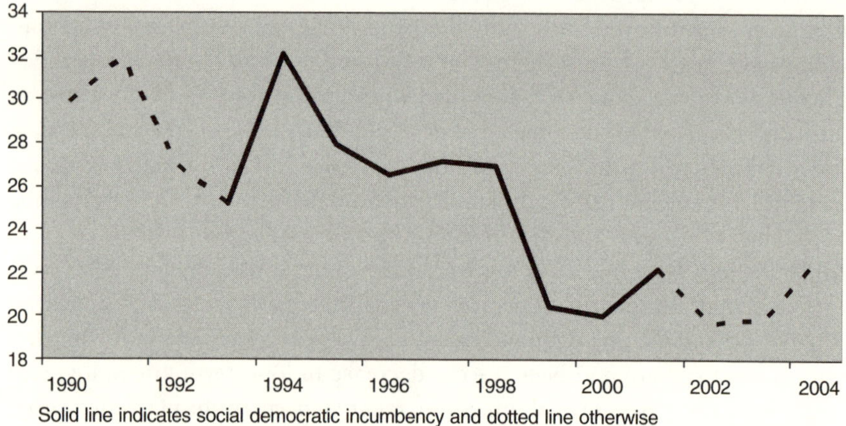

FIGURE 5.4. Unemployment with Duration of One Year and Over as Percentage of All Unemployed in Denmark 1990–2004 (*Source:* OECD 2007a).

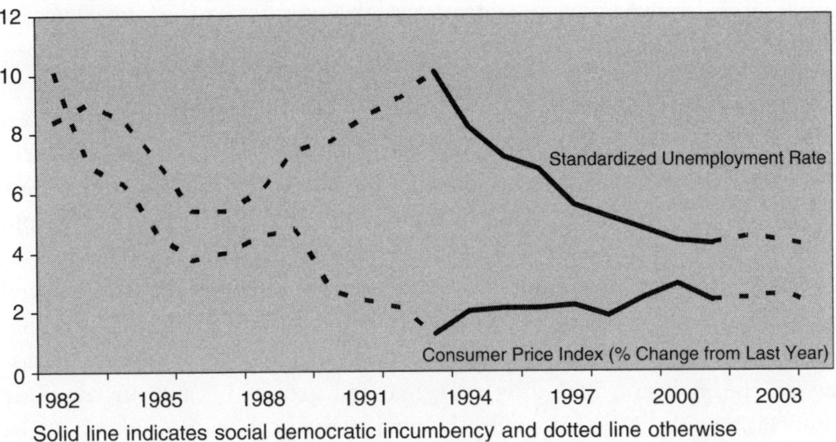

FIGURE 5.5. Relationship Between Unemployment and Inflation in Denmark 1982–2004 (*Source:* OECD 2007a [unemployment]; OECD 2007b [consumer price index]).

The success in the Danish ALMPs is closely related to the strong institutional basis for corporatist coordination among various actors. The dense network of unions, employers' organizations, regional Labor Market Boards, and individual firms cemented the exchange of information and reduced uncertainty over the strategic behavior of each other. Given the large number of players involved in the implementation of ALMPs, this corporatist framework is crucial for avoiding collective action failure and the problems it brings, such as shirking in training investment and cost shuffling among different players. As will be documented for other countries, where such corporatist institutions were nonfunctioning (such as in France and the UK), these very problems occurred, turning ALMPs into financial subsidies that firms exploit for hiring cheap labor (Clasen and Clegg 2006: 200; Martin and Swank 2004).

Despite the reform's success on a macro level, there is still unevenness in performance for individual programs and circumstances. Activation measures in the social insurance system had better success rates than those in the municipal (social assistance) system. A similar picture can be painted for offers of job training in the private versus public sector and for regular long-term education versus short-term vocational training (van Oorschot and Abrahamson 2003: 300). One key factor driving the variation in program performances was the nature of the target population to be activated. The weakest employment effect for ALMPs was on groups who had been receiving assistance or excluded from the labor market for the longest period of time (Rosdahl and Weise 2001: 178–179). These are the groups with the greatest need for state help in activation, due to their desperate situation of persistent exclusion. Therefore, to some extent, the ALMPs became least effective where they were most needed. This is not an isolated but general pattern, which also can be found in the activation reforms under New Labor and the Purple Coalition in the Netherlands. Partly for this reason, the focus of third way reforms in Denmark gradually went beyond straightforward activation to include non-labor-market objectives, such as social integration, enhancement of the quality of life, the overcoming of social problems, and investment in human resources. A long-term strategy focusing on the inclusion of highly marginalized groups became increasingly important in the social democratic agenda for activation (Trickey 2001: 290; Rosdahl and Weise 2001: 160).

Sweden

Given the fact that activation was already an institutionalized component of Swedish social policy throughout history, in the 1990s the active labor market reforms were less extensive relative to other Nordic countries, especially Denmark. Apart from a development guarantee for the young unemployed on municipal social assistance, no major new ALMPs were introduced. Changes to the existing welfare state were also relatively limited, with neither dramatic structural overhaul nor retrenchment (Hort 2001: 262). Nevertheless, today Sweden still spends more on ALMPs than any other OECD country. Indeed, despite minimal changes, Sweden already fulfills all of the three quantitative demands for employment polices of European Union (EU) member states: a minimum of 20% unemployed participating in ALMPs, the offer of ALMPs to all young unemployed after six months, and to unemployed adults after twelve months. The Swedish social democrats were confident enough in their activation principle to propose an employment union within the EU to counter the emphasis on the monetary union (Boesby, Dahl, and Ploug 2002: 41; Furåker 2002: 123; A. Gould 2001: 147).

Administered by the powerful National Labor Market Board (AMS), ALMPs in the Swedish context were typically incorporated, together with a solidaristic wage structure, into the Rehn-Meidner model. The solidaristic wages priced low-productivity industries out of the market. Active labor market measures were then used to stimulate both the demand (through subsidies to employers) and supply (through training) of the labor force.

Labor displaced from low-productivity sectors were moved into high-productivity ones through ALMPs. Growth in the economy as a result of increasing labor force participation was then used to finance a system of universal and generous social programs. Though ostensibly a tripartite institution, AMS was traditionally dominated by representatives from unions. The role of AMS in Rehn-Meidner was primarily job creation through either demand or supply-side measures, but the board also distributed subsidies to new industries, organized training, and offered financial compensation for those moving to regions with labor shortages. Therefore, Rehn-Meidner gives AMS an important role in both economic and employment policy (Lødemel and Trickey 2001: 13; Hort 2003: 249; Boesby, Dahl, and Ploug 2002: 19).

Designed for an economy dominated by high-productivity manufacturing industries, the Rehn-Meidner practice of solidaristic wages started to have the opposite effect as secular shifts to the low-productivity service sector deepened after the Golden Age. Arguably, suppression of wage dispersion now contributed to, instead of removing, unemployment, because while manufacturing industries shed jobs, low wage dispersion prevented the expansion of private service-sector employment. However, the overall impact of this change on employment was not significant because expansion of the public sector has increasingly become a key engine to sustain job growth in Sweden. Despite a generally high level of labor market activation, the 1980s were a lackluster decade for Swedish active measures when compared with the 1990s. Although ALMPs almost always dominate passive measures (unemployment insurance in particular) in the Swedish case, passive measures peaked during the late 1980s through such measures as further relaxation of eligibility criteria for unemployment insurance in 1987 and the abolition of its waiting period (Benner and Vad 2000: 430).

After coming to power in 1991, the bourgeois parties attempted to control the cost of public expenditure. The government shelved the expensive ALMPs, such as skill and competence development, and invented cheaper programs instead. This strategy resulted in a serious attenuation of ALMPs, and a growing proportion of active program participants were involved in cheaper measures. As Figure 5.6 shows, the bourgeois government, starting from 1991, led to a clear drop in labor market expenditure. The progressive retreat from public financial commitment to ALMPs under the center Right meant that by 1994, for the first time in postwar history, passive expenditure in unemployment insurance was greater than public expenditure on ALMPs. Such development was considered a major setback for the Swedish

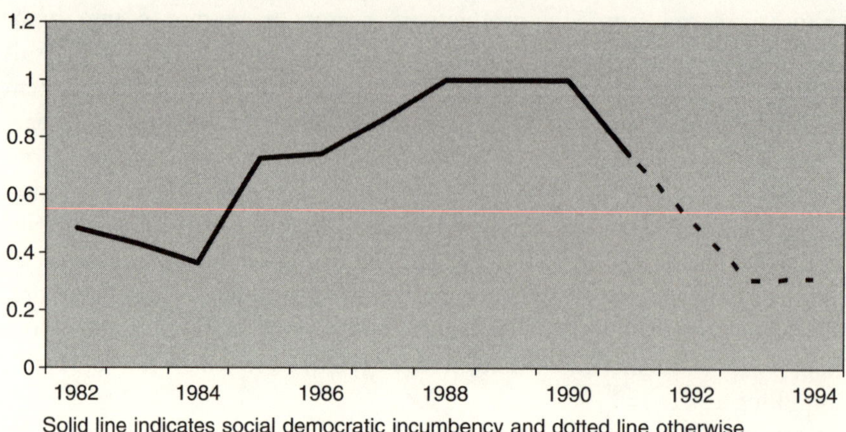

FIGURE 5.6. Active Labor Market Expenditure in Sweden as Percentage of GDP 1982–1994 (*Source:* OECD 2006a).

activation model (Hort 2002: 140; Hort 2003: 251). When the social democrats returned to power in 1994, the departing bourgeois parties handed over a combination of rapidly rising unemployment and budget deficit above 10% of the GDP. Despite this most unfavorable condition, the social democrats managed to quickly overturn the deficit problem, achieving a surplus at 2.9% of GDP by 1997 (OECD 2006b).

This fiscal recovery opened up new revenues for public expenditure, and in 1996 the social democrats grabbed this chance and relaunched their active labor market reform. The government put in place a new program aimed at cutting open unemployment in half by the year 2000, and later set another goal of achieving gainful employment for at least 80% of those between the ages of 20 and 64 by the year 2004. In relation to these targets, the government focused specifically on measures that offer training for the unemployed. As seen in Figure 5.7, expenditure on training has increased persistently since 1997. In 2000, in order to reduce long-term unemployment between the ages of 55 and 64, the government further provided financial resources for an additional 40,000 job creation placements with local governments, in the program Temporary Public Sector Jobs for Older Workers (OTA). During the same year, the social democrats also introduced a special program called Activity Guarantee targeted at those 20 years or older in danger of becoming long-term unemployed. This measure offers a place in various types of ALMPs, as well as the same level of compensation as unemployment insurance, and by refusing the offer of

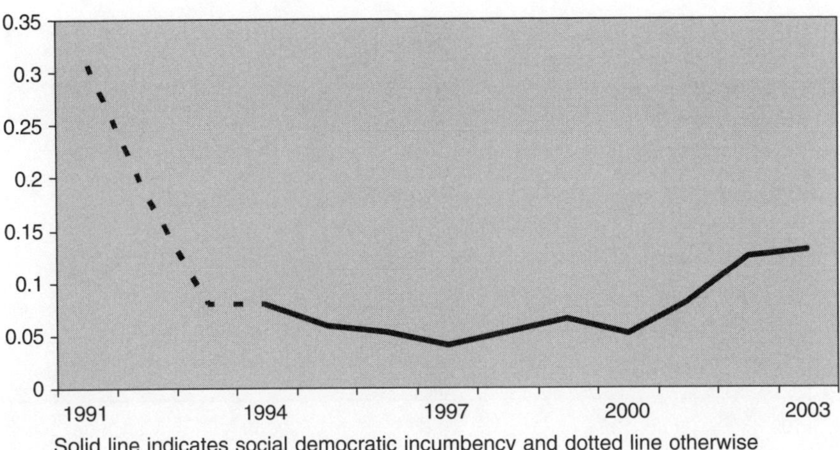

FIGURE 5.7. Labor Market Training Expenditure as Percentage of GDP in Sweden 1991–2003 (*Source:* OECD 2006a).

activation, the beneficiaries will lose the right to regular unemployment benefits (Wadensjo 2002: 399; Hort 2002: 141; Dios 2002: 12). While initially focused on the long-term unemployed, the Activity Guarantee was later extended to cover part-time unemployed (people working for involuntarily shorter hours), and it became an important strategy in combating the new social risks associated with persistent labor market exclusion or atypical working career patterns.

In a similar vein, the Swedish government set up a national reskilling program in 2003 (the *Kunskapslyftet*), which focuses on lifelong learning and further training, especially in terms of increasing the human capital endowments of those workers with only a basic level of education (Timonen 2004: 96). Though bundled into active labor market policies in general, all of the human capital measures mentioned here benefit not just the unemployed but in particular the high-risk groups of various types, ranging from the disabled and the young to the unskilled. As discussed in the theoretical Chapter 2, this demonstrates the positive externalities that these outsider groups can derive from the relatively strong organizational integration of the unemployed within the Swedish labor movement. As another example, the government reintegrated disabled people into the labor market through wage subsidies, sheltered jobs in the public sector, and Samhall (a publicly owned group of firms) (Drøpping, Hvinden and Vik 1999: 156). The impressive social democratic reduction in long-term unemployment seen in

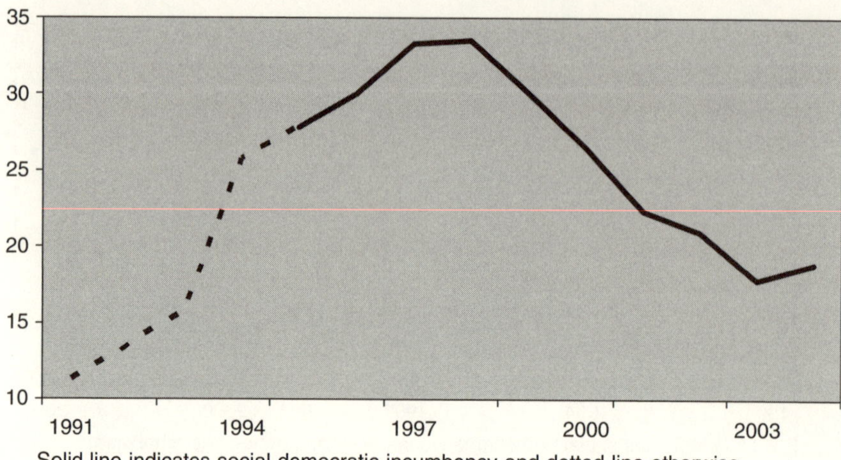

FIGURE 5.8. Unemployment with Duration of One Year and Over as Percentage of All Unemployed in Sweden 1991–2004 (*Source:* OECD 2007a).

Figure 5.8 demonstrates its success in reducing the segmentation between insiders and excluded outsiders.

After the social democrats returned to power in 1994, not only was there a quantitative expansion in the volume of ALMPs, but there was also a qualitative change in the principles and goals of the ALMPs. During the bourgeois period, the chief objective of government reforms was to keep the unemployment rate as low as possible so that as few people as possible could enter the welfare state. With the social democrats in power, the emphasis of active measures was focused instead on both matching the unemployed to the demands in the labor market and reducing the risks of circling between active and passive measures. With social democratic incumbency, the focus of labor market reforms turned increasingly to employability (Boesby, Dahl, and Ploug 2002: 41).

Generally, the Swedish social democrats had evaded the question about how low wages should fall for low-skilled jobs and instead kept wages at relatively high levels in practice. The consensus was that the state should not subsidize or encourage low-wage employment, and instead the state should work toward improving qualifications for workers so that they become more employable. Therefore, the Swedish ALMPs are a civilized version of workfare, which tries to offer empowerment to people through the right to work, and the goal of the original Rehn-Meidner model has always been to improve the political resources of the unemployed (Lindgren

1999: 54). In labor market activation as formulated under Rehn-Meidner, carrots are usually used rather than sticks, and the carrots in question are usually direct offers of job placement or training opportunities.

In the early 1990s when deficit problems were serious, the Swedish government was forced by dwindling state resources to reinterpret the work-first principle as a bridge-over principle, so that instead of a job offer, people were offered six months of paid employment, after which they became eligible for unemployment benefits again (Hort 2002: 148). This bridge-over principle has its own negative consequence of recycling the unemployed between ALMPs and unemployment benefits. It was precisely for this reason that, in Denmark, the social democrats decisively broke the "bridge" by severing the linkage between unemployment compensation and the participation in labor market programs. By contrast, in Sweden any attempt to separate benefits and activation was hampered by the social democrats' decision, under union pressure, to rescind the previous government's laws making unemployment insurance mandatory. By rescinding the bourgeois laws, all rules and regulations about unemployment insurance reverted to their pre-1994 status, including entitlement to continuous requalification for benefits by participating in active measures. Nevertheless, the Swedish social democrats later did go on to make some limited changes and weaken the potential for recycling beneficiaries. After 1996, it became no longer possible to qualify for the first period of benefits by participating in ALMPs, which could only count as work when an unemployed person was requalifying for the benefit (Boesby, Dahl, and Ploug: 2002: 22–33).

Since there was no dramatic increase or decrease in ALMPs overall, the general pattern of Swedish activation in the 1990s was mostly a shift in emphasis between existing programs. When the unemployment crisis escalated during the early 1990s, the government's initial response was to significantly intensify training and education programs in an effort to stop the potential rise of long-term unemployment. Later, ALMPs aimed at providing actual work experience became more prominent. After the mid-1990s, measures targeted at the young unemployed took center stage. By the end of the decade, both education-oriented and work-oriented programs were intensified. On a more general level, the emphasis on the obligation, rather than right, to activation was made stronger in the latter half of the 1990s, when the social democrats were in power, than during the earlier half, when the bourgeois parties ruled for most of the time. It was precisely because the social democrats enjoyed greater trust as guarantors of the solidaristic welfare state that their attempt to introduce some compulsion into active protection was less grudgingly accepted. Similarly, when it comes to the limited retrenchments carried out over the decade, the general pattern was for the bourgeois government to propose benefit reduction, only to be opposed by a united front between unions and the social democrats. Once in power, the social democrats actually implemented some of the cuts advocated by the bourgeois parties (Timonen 2003: 156; A. Gould 2001: 148).

Compared with other measures, it was the ALMPs targeted at the young that were less accommodating and carried a heavier undertone of coercion. In contrast to other ALMPs, compensation in youth programs is not linked to market wages but to replacement levels in either unemployment benefits or education programs, both of which are traditionally lower by comparison. Meanwhile, stricter obligations to either work or continue education were imposed only on the young unemployed. For this segment of the population, the social democrats introduced a Development Guarantee Program in 1998. This program placed the young unemployed under the ultimate responsibility of the municipalities, who were required to make an offer of either municipal work or a training program for up to twelve months. At the same time, the young unemployed themselves were obliged to accept any offer of activation or lose their benefits, even though the activation offer might involve terms inferior to the regular labor market and might not lead to entitlement to unemployment benefits. This strong attention on the young unemployed, and the adoption of comparatively harsher measures for them, is also true of third way reforms in several other countries (Timonen 2003: 100–101; Hort 2002: 263; Kildal 2001: 10).

Norway

During the 1990s, the first sign of resurgence for the activation principle was Labor's Social Services Act of 1991, which emphasized that benefits *may* be conditional upon willingness to work. Admittedly very tentative, this assertion of the duty to work was later expanded by Labor to cover recipients of not only social assistance but also benefits for unemployment, sickness, disability, old age, and single-parent families (Kildal 1999: 355). Formalization of the work-line approach started with Labor's 1992 White Paper on Rehabilitation, which focused on the increasing problems of exclusion from the labor market. The White Paper clearly set out the principle of work being the first choice, and a Green Paper issued shortly afterwards presented the concept of a reservation wage as an argument for introducing cuts to the replacement rates of unemployment benefits.

Up to the mid-1990s, Norwegian ALMPs in the spirit of *arbeidslinje* existed alongside, rather than at the cost of, generous passive welfare benefits. This characteristic is clearly reflected in a package of measures called Solidarity 2000. Launched in 1993, this was Labor's first major offensive against unemployment since the early 1990s. As it was designed during a period when unemployment in Norway had just peaked, Solidarity 2000's central objective was to reduce unemployment to a state of equilibrium by the year 2000, which the Ministry of Finance and Customs calculated to be 3.5%. The two core policy instruments deployed under Solidarity 2000 to combat unemployment were wage moderation, in the form of a slower wage increase than in other industrialized countries, and continuation of ALMPs. In Solidarity 2000, the government mentioned the possibility of "reassessing" both welfare benefits and subsidies to private industries as a way of controlling costs and consolidating the budget. However, no substantive action was taken on these fronts, and the government was ready to continue financing the ALMPs directly though public spending.

The ALMPs introduced since the renewal of *arbeidslinje* were marked by a particularly strong emphasis on enabling and requalification. Figure 5.9 shows the expansion in training measures under Labor in contrast to cuts under the center Right. In 1998, qualifying courses alone accounted for 75% of all participants in ALMPs (Halvorsen 2002: 166). As a demonstration of Labor's serious attention to the enabling dimension, during a period of high pressure from rising unemployment, the enabling active

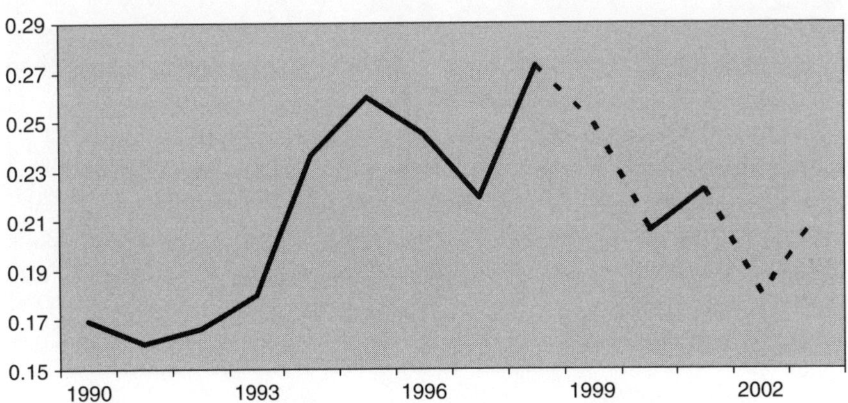

FIGURE 5.9. Labor Market Training Expenditure as Percentage of GDP in Norway 1990–2003 (*Source:* OECD 2006a).

labor market programs can even be restructured into purely training programs, with the objective of job placement temporarily removed from the program remit. For example, as Norwegian unemployment started to pick up in the late 1980s, existing work training ALMPs for the young and long-term unemployed became increasingly overwhelmed by the rapidly rising number of trainees. As a result, the National Employment Agency reformulated the objective of these programs. Originally, they were aimed at not only providing training but also eventually getting the trainees employed; now these programs only served to maintain working ability (Karlsen 1997: 153).

Beyond the "work line," another historical legacy of Norwegian welfare is the localized and generous social assistance schemes. This institutional heritage increased the effectiveness of ALMPs in reducing barriers between insiders and outsiders. The significant power and flexibility for local labor market authorities enabled them to extend the ALMPs, which were initially designed just for the insured, to various vulnerable groups on social assistance, such as the low-skilled. While such path dependency on the social assistance legacy did lead to a somewhat more coercive approach to activating the marginal people, these individuals were also provided with good employment opportunities they would not have had access to otherwise (Lødemel 2004: 218).

Another important set of measures against new social risks were targeted at the young, such as the Vocational Training Program introduced by Labor in 1985. As Figure 5.10 shows, this is another area where Labor

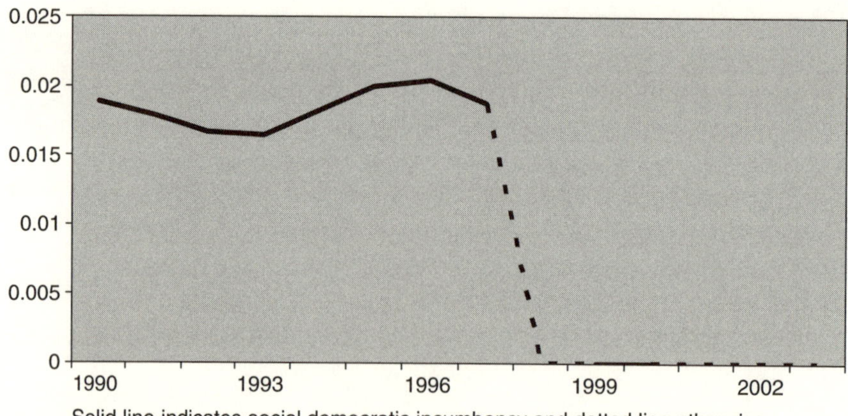

FIGURE 5.10. Labor Market Measures for the Young as Percentage of GDP in Norway 1990–2003 (*Source:* OECD 2006a).

is clearly differentiated from the center-right approach. In 1994, the government provided a statutory right to upper secondary education or training lasting up to four years for young people between the ages of 16 and 19, and there was a guarantee of placement in the labor market, a job, or education for people under 20. Those between 20 and 24 were also prioritized in receiving active labor market programs after 1995. Through wage subsidies and sheltered employment workshops, the government also tried to reactivate the disabled into the labor market (Drøpping, Hvinden, and Vik 1999: 151–156). For lone parents, the government introduced the OFO (follow-up arrangement for lone parents), which combines cash payments with education or employment under the guideline of "active benefit receipt." Most innovative in the OFO measure is the role of personal mediators offering counseling services for lone mothers. These unpaid mediators are themselves recipients of transitional benefits. From the vantage point of a similar background or experience, they help establish empathy and a bond with customers from the typically excluded new social risk groups (Skevik 2005: 54).

In order to encourage lifelong learning, during the 1990s Labor further introduced a program called "Competence Reform," under which employees become entitled to three years of unpaid leave for educational purposes (Solem and Overbye 2004: 34). This heavy emphasis on training and investment in human capital at the occasional expense of immediate job placement almost makes a mirror image of the neoliberal workfare practice, where the preoccupation with moving people off welfare results in low-skill jobs and poverty in work. The low-wage or low-benefit route to labor market activation is now clearly shunned by Northern European social democrats. Nevertheless, relative to Sweden and Denmark, the expansion of enabling programs in Norway was moderate, as unemployment problems facing the country in the early 1990s were less pressing by comparison.

Across Northern Europe, social democracy responded to rising unemployment in a similar fashion, by accelerating public investment and ALMPs and, initially, resorting to labour-market-clearing or early exit pathways. In other words, much of the expansion in active labor market measures in Scandinavia was unemployment-driven. As Figure 5.11 indicates, ALMP expansion in Norway after the late 1980s offers a graphic illustration of this pattern. Between 1988 and 1991, participation in Norwegian active labour market measures increased by 400% while unemployment rose by an unprecedented 90%, albeit very temporarily. While the ALMPs cost 1.1% of GDP in 1991, by 1993 they were costing about twice as much, at 2.6% of GDP, and by 1999, when the country was well on its

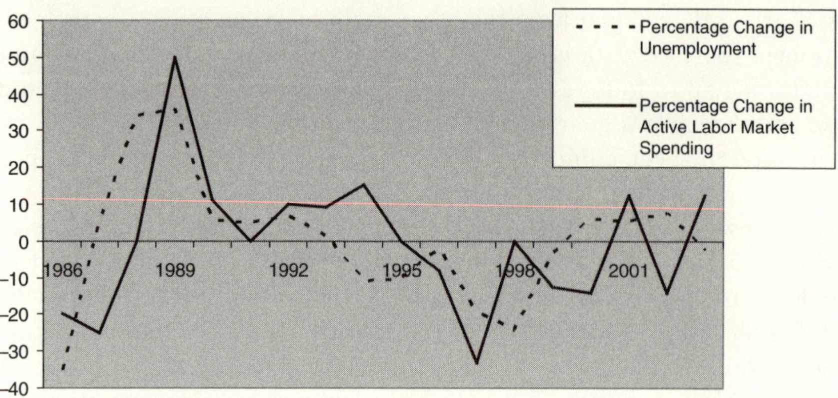

FIGURE 5.11. Relationship Between Unemployment and Active Labor Market Spending in Norway 1986–2003 (*Source:* OECD 2006a [labor market spending]; 2007a [unemployment]).

way to economic recovery, spending on the active labor market measures went back down to only 0.8% of GDP. Overall, Norwegian activation programs underwent significant fluctuations throughout the 1990s, and the government explicitly regarded this pattern as a necessary part of a "stabilization strategy": ALMPs were expanded or contracted in a countercyclical response to developments in the labor market and the macroeconomy more generally. In this sense, not only were the Norwegian active labor market measures unemployment-driven, they were deliberately so (Dolvik et al. 1997; Halvorsen 2002: 166; Dahl and Drøpping 2001: 281).

The unemployment problem in Norway during the early 1990s was less serious than in both Sweden and Denmark. Oil revenues largely shielded the economy from the external component of the unemployment crisis gripping the rest of Scandinavia. The Norwegian government also managed to avoid some of the macroeconomic mistakes made in Sweden, such as a credit boom quickly followed by a turn to hard currency. The domestic, and structural, component of Norwegian unemployment was temporarily but swiftly reduced with labour-market-clearing measures. Given this context, the need to increase public resources for activation was less urgent than both in Sweden and Denmark. Meanwhile, ALMP expansion under Labor was also overshadowed by a simultaneous increase in passive expenditure, including not only early exit pathways but also rising payments in unemployment benefits. For example, the total social expenditure on employment-related measures nearly doubled between 1989 and 1993, but unemployment benefits alone accounted for 54% of the expenditure in 1989, and around 60% by 1993 (Dolvik et al. 1997: 77).

The short interval of center-right government between 1997 and 2000 saw some retreat from the principle of activation, and instead there was renewed interest in passive labour-market-clearing measures and early exit pathways. In 1998, for example, the bourgeois government not only lowered the retirement age to 62 but also introduced a cash-benefit scheme for parents with children. This benefit was not tied to the employment contract, and was targeted specifically at parents who choose not to use public child-care facilities. As a result, about 20% of women with very young children took advantage of this scheme and reduced their labor market participation. Through measures like this, the bourgeois government worsened the fragmentation in task arrangements on work and reproduction between men and women (Halvorsen 2002: 173–175; Solem and Overbye 2004: 29). However, this reversal to labour-market-clearing passivity was short in duration, and after the center Right lost the following election, the returning Labor government refocused its policies onto intensifying *arbeidslinje*.

The Netherlands

The center-right Lubbers administration started reforming the social security system as early as 1987, but its strategy focused primarily on reducing the labor supply and redistributing available work. The main scheme for promoting employment during the Lubbers I and II administrations was a single program, *Loonsuppletie*, which offered a temporary wage supplement for all categories of the unemployed on condition that they accept a job with a wage below a previous wage level (van Oorschot 2002a: 112–114; Abrahamson and van Oorschot 2002: 4–7). Premised on low-wage and low-productivity jobs, these earlier measures of employment promotion failed to alter the balance between active and passive instruments, and despite repeated attempts at retrenchment, the volume of passive beneficiaries continued to increase after 1987. After the PvdA entered the government in 1989, a process of rethinking on employment policy gradually took place. Labor force reduction was gradually replaced with efforts to expand the actual supply of labor on the job market. While initially focused exclusively on stemming unemployment, the policy emphasis broadened to encompass issues such as net participation and employment/population ratio, which kept falling despite increasing female entry into the labor market. The earlier objective of redistributing unemployment also gave way to the goal of increasing labor market participation. In addition, the PvdA

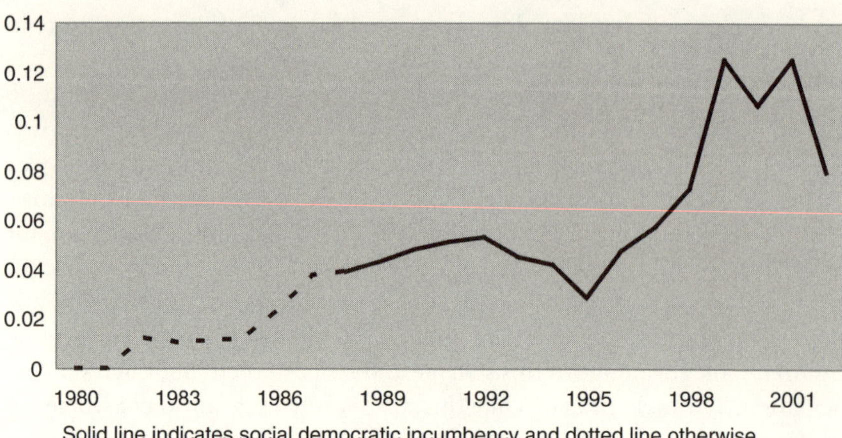

FIGURE 5.12. Active Labor Market Expenditure as Percentage of GDP in the Netherlands 1980–2002 (*Source:* OECD 2006a).

made social cohesion a crucial component of government policy (Green-Pedersen 2002: 106–107; van Oorschot 2002a: 107; Visser and Hemerjick 1997: 157; Hoop: 2004: 69–70). Overall, as Figure 5.12 shows, there was a clear expansion of active labor market measures after the PvdA came to power.

During the PvdA's period in office, the young unemployed were the first and foremost target for its third way activation reforms, and Figure 5.13 reflects the party's intensifying measures aimed at helping this vulnerable group. In 1992, the government introduced the Youth Employment Act (YEA), under which individuals between the ages of 18 and 22 who were unemployed for more than six months would see their entitlement to a minimum income replaced with an entitlement to minimum job rights. This change significantly strengthened the duties as well as rights of the young unemployed to participate in ALMPs. On the basis of stronger linkage between benefits and activation, the government sponsored a wide range of ALMPs aimed at improving skills for various types of benefit recipients, as well as creating demand at the lower end of the labor market.

A very large segment of these ALMPs offered placements in state-subsidized supplementary public-sector jobs, which implies a long-term increase of public investment in labor market measures. In addition, these programs' public-sector orientation also indirectly helped reducing the insider–outsider divide, as the electoral trade-off in conflicting preferences between insiders and outsiders is much smaller than in the private sector (Armingeon 2006).

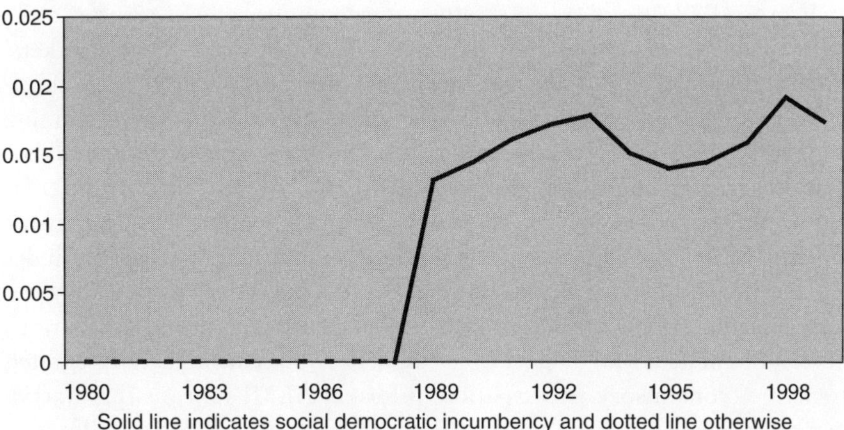

FIGURE 5.13. Labor Market Measures for the Young as Percentage of GDP in the Netherlands 1980–1999 (*Source:* OECD 2006a).

The Youth Work Guarantee, for example, offered training or public-sector jobs for young people up to 24 years of age who are not in regular education and are without paid employment. On the other hand, the *Banenpool* schemes were targeted at another key new social risk group, the long-term unemployed, by offering them subsidized jobs in the health care or welfare sector. In addition, job pools for the low-skilled were created with funding from unemployment benefits and government subsidies.

Among the most innovative ALMP schemes aimed at incorporating outsiders were the two Melkert job schemes, named after the minister of social affairs. Melkert-1 aimed to create 40,000 subsidized jobs in the most disadvantaged segment of the labor market. Under this scheme, temporary jobs were created in the public and subsidized sectors for a duration of six months to two years. These jobs were targeted at the long-term unemployed for 32 hours a week at the minimum wage or up to 20% above. Melkert-2 covered both public and private sectors by reimbursing half of wages for up to two years for employers who hired a long-term unemployed person for a new job. Handicapped workers, meanwhile, could work in sheltered workshops and sell products at market price while collecting a wage subsidy from the government. The remit of sheltered workshops had been expanded as an instrument of general labor market activation, so that these workshops also employed people who were unemployed without a handicap (Hartog 2000: 57–58; Visser 2001: 31; Beukema and Valkenburg 1999: 117–118).

In 1998, YEA and various other noncompulsory ALMPs for older individuals were merged into a major policy package, the Jobseekers' Employment Act (JEA). The three principal measures under JEA are subsidized regular employment, subsidized municipal employment, and training or "social activation" (Handler 2002: 30). The integration of different labor market schemes under JEA stopped the differential treatment of different age groups, and participation in ALMPs technically became obligatory for younger as well as older job seekers. The merger of different programs under JEA further broadened the scope of activation measures, so that they not only subsidized regular jobs but also offered training programs and various other unpaid activities as part of social activation. Given JEA's integrated structure, compulsory participation in formal ALMPs means that participation in these other social activation schemes also became obligatory. Along with increased obligatory requirement on job seekers, the government also committed itself to the task of offering ALMPs within a one-year period for all newly unemployed and of providing sufficient subsidized jobs/training opportunities. Similar to several other third way cases, the priority target under JEA was the young unemployed, followed by the long-term unemployed (van Berkel and de Schampheleire 2001: 31; Spies and van Berkel 2001: 105–128). Just as Figure 5.13 demonstrated the PvdA's efforts in activating the young unemployed, Figure 5.14 similarly shows its success in drastically reducing long-term unemployment.

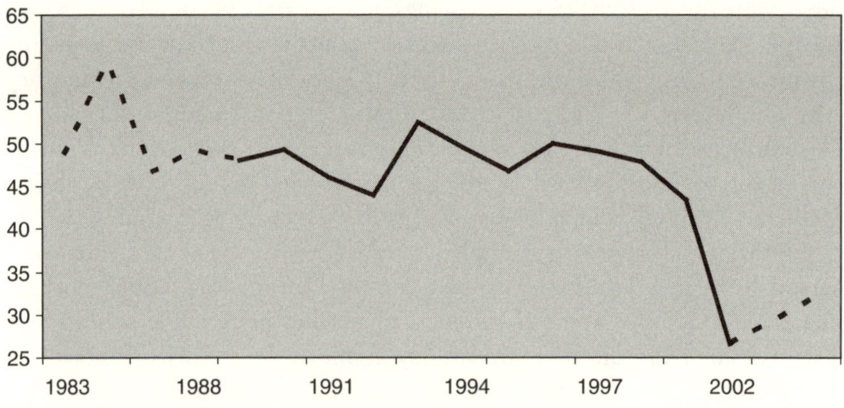

FIGURE 5.14. Unemployment with Duration of One Year and Over as Percentage of All Unemployed in the Netherlands 1983–2004 (*Source:* OECD 2006a).

Although the Netherlands underwent a clear economic revival and large employment growth after the mid-1990s, unemployment did not decline substantially among the older unemployed, the low-skilled, and other disadvantaged groups vulnerable to being shut out of the labor market. There was also no significant increase in the total volume of work. For this reason, activation remained on top of the government's social and labor market policy agenda. The two Purple Coalitions after 1994 placed growing emphasis on job creation for disadvantaged groups, such as the long-term unemployed, females, ethnic minorities, and the elderly. For this purpose, the government subsidized public-sector jobs at the lower end of the labor market. In addition, in both 1996 and 1997, the government was able to restore the net linking of minimum wages and social benefits (Visser and Hemerijck 1997: 118; van Oorschot 1999: 32).

The new Social Security Act of 1996 also enabled municipalities to experiment with activation programs targeted specifically at the long-term unemployed and their potential participation in a range of unpaid activities on a local level (van Berkel, Cohen, and Dekker 1999: 95–96). By the mid-1990s, local spending as a proportion of total public expenditure was reduced to less than 25%, but at the same time local taxing power was progressively updated, a move clearly aimed at compensating for the drop in transfers from the central government. This devolution in the source of public expenditure was in alignment with the governments' general attempt to decentralize responsibilities for ALMPs to local areas, so that it became easier to take into consideration the individual circumstance of the unemployed and design specifically tailored programs. Through the introduction of explicit activation duties and rights, plus integration across policy domains, JEA represented the culmination of the PvdA reforms to activate the labor market. The fundamental objective of social security was transformed, from passive protection to active participation. The numerous schemes subsidizing jobs for disadvantaged job seekers had in effect created a large secondary labor market, catering to vulnerable new social risk groups and reducing the insider–outsider divide (Fargion 2000: 72; Keman 2003: 129; van Berkel and de Schampheleire 2001: 31).

France

The first tentative work-based insertion program under the Socialists was the Collective Utility Work in 1984, but its impact remained minimal. It was only four years later that more serious efforts were made in activation, with the introduction of the Minimum Income of Insertion (RMI) under the Michel Rocard government. RMI was crucial in explicitly establishing the principle of insertion (into the labor market) as the main condition for receiving benefits. As a program of a dual nature, RMI is the only major social assistance benefit systematically integrated with publicly funded ALMPs to help recipients enter jobs or training (Barbier and Théret 2003: 150). In this sense, RMI is distinctive in being a major part of both passive and active protection. It is precisely for this reason that RMI will feature prominently again, in Chapter 6 on passive protection, where characteristics in its social assistance aspect will be emphasized more. In the current chapter, the focus is on RMI's active aspect, that is, the insertion requirements.

In the debates and negotiations leading up to the introduction of RMI in 1988, few unions were opposed to attaching the insertion requirements to the scheme. Since the insertion clauses prioritized the linkage between employment and income, it was a very welcome instrument for the unions, whose primary concern was to prevent the new social assistance schemes from becoming a long-term threat to the earnings-related social insurance system. Actually, unions lobbied against the institution of a RMI minimum income based on the principle of rights for all, and so imposition of the insertion condition made it much easier for unions to accept RMI (Clegg 2002: 218–222). The union attitude toward RMI reflected the electoral dilemma faced by the French Socialists in reconciling insiders and outsiders. Without the encompassing organizational capacity of its Scandinavian counterparts, the French labor movement had prioritized the core workforce in the social insurance system at the cost of other new social risk groups. The RMI-related passive social assistance benefits are valuable strategies for combating new social risks, but being segmented from the social insurance core, they also have limitations, and I will discuss this issue in Chapter 6 on passive social protection.

Claimants of RMI benefits are theoretically required to sign a contract, and the contract's content and enforcement varies with locality, target groups, or the organizations involved, given the decentralized administration of RMI. The major set of ALMP contracts under RMI are the Employment Solidarity Contracts (CES), which are temporary, part-time, and subsidized contracts involving 20 hours per week of work in the nonprofit sector for a period of three months to two years. The CES contracts in RMI were followed up in 1992 with the Consolidated Employment Contracts (CEC), which are targeted at more specific segments of the unemployed, and in 1995 with the Employment Initiative Contracts (CIE), which are regular contracts subsidizing private-sector employers. In any of these contracts, welfare recipients can gain regular employee status with all the corresponding rights and duties. After the National Employment Agency took over RMI administration in the mid-1990s, integration of social security and employment within RMI schemes intensified (Morel 2004: 118–119).

However, on the local level, enforcement of individual RMI contracts, and of the insertion principle more generally, tends to be very slack, which severely limits the effectiveness of this policy. Although contracts of insertion are technically required, all training and job activities under RMI are voluntary in practice, and access to these insertion activities are legally guaranteed to citizens. Since 1988, about half of the RMI beneficiaries did not sign the contracts, and only 5% to 6% of beneficiaries were actually sanctioned for noncompliance. Even so, there is increasing pressure within the parties on the Left, including the Socialists, for transforming RMI into an unconditional income allowance based on citizenship and completely suppressing the RMI insertion requirements (Barbier and Théret 2001: 162; Enjolras et al. 2001: 52).

Overall, the conditionality of work in French social and labor market policy has maintained an ambiguous and inconsistent profile. For the older uninsured, work-to-welfare requirements are attached (but in name only) to the primary activation scheme RMI; for the young, these requirements supposedly exist despite RMI, because the young are not eligible for RMI benefits. However, there is no clear rule of either sanctioning or compulsion to work for the young. Technically, for example, noncompliance with job search requirements can lead to cuts in unemployment insurance benefits, but social assistance entitlement is not conditional on participation in work-related programs (Spicker 2002: 116; Enjolras et al. 2001: 42; Daguerre 2004: 44; Barbier and Théret 2003: 150). The dual nature of RMI as a social assistance benefit and ALMP package also has its drawbacks, because it in effect subsidies low-skilled labor with its social assistance minima and encourages the formation of a secondary labor market of unstable and low-wage jobs. As the Socialists' key active labor market instrument, an additional limitation in RMI is that it only targets individuals over the age of 25, despite the fact that the group displaying the highest unemployment rate are young women under the age of 25 (Hantrais 1996: 65; Barbier and Théret 2001: 174).

As Figure 5.15 indicates, the gradual realignment of French ALMPs to the young unemployed gathered pace after the Socialists were returned to power under Lionel Jospin in 1997. Throughout its period in office, the Jospin government continued to insist on the the role of the state as the guarantor of employment, and direct job creation or subsidization by the state

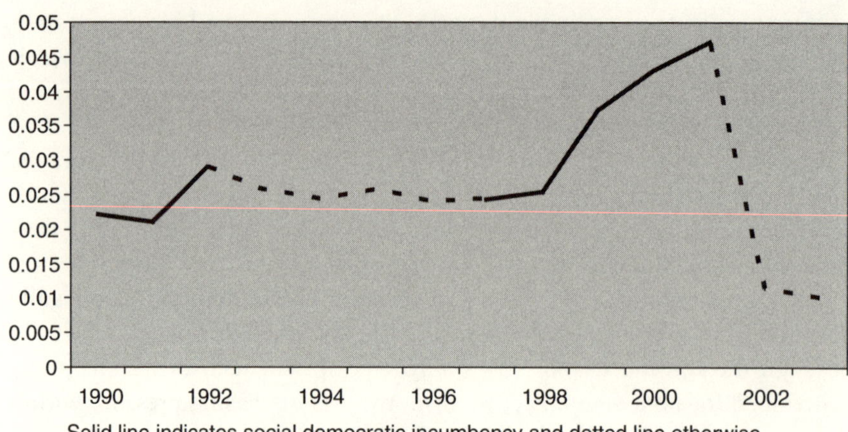

FIGURE 5.15. Labor Market Measures for the Young as Percentage of GDP in France 1990–2003 (*Source:* OECD 2006a).

remained an important component of employment policy (Clift 2004: 135). In the Socialists' 1997 election program, the two highest-priority policy initiatives were both aimed at facilitating job growth and labor market participation. One was the promotion of youth jobs in the social-service sector in order to reduce youth unemployment, and the other was shortening the working week to 35 hours (Sferza 2002: 137).

The largest-scale job creation scheme to emerge under the Jospin government was the Aubry Plan, named after Martine Aubry, minister for employment and solidarity. Passed in 1997, the plan proposed the creation of 700,000 minimum-wage and largely state-financed jobs, half to be in the public sector and half in the private sector. These jobs are five-year nonrenewable contracts targeted specifically at the young unemployed, and up to 80% of the wage and non-wage costs would be financed by state subsidies. More than 8 billion francs were allocated to the scheme. One year later, 100,000 such posts had already been identified and 60,000 filled. As the government's major job-creation instrument, the Aubry Plan is to some extent the most interventionist employment policy attempted in Europe, and it demonstrates that labor market activation goes to the very heart of the policy objectives for the Socialist government. During its entire period in office, the Jospin government increased the resources devoted to employment policy by 13%, reaching 4.5% of GDP by 2000. During the 1997 to 2000 period, the Socialists devoted considerably more public funds to subsidized employment (at 1.7% of GDP) than did their German (0.8%)

or British (0.015%) counterparts (OECD 2006a; Morel 2004: 120; Sferza 2002: 141; Enjolras et al. 2001: 62).

By March 2001, the Aubry Plan had led to 274,900 new jobs in the public sector and 308,000 in the private sector. The number of French workers enrolled in public labor market programs had expanded two and a half times, and aggregate spending on ALMPs showed a similar increase. An important character of these job creation or subsidization plans was that their financing was openly predicated on increased public expenditure. The Socialists made it clear that the financial burden for supporting these measures would not fall on either wage earners or employers, but instead on the state (Levy 2002: 8–14; Clift 2003: 168). While innovative for the focus on activating the unemployed, the Socialist expansion of labor market programs also revealed a pattern of path dependency on the French historical legacy of statism in public policy. In macroeconomic policy, the Mitterrand U-turn indeed brought an end to traditional *dirigisme*. However, Figure 5.16 shows that state involvement in active labor market measures did not decline under the Socialists. Rather than a retreat of the state, it was simply redeployed for a difference purpose. Due to the persistency of high unemployment, starting from 1988, labor market programs began to expand, especially those with an enabling feature, such as training and subsidies for youths and the long-term unemployed. Between 1984 and 1999, the number of workers enrolled in public labor market programs had shot up from 1.2 to almost 3 million (Levy 2005: 107–109).

While the statist legacy helped significantly expand active labor market measures, the same legacy also negatively affected the effectiveness of these measures. As Figure 5.17 indicates, the various changes made by the Jospin government had proved inadequate to significantly dent either total unemployment or long-term unemployment. One key problem is ineffective obligation enforcement in active labor market measures. The government's reluctance to enforce an individual duty to accept activation offers can be explained by the traditionally strong emphasis on the state as employer of last resort. Unemployment and its consequences are typically treated as collective issues for the French society, rather than a question of personal incentives for the unemployed individual. This statist principle led to ambiguous interpretations of what activation implies. General integration into activities in society, known as social activation, is often regarded as sufficient, even though it does not result in actual participation in the labor market. Throughout the past two decades, a persistent emphasis on the state's responsibility to take care of its citizens has also resulted in very

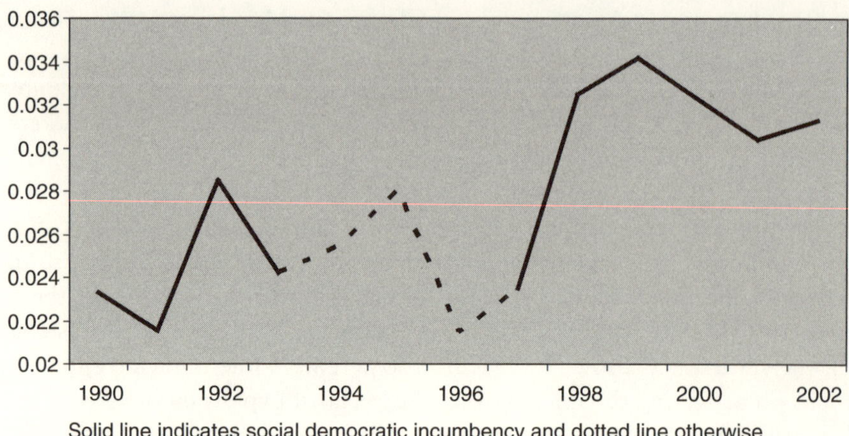

FIGURE 5.16. Active Labor Market Expenditure as Percentage of GDP in France 1990–2002 (*Source:* OECD 2006a).

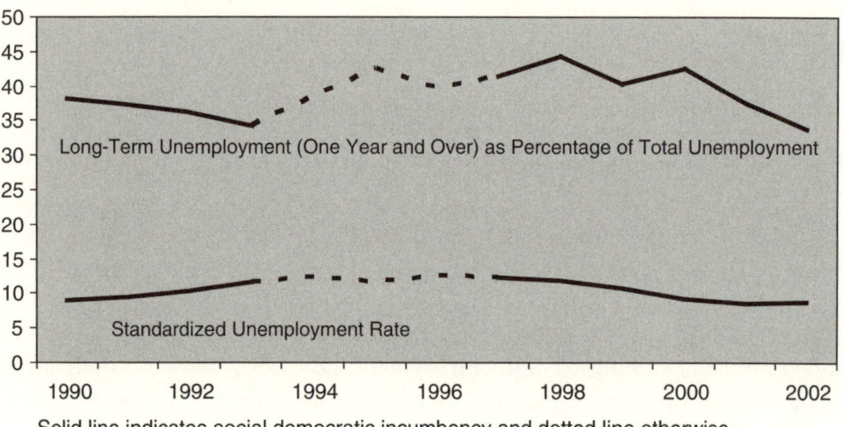

FIGURE 5.17. Total Unemployment and the Share of Long-Term Unemployment in France 1990–2002 (*Source:* OECD 2007a).

limited changes to passive benefits, such as unemployment compensation, in terms of both generosity and eligibility.

The Socialists' statist orientation is clearly reflected in their ALMPs targeted at youth unemployment. Unlike the New Deal in Britain or JEA in the Netherlands, the French policy instrument encompassed a series of gigantic direct job-creation or subsidization schemes, where the obligation of activation fell almost completely on the state rather than on the individual being helped (Merkel 2001: 70). The statist institutional legacy also accounts for the unique characteristic of RMI insertion clauses, where it is compulsory for the state to offer ALMPs but there is no corresponding obligation on the individual to participate or accept the terms of the offer. The dependency on social assistance that the Socialists tried to eliminate through the RMI insertion clauses was merely replaced with another form of dependency, on massive use of state-sponsored job-creation or subsidization measures (Barbier and Théret 2001: 157; Farvaque 2002: 5). In addition, although RMI includes a component of reinsertion into the labor market, in implementation it is interpreted often as general social reinsertion, rather than actual integration into employment. Therefore, under RMI, the unemployed are required to demonstrate a willingness to participate in society as a whole, rather than in the labor market, or to accept a specific job offer. This characteristic of RMI insertion clauses reflects the emphasis in French employment policy on the social treatment of unemployment, rather than on the actual promotion of labor market participation. The attention on the social dimension shows some similarity with Scandinavian employment policies, but the Scandinavian approach emphasizes labor market as well as social integration. By contrast, by the mid-1990s, the main French social question had become not transferring people to work but, given the lack of jobs available, the provision of welfare for those excluded from the labor market (Barbier 2001: 15).

The legacy of statism in France also indirectly affected the institutional basis for collective action in policy innovation. Just as power and resources have been concentrated in the central state, by comparison interest groups, such as unions and employers' organizations, are correspondingly both weakened and divided in organization (Levy 1999a). This lack of corporatist institutions led to failure in cooperation between social partners, and impeded in particular the introduction of active labor market training programs. Unlike in neighboring Germany, where historically employers' organizations had played a crucial role in passing on information, setting criteria, guaranteeing standards, and monitoring the content of labor market programs, in France labor market training depended from the start on lawmaking and subsidies from the state. In 1984, the Socialist government legislated for Contracts of Qualification (CQ), which were youth vocational training contracts that serve a purpose similar to conventional apprenticeship contracts. However, most of the French firms adopting CQs were simply using them as a method of hiring relatively cheap youth labour, rather than investing in training as the government intended for these measures.

Consequently, the actual improvement in skills and education levels was negligible among the young who were enrolled in these programs.

The core problem, as Pepper Culpepper points out (2003), was the inability by firms to coordinate and invest in a high-skill equilibrium. This cooperation failure was, in turn, due to the lack of strong corporatist institutions, whose role in centralizing information and enhancing communication would have been crucial in reducing uncertainty about each firm's strategic intention and choice. French employers' organizations were not organized on the level of the *région*, the local jurisdiction to which labor market policy administration was devolved in the 1980s. On the union side, there was a similar problem of weak organizational strength. Without a peak association, unions were led, on the basis of sectoral differences, by three different peak confederations, the *Confédération Générale du Travail* (CGT), the *Confédération Française et Démocratique du Travail* (CFDT), and the *Confédération Générale du Travail-Force Ouvrère* (CGT-FO). With firms unable to mutually coordinate, attempts to shirk and claim funding without investing in skills were rampant. Control over the resources to finance the training centers, rather than the standard or content of the training, became the key issue of dispute between unions and employers (Culpepper 2003: 66–67; 134–135).

Another victim of collective action failure was the Plan to Help the Return to Employment (PARE), signed by the social partners in 1999. This scheme stipulated that labor market institutions would do their utmost to find jobs, and the unemployed would make similar efforts in accepting the jobs or training offered. However, unions believed that the distribution of obligations in the agreement was not symmetrical, with no specific requirements for the behavior of employers. Two trade unions therefore refused to sign the deal. This led to the rejection of the initial version of PARE. This contract was later watered down so that there were no longer obligations for the unemployed to sign a PARE, which was instead based on free acceptance induced by financial incentives. Although the Socialists were able to implement some changes in labor market policies, these often had to occur in an implicit and incremental manner in order to placate the social partners. For example, the government's attempt to use a single gateway (similar to ONE under New Labor or Jobcentre Plus under the ALP) to integrate benefit services for all claimants and strengthen the linkage between welfare and work was largely ineffective. For social partners, this concept of joined-up government was difficult to reconcile with existing and entrenched divisions of responsibility between themselves and the state (Ughetto and Bouget 2002: 99, 105; Clasen and Clegg 2003: 374).

Germany

Similar to several other third way cases, the primary target of activation reforms in Germany was the young unemployed. During the first term of the Red-Green coalition, the major ALMP to combat youth unemployment was the scheme Youth with a Perspective (JUMP), introduced in 1998. Its two billion deutsche marks of annual budget came partly from a federal subsidy and partly from the European Social Fund. The fact that the federal government picked up the tab for almost the entire German portion of the budget represented a significant financial commitment by the Schröder government. Reflecting a general pattern of the SPD's activation policies, JUMP was characterized by a heavy reliance on state-subsidized employment measures, such as direct job creation or subsidization (Vail 2002: 11; Schröter 2004: 23).

JUMP made extensive use of financial incentives, in the form of state subsidies, to encourage employers to create new jobs for the young unemployed, especially for those in the new *Länder*. In addition, for the young unemployed, the scheme also offered individual counseling, training, and apprenticeship opportunities. Figure 5.18 shows that despite the constraint of the Stability and Growth Pact, the Red-Green coalition presided over an increase in expenditure on programs for both the young and labor market training. JUMP was originally intended to serve up to 100,000 workers under the age of 25, but after its inception in 1998, more than

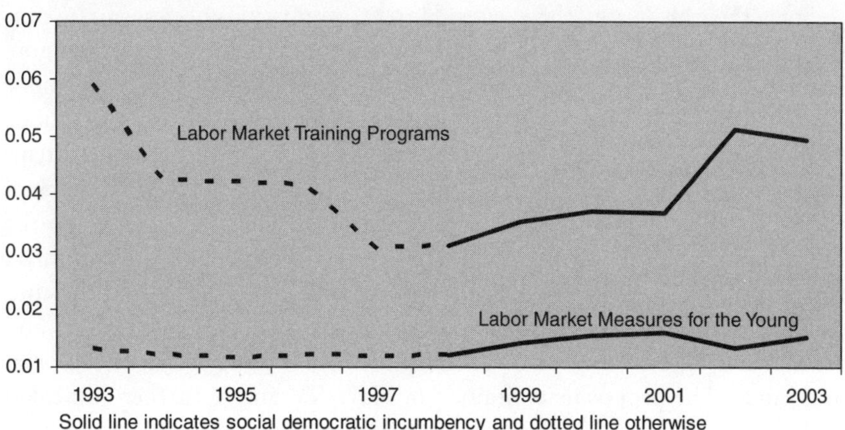

FIGURE 5.18. Training and Youth Employment Programs Expenditure as Percentage of GDP in Germany 1993–2003 (*Source:* OECD 2006a).

300,000 young unemployed individuals had participated in it, and from 1999 to 2001, it subsidized between 100,000 and 140,000 jobs or training places. However, it remained unclear how many of these were actually new jobs that would not have materialized without the intervention of JUMP (Schröter 2004: 23; Voges, Jacobs, and Trickey 2001: 98; Bispinck and Schulten 2000: 205–206).

Despite JUMP's scale and ambitions, the scheme was not compulsory, and although the employment-service officers do have the discretion to sanction benefit claimants for refusing to accept suitable training or job opportunities, JUMP itself relied entirely on voluntary participation by the young unemployed. This, to some extent, limited the program's effectiveness, and it was unable to induce a change in either administrative or young job seekers' behavior (Schröter 2004: 24). In parallel with JUMP on the national level, the SPD also introduced a range of local job-subsidization schemes called "Help Toward Work," which subsidize either regular jobs under an employment contract or casual jobs not subject to an employment contract for a limited period (Handler 2002: 39).

Apart from these individual programs, the SPD also tried to make its active labor market measures more systematic and efficient as a whole, and for this purpose, the government increased investments in ALMP research and design. Partly in response to the breakdown of Alliance for Jobs negotiations, the government decided to bypass the social partners, and it appointed the Hartz Commission to draft new proposals for active labor market reforms and for correcting inaccuracies or mistakes previously discovered in employment services.

Since their inception, the various Hartz Commissions became an institutionalized part of ALMP design and a source of advice for the Schröder government, touching on a wide range of issues connected to social and labor market policies. Hartz I and III focused on the reorganization of public employment services to increase efficiency, and Hartz II highlighted temporary employment as an instrument of job placement in ALMPs, through the establishment of Personnel Service Agencies. Hartz IV and V, on the other hand, pushed toward much stronger enforcement of obligation on the part of job seekers. These latter two commissions emphasized the contractual nature of the relationship between labor market institutions and ALMP clients, and they also recommended important cutbacks to social assistance. The proposals contained in Hartz IV and V further coincided with objectives in new activation measures introduced by the second Red-Green coalition. Along similar lines, in 2003 the commission known as Hartz I+II also recommended measures that promote marginal part-time work for mothers by lowering tax rates on these so-called mini-jobs. In addition to Hartz, the Red-Green coalition also appointed a separate commission in 2002 to develop long-term sustainable social security reform. Recognizing the problem of lax enforcement in existing ALMPs, the Hartz Commission also proposed an increase in demands on regional mobility, especially for the younger and single unemployed, as well as lengthened benefit-ineligibility periods as a sanction for violating job-search conditions. In order to make sanctions in ALMPs easier to impose, the commission suggested that ineligibility duration be staggered over a period of time (Dingeldey and Linke-Sonderegger 2004: 27–31; Leibfried and Obinger 2003: 213; Weinkopf 2003: 247–253).

Partly based on momentum from the Hartz Commissions, labor market activation intensified after the start of the government's second term. The most important innovation in this area was the introduction in 2002 of the Law for Job-Activation, Qualification, Training, Investment, and Placement (Job-AQTIV), which was directly drawn from recommendations in Hartz IV and V. This policy package focused on enforcement and incentives in ALMPs, and it also redirected government's employment strategies, from reducing labor supply to labor market activation.

Compared with previous measures, Job-AQTIV included noticeably sharpened rules about "reasonableness of work" in job-search criteria in ALMPs, and it also emphasized the use of intensive advice and individualized guidance for the unemployed. Making extensive use of the methodology of profiling, pilot projects of individualized support were carried out in a number of local settings, and Job-AQTIV explicitly stipulated that public employment services should apply instruments of this nature. In order to expand the capacity for ALMP job placement and employment service counseling, Job-AQTIV also proposed an increase in the involvement of third parties, such as private placement agencies or training institutions, in the active labor market measures. This development dovetailed with earlier recommendations from the Hartz Commissions during the coalition's first term of office, especially the plan for a one-stop-shop Job Center to integrate the duties of various employment and social-support services. Such one-step service was already implemented by the British and Australian social democrats as part of their third way reforms, and in 2000 a law was passed in Germany to a similar effect, so that social assistance and unemployment placement administrations were merged (Weinkopf 2003: 251–266; Handler 2002: 39).

As seen in Figure 5.19, the introduction of Job-AQTIV in 2002 led to a renewed increase in active labor market expenditure. The program led to

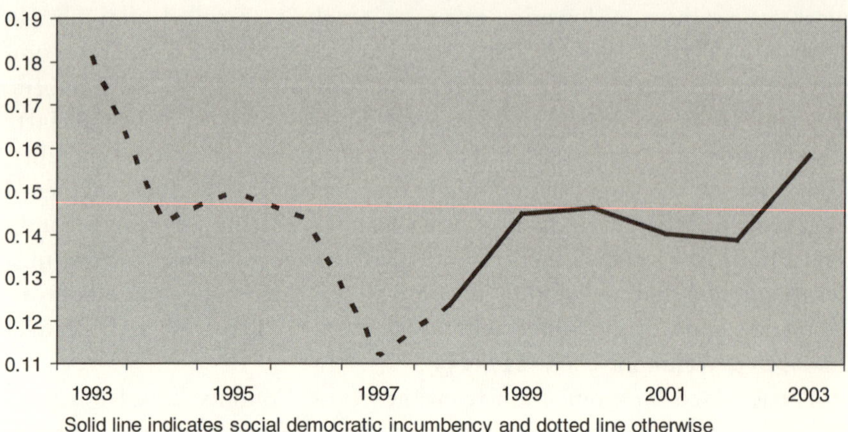

FIGURE 5.19. Total Active Labor Market Measures as Percentage of GDP in Germany 1993–2003 (*Source:* OECD 2006a).

the restructuring of job-placement services belonging to the Alliance for Jobs, and it also brought a much more aggressive and contractual approach to activating the unemployed. Under Job-AQTIV, reinsertion plans had to be worked out between the unemployed and the local labor officer. Based on personalized profiling for each individual job seeker, the contract clearly set out obligations on both sides. The local authorities became committed to offering suitable job openings plus individualized advice and counseling, and the clients committed themselves to accepting reasonable job offers or making clear efforts to search for jobs. For clients who fail to meet their obligations, the potential sanctions are in the form of complete benefit removal for up to 12 weeks. Taking over some responsibilities for financing and policy design previously given to the Alliance for Jobs, the government became more active in applying pressure on the unemployed to accept job offers (Vail 2002: 11; Handler 2002: 39; Vail 2003: 49).

In addition to a clearer conceptualization of rights and obligations, Job-AQTIV also encourages both more training investments and greater labor market flexibility, by means of job rotation schemes, for example. With recommendations from Hartz I+II in 2003, training vouchers were created to increase competition among the suppliers of training measures and to improve transparency, and state subsidies were provided for training programs. With measures like this, the Red-Green coalition hoped to make it easier for individual clients to select training programs for themselves. Although the emphasis on the enabling dimension of activation grew through time, the SPD's labor market measures still tended to focus more on manipulating pressure and incentives for the unemployed than on requalification, training, and long-term investment in human resources, especially compared with Scandinavian social democracy (Dingeldey and Linke-Sonderegger 2004: 29–38; Hanesch 2003b: 214–216). The Schröder government's active labor market training policies were largely irrelevant to the new social risk groups, with JUMP as one exception. Most training and up-skilling measures continued to be biased toward those who have enough contribution history to be covered by the social insurance system.

Reflecting the persistence of insider–outsider problems in Germany, Figure 5.20 shows that long-term unemployment continued to increase throughout the late 1990s and onward. The inability of the German government to extend an encompassing and undifferentiated system of labor market activation can be accounted for by problems of corporatist coordination in this policy arena. Germany does enjoy considerable advantage over countries like France or the UK (also documented in this chapter) in the ability of its employers' associations and unions to coordinate training. However, such corporatist institutions were absent in active labor market policies. These policies were funded jointly with, and therefore affected by, passive social insurance, which had a highly fragmented and multi-level governance structure. Given the large number of players (including the Federal Labor Office, local authorities, and social partners running each separate social insurance scheme) involved in this process, their inability to centrally communicate and coordinate led to serious collective action failure, and there were frequent attempts at cost shifting among one another (Clasen and Clegg 2006: 202–3).

Figure 5.20 indicates that, overall, the SPD's ALMPs were ineffective in combating unemployment in Germany. The collective action failure of policy implementers was part of the problem, here and in France (as shown earlier). In addition, due to the contributory nature of social security in Germany, ALMPs are financed through unemployment insurance funds, rather than general taxation. As a result, when economic growth slows down, these programs automatically run into financial difficulties. Since insurance benefits and ALMPs are jointly financed, the former tend to crowd out the latter whenever unemployment is on the rise. There is neither legal entitlement nor obligation to participate in many of these training or job programs, and the labor market measures easily become a pro-cyclical instrument of cost control (Manow and Seils 2000a: 149–150; Clasen 2000: 104).

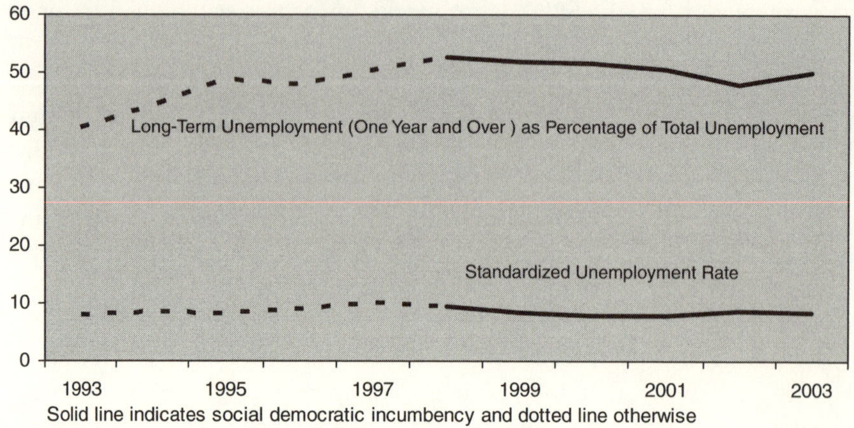

FIGURE 5.20. Total Unemployment and the Share of Long-Term Unemployment in Germany 1993–2003 (*Source:* OECD 2007a).

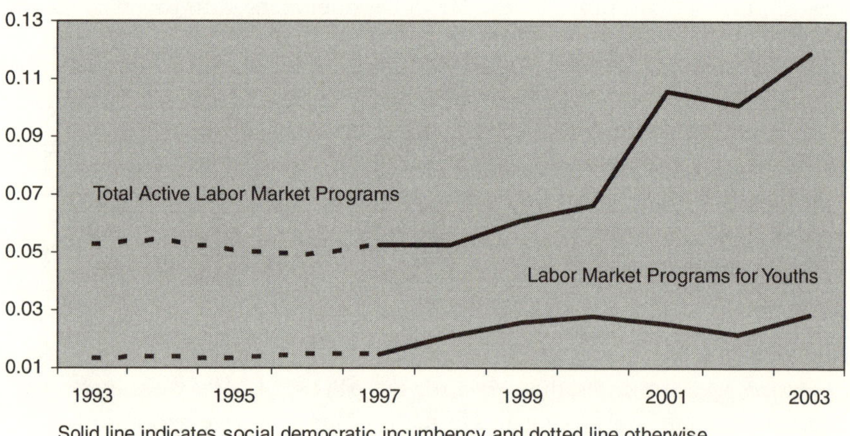

FIGURE 5.21. Labor Market Programs (Total and for Youths) as Percentage of GDP in the UK 1993–2003 (*Source:* OECD 2006a).

United Kingdom

Figure 5.21 highlights New Labour's record in expanding both active labor market measures in general and policies for the young in particular. The youth measures are important as the first major focus under the New Deal, an ambitious and comprehensive set of activation measures. There are six

New Deal programs targeted at different groups, but they share some common characteristics. Firstly, all New Deal programs include a "Gateway Period," during which intensive job-searching help is offered to the unemployed. Secondly, if the participants remain unemployed on the expiration of the Gateway Period, there are four follow-up activation options for the individual to choose from: subsidized employment, self-employment, voluntary work, and 12 months of free training. Crucially, there is "no fifth option," and so activation of some sort is theoretically required of all participants. In 2003, the Gateways for the six programs were merged into a single service called Jobcentre Plus. The merger of the six Gateways also combined the previously separate welfare and employment services, and this process contributed significantly to the unification of the New Deal. Thirdly, all New Deal programs are supply-side programs focused on the specific needs and circumstances of different population groups to be activated. All these programs emphasize the importance of making the welfare system responsive to the individual needs of beneficiaries, in the form of Individual Action Plans. In an Individual Action Plan, personalized counseling is offered to clients as a method both of enabling and of control (Dingeldey and Linke-Sonderegger 2004: 18–21).

Therefore, all the New Deal programs rely heavily on one-on-one communication between New Deal targets and personal advisors familiar with the specific circumstances of individual beneficiaries. Given the depth of knowledge and interpersonal skills required for these personal advisors, their growing influence through the New Deal has gradually changed the institutional tradition of British social protection. There is less impersonal and stigmatizing means testing, but more flexible consultation with the unemployed. Furthermore, as seen in Figure 5.22, the New Deal has also achieved tangible results in labor market activation, cutting long-term unemployment almost by half and reducing total unemployment as well.

Similar to several other third way cases, New Labour started its active labor market reforms with the group generally considered least difficult to activate: the young unemployed. Not only did the government provide special public resources for this group, but the growing emphasis on coercion and compulsion was also primarily targeted at them. Among the six New Deal programs, the New Deal for Young People (NDYP) is the first to be introduced by the government. Initially, New Labour funded NDYP through an earmarked tax from private utilities, so that starting expenses of the program were front-loaded. With increased labor market participation expected, the program becomes self-funding afterwards and will not become a burden on the general taxation system (Trickey and Walker

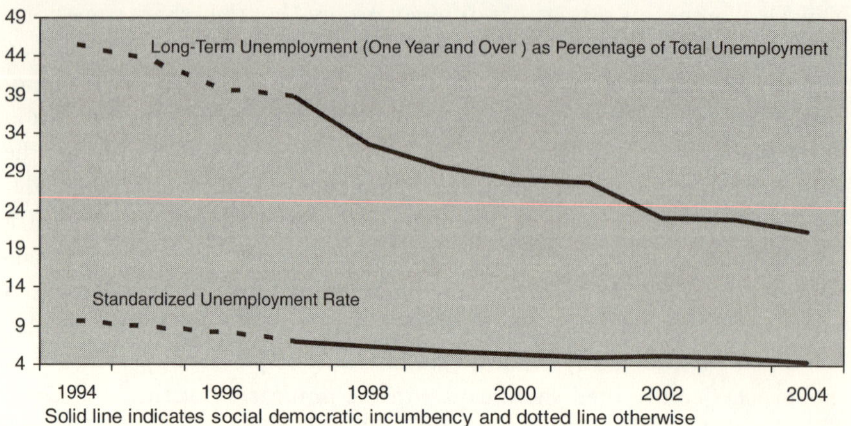

FIGURE 5.22. Total Unemployment and the Share of Long-Term Unemployment in the UK 1994–2004 (*Source:* OECD 2007a).

2001: 181; Peck 2001: 280–323). The second New Deal program to come into effect is the New Deal for Long Term Unemployed (NDLTU), which explicitly offers employer subsidies for taking on long-term unemployed workers for a period of six months. These subsidies are offered to employers to reduce the potential wage cost and encourage them to create more job opportunities (Wood 2001: 58; Grover and Stewart 2000: 241).

Eager to see outcomes quickly from the activation measures, the government concentrated its financial resources on those most likely to be activated. Other less easily activated groups were filtered down to newer and less well-resourced New Deal programs. Overall, NDYP and NDLTU are much better funded and more clearly structured in design than the remaining four New Deal programs. NDYP, in particular, takes up the bulk of the government's spending in New Deal programs. Out of the six New Deal schemes, only these two are compulsory in participation. Partly because of better financial resources, these two New Deal measures focus on work as well as employability, and therefore there is a strong emphasis on human capital and job quality, matched by public investments in training and job-placement services. NDYP and NDLTU, especially the former, incorporate a diverse set of instruments for labor market activation: wage subsidies, job-search assistance, training, and direct job creation. Consequently, in policy outcomes, NDYP is one of the most effective in reintegrating the target population into employment, and it is also the New Deal program with the greatest potential to become self-financing in the long term (Peck 2001: 313–315; Finn 2003: 116–120).

The remaining four New Deal programs are the New Deal for the Unemployed Aged 50 and Above (ND50+), New Deal for Lone Parents (NDLP), New Deal for Disabled People (NDDP), and New Deal for Partners (NDP). The gradual introduction of these programs reflected New Labour's ambition to extend activation to not only the officially unemployed but also the economically inactive sectors of the population. However, such ambition has not yet been matched by corresponding investment. Participation in all of these four programs remained voluntary, although since 2002, attendance at work-focused interviews has been mandatory in NDLP. With inadequate public investment, these New Deal programs focus more narrowly on reducing the barriers to work. There is also relatively less attention to the issue of direct job creation or upgrading human capital (Oppenheim 2001: 79–80; Millar 2002b: 271–272).

The imbalance in government investment among the six New Deal schemes means that the New Deal will be most effective for the most employable, many of whom will probably enter the labor market eventually anyway. By contrast, the programs will be less effective for those who are least employable and therefore need activation most urgently (Barbier 2001: 15). Nevertheless, the six New Deal programs as a whole do represent a qualitative change of direction in activation policy since the last Conservative government. Regardless of financial resources, the ultimate focus of all six New Deal programs is on integration into employment, rather than simply reducing the cost of welfare claims. Although these programs, especially NDYP, inherited some compulsory mechanisms from the Conservatives, increased public funding through windfall taxes (and later increases in direct taxes) is an important policy innovation (Trickey and Walker 2001: 194–206). In addition, there is also increasing coordination and integration between the New Deal measures and corresponding tax reforms. Reductions in lower marginal tax rates helped reduce the poverty trap, and tax credits helped remove the unemployment trap.

Overall, fiscal welfare in combination with the New Deal has helped in removing barriers to work, and as Figure 5.22 showed earlier, declining unemployment became New Labour's major achievement during its first term of office. Despite a relatively positive record in delivering a strong employment performance, New Labour's activation measures also have clear vulnerabilities. Given their supply-side emphasis, ALMPs cannot be effective if the labor market (and the local economy) itself shrinks from the demand side. For this reason, the government made extensive use of employer subsidies in the New Deal, as an incentive for businesses to directly create more jobs and take on unemployed people (Peck 2001: 313–324; Trickey and Walker 2001: 194–206).

The institutional legacy of a liberal welfare state deeply shaped the path-dependent implementation of the New Deal. Over time, the highly targeted and means-tested nature of British welfare strengthened the Dwotkinian emphasis on deserts and moral responsibility. In shifting the policy paradigm from neoliberal cost control to labor market integration, New Labour adopted a discourse with a heavy emphasis on personal responsibility, incentives, and the threat of a dependency culture. Characterized as "tough love," this social-policy principle made it clear that although benefit recipients should be cared for, they should also reciprocate by taking responsibilities for themselves. Activation under New Labour, in other words, is a form of top-down social engineering based on human rationality (Mullard 2000: 4; Clasen 2000: 97; Jordan and Jordan 2000: 24–33). Within the framework of this new communitarian look at social justice, New Labour started to embrace nonstatutory welfare in the form of voluntary and community organizations, many of which are organized through the government's new National Citizens Service Program (Brunsdon and May 2002: 61–63). Overall, as seen in Figure 5.23, New Labour devoted significantly fewer resources to enabling strategies, such as training, than its did German and French counterparts. Instead, its activation methodology is

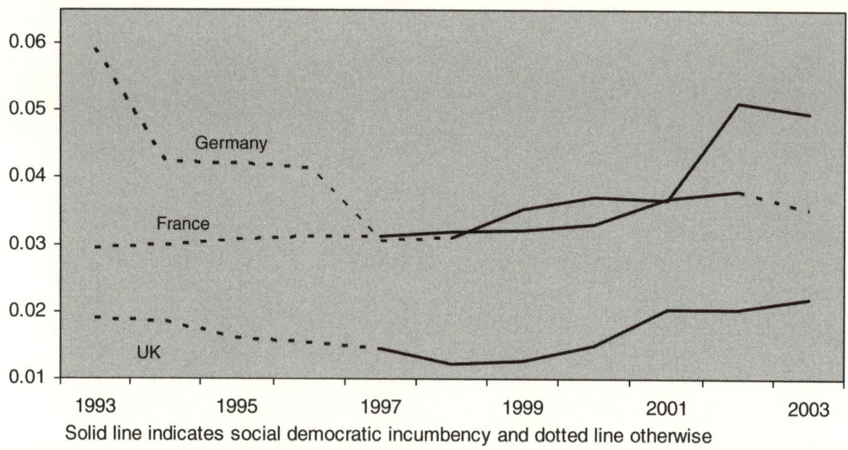

FIGURE 5.23. Labor Market Training as Percentage of GDP in the UK, France, and Germany 1993–2003 (*Source:* OECD 2006a).

characterized by a stronger form of conditionality, moral undertone, and compulsion.

This path dependency on the institutional legacy of poor relief also affected the attitudes of firms toward the New Deal measures. The take-up rate of firms in the ALMPs has been low by international standards. Unlike countries such as Denmark where firms made genuine efforts to invest in training and up-skilling, in the UK, firms viewed the beneficiaries of active measures more harshly as undeserving individuals with incentive problems. Because these programs covered only a small segment of the unemployed population, firms also had little trust in the government's promise to raise the British skill equilibrium through these measures. The New Deal was also affected by the institutional constraint of large numbers: Without any coherent peak authority in coordinating firm strategies, free riding was rampant, and firms largely used these active measures as an opportunity to hire cheaper labor, rather than enriching human capital for their employees. In general, without the corporatist mechanism of mutual monitoring and communication, there was a strong incentive to poach skills from each other and little desire to train as a result (Martin 2004). As shown elsewhere in this chapter, this problem of collective action failure occurred in other similar cases where corporatism was in decline or absent, such as in France and Germany.

Australia

The overall objective of the ALP government was to realign both social security and labor market policies along the principle of the OECD's Active Society recommendations. In a clear departure from the previous center-right tradition of program design within isolated policy domains, the ALP recognized that activation required an interconnected set of different policy arenas, rather than monetary or fiscal policy alone. Under the ALP, social, labor market, economic, and incomes policy became highly coordinated within the overarching theme of third way activation (Gibson 1990: 184–186; Carter 1993: 266).

The constraint of the Accord, and the strong influence of unions inside the parliamentary ALP through different factions, led the Labor government to pursue an incremental and highly corporatist approach to labor market activation. The government promoted employment participation in the context of trade-offs between wage restraints and increased social wages. Changes in the social wage ensured that targeting would be tightened but was aimed mainly at the better-off. Meanwhile, greater social spending and new programs protected the most vulnerable. In addition, the heavily regulated nature of funds for occupational pensions, known as Superannuation, plus the compulsory nature of the contribution to Superannuation funds, all reflected a pattern of active state intervention that traditionally characterized the Australian welfare state. The ALP's third way reforms "refurbished," rather than retrenched, the traditional wage earners' welfare state (Pierson and Castles 2001: 8–9; Castles 1994: 132–133). Electorally, the Accord framework helped the ALP to juggle the balance between public versus private, skilled versus unskilled, and sheltered versus exposed sectors till 1996 (Schwartz 2000: 120–122). The mass defection of the labor movement was held off for more than a decade because of good employment performance delivered through active labor market measures. The ALP's reforms were targeted very specifically at one group that is typically considered as excluded outsiders: the long-term unemployed.

Figure 5.24 indicates that under the ALP, the biggest expansion in active labor market measures occurred after Paul Keating became prime minister in 1991, while over the entire ALP period, resources devoted to labor market training increased steadily. In 1991, the Unemployment Benefit was replaced with two new forms of activation measures: the Job Search Allowance and the Newstart Allowance. Both these programs were linked to other ALMPs, required new job-searching commitments, and offered new forms of cash support for people in short- or long-term unemployment to encourage job searching (Saunders 1995: 47).

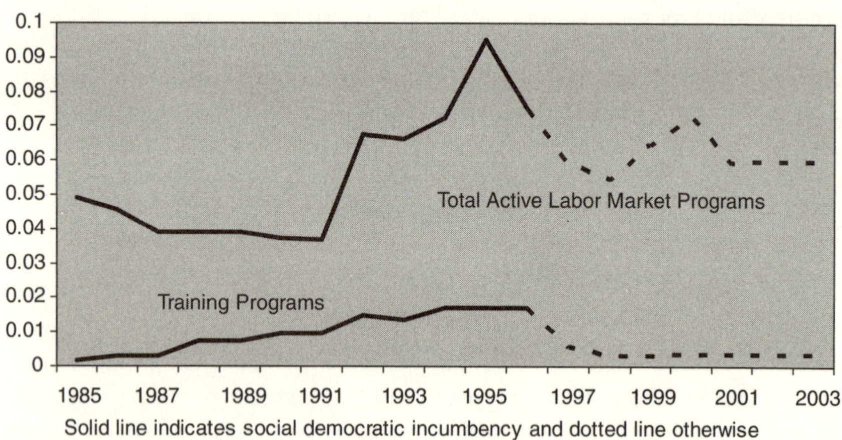

FIGURE 5.24. Labor Market Programs (Total and Training) as Percentage of GDP in Australia 1985–2003 (*Source:* OECD 2006a).

Then, in 1994, Keating launched the comprehensive program package Working Nation, which anticipated much of the New Deal under Blair's New Labour. Working Nation represented a major intensification of Labor's ambition and financial commitment to activating the labor market, involving a real increase in budget projections of 6.5 billion Australian dollars (Finn 1999: 58). Working Nation gave the clearest indication ever in Australia for an employment-oriented approach to social justice. The scheme contained major reforms in both labor market and income support policies. The ALP moved on from Bob Hawke's earlier emphasis on the most easily activated (the young unemployed). Instead, the primary focus of Working Nation fell on the long-term unemployed (18 months or longer). The package's key component was a job guarantee called Job Compact, through which all long-term unemployed were offered active assistance, and reciprocally they were obliged to accept reasonable offers (Junankar and Kapuscinski 1997: 3). The government also offered wage subsidies to employers to encourage hiring the long-term unemployed, with the amount of the subsidy going up as the duration of unemployment lengthened. As a whole package, Job Compact provided individual case management, training, a job for six to twelve months, a training wage, and intensive job-search assistance. Active assistance through these programs and wage subsidies were crucial in helping the long-term unemployed leave the welfare system. Just wage subsidies alone accounted for 80% of successful placements of the long-term unemployed.

By the time Labor came to power in 1983, the Australian labor market had become increasingly segmented by gender, as well as by full-time versus part-time status, and such segmentation significantly contributed to the incidence of long-term unemployment (Saunders 2002: 91). In response, the ALP introduced a wide variety of activity tests characterized by flexible criteria. Immediate job-seeking requirements were relaxed to allow individuals to pursue a wide range of approved activities outside formal and full-time employment, such as self-employment or participation in community-based cooperatives, unpaid voluntary work, or education and training courses. These measures made important contributions to the activation of part-time and casual unemployment. The 1989 Social Security Review formally replaced a work test with an activity test, thereby acknowledging part-time as well as full-time work. And after 1991, the Working Nation package carried the measure further, to a participation test, rather than a simple job-activity test (Finn 1999: 58–68; Marston, Larsen, and McDonald 2004: 5–6; C. Pierson 2001: 8). Under Working Nation, it also became easier for workers to report earnings and quicker for income allowances to be reinstated on the termination of a casual job, so that the unemployed were encouraged to take up part-time or casual jobs. The general assessment of income was changed so that individuals were allowed to keep a part of any casual earnings, a move that facilitated people looking for part-time or casual jobs while retaining an incentive for full-time jobs (Harbridge and Bagley 2002: 180–183; Saunders 1995: 52–53; Shaver 2002: 335).

However, the potential effect of Working Nation in activating the labor market was abruptly curtailed when the center-right coalition returned to power in 1996 and dismantled the package on cost grounds. Replacing Working Nation in 1997, the government put in place Work for the Dole. This new scheme was a form of harsh but ineffective workfare, especially weakened by the contradiction between compulsory state sanctions and minimum state involvement in the labor market. The government's policy focus shifted from ALMPs to a mandatory system of punishments, and the primary objective now became to reduce the number of people on the welfare payroll. With welfare dependency now being the center of attention, the coalition government emphasized being tough on welfare cheaters, backed up by an explicit appeal to public opinion (Saunders 2002: 64). The center Right reduced spending on active labor market measures by 24%, and in order to reduce state intervention in employment services, it introduced Job Network, which opened contestable markets into employment services that were previously publicly funded. The government also introduced Centrelink, a one-stop shop for government income support (Pierson

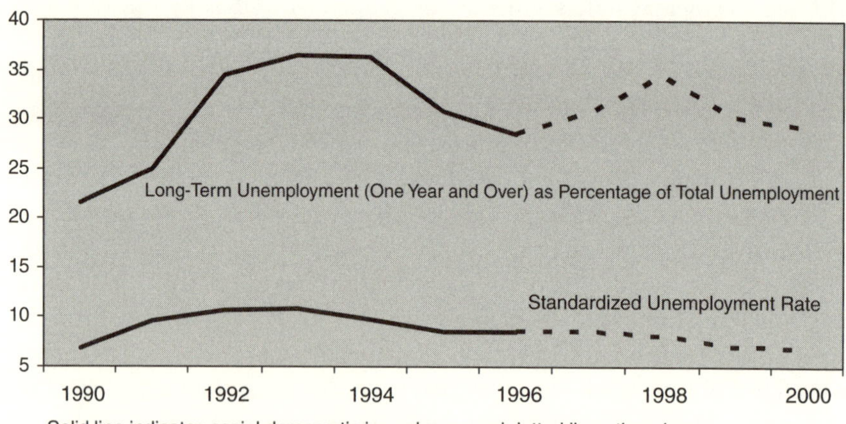

FIGURE 5.25. Total Unemployment and the Share of Long-Term Unemployment in Australia 1990–2000 (*Source:* OECD 2007a).

and Castles 2001: 13; Finn 1999: 65). Work for the Dole was designed to not compete with any regular form of employment, and so there was little room for integrating new social risk groups with marginalized labor market opportunities. The Howard government was especially reluctant to encourage women to enter the labor market. Still somewhat attached to the traditional breadwinner model of social security provision, the Liberal Party increased fiscal incentives for women to stay at home (M. Jones 2002: 18–25).

Even within its short duration of two years, Working Nation under the ALP delivered good results in labor force participation for the excluded outsiders it set out to activate. Long-term unemployment fell by a massive 20% by June 1995, only one year after Working Nation came into being. Figure 5.25 shows that Labor managed to reverse the rising trend of both total and long-term unemployment during the last three years of its term. Overall, Working Nation left valuable lessons in how to activate the labor market in the Australian context. Performance evaluation of the policy package demonstrated that employment and training programs could indeed accelerate labor market entry, but effectiveness depended on whether the program was sufficiently tailored to the specific circumstance of the unemployed individual. More importantly, program performance was also contingent on the state of the economy: When there is an economic decline, it becomes much harder to activate the labor market. Therefore, supply-side

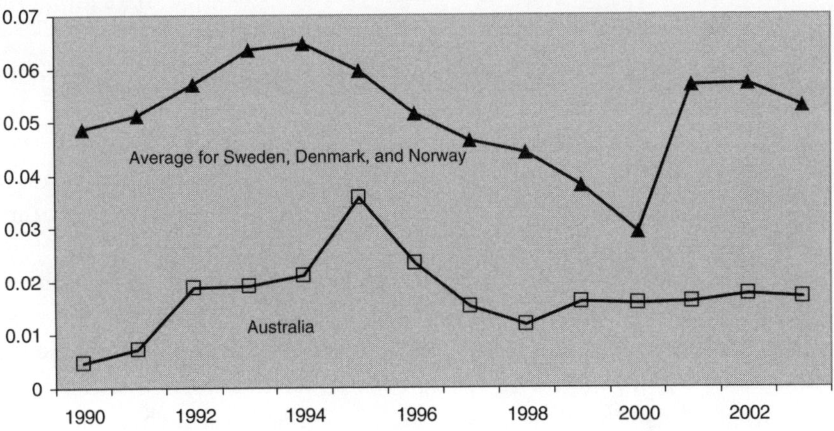

FIGURE 5.26. Employment Subsidies as Percentage of GDP, Australia and Scandinavia Compared 1990–2003 (*Source:* OECD 2006a).

reforms such as Working Nation need to be linked with macro-demand-management measures and direct job creation (Finn 1999: 66–69).

Demand-side job creation remained weak under the ALP. Believing that there is a direct connection between unemployment and insufficient personal incentives, the government focused predominantly on the supply side while ignoring the demand side in subsidizing job creation. Partly in reaction against the ineffective interventionist polices of the preceding coalition government, Hawke abandoned Fraser's measures in public-sector job subsidization (Saunders 2002: 220). The general neglect of direct job creation is one distinctive feature that sets Australian ALMPs apart from the Scandinavian approaches. Figure 5.26 shows clearly that the ALP spent much less on subsidizing employment creation than did its counterparts in Northern Europe.

New Zealand

Contrary to most other cases in this book, the fourth Labour government consciously avoided the third way approach premised on public investment in ALMPs. Instead, it adopted a neoliberal strategy toward reducing unemployment, through monetarist policies and downsizing the state, the only exception in this book to the general connection between social democracy and the third way paradigm. The historical origin of this unusual outcome is a combination of ideological hijacking by neoliberals within the parliamentary Labour Party and the crisis of state intervention prior to Labour's incumbency. I have discussed these two background factors in greater detail respectively, in Chapters 2 and 3, and here I examine the strategies that Labour adopted as an alternative to ALMPs.

Labour had a clear policy framework and strategic planning in economic liberalization, but it carried out social and labor market reforms in an ad hoc and minimalist manner, with little overall structure. Overshadowed by the government's attention to the economy, these social issues were more or less used as a foil, to cushion the impact of rapid deregulatory reforms. Labour's changes in social security were largely limited to some tightening of the access to welfare services, for the purpose of cost control (Koopman-Boyden 1990: 227–230; O'Brien 1993: 14; Boston and Holland 1987: 7–8). As a general pattern, Labour went ahead with extensive reforms where the immediate political costs were low or benefits certain, but it was more cautious where the political costs were big and immediate, such as industrial relations or social policy. Labour believed that working-class votes could still be retained despite its economic fundamentalism. This could happen as long as it spared the social security and industrial-relations systems from

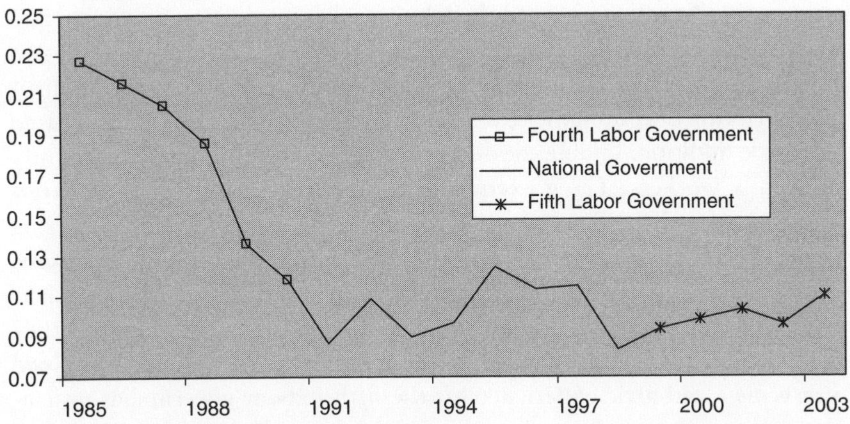

FIGURE 5.27. Active Labor Market Expenditure as Percentage of GDP in New Zealand 1985–2003 (*Source:* OECD 2006a).

the reforms, on top of taking a progressive stance on noneconomic issues such as the environment (Cheyne and Belgrave 1997: 42; Harbridge and Walsh 2002: 200–201).

Figure 5.27 makes clear that the fourth Labour government ushered in a sharp decline in labor market expenditures in New Zealand. Shortly after it came to power, Labour abolished a wide range of job creation and wage-subsidy schemes on the grounds that they distorted market incentives. The government completely ruled out direct state intervention in the labor market, and turned its focus instead to what it perceived as a lack of personal incentives. In place of the abolished ALMPs, Labour installed a heavily targeted scheme called ACCESS aimed at removing behavioral barriers, backed up by substantial reduction and tightening of benefits. Based on a "less eligibility" principle, the government's publication "Benefit Reform" recommended a persistent income gap between benefits and wages (Higgins 1999: 261–265; O'Brien and Wilkes 1993: 87–88).

As a general pattern, since 1985 the government had attempted to bypass direct labor market intervention using a series of alternatives, first by modifying individual behavior in ACCESS, then by controlling the money supply. When this policy clearly failed in 1988, the focus then moved to controlling interest rates (O'Brien and Wilkes 1993: 133–135). The primacy of cost control over public investments for enabling labor force participation created additional barriers to work for people with caregiving responsibilities. In the Scandinavian approach to third way activation, the expansion of child-care facilities significantly enhanced the labor market integration of women and persons with caregiving duties. By contrast, in New Zealand, deregulation under Labour and its National successor led to the comprehensive de-institutionalization of community care. To reduce expenditures, Labour refused to provide additional public resources for the sector of unpaid community and family workers. The government also actively encouraged the externalization of welfare burdens onto the informal sector, which, consisting largely of women, was more or less confined within the limit of the family.

Ten years of hard-hitting deregulation by both major parties, their nonconsensual approach to reform, and the massive public anger they aroused, plus the drastic change in the electoral/party system, combined to serve as a cathartic experience for the fifth Labour government returning to power in 1999. The emphasis on work instead of welfare, which had been highlighted by Labour in the previous two decades, was continued after 1999, and the party reaffirmed its commitment to full employment. However, there is now a clearer departure from past practice in how the work emphasis should be implemented. Representing the first real change in policy direction since 1984, the fifth Labour government removed past workfare measures that were narrowly based on mandatory sanction, and it also restored to the agenda the issue of child poverty. The first major reform in welfare benefits, to be fully implemented by March 2008, significantly increased the financial rewards for working families. The government reduced the rate at which benefits are withdrawn and put in place a wide range of tax credit programs to make work pay (Mackay 2003: 105; Buchanan and Nicholls 2003: 105–106). Going even further than Blair's coy approach of increasing stealth tax, the government under Helen Clark explicitly pledged an increase in direct taxes as a source for renewed public spending. Nevertheless, it has not yet introduced new major ALMPs, the most important component of third way activation. Currently, Labour's main efforts are limited primarily to expanding in-work incentives, which I discuss in greater detail later in this chapter.

Analysis of ALMPs

As the most revolutionary aspect of active social protection, active labor market programs demonstrate the clearest contrast between social democratic enthusiasm for expansion and center-right reluctance or occasional rollback. A few common patterns in policy paradigms can be observed in social democratic ALMP reforms. Meanwhile, within the context of these common patterns, policy implementation and outcomes are different across country cases. The general consistency of these social democratic ALMP patterns across cases reflects the power resources logic, while the diversities in policy implementation reflect the logic of path dependency.

Social democratic governments either continued the budgetary discipline, anti-inflation, and cost-control principles from their center-right predecessors, as in Britain and the Netherlands, or pioneered these principles themselves, as in Australia and New Zealand. However, in most instances, this cautious economic approach went hand in hand with, rather than at the expense of, increases in public expenditures for active labor market measures, especially those with long-term-enabling or social-investment objectives (Bonoli 2004: 203). By comparing the major ALMPs covered in the case studies, several general patterns emerge.

First of all, in designing their ALMPs, social democratic parties have placed increasing emphasis on balancing obligations with rights to accept offers of activation, and have shown a growing willingness to enforce obligations through compulsion. Examples of this pattern can be found in the British New Deal, Dutch JEA, ALMPs based on the Social Services Act in Norway, and Danish ALMPs. The emphasis on the right to activation is particularly strong in Scandinavia plus France, but the interpretation about rights to activation is more ambiguous for the New Deal and the Dutch JEA, whereas such entitlement does not formally exist in Norwegian workfare programs related to social assistance benefits. As alluded to in Chapter 2, the relatively uncompromising attitude toward vulnerable social-assistance recipients in Norwegian activation can be accounted for by the unusually weak (by Nordic standard) organizational integration of the unemployed in the labor movement. For 1998/2002, the unemployed/employed unionization ratio is 0.27 in Norway but 0.84 and 0.93 for, respectively, Sweden and Denmark (Ebbinghaus 2006). Organizational integration of the unemployed is crucial for bridging the insider–outsider divide, and the Norwegian case shows that where organizational integration is thin, social democratic policies also focus less on providing human capital resources for the vulnerable marginal groups.

Patterns of policy implementation clearly reflect variation across cases in the emphasis on rights versus duties for labor market activation. For example, while Danish ALMPs have an in-built element of compulsion, the unemployed can choose from a wide range of activation options, and the government actively seeks to enhance the skills of the unemployed through training offers. Sanctions, while they exist, are not at the forefront of Danish ALMPs. The New Deal, by comparison, is clearly ready to impose sanctions, especially on the young. At the same time, measures in the New Deal are also more tolerant of low wages and labor market inequalities. The linkage between fighting unemployment and skill development in the New Deal, though rapidly developing, is still weaker than in Danish ALMPs. Between the most integrative and most coercive ALMPs, the French RMI and American workfare programs tend to occupy the polar ends (Etherington 1998: 156–158; Trickey 2001: 254–256).

Another cross-case common pattern is that there is a relatively consistent hierarchy of priorities in social democratic ALMPs. The young unemployed are usually the first target, provided with the most substantial public resources in training and job offers but also with the most coercive enforcement rules. Actually, a lot of the flagship ALMPs started off as programs for the young and later were expanded to become comprehensive measures (Trickey 2001: 258). Typical examples of this pattern are the New Deal in Britain and the JEA in the Netherlands, and participation in these specific programs is universal for all of the young unemployed. Given the amount of resources and attention, youth activation also tends to be most effective when compared with other target groups. Next to the young, the long-term unemployed constitute a second major activation target because of their especially close connection to the increasingly salient issue of social exclusion. A typical ALMP tailored to this segment of the population is the Working Nation package under the ALP in Australia.

In a closely related pattern, some social democratic parties have gradually expanded the coverage of their ALMPs to include outsiders: the new social risk groups suffering from various labor market disadvantages. Most of them organized weakly on their own, these marginal groups often have to depend on positive externalities from the organizational integration of stronger groups with somewhat similar risk portfolios, such as women and the unemployed in general. However, outside Scandinavia these latter groups are themselves mostly weakly organized. There are some exceptions, such as France's strong female unionization (female/male union density ratio 0.91) or feminist politicians' significant influence within the Dutch PvdA government. The positive externalities of such organizational integration can be seen not only in the well-known generosity of French public child care but also in part-time-friendly flexicurity reforms and gender-friendly incentives in the Netherlands (more on the Dutch case later in this chapter). However, in general, it is the Scandinavian ALMPs that have gone furthest in activating the really difficult cases, such as the low-skilled or long-term unemployed. Of course, as noted earlier, Norwegian activation measures for marginal social-assistance recipients rely relatively heavily on coercion, and I will describe the social-assistance reforms in greater detail in Chapter 6 on passive protection.

2. IN-WORK INCENTIVES

As its name suggests, active protection primarily operates by facilitating labor market entry for the unemployed and those out of the labor force. In addition to ALMPs, there are some supplementary measures that serve the same purpose. They offer a passage into the labor market more indirectly. Unlike ALMPs, they cannot directly create the physical and concrete venues where the unemployed and the labor market could interact. Nevertheless, were this labor market interaction to occur, the supplementary measures could increase its financial returns, or decrease its family-related personal costs. Programs serving these purposes are in-work incentives, which can encompass not only tax credits, minimum wages, and reductions in social security contributions but also the provision of public child-care places or individualization in tax/benefit assessments.

The focus of this book is the period since the 1980s. At the outset, it is important to emphasize that countries with already generous public child-care or protection against low wages (through centralized bargaining) do not urgently need in-work incentives, such as statutory minimum wages. For this reason, across Nordic countries there were no further major expansions in in-work incentives, and these countries do not feature in this section's analysis. Where social democrats did introduce important new in-work incentives since the early 1980s, their implementation demonstrates a strongly path-dependent pattern. Continental European measures have relied heavily on reductions in social security contributions, whereas negative income taxes (essentially means-tested benefits) have been more typical for social democrats in liberal welfare states. Meanwhile, as evidence for power resources, there are still some noticeable policy contrasts between different parties. For example, compared with social democracy, the center-right governments tend to be much less enthusiastic about increasing positive financial incentives for female employment or increasing the minimum wage. Table 5.2 provides an empirical and theoretical roadmap for the analysis of in-work incentive policy changes.

The Netherlands

Among the various financial incentives deployed by the PvdA to encourage labor market participation, many were actually directed at employers rather than employees. In general, few of the government's activation

TABLE 5.2. *Key In-Work Incentive Developments, by Country and Theoretical Implications*

Key policies in order of appearance in the chapter	Theoretical Implications ⇒	Power Resources	Path Dependency
	Netherlands	Employer subsidies; incentives for part-time parents	Continental→ heavy reliance on reductions in social security contributions
	France	Employment Premium; further expansion of female-friendly policies	
	Germany	Various schemes to reduce social security contribution	
	United Kingdom	Working Families' Tax Credit; National Minimum Wage	Anglo-Saxon→ heavy reliance on negative income tax (means-tested benefits)
	Australia	Liberalized income tests; various new means-tested benefits introduced	
	New Zealand	Working for Families	
	Denmark	Generous wage protection and public child care (social democratic tradition)	
	Sweden		
	Norway		

Note: Countries in shaded areas have no major policy innovation during period under examination and do not feature in the analysis.

measures were solely aimed at modifying the behavioral pattern of unemployed individuals without requiring direct cooperation from employers. For the PvdA, apparently the work barrier, especially for the long-term unemployed, lies more in the perceptions and attitudes of employers than in the personal initiatives of the unemployed. The government's policy premise was that by far the vast majority of unemployed people were eager to find a job, but employers were especially prejudiced against hiring the long-term unemployed. Therefore, employment subsidies, especially in the form of reductions in social security contributions for employers, were introduced on a large scale (van Oorschot 1999: 32–33; Hemerijck, Unger, and Visser 2000: 226). To encourage businesses to hire more low-skilled workers, the government in 1993 increased the Special Reduction in taxes for people with wages below 115% of the minimum wage. In addition, two new pieces of legislation, the Law on the Use of Jobseekers and the Law on the Reintegration of Handicapped People, offered companies subsidies to create special jobs that would not compete with regular jobs, in both the public and private sectors. Employers were also subsidized if they were willing to create jobs on an experimental basis. The total reduction in social security contributions cut wage cost by 10%, and in combination with reductions targeted at long-term unemployment contributions, the total cuts in wage costs amounted to as much as 23% (Keizer 2003: 294–295; Hartog 2000: 59). Overall, as seen in Figure 5.28, the PvdA was able to sharply reduce the tax wedge during its time in power.

Since the 1970s, subsidized labor had been used to temporarily or permanently compensate for shortfalls in the labor market. With the PvdA now in government, subsidies for jobs became more flexible and tailored to the individual circumstance of the unemployed. The policy

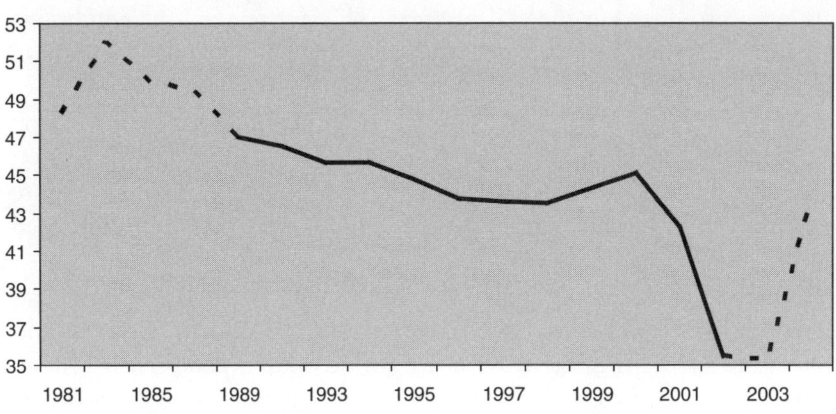

FIGURE 5.28. Tax Wedge for Average Production Worker (APW) in the Netherlands 1981–2004 (*Source:* OECD 2005a; figures [percentages] include employers' social security contributions).

principle underlying these subsidies also broadened, from simply reducing unemployment numbers to enabling labor market reintegration. Most of the various in-work incentives were later integrated under two framework laws, the Act on the Integration of Jobseekers and the Act on Reducing Contributions. The reformed Dutch tax system now provides new forms of tax credits and reductions to which only those employed are entitled (de Schamphelerie and van Berkel 2001: 51–52; Hoop 2004: 69–70; van Oorschot 2002a: 112–114).

In addition to pure financial in-work incentives, the PvdA also improved in-work incentives by decreasing the family-related cost of entering the labor market. Reconciliation between work and family had been a core objective since the start of PvdA's active labor market reforms. This, as discussed in Chapter 3's case studies of third way ideologies, can at least partially be attributed to the political influence of Dutch feminists within the PvdA, as well as the unusually strong impact their campaigns made on society. On this basis, the party proposed an entitlement to part-time work for parents, and it promised to extend maternal leave and to introduce paid parental leave of six months. After becoming the dominant coalition partner in the Purple Coalition in 1994, the PvdA proposed a "combination scenario," which focused on the division of tasks inside households with children. The "combination scenario" recommended that each partner work for 30 to 35 hours a week and carry out caregiving tasks for 20 to 25 hours a week. Within this framework, it is envisaged that each employee can realize a new balance between working and caregiving responsibilities. In line with the "combination scenario," an Enabling Act of Labor and Care was introduced at the end of 2001. This act relaxed the conditions for various parental leave schemes and coordinated their implementation. A system for career interruption was also set up so that employees have the right to break off their career for a certain period of time for the purpose of taking care of children, family, or friends (van Oorschot 2004: 219; Seeleib-Kaiser, van Dyk, and Roggenhamp 2004: 27–29). Overall, Figure 5.29 clearly indicates that parental-leave schemes were massively expanded after the PvdA came to power.

With the tax reform in 1990, the government reduced the basic tax allowance for breadwinners and integrated social security with the taxation system, lowering the disincentive for second earners to work more hours. The institutionalization of a statutory minimum wage helped narrow the wage differentials between men and women, as well as between part-time and full-time workers (Visser 2001: 27–28).

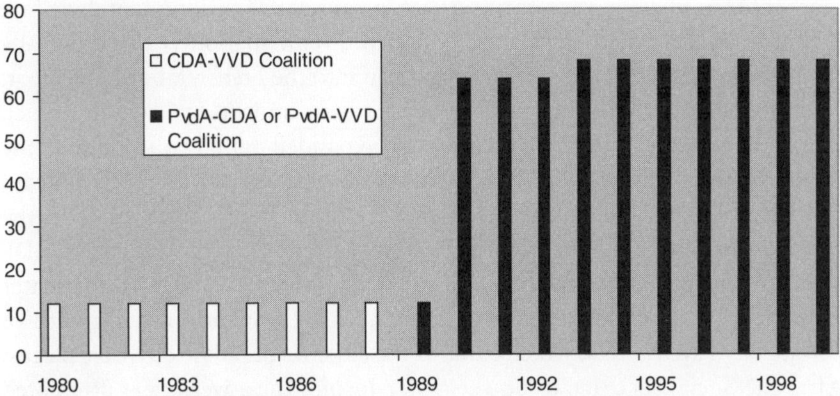

FIGURE 5.29. Total Weeks of Parental and Child-Care Leave Schemes in the Netherlands 1980–1999 (*Source:* Gauthier and Bortnik 2001).

France

After the Jospin government came to power in 1997, the use of financial incentives to stimulate employment among disadvantaged groups grew significantly. In order to facilitate small and medium firms in hiring new employees, especially in low-wage jobs, the government tried to lower labor costs by reducing or exempting social security contributions for employers. Financial incentives were also targeted at employees, with the key instrument being the Employment Premium (PPE). Introduced in 2001, PPE is a means-tested new wage supplement funded from general taxation. It is targeted at low-income earners in the form of a tax credit covering those whose wages do not exceed 1.4 times the minimum income guarantee. By compensating low-paid workers for some of their income and social security payments, PPE increases the financial returns from work in low-wage jobs. In addition, the government introduced tax cuts targeted specifically at the lower end of the income scale. For example, lower salaries were progressively exempted from a professional tax, and the General Social Contribution and the habitation tax on lower earners were also reduced in order to remove the poverty trap for people coming off the means-tested basic income benefit RMI. Income disregards for RMI were also strengthened (Morel 2004: 120–121; Clasen and Clegg 2003: 370; Clift 2001: 176).

In addition to offering purely financial incentives, the Socialist government also tried to help reduce the potential family cost of entering the labor market for mothers. Such reforms are atypical relative to continental welfare regimes, and as noted earlier, one important explanation is the unusually strong organizational integration of women into the French labor movement. The model of the working mother occupies an important place in French family policy, and public day care was expanded rapidly throughout the 1970s. In the 1980s, the Socialists removed the provisions in family policies that discriminated in favor of particular gender or family roles. In 1987, the center-right government introduced a new child-rearing allowance (AGED). This scheme marked a turning point in French family policy. It led to greater diversification in child-care arrangements, and it resulted in the growth of private day-care centers, which came at the expense of public day-care places. After the Socialists came to power under Jospin, the government attempted to make child-care benefit arrangements more progressive and redistributive toward the worse-off, and to align child-care policies with the general efforts by the government to activate the labor market. For these purposes, the Socialists introduced a new benefit in 2001 to supplement child-care costs for women returning to work. The number of child-care places was also expanded. In an effort to make child-care support more progressive, the government excluded higher earners from the benefit by means testing, and it removed the tax deduction for in-home child care. However, the government was later forced to withdraw the means testing of child-care benefits after concerted opposition from both center-right parties and the social partners (Daguerre and Taylor-Gooby 2003: 633–634; Levy 1999b: 247–252).

Germany

In order to promote employment, the Red-Green coalition offered financial incentives to employers as well as employees. For employers, the government subsidized a reduction in social contributions to the pension scheme, in order to reduce non-wage labor costs and to make the hiring of new workers more financially attractive. For employees, the government reduced the basic rate of the personal income tax and introduced new exemptions for both income taxes and social contributions below a certain wage threshold, so that low-income earners could get significantly greater return from work. The general wage threshold for social contribution exemptions was raised in 1999 with union support, and the application of these exemptions was also extended into areas of casual employment and self-employment (Leibfried and Obinger 2003: 212; Seeleib-Kaiser 2004b: 128; Vail 2002: 14). As seen in Figure 5.30, the consistent and sharp increase of the tax wedge in Germany in the late 1970s was kept at bay after the Red-Green coalition came to power.

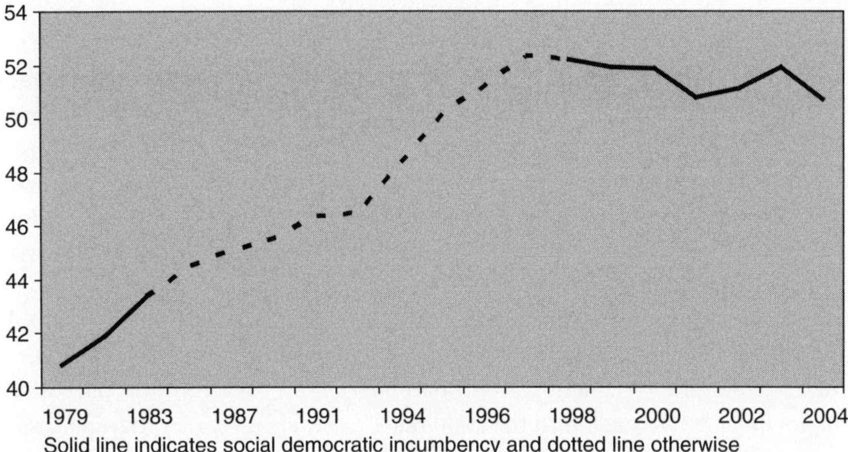

FIGURE 5.30. Tax Wedge for Average Production Worker (APW) in Germany 1979–2004 (*Source:* OECD 2005a; figures [percentages] include employers' social security contributions).

After its reelection in 2002, the Red-Green coalition devoted increasing resources and attention to the creation of and experimentation with different financial incentives to work for employees. Based in several localities, various model projects were designed for this purpose. For example, the Einsteigsgeld and PLUSLohn models were respectively tested in Baden-Württemberg and in North-Rhine Westphalia's Duisburg employment office, the former making it easier to claim social assistance while earning a wage for 12 months and the latter offering in-work benefits for 12 months. On the national level, the Mainz model was in use, which worked under the slogan "Work Must Be Worth It" and offered federal subsidies in the form of reimbursement for social security contributions or increases in child benefits to low-wage earners for up to 36 months. An important characteristic of these model projects is the very high proportion of women enrolled in them, for example, 64% in Mainz and 77% in Einsteigsgeld, and these schemes are important measures in activating the female labor force. Both the Mainz and Einsteigsgeld models, for instance, encouraged greater in-work support for women with children or part-time work. For this purpose, the assessment of benefits in these model projects was related not to a specific hourly rate but to the highest achievable monthly household income. Both the Mainz and Einsteigsgeld subsidies represented monetary transfers intended specifically to bring about a direct improvement in the income position of family households (Weinkopf 2003: 255–257; Vail 2003: 52; Spiess and Wagner 2003: 306).

By international standards, Germany has not only an above-average unemployment rate but also a low employment rate. A very important contributor to this situation is the below-average female employment rate, which is itself due to the large number of domestic and caregiving service jobs being performed on an unpaid basis by women outside the labor market. To alleviate this situation, the Red-Green coalition in its first term increased child allowances in several steps and substantially raised the income limits for claiming the full amount of means-tested parental allowances. The government also proposed an expansion in child tax credits and enacted an entitlement to both parental-leave provisions and part-time employment for parents until the child reaches the age of three. Shared access to parental leave, meanwhile, was made easier for both parents. There is, in addition, a means-tested parental benefit available for the first two years after childbirth (Weinkopf 2003: 261–262; Seeleib-Kaiser 2004b: 137–139). Figure 5.31 shows that, overall, the social democrats were relatively consistent in expanding resources to help families with children.

With the SPD's measures targeted at families and children, the state became increasingly willing to deliver family support directly through public policy, instead of leaving family risks to be redistributed within the household, as in past practices. Family policies, therefore, underwent a process

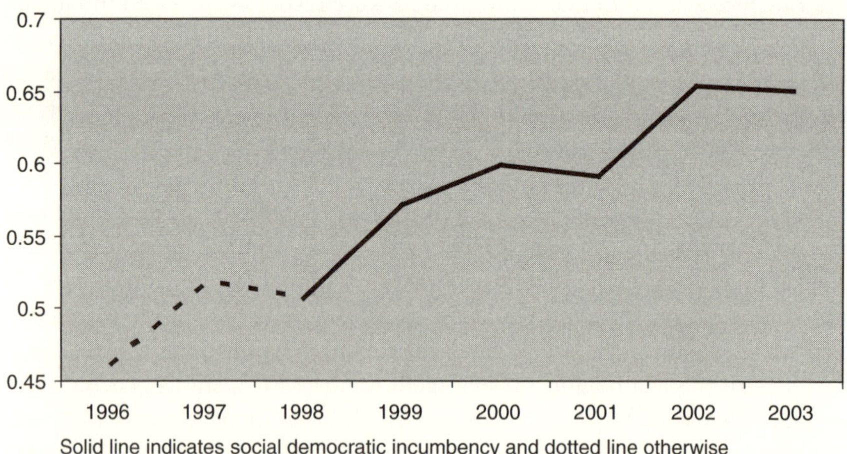

FIGURE 5.31. Public Transfers on Assisting Families with Children as Percentage of GDP in Germany 1996–2003 (*Source*: OECD 2006a).

of expansion as well as adjustment in their functions, so that they were aimed less at securing the standard of living for wage earners and more at meeting the actual needs of families (Seeleib-Kaiser 2002: 34–35; Seeleib-Kaiser 2004b: 127–128; Leibfried and Obinger 2003: 212). The employability of mothers was emphasized in Job-AQTIV, the major activation package during the second term of the Schröder government. The new legislation introduced equal treatment of child-care periods and contribution periods in unemployment insurance, so that mothers have entitlement to unemployment benefits as well as access to ALMPs. For families with children, the government also made available a new option to combine part-time work of up to 30 hours a week with parental leave for both parents for three years. After 2002, the general remit of ALMPs was extended from status-equivalent reemployment of the unemployed into new areas, such as an atypical employment relationship or subsidized self-employment (Dingeldey and Linke-Sonderegger 2004: 30; Clasen and Clegg 2003; Seeleib-Kaiser 2004a: 16).

During its second term, the government treated as a top priority the expansion of new child-care facilities and schools with an all-day schedule. By emphasizing the role of public institutions in child care, the social democrats clearly distinguished themselves from the Christian democratic emphasis on the choice to buy child care on the market or self-service at home. The Red-Green coalition expected that by the end of its child-care expansion reforms, publicly financed child care would be available for 20% of all children under the age of three. However, as the provision of child-care facilities had been severely underdeveloped historically in Germany, the SPD's efforts were insufficient to have a clear impact on the activity rate of women or mothers in particular (Bäcker 2003: 302; Seeleib-Kaiser 2004b: 139–141; Weinkopf 2003: 261–262).

Another impediment existing in the current German system is the differential treatment of family status for tax purposes, resulting in a high marginal tax rate for a second earner, which significantly reduces the likelihood for full-time employment for married women (Dingeldey and Linke-Sonderegger 2004: 31). Furthermore, with regard to the new social risk of low-skill unemployment, the social democratic reforms had made little relevant impact, especially in providing in-work incentives for low-skill jobs. Reflecting the social democratic electoral dilemma of the insider–outsider divide, this failure was largely due to the refusal by unions to subsidize low-wage jobs for fear of compromising the high-skill equilibrium in the core industries, where workers are protected by the primary social insurance system (Aust and Bönker 2004: 45). The labor market experience of young

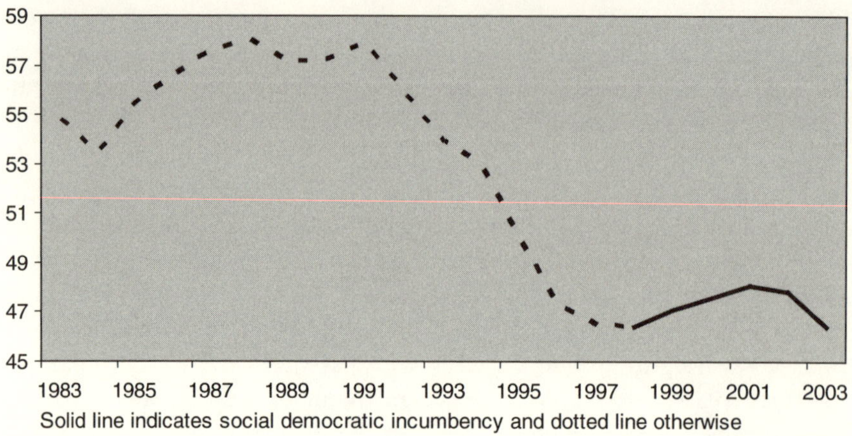

FIGURE 5.32. Labor Force Participation for Females 15–24 Years of Age in Germany 1983–2003 (*Source:* OECD 2007a).

female members of the labor force, a typical new social risk group, highlights the persistence of the insider–outsider divide problem in Germany. As seen in Figure 5.32, although this group's sharp decline in labor force participation stopped after the Red-Green coalition came to power, the social democrats had not been able to reverse the trend.

United Kingdom

Since it came to power, New Labour has introduced a wide range of in-work incentives, especially for those in the lowest-paid sector. One of the most important measures in this regard is the National Minimum Wage, implemented in 1999. This represents a significant development in government strategies toward promoting employment and preventing poverty in work, the first time that a national minimum wage rate has been set in Britain. In addition to the minimum wage, there are also reductions to starting tax rates, lower tax bands, and cuts in national insurance contributions for low-paid workers (Millar 2000: 342; Millar 2002b: 273; Rhodes 2000b: 181).

In its efforts to extend in-work incentives, New Labour has been distinctive in devoting focused attention on the activation of single parents and various other disadvantaged family types. As weakly organized outsiders suffering from typical new social risks, these atypical families clearly benefited from the positive externalities of organization integration (of women) theorized in Chapter 2. Despite their limitations, Labour's policies for disadvantaged families were in no small measure related to the organizational influence of female members of Parliament (MPs) within the party. This was the largest female representation in Parliament in the country's history, and Harriet Harman served as the first minister with portfolio on social policy. In addition, feminists outside the party were also regularly consulted. With the publication of the White Paper Fairness at Work in 1998 and the Employment Relations Bill in 1999, the government formally started to push actively for reforms helping families on low incomes. In order to activate single parents and low-income earners in couple households, the government introduced a stream of measures under the headline of "Making Work Pay." The most important initiative under "Making Work Pay" is the introduction of the "Working Families' Tax Credit" (WFTC) in 1999. WFTC is a form of negative income tax paid by the Inland Revenue, a form of in-cash transfer aimed at removing the poverty trap and increasing disposable market income with reference to the number of children in the household. WFTC replaced the Family Credit introduced by the previous Conservative government. The key difference between Family Credit and WFTC is that the latter is paid through the wage package, so that there is a psychological effect of linking benefits to work. As a form of means-tested benefit, WFTC is also markedly more generous than the Family Credit (Deacon 2003: 106).

As a form of negative income tax, WFTC appears as lower taxation, rather than higher public spending. Since the negative income tax is counted as a tax reduction rather than a cash payment, WFTC does not count as a formal part of public expenditure. This situation is consistent with Labour's 1997 election promise not to increase the income tax or public spending beyond the limits of the previous Conservative government, and so tax credits have become an increasingly acceptable "costless" way of offering in-work incentives. Reflecting path dependency on means-tested institutional legacies, the growing use of fiscal welfare to provide in-work incentives, especially through the taxation system, also features strongly in other liberal welfare states (Rhodes 2000a: 61–62; Parry 2000: 99; Adler 2004: 97–102). With increases in financial support announced in the 2000 budget, WFTC provided a guaranteed minimum income for one-earner families working either full time or part time. In 2003, there was a significant rationalization of the tax-credit system, as the government introduced a single Working Tax Credit (WTC) for all working adults. Meanwhile, Labour also created a separate Child Tax Credit (CTC) for families with children, which achieved a major reduction in the financial costs for child care (Dingeldey and Linke-Sonderegger 2004: 24; Oppenheim 2001: 84).

With the large-scale introduction of negative income taxes into the wage system, income supplementation gradually became the main responsibility of the tax, rather than the social security system, and both the level and coverage of income supplementation kept increasing (Millar 2000: 342). Figure 5.33 highlights the clear increase in public expenditures on tax-credit measures since New Labour came to power. By 2003, WFTC had reduced the tax bill of about one million low-paid families by 20 pounds a week, whereas the CTC amounted to a 2.5% tax cut in value (Evans and Cerny 2003: 38). WFTC and CTC, along with the Disabled Persons Tax Credit (DPTC), are all work-based tax credits paid by an employer as a supplement to wages. They are paid at a higher rate than means-tested out-of-work benefits, and so these tax credits offer significant in-work incentives. While WFTC marked the first significant step in the British welfare state to integrate the previously separate tax and social security systems, the 2003 merger of all tax credits into WTC marked the completion of the integration process. Crucially, this integration of tax and social security systems went hand in hand with the integration between benefit and employment services, primarily through the "Gateway" services of the six New Deal programs. The linking of the New Deal with tax credit reforms is a major innovation of the New Labour government. With the integration of all six New Deal Gateways into one Jobcentre Plus as the single point of

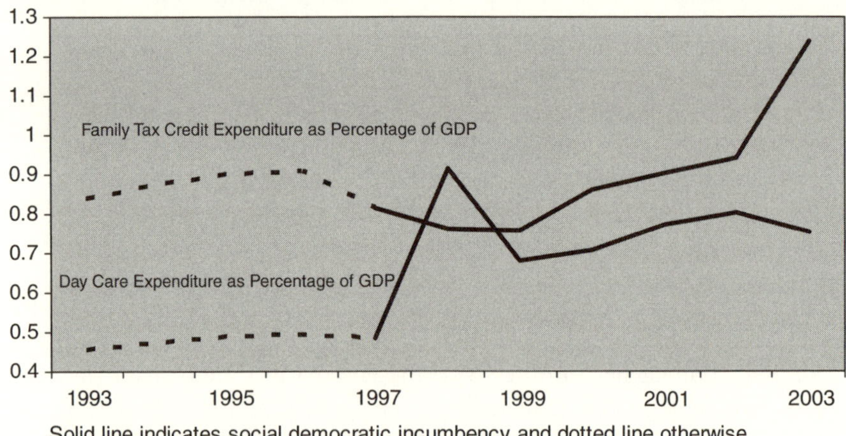

FIGURE 5.33. In-Cash and In-Kind Incentives for Work in the UK 1993–2003 (*Source*: OECD 2006a).

access, there is now an unprecedented degree of coordination and coherence in New Labour's activation strategies in employment, taxation, and social security domains (Hewitt 2002: 192–194; Adler 2004: 103–104).

Another important initiative in increasing in-work incentives is the replacement of the Married Couples Allowance, which was assumed to discourage labor market entry for married women, with a flat-rate Child Benefit. In addition, the government also expanded the scope of its flagship New Deal programs to include a New Deal for Lone Parents (NDLP). The implementation of these programs indicates that the social policy conceptualization of the family has started to shift, from the traditional breadwinner model to adult worker families (Cressey 2002: 355; Hewitt 2002: 194). The government, as Figure 5.34 shows, significantly increased spending on parental-leave schemes. On top of all these financial incentives as carrots, there is also increasingly the stick of compulsion, which is being extended to single parents, as well as people with disabilities, so that they are now obliged to attend work-focused interviews. Further expansion in the scope of compulsion remains very likely (Walker and Wiseman 2003: 23).

There are, however, some clear weaknesses in New Labour's attempt to promote labor market activation for families with low incomes. First of all, at the moment the government does not have a clear strategy for women's activation. In New Labour's ALMPs for families on low income, the policy focus is on workless households, rather than workless individuals (Millar 2002b: 279). The lack of individual means testing, individual claims, and

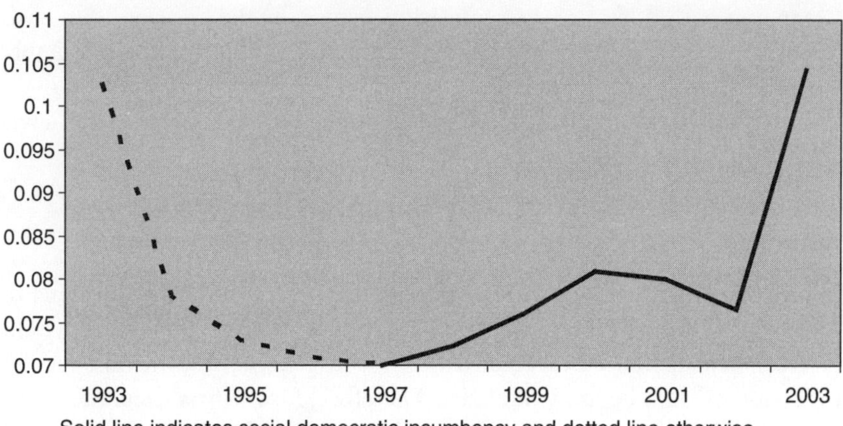

FIGURE 5.34. Public Expenditure on Parental Leave as Percentage of GDP in the UK 1993–2003 (*Source:* OECD 2006a).

individual payments, all of which were important elements of the Working Nation package for the ALP in Australia, means that New Labour has been less successful than its Australian counterpart in encouraging the labor market participation of females. Secondly, NDLP lacks sufficient resources to finance substantive policy initiatives. Significantly less well funded than other more established New Deal programs such as NDYP, the NDLP package has been largely limited to the offer of information and advice for single parents, without any form of job guarantee, in-work incentives, or incentives for employers to take on single parents (Millar 2000: 343).

A more serious weakness in Labour's activation of low-income families, however, is in the area of child care. There was some expansion of public child care places since 1998, with the establishment of the National Childcare Strategy (NCS), which proposed more nurseries and after-school care. However, although NCS marked the first attempt by a British government to formally address the issue of child care, NCS's various funding schemes, known as Sure Start, focused primarily on the stimulation of private or community child care. More generally, the government clearly devoted more financial resources to tax credits (WFTC, for example) than to public child care as the primary in-work incentives for female labor market activation, as shown in Figure 5.33. Instead of offering more child-care places, NCS uses the tax credits paid through WFTC as additional funds for parents to meet the cost of child care (Daguerre and Taylor-Gooby 2003: 635; Dean 2002: 6). For this reason, the net impact of NCS has been uncertain, with the number of child-care places for 8-year-olds and younger continuing to decline even after the scheme was introduced. Compared with other areas of activation, especially the creation of in-cash incentives for work, the money allocated to public child care is considerably less, and questions of education and individual development for younger children has been largely ignored in Labour's child-care strategies (Lewis 2003: 86; Taylor-Gooby and C. Larsen 2004: 67).

Australia

In order to provide in-work incentives to encourage female job searching in Australia, Working Nation ensured that spouses of the unemployed would receive payments based on their own job activity, and that income testing for couples would be individualized. Therefore, for the first time, the tradition of the breadwinner was broken in Australia, and partners were treated as separate individuals. Labor's reform of means testing took on all aspects of the individualization agenda: individual claims, individualized means testing, and individual payments. Introduced after 1995, these measures in individualizing means testing led to a significant transfer of payments from men to women (Millar 2003: 70). Next to females, another major target for the ALP government's in-work incentive policies was families on low incomes or persons with caregiving responsibilities.

On this front, the government tried to liberalize income tests and reduce poverty traps for families working on very low wages. Labor introduced the Family Package, a program targeted specifically at low- to average-income families with significantly increased levels of payment. Social-assistance programs were designed as a wage top-up for those working for decreased wages. In addition to using supplementary social assistance to top up single or no-income families, for better targeting the government also transformed the universal child benefit into a means-tested family benefit called the Family Assistance Supplement (FAS). For unemployed single parents with older children, the government introduced not only a Parenting Allowance but also Jobs, Education, and Training (JET), a voluntary program involving targeted counseling, assistance with child care, training, and education. Another important measure that played a role in easing the transition from welfare to work for families was the restoration of national health insurance (Medicare), which was abolished by the previous coalition government (Hemerijck and Schludi 2000: 195–199; Schwartz 2000: 118–119; C. Pierson 2001: 9–10). The means-tested health-benefit system under the coalition government had created work disincentives as people were in danger of losing their health benefit when going back to work, and the reestablishment of national health insurance under ALP helped to reduce such work disincentives.

In the attempt to provide in-work incentives for part-time workers and unpaid employment more generally, the ALP focused almost exclusively on relieving the *financial* burdens of dual or one-and-a-half earner families, by offering them incentives in cash. Apart from Medicare, the government did relatively little to directly relieve the *caregiving* burdens of these transitional families. Figure 5.35 highlights the sharp gap between Labor's in-cash and in-kind types of work incentives. Like the fourth Labour government in New Zealand, the ALP tried to externalize in-kind responsibilities onto the family and merely remain the primary provider of cash benefits. The reluctance of the Australian (and New Zealand) state to be involved directly in delivering social services led to a massive undersupply of child-care facilities and funds (Gibson 1990: 184–200; Hemerijck and Schludi 2000: 195–199). On the one hand, individualization of spousal income and means testing through Working Nation removed female financial dependence; on the other hand,

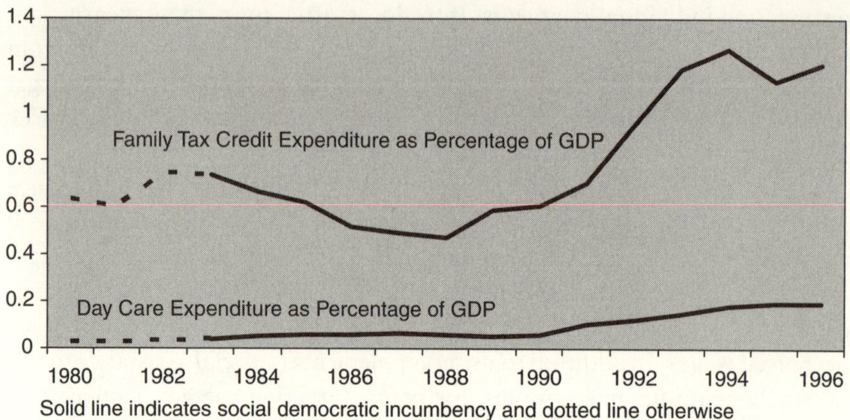

FIGURE 5.35. In-Cash and In-Kind Incentives for Work in Australia 1980–1996 (*Source:* OECD 2006a).

there was little effort to remove the unpaid caregiving obligations within the family. As the experience in Scandinavia demonstrates, activation of women and, to a lesser extent, dual or one-and-a-half earners as well as part-time workers, cannot be fully effective without adequate public child-care provision. Removing barriers to female employment, therefore, became one unfinished agenda under the Hawke and Keating governments (Castles 1994: 140; Harbridge and Bagley 2002: 191). For instance, as Figure 5.36 indicates, the ALP government had achieved no clear improvement over unemployment for the vulnerable social category of young females.

New Zealand

The fifth Labour government sent a clear signal in reversing the coercive workfare programs implemented by the previous National and fourth Labour governments. In terms of principle, labor market activation and employment has been at the top of the party's agenda since the fourth Labour government. In terms of policy practice, prior to the Clark government, the primary focus had been on making welfare less attractive, rather than on making work more attractive, and this was a typical neo-liberal workfare orientation endorsed by Anglo-Saxon secular-right parties. Through the Working Towards Employment Bill (later known as the Social Security Amendment Act), the fifth Labour government signaled its intention to reject this neoliberal paradigm. The government removed or

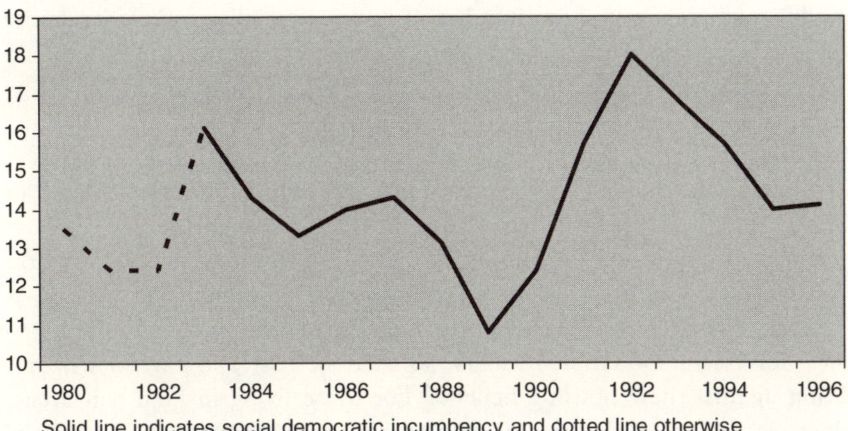

FIGURE 5.36. Unemployment Rate for Females 15–24 Years of Age in Australia 1980–1996 (*Source:* OECD 2007a).

put under review many of the harshest elements of workfare, especially those based on mandatory sanctions, such as compulsory work testing for single parents. Labour also discontinued a mandatory trial of work capacity in the event of sickness, injury, or disability. The community wage scheme, where the unemployed are required to participate in community work for less than the minimum wage, will be superseded by a voluntary scheme, and there are separate benefits reestablished for both the sick and the unemployed. Meanwhile, the government also raised the minimum wage, by 36% between 2000 and 2005 (St. John and Rankin 2002; Mackay 2003: 104–107; McClelland and St. John 2006: 182; Cooper and May 2005: 4).

The fifth Labour government shifted the focus of labor market activation from negative to positive incentives, by increasing the financial returns from work for low income families as well as decreasing the family-related cost for them. This is the biggest item in the government's social security reform, costing $1 billion (NZ) per year, and it is the most significant step in Labour's third way changes so far. It emerged relatively late, in the form of a policy package called "Working for Families," through the 2004 budget statement. The actual full implementation was not to be complete until March 2008. This program is targeted at low- to middle-income families with dependent children (Nolan 2004; Perry 2004).

The government replaced the Child Tax Credit with the In Work Payment, which, while significantly more generous than the previous tax credit, requires a minimum number of hours worked per week (20 hours for single parents and 30 hours for couples). Compared with the Child Tax Credit, working families under the In Work Payment are better off by $45 per week (one child), $35 (two children), or $15 (all other working families). A lower benefit-eligibility income threshold of $20,000 was abolished, and income testing was rationalized to one single level of $27,500, with a benefit clawback rate of 30% above this level. The government also adjusted the Family Tax Credit in favor of people in work, and working families have had a guarantee of minimum net income at $17,000 since 2006. Furthermore, Labour relaxed income-testing criteria for Accommodation Benefits, so that the first $80 earned will not count against these housing benefits. For those living in high-rent areas, the government reduced the means-tested clawback rate and increased the payment rate. At a cost of $31 million, Labour also increased subsidies for child care and relaxed means-testing criteria for these subsidies. For the similar purpose of increasing female labor force participation, legislation for paid parental leave was introduced, available for both the husband and wife. Also on the party's agenda was the issue of pay equity between men and women (St. John and Craig 2004; Curtin and Devere 2006; Spoonley 2004: 12). Under the fifth Labour government, there is now a clear distinction from the Nationals in policy priority, between labor market activation, on the one hand, and downsizing the state, on the other hand. In the 2005 election campaign, while Labour offered further tax credits for working families and interest-free loan for students, the Nationals offered instead blanket tax cuts for all (McClelland and St. John 2006: 182).

While the Working for Families package was innovative in significantly increasing the financial returns for working families, it did not totally break from the institutional reliance on coercion typical of liberal welfare states. Measures in the policy package continued to rely on maintaining and further increasing the income gap between working and nonworking families. This was achieved not only by increasing income for the former group, but also by reducing or removing benefits for the latter, who tend to be at the bottom of the income scale. Among this worst-off group were a large number of single parents. For a single parent to lower the number of hours worked below 20 or stop working, there is the risk of losing both the In Work Payment and the Family Tax Credit. Some 175,000 of the poorest children were in nonworking households facing either an income increase of less than $10 per child per week or simply no increase at all for a three-year period (St. John 2004; St. John and Craig 2004; Porter and Craig 2004).

Analysis of In-Work Incentive Strategies

Similar to ALMPs, policy changes in in-work incentives across the country cases demonstrate the combined influence of power resources and path dependency. On the one hand, social democratic governments took greater initiatives than their center-right counterparts in introducing various in-work incentive schemes; on the other hand, diverse institutional legacies clearly left their imprint on the implementation of these incentive policies.

One of the most prominent examples of in-work incentives is the minimum wage. With the relaxation of traditional wage egalitarianism in the workplace, the rising prominence of the minimum wage reflects the growing prioritarian orientation in social democratic egalitarianism, where a departure from equality can be allowed as long as it results in better protection for the worst-off. In Britain, the minimum wage was formally introduced for the first time under New Labour, whereas it had been increased on a regular basis in Australia under the Hawke and Keating governments throughout the 1980s and early 1990s. Similarly, the indexation of a legal minimum wage to price and wage developments under both the French Socialists and the PvdA has helped prevent individuals from working in abject poverty. Where a minimum wage is absent, high unemployment benefit-replacement rates often serve as a substitute for income redistribution and social protection. High replacement rates can further serve as an instrument of labor market activation, especially when there is at the same time a high degree of flexibility in the labor market and extensive ALMPs available, with the Danish "golden triangle" as an example (Wren 2001: 254).

Another relatively innovative form of financial incentive is the negative income tax (NIT). Theoretically, the NIT promotes work incentives through two methods, either by specifically targeting individuals who meet minimum working conditions or by saving a part of the extra income from deduction once the individuals start to earn more income (Bonoli and Sarfati 2002: 464). Tax credits of this type feature primarily in liberal welfare regimes, due to the institutional predominance in these countries of means-tested benefits and the general reluctance of Anglo-Saxon social democrats to increase direct taxes openly. For New Labour, the ALP, and the fifth Labour government in New Zealand, NITs take up a large portion of new financial incentives to work, in the form of the British Working Families' Tax Credit, the Australian Family Assistance Supplement, and the In Work Payment in New Zealand. Overall, NITs have demonstrated their positive effect on increasing work incentives, especially for low-wage earners. Decline in low wages is compensated through the NIT, which usually has a low withdrawal rate. Therefore, the combined income would be higher than the basic NIT rate (Hanesch 1999: 78–79). By reducing the impact of low wages and increasing wage mobility, the government opens an important channel for activating outsiders: those in a very disadvantaged position with regard to the labor market, such as the long-term unemployed, the disabled, and those with low levels of skill.

Reflecting the growing maturity of NIT practices in liberal welfare regimes, governments in these countries have gradually moved further ahead by integrating different NITs into a coherent package and broadening its overall scope. For example, Australia has seen tax credits catering to families with one earner transformed into common family benefits or tax credits, regardless of work status. New Labour, similarly, has also replaced WFTC with a Working Tax Credit available for all adults (Sinfield 2002: 349–350). Although most intensely used within the liberal welfare circles, tax subsidies have also left a footprint in other social democratic cases. The Employment Premium (PPE) introduced by the French Socialists in 2001, for example, is paid by the tax authorities for those earning less than 140% of the minimum wage.

The popularity of NITs with Anglo-Saxon social democrats is path dependent on the institutional legacy of benefit financing in liberal welfare regimes. The same is true for social security contribution reductions as a form of targeted wage subsidies for the Dutch, French, and, to a lesser extent, German social democrats, simply due to the historically contributory nature of their social security systems. In these countries, the proportion of total labor costs accounted for by the tax wedge has become a crucial contributor to real wage rigidities in the labor market. This was partly a result of collusion between social partners in externalizing the cost of economic adjustment. The contribution rates were by the mid-1990s unacceptably high and left ample space for restructuring. By exempting employers from social security contributions for low-skilled workers, these regressive employment subsidies achieve roughly the same purpose as NITs. They help in reducing the tax wedge, encouraging wage mobility, and activating those traditionally excluded from the labor market because of low skills or reduced work capacity (Ferrera and Hemerijck 2003: 112; Bonoli and Sarfati 2002: 465; Lodovici 2000: 42).

Finally, in-work incentives for women, especially those with child-rearing responsibilities, are more complex, as they include not only in-cash incentives but also in-kind measures to reduce the family-related personal cost of working. For in-cash incentives, an important characteristic in Scandinavian countries has been the large degree of individualization in social and taxation policies. As far as the tax system is concerned, the female labor supply is closely influenced by the unit of calculation for taxation purposes, the distribution of tax allowances for spouses or partners, and the way these allowances alter when the second partner has an income (Kvist 2000: 12; Daly 2000: 495).

Even more significant seems to be the role of in-kind measures, which can reduce the burden for child-rearing for mothers entering employment. In female activation, the unambiguous message is that the wide availability of child-care services is the indispensable contributor, without which both low fertility and low female labor market participation will result. Child-care services can be offered either through the public sector (as in Scandinavian countries) or through low-cost services in the private sector (as in liberal welfare regimes). Regardless of private or public, the provision of in-kind services is positively correlated with female employment rates (Lodovici 2000: 44).

Despite the between-regime difference in emphasis on public versus private child care, social democratic governments across welfare regimes have made efforts to expand public child-care places. This is seen in New Labour, PvdA, and the French Socialists, as well as in the traditional strong performers in Northern Europe. What is more, the experience of disadvantaged families demonstrates clearly the logic of positive externalities from organization, in bypassing the electoral dilemma of the insider–outsider divide. New social risk groups like single parents are archetypical outsiders, who are weakly organized politically across all these countries. However, their social exclusion has been reduced as an indirect result of the better organizational integration of women, within the labor movement in Scandinavia and within the parliamentary party in the UK and the Netherlands. The same logic helps explain the success of labor market flexibility reforms by these governments, to be discussed next.

3. FLEXICURITY

While in-work incentives operate as important supplements to ALMPs, there are other mechanisms serving a similar purpose. These measures again cannot directly create a venue bringing the unemployed and the labor market together. However, they do help to increase the possibility for interaction between the labor market and individuals, especially those who cannot work in normal conditions or on regular schedules. For these atypical workers, their labor market entry is eased by the relaxation of hiring rules. Once they enter the labor market, their job security is protected, and those temporarily excluded from the labor market are also offered protection, through the social security system. Measures serving these purposes can be called labor market flexicurity measures, a combination of flexibility and security (Wilthagen 1998).

As with in-work incentives, flexicurity reforms are not carried out by all countries. Countries that already have very flexible labor markets do not urgently need additional flexibility, and for this reason none of the Anglo-Saxon countries feature in the analysis here. In addition, by the 1980s, both Denmark and Norway also had a labor market that was by no means rigid, due to loose employment protection in the former case and a flexible working-time arrangement in the latter. The main venue of action in flexicurity, therefore, is in continental Europe. The analysis here focuses predominantly on the three conservative welfare states, followed by a brief discussion of the situation in the three Nordic countries.

Compared with ALMPs and in-work incentives, flexicurity reforms offer somewhat stronger evidence for path dependency, and on this policy issue corporatist breakdown was a particularly important contributing factor to path-dependent paralysis. The relaxation of employment protection struck at the heart of continental trade unions, which are largely biased in favor of insiders. On top of this major disincentive to change, the large number of actors involved in this process further creates enormous incentives for shirking and leads to collective action failure. Where a corporatist framework is lacking, social democratic parties struggle to obtain union support for their reforms in order to loosen up the labor market. This, of course, feeds back into and worsens the social democratic electoral dilemma between insiders and outsiders, since preference conflicts between these two groups are more intense in economic institutions with heavier employment protection. In addition, evidence for power resources here is less clear-cut than for ALMPs or in-work incentives, since in continental Europe, parties from both the Left and Right have attempted to reduce labor market rigidity. Still, there is some limited empirical support for the logic of power resources. Compared with social democrats, the Christian Democrats have been more strongly attached to the tradition of employment security and the insider–outsider segmentation it creates. The most successful flexicurity reform so far has been carried out by the PvdA in the Netherlands, who were vitally aided by the corporatist revival through the Wassenaar agreement. In both France and Germany, malfunctioning corporatist institutions have gone hand in hand with limited outcomes in government attempts to reduce labor market rigidity. Table 5.3 summarizes the main policy developments in flexicurity across countries.

TABLE 5.3. *Key Flexicurity Developments, by Country and Theoretical Implications*

Key policies in order of appearance in the chapter	Theoretical Implications	Power Resources	Path Dependency
	Netherlands	Flex Act of 1999	Corporatist cooperation was crucial for reform success
	France	35-hour week	Corporatist cooperation was crucial for reform success
	Germany	Limited change, relied on various work-sharing schemes	Corporatist cooperation was crucial for reform success
	Denmark	Labor market already flexible ("golden triangle")	
	Norway	Labor market already flexible (working-time arrangements)	
	Sweden	Fixed contract (watered down version)	Limited success (union resistance)
	United Kingdom	Labor market already highly flexible	
	Australia	Labor market already highly flexible	
	New Zealand	Labor market already highly flexible	

Note: Countries in shaded areas have no major policy innovation during period under examination and do not feature in the analysis.

The Netherlands

The PvdA did not approach labor market flexibility through straightforward deregulation. Instead, it balanced flexibility with security, in terms of decent employment protection for part-time and temporary workers. Since the flexicurity measures were implemented primarily to activate atypical employment, these measures focused on the legal position of employees with respect to job security, rather than on the after-the-fact provision of passive social security once the workers were easily dismissed from the labor market (Wilthagen 2004: 1). Most of the policy changes aimed at introducing flexicurity resulted from lengthy processes of negotiations among social partners and between them and the government. A crucial reason why unions and employers were willing to embrace the principle of flexicurity was the corporatist foundation laid years ago by the Wassenaar agreement. As we will see shortly, in cases where such corporatist framework declined (such as in Germany and Sweden), collective action failure among social partners indeed left flexibility reforms largely stalled. On the one hand, Wassenaar revitalized and entrenched the Dutch corporatist practice in industrial relations. On the other hand, through repeated interaction in negotiating wage restraints in exchange for working-time flexibility or part-time jobs, both unions and employers came to accept the concept of flexibility as the key to creating more jobs. With the continuing development of flexicurity, the initial Wassenaar settlement of "wage restraint for reducing the working week," was gradually replaced with "wage restraint for part-time work," in a more or less smooth fashion.

The first major move toward flexicurity was the collective agreement for temporary workers signed by unions and employers in 1995. Under this agreement, temporary workers were given the right to continued employment and pension insurance after 24 months. Then, in 1997, the government took on board most of the recommendations emerging from corporatist negotiations between social partners and consolidated these elements into the Flexibility and Security Bill. This bill involved compromise between employers and employees, as well as within unions between insiders with stable jobs and outsiders on the periphery of the job market. Proposals contained in the bill included modifications to the dismissal protection enjoyed by the core labor force, removal of the permit system for temporary work agencies, and a strengthening of the legal position for temporary workers. In 1999, the bill came into force as the Flexibility and Security Act (often known as the Flex Act). The act was the culmination of the PvdA's efforts to introduce flexibility and security into the temporary and part-time segment of the labor market. It represented by far the most comprehensive and faithful application of the principle of flexicurity (Visser and Hemerijck 1997: 44; Hemerijck and Visser 2001: 198–199).

In offering better security, the act clarified whether an employment agreement exists in the case of flexible labor. A temporary work agreement signed with a temporary work agency is now considered an employment agreement, and after six months all regulations regarding an employment agreement fully apply. The extension and eventual conversion of temporary into permanent contracts becomes automatic, and so temporary employees are protected from dismissal unless under very special circumstances. In allowing greater flexibility for employers, the act reduced the trial period in an employment contract from two months to one month in the case of temporary contracts. Issuing a notice for dismissal also becomes easier, as employment duration becomes the only factor determining the term of notice. In addition, procedures are shortened and simplified for employers who need to request permission from the public employment service for dismissal. On the one hand, the act ensured that a worker's legal position becomes stronger the longer he works on a temporary basis; on the other hand, it gave greater flexibility to the use of agency workers (Zwinkels and Peter 2001: 138–140).

Since the PvdA initiated the flexicurity reforms, there has been a massive expansion in the number and variety of flex jobs, many of which are very innovative in design. The typical flex jobs now available include not only temporary agency jobs and part-time work but also on-call work (where workers work only when there is an actual need for additional labor), fixed-term work, and subsidized employment such as the ID jobs ("Inflow and Throughflow" jobs). These ID jobs are based on a permanent contract but with the option of a fixed-term one-year contract for the first year of employment. Since the 1999 Flex Act, there have been an increasing number of job pools, whereby employees are rotated between different tasks depending on the various peaks in production. Or, alternatively, job-pool agencies can take on, for three years, people who have left the local labor market, while supplementary wages during this period are provided by the original employer. Under the slogan "From Job Security Toward Employment Security," trade unions are actively involved in innovative experiments combining different elements of flex jobs. The unions' strategies reflect a considerable degree of forward looking and ready acceptance of the skill-based society. For example, "investments contracts" enforce on both employers and employees the mutual responsibility to invest in education and training. Instead of an employment offer with just one job, employees are offered job opportunities within a certain job domain (Wilthagen 1998: 18–20; Wilthagen 2004: 4–6; Beukema and Valkenburg 1999: 116–117).

However, the activation effectiveness of these employment subsidy measures is uneven. The flow from subsidized to regular jobs decreases as the subsidy period lengthens. There seems to be a lack of either incentives or possibilities to move on once a client is placed in a subsidized job. These measures appear to be least successful with regard to the elderly and those with lower education, and they can potentially even be counterproductive for disabled workers (van Oorschot 2002b: 402–403).

With reforms increasingly oriented toward flexicurity, the main tool of labor market job redistribution has gradually shifted, from across-the-board labor time reduction, as was planned in the original Wassenaar agreement, to more weight being put on part-time work (Hemerijck, Manow, and van Kersbergen 2000: 116–117). Nevertheless, the PvdA still took a series of measures to further relax regulations over working time. In 1996, the government introduced the Law Governing Working Hours, under which a series of important new changes were put in place to facilitate working at irregular hours and to allow for individual variations in the length of the working week. These changes were further consolidated in July 2000, when the government introduced the Law on the Adjustment of Working Time. This new act gave workers who have worked for their current enterprise for one year the right to alter their weekly working hours either upward or downward, and the employer is generally obliged to comply with the request for altering working hours, unless for important business or operational reasons. Since the start of 1998, an average working week of 36 hours has been extensively applied, covering 2.8 million employees (Delsen 2002a: 317; Gorter 2000: 191; Plantenga and Dur 1998: 682; Beukema and Valkenburg 1999: 121).

Most of the flexicurity reforms, as explained earlier, focused on the legal position of atypical workers, but these core measures were also supplemented by improvements in related policy areas, such as wages, training, and parental leave. As part of the omnibus 1999 Flex Act, workers on a fixed-term contract and temporary agency workers have the same entitlement to leave schemes as workers on a permanent contract. Coverage for social insurance, health care, and additional pension schemes is now readily available for part-time workers, and the New Labour Act of 1996 also requested employers to take into consideration the caregiving duties of employees. By 1997, temporary work agencies had provided employment for more than 200,000 person-years (Green-Pedersen, van Kersbergen, and Hemerijck 2001: 317; Wilthagen 2004: 22–23).

With regard to wages, in 1993 the government repealed the "one-third criterion" in minimum wage and minimum holiday entitlement. This old criterion stipulated that employees working less than one-third of full-time hours were not entitled to minimum-wage or holiday payments. All similar exclusionary clauses in collective agreements were removed in 1994. As a result, the legal minimum wage becomes applicable to all employees of working age. In 1996, the entitlement of part-time workers to equal treatment was extended to overtime payments, bonuses, and training, and since the 2000 Working Hours Act, equal treatment of part-time workers has been extended to all areas negotiated by social partners, including not only wages and social security but also holiday pay, subsidized care provision, and second-tier pensions. With the implementation of all these measures, the earnings difference between full-time and part-time jobs has been narrowed to 7%. Then, in

2002 further provision became available for paid care leave and paid adoption leave on a short-term basis (Plantenga and Dur 1998: 682; Visser 2001: 26–28; Ferrera and Hemerijck 2003: 112).

These series of efforts to introduce flexicurity into the Dutch labor market have produced impressive results in terms of job creation, but the limitation of such instruments is also clearly emerging. Under Wim Kok's leadership, the Dutch government was able to reach its target of creating 350,000 new jobs one year ahead of time in 1997. Value added in the total economy grew by 31% between 1987 and 1996 (Visser and Hemerjick 1997: 151; Hemerijck, Unger, and Visser 2000: 229). However, the new jobs created are primarily part-time jobs occupied mostly by women, and what is called the Dutch miracle in reality amounts to an increase of only 10% in total available work. For better or worse, the fundamental nature of the Dutch miracle is the change in the structure, rather than the volume, of Dutch employment. This change in employment structure is in reality a "giant redistribution of work available," (van Orschoot: 2002a: 117), as full-time jobs held by men in manufacturing sectors are replaced by part-time or temporary jobs by women in service sectors. As Figure 5.37 shows, not only part-time work in general, but also part-time work for females and youth all steadily increased their share of total employment since the early 1980s. For this reason, when measured in total work amount per capita, the Netherlands remains close to Germany, despite a now much higher labor force participation rate. Although Dutch employment volume increased by 33% in the sheltered sector, it dropped by 7% in the exposed sector. The

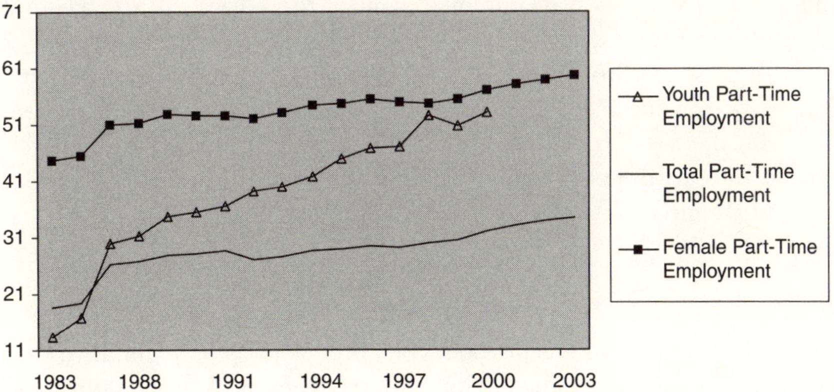

FIGURE 5.37. Part-Time Employment as Percentage of Total Employment in the Netherlands 1983–2003 (*Source:* OECD 2007a).

impressive job growth virtually happened within the low-productivity segment of the labor market. The successes of the Dutch economy since the
early 1990s, therefore, were not based on genuine improvement from the
supply side, and the country's job creation achievements can only be evaluated in relative terms (Goul Andersen and Jensen 2002a: 32–35).

In evaluating the overall performance of Dutch flexicurity reforms, it is
important to consider the advantage of backwardness. For the scope and
speed of changes to labor market regulations, the record had been impressive
after the PvdA came to power in 1989. However, if one considers absolute
levels rather than the extent of change, what the Dutch government achieved
amounted primarily to moving the country up to the European average.
Until 1980, Dutch labor force participation remained the lowest among
OECD countries, and the social security system was firmly grounded on the
breadwinner principle (Huber and Stephens 2001: 285). The Netherlands
now occupies the top position in part-time work, but it was only until the
1980s that it overtook other countries performing strongly in this area,
such as Sweden, Denmark, and the UK. Although it provides above-average
opportunities for flex jobs as a whole, it is still below the European average
on most other criteria of labor market flexibility, such as night, weekend,
and home work or on extra hours. During the 1990s, the scale and speed
of increase in female employment overtook all other European countries,
but these changes were only sufficient to transform the country from a
European laggard to an average performer. In addition, Figure 5.37 has not
distinguished between left and right government periods because, clearly,
the start of the rapid growth in Dutch part-time jobs preceded the PvdA's
policy intervention. The fundamental momentum behind increasing part-
time employment was probably due as much to policies as to behavioral
changes in women, especially later entry by married women into the labor
force. Because of chronic lack of child-care facilities in the country, part-
time work became the dominant coping solution for mothers. Nowhere
else in Europe was female activation so exclusively accounted for by developments in part-time employment in low-skilled service jobs (Daly 2000:
472–483; Hemerijck and Visser 2000: 238; Visser 2002: 24).

France

Under the Jospin government, there was one major policy initiative that
had some effect in increasing flexibility in the labor market: the shortening
of the work week to 35 hours. As an example of explicit state intervention to reduce working hours across industries through direct legislation,

the French 35-hour week became a radical instrument of job creation in Western Europe. Both sides of the social partnership were resolutely opposed to this change, the unions for wage- and work-regulation concerns and the employers for initial fears of excessive rigidity. In order to make the reform palatable to the social partners, the Jospin government took a highly incremental approach in putting the measures in place. After the legislation was unveiled in October 1997, the actual mechanisms for reducing working time were left to the social partners in bargaining agreements at the industry or company level. The government proposed a reduction in the work week from 39 to 35 hours in a gradual manner over a period of time, and this change would be coupled with an annualization of working hours in order to retain a high level of flexibility in working time (Hemerijck and Schludi 2000: 171; Sferza 2002: 142; Freyssinet 1998: 645–652).

To encourage social partners to accept this change, the government partially funded the transition process, offering significant subsidies to companies that signed agreements with unions to reduce time that would result in either creation or preservation of jobs. To be eligible for subsidies, the companies needed only to forgo planned layoffs rather than having to hire new employees (Levy 2000: 339). Overall, implementation of the 35-hour week did not further increase rigidity in the labor market, but instead introduced a considerable amount of flexibility in working patterns. To reassure employers, the government made it clear that the financial costs of transition to the 35-hour week would be shouldered by either the state or employees, but not firms. Based on this premise, the government accompanied working-time changes with new measures to subsidize structural labor costs, especially through social security contribution reductions for employers. These policies further contributed to the reduction of indirect labor costs. To encourage bargaining over the implementation of working-time reduction, the Socialists created a new system of state–company agreements, whereby state aid would be granted to companies that signed an agreement to reduce working time by at least 10%. On the other hand, companies that did not reduce contractual working hours by a certain deadline would have to treat hours worked in excess of 35 as overtime and more expensive (Barbier 2001: 14; Schröter 2004: 21; Clift 2001: 177). This particular success in increasing labor market flexibility, however, turned out to be the exception rather than the norm. The government's other attempts at labor market regulatory reforms were marred by failure due to resistance from the labor movement.

The historical legacy of statism posed further difficulties for flexicurity measures. With the persistent emphasis on the role of the state, French activation policy was pushed forward in a contradictory and not wholly efficient manner. Flexibility in labor market regulation, the obligation to participate, or anything else that emphasized the obligation of the unemployed at the expense of their rights were rejected for resembling American workfare. While there were indirect attempts to dismantle existing employment protection or weaken Bismarckian contributory mechanisms, the extent of the change was limited because the government was ultimately held socially responsible for protecting workers' welfare. As a result, despite some isolated cases of flexibilization, such as the easing of fixed-term contract termination rules or tax breaks for part-time contracts, the French labor market today remains highly regulated (Barbier and Théret 2003: 155; Merkel 2001: 70). In fact, as Figure 5.38 shows, labor market protection for regular employment in the core sector further intensified after the late 1990s, worsening the insider–outsider divide.

Germany

To increase the flexibility of labor contracts, the Schröder government made it legal, after January 2001, for employees to transform their full-time jobs into part-time ones without the approval of their employers. This change implemented European directives on part-time work and short-term employment contracts. The de facto creation of a legal right to part-time employment

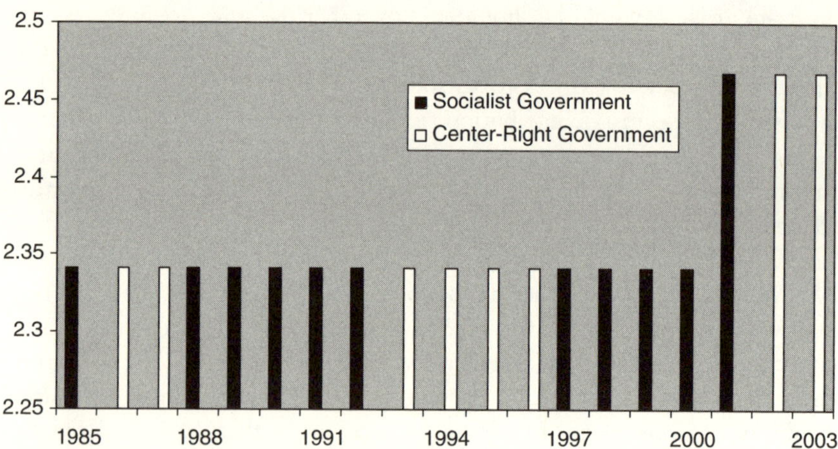

FIGURE 5.38. Protection for Regular Employment in France 1985–2003 (*Source: OECD 2004[1]*).

1 Data from OECD Employment Outlook (2004). Coded between 0 and 5, higher values of the indicator reflect more strict employment protection. The same applies to Figure 5.39.

reflects the determination of the government to intervene in the domain of wage contracts, where the principle of *Tarifautonomie* still dominates. Emulating the Danish leave schemes, the SPD introduced a job rotation scheme in 2001, by which the unemployed temporarily replace existing workers who use the time to participate in job-training or education programs (Vail 2002: 15–16; Vail 2003: 52). However, beyond these measures, the social democrats had failed to significantly change the labor market rigidity situation in the country. In fact, Figure 5.39 shows that the relaxation in overall employment protection in Germany after the late 1990s was a combination of a *further increase* in protection for the core regular employment sector and a *sharp decline* in protection for the vulnerable temporary employment sector. This, obviously, has done nothing but further intensify the already serious insider–outsider divide problems in German labor markets.

For countries that lack a tradition in corporatist accommodation between social partners and the government, it is difficult to produce trade-offs and compromises that can help all sides reach agreements on labor market flexibility arrangements. The ability to produce the necessary trade-offs appears to correlate with the strength of corporatist institutions or other similar consensual practices by social partners. In this regard, it was not very surprising that when the European Commission introduced the 1997 Green Paper proposing the balance between security and flexibility, there was a favorable response from the unions in Finland, but in Germany and France the union response was much more negative (Wilthagen 2003: 25). Similar to the experience of the French Socialists, union resistance in Germany not only played a role in the Schröder government's limited

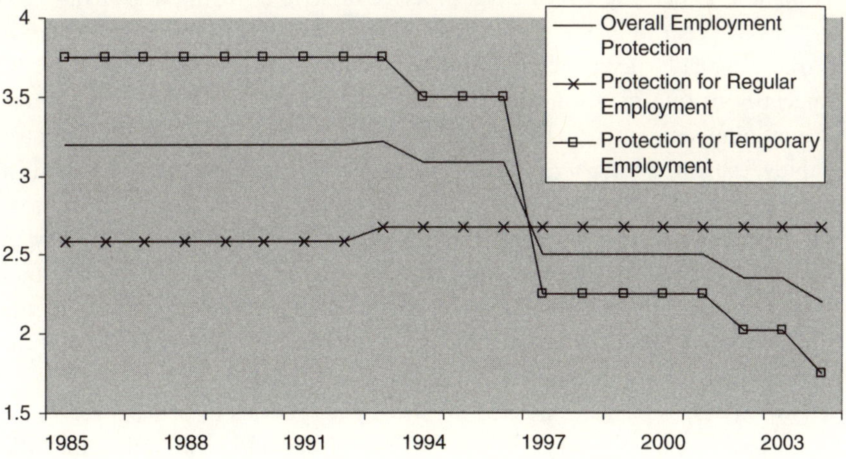

FIGURE 5.39. Employment Protection in Germany 1985–2004 (*Source:* OECD 2004).

success in labor market flexibility, but it also forced the government to further intensify job security for the core labor force, which in turn worsened overall rigidity in the labor market. Under the SPD, dismissal protection, which had previously been relaxed by the center-right coalition, was restored for companies engaging six to ten employees (Leibfried and Obinger 2003: 212). Overall, under the Red-Green coalition there had been limited progress in deregulating the labor market and introducing more flexibility. The government relied primarily on designing different ways of work sharing as its main instrument for combating rigidities in the labor market and promoting employment. Employers were encouraged to reduce working hours in exchange for greater flexibility in working practices. But on employment protection, the social democrats did not make any effort to ease the mechanism of hiring and firing (Hall 2002: 48–49).

Denmark and Norway

In addition to ALMPs, the success of Danish activation reforms since the early 1990s has been closely related to the traditional combination in Danish social and labor market policy arrangements known as the "golden triangle." The three main components of the golden triangle are flexibility, social security, and active labor market measures. The Danish employment system, therefore, is a kind of hybrid institution, with a high level of job mobility similar to that in Anglo-Saxon countries, but with a generous unemployment benefit system and well-established ALMPs similar to those in other Nordic welfare states (Madsen 2002: 245; Madsen 2004: 189). In its attempt to increase job security for workers, the social democratic government shunned the continental practice of stricter hiring and firing procedures, for fear of eroding the existing flexibility and mobility of the labor market. Instead, the government turned its attention to expanding ALMPs, especially in qualification and training schemes, as the alternative source of employment security. This type of job security is more sustainable for employees from a long-term perspective because of the productivity gains it involves (Larsen and Bredgaard: 2004: 9). In addition to flexibility in moving in and out of employment, there is also a high degree of flexibility in transiting between part-time and full-time jobs, made possible by the fact that part-time work is regulated by the same legal and collective rule as full-time work (Madsen 1998: 699). For this reason, there is little need for further flexicurity innovations in the Danish third way.

Norway faces a similar situation. During its periods in office after 1990, Labor had made only very limited efforts to bring more flexibility into the labor market. The government's most significant change in this area was the introduction in 2000 of the right to a temporary leave for up to three years for the purpose of pursuing education. At the same time, the government also encouraged the use of time accounts. However, under Labor there was no attempt to liberalize the labor law or to make it easier to sign fixed contracts, and there was no relaxation in employment protection legislation (Halvorsen 2002: 170–172). To comprehend the limited extent of reform by Labor, it is important to consider that there was traditionally a high level of flexibility in the Norwegian labor market. The already prevalent existence of part-time work, flexible working-hour arrangements, and leave schemes, plus an internationally very high degree of labor mobility (close to that in the United States and Canada), have together canceled out any serious rigidity problems that the high degree of employee security may have caused (Dolvik et al. 1997: 59, 69–71). Similar to the limited ALMP reforms by the Swedish social democrats, Labor's inaction in flexibility reforms can be accounted for by the presence of a more or less satisfactory status quo.

Sweden

By the mid-1990s, the traditional corporatist practice in Sweden had ceased to function very effectively, after the unilateral withdrawal of the employers' organization from centralized bargaining, as well as from all state agencies. After substantial decentralization in bargaining, there was no longer any strong coordination of negotiating strategies on either side of the social partnership. The incapability of the social partners to reach consensual decisions based on compromises or trade-offs was further aggravated by a strong union influence within the social democratic party. There was, in other words, very little immediate pressure on the unions to avoid direct confrontation with the government, and union opposition to changes they did not approve of tended to be very uncompromising. A typical example here is the social democrats' prolonged attempt to relax employment rights in order to create the possibility for more job creation, which was a continuation of policy strategies from the previous bourgeois government. After the social democrats proposed in 1995 a revision of the rules on employment rights, the relationship between the party and the unions deteriorated seriously. The LO staged mass campaigns in an attempt to influence public opinion against the party. In the end, not only were there significant defections within the party toward the unions, but the unions also managed to ally with the Left Party in opposition to the changes. What finally passed in parliament was a compromise solution, whereby for each employer a maximum of five individuals could be hired on a fixed contract for up to a year, by the end of which the employment could either be terminated or renewed into a permanent contract (A. Gould 2001: 150–151). In addition, in 1995 the social democratic government also abolished both of the two measures introduced by the previous bourgeois parties aimed at relaxing rules for layoffs and probationary periods of hiring (Bjorklund 2000: 157).

These developments show that, at least in the short-term future, the social democrats have become either reluctant or simply powerless to put through any changes that can be interpreted as threatening job security for workers. Even on a European level, the Swedish social democrats have taken the somewhat unusual stance of criticizing the idea of a flexible workforce by arguing that it involves less job security (Hort 2001: 261). A similar situation can be seen with regard to the party's approach to flexible working time. When the social democrats set up a commission to investigate an increase in flexibility in working time, there were serious divisions within both the party and the unions, and the final recommendation of the commission was very mild; the existing work week of 40 hours was kept, but a degree of flexibility in its application was allowed. There were, furthermore, strong disagreements between the unions and employers about the implementation and interpretation of the commission recommendations, with employers always expecting more flexibility and unions fearing a loss of control over working time. Few unions had managed to negotiate an agreement with the employers on this issue. The inability of the two sides to reconcile forced the social democrats to postpone legislation over this issue, as well as several other measures aimed at increasing labor market flexibility (A. Gould 2001: 152–153).

Analysis of Flexicurity Strategies

Reflecting institutional path dependency, there is clear variation in the outcomes of social democratic flexicurity reforms across cases. Whereas Denmark and the Netherlands clearly went down the road of flexibilization, similar reforms in Germany, France, and Sweden had largely stalled. The consequence of stalled reform was less serious for Sweden, given its relatively flexible labor market to start with, but for the other two countries it was a major setback, further contributing to the already serious insider–outsider problems in these economies. Here, the one particularly important factor in contributing to path dependency was collective action failure by social partners due to corporatist problems, which is relevant to all the three countries with limited policy outcomes. In addition, flexibility reforms are more effective when combined with stronger employment protection for temporary workers, plus increased social protection in general. Therefore, it is no wonder that the two most successful cases of reforms occur where the integration between flexibility and security is most tight, seen in the golden triangle of Denmark and the flexicurity reforms in the Netherlands. In most other instances, the combination of flexibility and security still tends to be underdeveloped, as one of the two dimensions tends to dominate the other. For example, whereas Anglo-Saxon countries have flexible employment-protection rules but ungenerous unemployment protection, Germany has generous unemployment compensation but strict employment protection. Compromises and trade-offs across policy domains constitute an important condition for smoothing the process of negotiations in flexicurity reforms. For example, reducing working time without cutting wages is harder for employers to accept than measures that blend working-time reduction with policies enhancing business competitiveness, such as firm-level work-sharing arrangements and leave schemes (Compston 1997: 204).

Most of the action will be within the company when it comes to implementing flexicurity measures. For this reason, decentralization and devolution of policy responsibilities to the region or local level can also enhance the effectiveness of flexicurity reforms, as long as there is at the same time strong coordination at the central level. In this sense, the two top-performing cases of the Netherlands and Denmark are also where there has been a consistent and mature development toward "centralized decentralization" in collective bargaining in recent years. By contrast, the less satisfactory progress toward flexicurity in Germany is partly related to the lack of central coordination in negotiations, which is itself a legacy of the strong *Tarifautonomie* principle. In addition, the Dutch and Danish cases also demonstrate that by broadening the agenda for flexicurity negotiations, it becomes easier to reach agreements, based on a wider range of trade-offs and compromises for both sides of the social partnership (Wilthagen and Tros 2003: 29–31).

Social democratic governments attempted to introduce greater labor market flexibility in order to promote employment. Nevertheless, the direct effect of flexibility is more on the structure than on the total level of unemployment because labor market rigidities, such as strict employment protection, serve mainly to create an insider–outsider divide in terms of differential employment access for different job applicants. In this sense, in the long run greater flexibility is an effective strategy in reducing *long-term* unemployment, but only indirectly so, by altering the structure of the labor market (Goul Andersen and Jensen 2002a: 40; Goul Andersen and Jensen 2002b: 85).

In addition, employment protection only starts to have a significant effect on employment structure at very high levels of protection, for example, in Southern Europe. By contrast, in both Norway and Sweden, nominally strict employment protection has not led to a severe insider–outsider divide. For both countries, job security can be negotiated on an individual basis on the company level, and the actual extent of flexibility in employment protection is quite high. Over the two decades between 1980 and 2000, the average ratio between adult and youth unemployment, as an indicator of the insider–outsider divide, is, respectively, 2.62 and 4.00 for France and Germany. By contrast, for Sweden and Norway it is only 1.79 and 1.36, not very different from the liberal market economies of the United States (1.50) and UK (1.86) (OECD 2005b). The relatively good employment performance of the Nordic labor markets since the mid-1990s indicates that combining a strong work line with generous social security is an effective alternative, to both the classic flexicurity approach in the Netherlands and the low-wage deregulatory approach in liberal welfare regimes (Clasen and van Oorschot 2002a: 236).

On a more general level, flexibility is more regulatory reform than simply deregulation. While rules for hiring temporary workers or people with reduced work capacity were relaxed, rules for retaining them (in other words, regulation for their job security) have been correspondingly tightened (Regini 2000: 14). The increasingly common strategy of regulatory reform seems to be partial deregulation targeted primarily at outsiders while leaving the core workforce intact. By sparing insiders from most of the changes, this approach is helpful in encouraging cooperation from unions. By targeting outsiders for the reforms, this strategy is highly efficient because, as discussed earlier, labor market rigidities primarily affect the structure of employment and perpetuate the insider–outsider divide, reflected in inferior job access for outsiders. In other words, the very groups most likely to be affected by labor market rigidities are the reforms' target groups: youths, women, low-skilled, and various other new social risk categories. Flexibilization can also be more effective if the decline in wage and job security is coupled with some subsidization, especially for training and education. This way, there remains a good chance for the loosely attached to ultimately migrate into the core labor force. Fundamentally, it is difficult to find a long-term solution to unemployment in a low-skill equilibrium, unless at the cost of considerable income inequality, as is the case in the United States (Esping-Andersen and Regini 2000a: 6; Esping-Andersen and Regini 2000b: 337–340).

4. ANALYSIS OF ACTIVE PROTECTION

Active social protection, especially the expansion of ALMPs, is the most important component of the third way policy paradigm. By activating the unemployed and preventing labor market exclusion, it directly reflects the fundamental third way ideology of productivist solidarity and prioritarian egalitarianism. The doctrine of hard work is nothing new, as laissez-faire liberals have traditionally embraced this principle in their advocacy of a less interventionist government. In other words, moving people from welfare to work can be compatible with cost cutting and state downsizing, if it relies on eliminating benefits and forcing people to work. However, activation can also be enabling, through human capital investment, job search help, and in-cash or in-kind incentives for working. Rather than cost retrenchment, these enabling measures all require further and long-term expansion in public investment. This clear prioritization of collective resource mobilization in delivering social justice is a principle that one cannot identify with either the secular or religious Right, and this is the fundamental reason why the third way continues to be social democratic at its core. On this basis, empirically, public expenditure on active labor market policies should be a distinct feature strongly associated with social democratic incumbency.

Because of their employment-centered orientation, third way reforms constitute a highly effective strategy for achieving productivist solidarity and prioritarian egalitarianism. However, this heavy reliance on employment also brings important challenges to the successful implementation of third way reforms. Not all of the unemployed are equally easy to activate by means of enabling measures. Some vulnerable social categories, such as the low-skilled, single mothers, and disabled, or those who cannot work full time, are more costly and difficult to activate. These also happen to be groups with weak political representation within the labor movement. To the extent that these new social risk groups most need solidarity and prioritarian help, if core blue-collar workers prevent social democracy from extending activation resources to them, then the third way reform will have failed to live up to its principles. If, as David Rueda (2007) points out, the insider–outsider divide is indeed a problem intrinsic to social democracy, then this would impose the ultimate limitation on the value of third way reforms.

However, as the various country cases in this chapter have shown, it is possible for social democracy to overcome this problem. The stronger the labor movement, the broader its organizational capacity, and the more likely for outsiders to be in. For example, where women and the unemployed become organizationally integrated (such as in Scandinavia), social democratic governments invest strongly in measures like training and flexible labor markets. Due to overlapping preferences, these are benefits that spill over to even those who still cannot organize, such as the low-skilled or single mothers. Based on the same logic, the political influence of feminists within British and Dutch social democratic parties all led to policies whose benefits flow to marginal groups, such as low-income families or part-time workers, male or female. Of course, the positive externalities of organization only provide the *possibilities* for bridging the insider–outsider divide. Where organizational encompassment is weak (such as in Germany), activation has failed to reach most outsiders. As we will see in the next chapter, passive protection, such as means-tested minimum income replacement, can also help the outsiders, but since the root problem of new social risks is labor market exclusion, it is active protection that will make the fundamental difference in solving this problem.

Therefore, while it is vital to establish the empirical association between social democracy and public expenditure on ALMPs, it is equally important to evaluate, within the same analytical framework, whether social democracy is empirically associated with measures that worsen the insider–outsider divide. Here I focus on two such measures: employment protection and social security contribution/payroll taxes. The former measure increases firing (and hence hiring) costs, and the latter increases non-wage labor costs, all of which diminish labor market entry opportunities from the lower end, where marginal and atypical workers are concentrated. Furthermore, the reduction of the former (flexicurity) and the latter (in-work incentives) happens to represent the two key supplementary active protection methods besides ALMPs. Case materials in this chapter offer no clear evidence for a straightforward association between social democracy and divide-deepening measures. Instead, given its social and religious origins, Christian democracy is more likely to be behind these policies. As discussed in Chapter 2, large and concentrated landownership, characterizing Catholic strongholds, helped retain a feudalist social structure, leading to a strong preference for the preservation of existing social status, based on the accumulation of an uninterrupted employment career. Both strict employment protection and contribution-based social security help perpetuate such uninterrupted career accumulation. The priority of God's natural communities further increases the Christian democratic reluctance to ease employment access for women by relaxing employment protection.

In short, here I try to establish the empirical association between social democracy and ALMPs, and the absence of such association with either employment protection or payroll taxes, which, instead, should be identified with Christian democracy. These are questions that reveal the relationship among social democracy, activation, and the insider–outsider divide on a fundamental level. Therefore, I examine these issues through a pooled time-series analysis, which, with data availability for all control variables considered, covers seventeen OECD countries, starting from 1980 (for ALMP and employment protection) and 1961 (for payroll taxes).[2] This quantitative analysis is based on Huo, Nelson, and Stephens (2008). The variable for ALMP is measured as expenditure on active measures as percentage of GDP, divided by the unemployment rate. Employment protection legislation is a composite score that measures the notice period required before layoffs occur, the right to and level of severance pay, fines suffered by companies that lay off older workers, restrictions on fixed-term contracts, and the ability of temporary work agencies to operate.[3] The variable for payroll taxes is payroll and social security taxes as a percentage of GDP.[4]

The independent variables included in the analysis are two partisanship variables and a set of economic, demographic, and political control variables taken from Huber and Stephens (2000, 2001, 2006). The partisan variables measure the cumulative percentage of cabinet seats that the Left and Christian democratic parties have held in the governing coalition since 1946.[5] The economic variables are GDP per capita, inflation, military spending, foreign direct investment, trade openness, and unemployment. The measurement for all these variables is straightforward and follows the standard formulas. GDP is the total volume of goods and services produced by national residents measured in current U.S. dollars per capita. Inflation is measured with the consumer price index. Military spending is expenditure on military goods and services as a percentage of GDP. Foreign direct investment is a measure of the investment made by an individual or company in the country in question in the productive capacity of another country as percentage of GDP. The variable measures outflows of foreign direct investment. Trade openness is the total volume of imports and exports as

---

[2] These countries are: Australia, Austria, Belgium, Canada, Denmark, Finland, France, Germany, Italy, Ireland, Japan, Netherlands, Norway, Sweden, Switzerland, the United Kingdom, and the United States.

[3] Additional information on coding can be found in OECD (2004), Table 2.A1.2.

[4] Data based on Huber et al. (2004a), with original data from OECD.

[5] For the variable on left cabinet seats, it is scored 1 for each year when the Left is in government alone, scored as the fraction of the Left's seats in parliament of all government parties' seats for coalition governments, cumulated from 1946 to date. The variable for religious parties' government share is coded in the same procedure as for left parties.

percentage of GDP. Unemployment is percentage of the labor force that is unemployed according to the OECD standardized unemployment rate.[6]

The final group of variables includes constitutional structure, women's mobilization, percent aged, voter turnout, strikes, and authoritarian legacy. Constitutional structure is an additive index of federalism, presidentialism, bicameralism, and the use of popular referenda as a normal component of the political process.[7] Women's mobilization measures the propensity for women to join (nonreligious) organizations, with values estimated by women's organization regressed on percentage of seats in parliament held by women and the electoral system (proportional representation [PR] or single-member district).[8] Percent aged is the percentage of population 65 years of age and older. Voter turnout is the percentage of the electorate that voted in the most recent national election. The variable for strikes is the number of working days lost per 1,000 workers. Finally, the measure of authoritarian legacy is the nature of the political regime in 1900, coded according to Rueschemeyer, Stephens, and Stephens (1992).[9] As noted, the controls are a standard set that Huber and Stephens (2001, 2006) adopt to operationalize extant theories of welfare state development. Since they serve as controls to assure that the findings for the two partisanship variables are not the result of omitted variable bias, I do not discuss the hypotheses underlying their inclusion, and thus I employ two-tailed (nondirectional) significance tests for the controls.

Hicks (1994: 172) notes that "errors for regression equations estimated from pooled data using OLS [ordinary least squares regression] procedures tend to be (1) temporally autoregressive, (2) cross-sectionally heteroskedastic, and (3) cross-sectionally correlated as well as (4) conceal unit and period effects and (5) reflect some causal heterogeneity across space, time, or both." I follow Beck and Katz's (1995) recommended procedure, using panel-corrected standard errors, corrections for first-order auto-regressiveness, and imposition of a common rho for all cross sections. Since

---

[6] Data for all these six control variables are from Huber et al. (2004a). For foreign direct investment, original data are from Swank (see Swank 2002), originally coded from *IMF, Balance of Payments Statistics*, various years. Data for 1960–1961 are coded by John D. Stephens and Evelyn Huber from the same source.

[7] Data from Huber et al. (2004a). The precise construction of the additive index is discussed in Huber and Stephens (2001), pp. 55–56.

[8] Data from Huber et al. (2004b). The precise construction of the women's mobilization variable can be found at Huber et al. (2004b, 2006).

[9] Variables for constitutional structure, percent aged, voter turnout, strikes, and authoritarian legacy are based on Huber et al. (2004a), with original data for percent aged from OECD.

there is some trend in the data, I do not include a lagged dependent variable as recommended by Beck and Katz (1996) because in this situation, the lagged dependent variable inappropriately suppresses the power of other independent variables, as Achen (2000) has shown.[10] Beck and Katz (2004: 16–17) have shown that correcting for first-order auto-regressiveness actually does include a lagged dependent variable on the right-hand side of the equation (known as Prais-Winsten estimations). Thus, it does deal with the problem of serial correlation but without suppressing the power of other independent variables.

Beck and Katz (1996) and others have argued for the inclusion of country dummies in order to deal with omitted variable bias. However, Plümper, Troeger, and Manow (2005: 330–334), in their recent treatment of this issue, have countered that this procedure (1) eliminates any variation in the dependent variable that is due to time invariant factors, such as difference in constitutional structures; (2) greatly reduces the coefficients of factors that vary mainly between countries; (3) eliminates any differences in the dependent variable due to differences at t1 in the time series; and (4) "*completely absorb*[s] differences in the level of the independent variables across the units" (p. 331, emphasis in the original). Elaborating on this last point, they argue that if the level of the independent variable has an effect on the level of the dependent variable (e.g., partisan incumbency and ALMP expenditure), "a fixed effects specification is not the model at hand. If a theory predicts level effects, one should not include unit dummies. In these cases, allowing for a mild bias resulting from omitted variables is less harmful than running a fixed effects specification" (p. 334). For this reason, fixed effects estimation or the inclusion of country dummies is not appropriate for the analysis here.

To check results for robustness, all three dependent variables were reestimated with OLS estimation of the regression coefficients, which provides consistent estimates of the regression coefficients, and *robust-cluster* estimators of the standard errors. The robust-cluster variance estimator is a variant of the Huber-White robust estimator that remains valid (providing correct coverage) in the presence of *any* pattern of correlations among errors *within* units, including serial correlation and correlation due to unit-specific components (Rogers 1993). Thus, the robust-cluster standard errors are unaffected by the presence of unmeasured stable country-specific factors

---

[10] In these data, the lagged dependent variable explains 98% of the variation in the dependent variable.

TABLE 5.4. *Prais-Winsten Estimates of ALMP Expenditure, Employment Protection, and Social Security/Payroll Taxes*

	ALMP Expenditure	Employment Protection	Social Security/ Payroll Taxes
Left cabinet	.010**	.014	−.004
Christian democratic cabinet	.000	.040***	.324***
Constitutional structure	−.016	−.153*	−.084
Women's mobilization	−.006	.004	.071
% Aged	−.029**	.029	.1.007***
Voter turnout	−.003	.017*	−.086*
Strikes	−.022	−.378	−1.889
Authoritarian legacy	.037*	−.055	−.605
GDP per capita (1,000s)	.011**	−.072***	−.079
Consumer price index	−.020	−.083	.381*
Military spending	.011	−.066	.121
Foreign direct investment	.003	−.003	.013
Trade openness	.000	−.007***	−.005
Unemployment		−.034**	.101**
Constant	.553*	2.835*	0.830
Common Rho	.86	.90	.94
R-square	.18	.67	.18
N	304	254	653

Note: Level of significance: *** = .001, ** = .01, * = .05 (two-tailed test, except for partisanship variable)

causing correlation among errors of observations for the same country, or, for that matter, any other form of within-unit error correlation. The robust-cluster estimator requires errors to be uncorrelated *between* clusters. The latter assumption might be violated if unmeasured factors affect the dependent variable in all units at the same point in time. Global economic fluctuations could produce such contemporaneous effects. To evaluate the potential impact of such unmeasured period-specific factors, the models were reestimated with indicator variables for the oil crisis period (1974–1979), the 1980s, and the 1990s; the baseline category corresponds to the Golden Age of postwar capitalism (1961–1973). None of the three indicators reached significance in any of the models, suggesting that period-specific effects are not present. The robust cluster OLS estimations were substantially the same as the Prais-Winsten estimations.

Estimation outputs are in Table 5.4. As hypothesized, social democratic incumbency is positively related to active labor market policy expenditure, and it is not related to either social security/payroll taxes or employment protection, which, instead, are strongly associated with Christian democracy. In other words, active protection based on public investment, rather than cost cutting, is indeed the fundamental principle with which third way social democracy strongly identifies. Although there might be instances where social democratic governments clearly failed to address the insider–outsider divide (such as in France and Germany), case materials in this chapter have shown that it is not a situation intrinsic to social democracy. This conclusion is corroborated here by the quantitative analysis. Policies that cement the status of insiders (and hence further diminish the access of outsiders), such as employment protection and payroll taxes, emerge as unambiguous hallmarks of Christian democracy. Therefore, to counter the Rueda thesis, if there has to be an identifiable sociopolitical basis for the insider–outsider divide and the limits it imposes on third way reforms, it will be Christian democracy and the conservative welfare state institutions it helped to perpetuate.

6

Restructuring Passive Protection

This chapter turns the focus from the active to the passive side of social protection. While active protection enhances the possibility of labor market integration, passive protection can potentially facilitate exclusion from the labor market. Compared with the active side, the partisan difference in passive protection reforms is noticeably smaller. The fundamental reason behind this narrower partisan difference is precisely the passive nature of these measures. On an ideological level, massive labor market exclusion goes against not only the third way principle of productivist solidarity and prioritarian egalitarianism but also the secular-right advocacy of social Darwinism through hard work and competition. On a policy level, low labor force participation was the key factor contributing to the fiscal crisis of social security across all welfare state types. Fiscal pressure on social security was especially serious where ideological sympathy for labor market detachment has traditionally been strong: Christian democratic welfare states. In short, no OECD government can afford not to make some changes to passive protection. The attempt to restructure, or worse, retrench, was almost universal across partisan colors.

Therefore, as evidence for power resources, partisan difference in passive protection was not nearly as drastic as in active protection. Having clarified this overall pattern, it is nevertheless still possible to notice some contrasts between social democracy and the center Right in how they approach passive social reforms. Again, while the center-right strategy is more or less divided between secular-right cost cutting and Christian democratic inaction, the social democratic strategy is action, but without exclusive emphasis on cost cutting. The main agenda for social democratic reforms is more restructuring than retrenchment. In reforming passive protection, the logic of path dependency receives strong empirical support. The constraint of

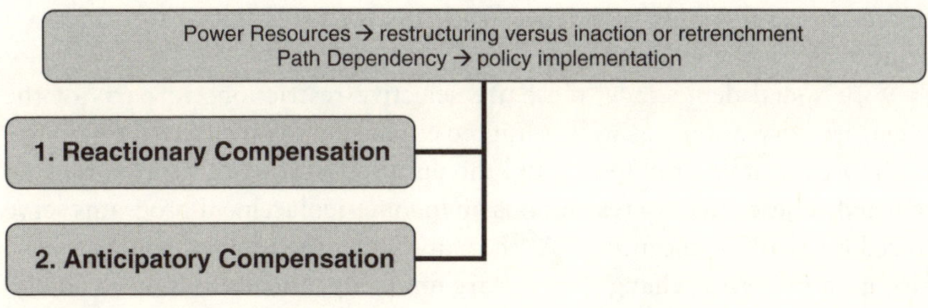

FIGURE 6.1. Overall Organization for Chapter 6

historical welfare institutions, sometimes confounded by collective action failure from social partners, limits the extent of reforms. The role of social partners (and corporatism) is often important for changes in early exit pathways, such as disability or early retirement benefits, especially in continental welfare states. Here, not only do the changes involve direct removal (more than just restructuring) of preexisting benefits, but social partners also collude in using these measures to externalize the cost of economic adjustment.

Just like active protection, it is possible to break passive protection down into subcomponents: reactionary and anticipatory income compensation. The former includes all benefits that are delivered after the individual in question is already ejected from the labor market, and serves purely as compensation for income lost, fait accompli. The latter is anticipatory, in the sense that it actually has the potential to take individuals who are still in the labor market out of it, by offering them benefits. As Figure 6.1 shows, this chapter is organized around these two distinct policy themes.

1. REACTIONARY COMPENSATION

The most important example of reactionary compensation is unemployment benefits. Loss of employment precedes this type of income replacement, and the benefits, are in this sense, reactionary rather than anticipatory. Reactionary compensation helps prevent social misery in the event of work termination. However, perpetuation of such benefits can reduce the incentives to work and, in turn, perpetuate the status of exclusion from the labor market. For this reason, social democratic governments have, in general, not stayed inactive with regard to these passive measures. However, their main reform agenda is not radical dismantling for cost saving but, instead, restructuring not only to remove work disincentives but also to increase protection for the worst-off.

With social democracy, there are selective restrictions to parts of the social security system, as well as limited expansion to other parts. Eligibility is almost inevitably tightened, and the duration or level of benefits is often reduced. These selective restrictions on income-replacement programs serve to reduce work disincentives. At the same time, the social democrats have also used targeting, changes in welfare financing, and various other adjustments to further increase a basic level of protection for the most needy. Reflecting the growing prioritarian emphasis in third way egalitarianism, better protection for the worst-off in income-transfer programs compensates for the overall restriction in social security generosity.

Unlike their Christian democratic counterparts, social democratic parties do not remain ideologically attached to the labor-market-exit potential of income-replacement programs. Unlike the secular Right, they have no plan to drastically retrench these programs to cut costs. The logic of power resources is reflected in the distinctive association of social democratic incumbency with a passive protection paradigm focused on restructuring benefits. The paradigm's actual implementation also displays clear evidence for path dependency on given welfare institutional constraints. Benefit restructuring follows distinct patterns across three welfare state regimes. Scandinavian social democrats favored the tying of benefits to the acceptance of job and training offers, Anglo-Saxon governments manipulated means-testing instruments, and their continental counterparts have kept the insider-biased social insurance component almost intact, while supplementing it with a tax-funded minimum tier. Furthermore, in some cases, lack of corporatist cooperation further reduced the room for reform, and contributed to the path-dependent reinforcement of traditional policy institutions. Table 6.1 provides the key policy details for each country and their theoretical implications.

Denmark

Before the social democrats returned to power in 1993, the Danish unemployment benefit system had been not only passive rather than active in nature but also extremely generous, embodying a culmination of the social rights notion of citizenship. Access to full benefits, for example, was available for the unemployed for more than nine years. The labor market reform launched in 1994 signaled the first major attempt to change the main functions of Danish social security. Targeted specifically at recipients of

TABLE 6.1. *Key Reforms in Reactionary Income Compensation, by Country and Theoretical Implications*

Key policies in order of appearance in the chapter	Theoretical Implications	⇒ Power Resources	Path Dependency
	Denmark	Significant reduction in benefit duration; high benefit level maintained	Nordic→ emphasis on restricting duration, not level, of benefits; restructuring of benefits closely integrated with more enabling measures from the active side
	Sweden	Eligibility rules tightened; high benefit level maintained	
	Norway	Social Services Act; benefits tied to acceptance of activation offers	
	Netherlands	From "price" to "volume"	Continental → growing segmentation in welfare arrangements for social insurance versus assistance recipients
	France	RMI, financed by a new General Social Contribution	
	Germany	Hartz I-IV	
	United Kingdom	Fiscal welfare to combat social exclusion and child poverty	Anglo-Saxon → emphasis on tightening or relaxing means testing
	Australia	Means testing from above; social wage increased persistently	
	New Zealand	Indirect restructuring of passive benefits through the tax system	

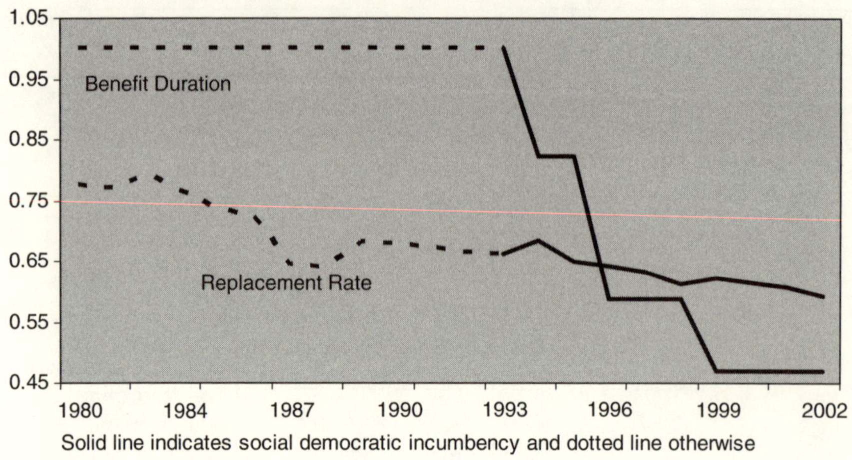

FIGURE 6.2. Unemployment Benefits Replacement Rate and Duration in Denmark 1980–2002 (*Source:* Scruggs 2004; benefit duration in 1980 [442 weeks] re-coded as "1").

unemployment benefits, the reform was carried out in three phases in 1994, 1996, and 1999, respectively. Throughout the three phases of the reform, its most conspicuous character was a growing emphasis on the obligation to accept job offers in return for the continuation of unemployment benefits. Each phase represented a further expansion in the number and type of unemployed persons to be involved in the changes. As Figure 6.2 shows, instead of sharply reducing the actual level of benefits (as was the practice under the bourgeois government) or creating a low-wage labor market, the social democrats followed the example of their Swedish counterparts, by focusing on shortening benefit duration, supplemented with strengthening demands on job search (Dahl et al. 2002: 34; Lind 2000: 145).

While the Danish unemployment benefit system had previously been characterized by very generous replacement rates and extremely long duration, the social democratic reforms drew Denmark closer to, but still above, the European average (Madsen 2003: 76). On the one hand, as a Ghent system, unemployment funds are tied to unions, which retain significant control over the management of these funds. On the other hand, the fact that the pre-reform Danish social security system was already close to being purely tax-financed reduced the opportunities for unions to make proprietary claims on the social security system. Corporatist cooperation from social partners was therefore also less relevant in preventing collective action failure and delivering reforms in this area. This forms a contrast with insurance-dominated social security systems and their comparatively more difficult process of reforming income-replacement programs, for example, in continental welfare regimes (Goul Andersen 2002a: 156; Goul Andersen and Jensen 2002b: 284; Kvist 2000: 32).

Under the social democratic governments, the duration of unemployment benefits was first limited to seven years in 1995, and then to five years in 1996 and four years in 1999. These changes were revolutionary in the Danish context because unemployment benefits had been virtually indefinite prior to the labor market reforms. The decision in 1994 to cap maximum length at seven years was the first time in history that a formal limit was placed on the duration of unemployment compensation. Overall, total enrollment time for various passive income-replacement schemes had been reduced from nine years in 1993 to four years in 2000. In addition to shortening the benefit period, the government also imposed stronger working conditions for eligibility, in the form of 6 months of nonsupported employment in 1995, lengthened to 12 months in 1996. While the coercive part of the changes fell primarily on the unemployed, there were also similar measures targeted at employers, such as making temporary layoff more costly by requiring employers to pay for the first two days of unemployment compensation (Stephens 1996: 55; Bjorklund 2000: 155–156; Loftager and Madsen 1997: 124–125; Kvist 2002: 21–22).

Whereas the three-phase labor market reforms primarily focused on changes to unemployment benefits, the government also made targeted efforts to readjust the social assistance system, with the introduction of the 1997 social assistance reform. In the reform, there was little direct change to the level or eligibility for social assistance benefits per se. Instead, the focus was on further integration between the social assistance system and the newly expanded active labor market measures. All recipients of social assistance were now required to participate in drawing up individual action plans and to accept offers of activation, including job placement, job training, and education. The government imposed particularly strict rules on young social assistance recipients in their obligation to accept active offers. Social assistance recipients under the age of 30 were expected to be activated within the first 13 weeks of welfare, and benefit reductions of up to 20% would be imposed on those who refused a fair offer of activation measures. For those over 30 years of age, activation was required within one year of unemployment. Alongside this growing emphasis on obligations for social assistance recipients, the government also made employment more attractive, by reducing taxes (and the work disincentives they generate) for low-wage earners. Local officials, meanwhile, were now required to provide those on unemployment benefits with both a job-searching plan and eventually an employment situation (Ploug 1999: 97; Benner and Vad 2000: 458; Rosdahl and Weise 2001: 169).

The 1997 social assistance reform was later supplemented with both a new Social Assistance Act and an Activation Act. With these two new laws, social assistance recipients who refused to accept job or training offers would have their benefit levels cut, but those who complied with the activation obligations would receive a wage protected by a collective labor market agreement. The age limit of immediate activation after being placed on social assistance, meanwhile, was also raised from 25 to 30 years (Kildal 2001: 8). At the time of the first government attempt to reform the social assistance system, the ambition was modest, in the form of the Youth Allowances Scheme under the bourgeois parties in the early 1990s, and the only group affected were the very young, between 18 and 19 years. Now, after more than a decade of social democratic labor market reforms, the integration of social assistance with labor market activation has encompassed increasingly broad age bands. With the introduction of the Activation Act, participation in activation became compulsory for all beneficiaries of social assistance (Abrahamson and van Oorschot 2002: 10).

In addition to unemployment benefit and social assistance, the social democrats also made corresponding adjustments to the fiscal side of the welfare state. The tax reform of 1994 transformed both social assistance and state old-age pensions from partially tax-exempted to fully taxable benefits. While the government restrained entitlement to these benefits through tax changes, it also raised actual benefit levels to more than compensate for the tighter entitlement requirements. The retrenchment implemented through tax changes was aimed not so much at cost control as increasing work incentives for the elderly and avoiding long-term passivity (Ploug 2000: 5; Green-Pedersen 2002: 125).

Despite a growing emphasis on the obligation to work backed up by sanctions, social security restructuring under Danish social democracy did not aim primarily at coercing the unemployed. On the contrary, the reforms included complementary elements of both social discipline and social integration, although social discipline was given increasing emphasis at the expense of integration over time. As unemployed individuals pass through various stages of the social protection apparatus, the first stop is almost always an offer of carrots. Besides opportunities for human capital upgrading, such carrots also include individualized counseling, planning, and various other job-search services financed by the government. As Figure 6.3 indicates, public

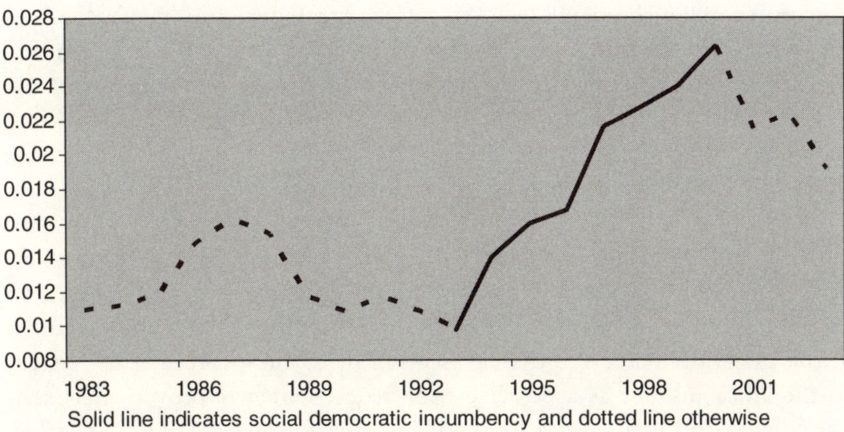

FIGURE 6.3. Employment Service Expenditure as Percentage of GDP in Denmark 1983–2003 (*Source:* OECD 2006a).

expenditures on employment services has increased sharply during social democratic incumbency. The primary objective for benefit recipients is to offer them incentives to acquire qualifications and be active. As part of an enabling strategy, beneficiaries are activated by means of skill-related initiatives, rather than further cuts in the financial support they currently rely on. In dealing with the potential problem of low productivity, the social democratic qualitative approach, by raising the level of qualifications, is a clear contrast with the neoliberal quantitative approach of lowering wages. The sticks, in the form of sanctions in this sense, are only used as a second-best option, when benefit recipients refuse to take the activation and training offers. In other words, sanctions in social security are *negotiated* sanctions based on a two-way contract. Apart from reducing or removing benefits when fair offers of activation are refused, the state rarely goes out of its way to check upon mobility, availability or job-searching activities for those on benefits (Lind 1999: 195; Barbier 2001: 19; C. Larsen 2004: 11–15).

The restructuring of reactionary compensation programs under Danish social democracy did not compromise the role of the state as the provider of generous benefits and employer of last resort. On the contrary, the social democratic state took an even more interventionist role in the lives of those in the social security system, as evidenced by the government's determination to commit resources to action plans that are tailored down to the specific circumstance of each unemployed individual. For this reason, the Danish social security reform strategies are "neostatist," in the sense that the state remains the main actor and, most importantly, financier, in the various schemes designed to change the behavior of the unemployed. By contrast, in American and British Thatcherite workfare measures, the main actor belonged to the market, operating through the downward mobility of wage levels (Torfing 1999: 18; Barbier 2001: 19; Loftager 1998: 14). The social democratic reforms enabled individuals to gain control over their own lives rather than pushing them toward workfare. This is also largely the perception among those who were subjected to the impact of government reforms. Participants in labor market programs generally perceived their transition from the social security system to the labor market as a positive experience, which improved their self-confidence and competitive potential on the job market. Here, the key factor in enabling the beneficiaries to take control seems to have been the personalized action plan drawn up between the individuals and the labor market authorities (Jensen 1999: 14).

More generally, the fundamental rationale of the unemployment benefit system has gradually shifted, toward a growing emphasis on the needs criteria, the duty to work, and the communitarian notion of citizenship based on participation. The social democratic reforms since 1994 gradually transformed the Danish social security system from universal, passive, and centralized to selective, active, and oriented to individual needs. In addition, whereas the traditional Danish welfare state was highly de-commodifying, the activation reforms recommodified labor to some extent (Loftager 1998: 2; Goul Andersen 2002b: 69–72; Jensen 1999: 1–5). These achievements of the reforms look only more remarkable when one considers the fact that no significant reduction in replacement rates actually occurred during the entire reform process. This also casts doubt on previous bourgeois strategies that placed more emphasis on cutting the level of benefits. Given this revelation, since the 1994 labor market reform, no serious discussion about reducing the level of financial support had taken place until late 2003, regardless of which party headed the government (Madsen 1999: 56; Torfing 1999: 18; C. Larsen 2004: 16).

Although the Danish unemployment insurance system was somewhat retrenched as a result of social democratic reforms, it remained one of the most generous among the OECD. The tightening of eligibility condition was relatively moderate (changed from 26 to 52 weeks of paid work during the three years prior to benefits), and the benefits remain wide in their coverage (up to 80% of the population), providing highly undifferentiated social protection by international standards. The undifferentiated, rather than segmented, coverage of unemployment benefits has helped in reducing the new social risks for marginal groups on and off the labor market (Clasen and Clegg 2006: 200). As we will see later, continental European social democratic governments are, by comparison, much less successful in providing undifferentiated passive protection, and the growing segmentation between social insurance and assistance has further worsened their insider–outsider problems.

Sweden

Under the social democratic government after 1994, the increase in active expenditures, such as labor market training, had not been accompanied by significant cuts in passive programs. Instead, expenditures on active and passive measures had gradually moved to very similar levels. In benefit generosity, the Swedish social security system did not experience any dramatic overhaul during the 1990s. Given the serious economic and fiscal crisis at the beginning of the decade, a number of cutbacks were imposed. The timing of these cutbacks indicates that they were more likely driven by a typical social democratic concern for (especially sustained) unemployment than by a typical neoliberal concern for economic competitiveness (Stephens 1996: 44–45; Huber and Stephens 2001: 250; Boesby, Dahl, and Ploug 2002: 31–45). The government's primary strategy in the early 1990s was indeed to reduce benefit levels and tighten eligibility conditions. However, as seen in Figure 6.4, after unemployment started to decline, the social democrats went on to reverse the cuts to benefit levels introduced by the previous bourgeois government. For this reason, ultimately there was no dramatic decline in benefit generosity between the beginning and end of the decade (Hort 2003: 263; Palme et al. 2002: 341). By comparison, bigger changes took place in the pensions system than in unemployment benefits.

In reforming unemployment compensation, the Swedish social democrats focused more on changing its structure than its level. Instead of massively cutting replacement rates, the party used a combination of high replacement rates and tightened eligibility rules (Boesby, Dahl, and Ploug 2002: 42–46). This method of keeping benefits relatively generous but more demanding in work conditionality is a strategy also adopted by the Danish social democrats in their social security reforms. In the Swedish context, a representative example of this strategy is the Uppsala model, implemented for social assistance recipients. Named after the municipality of Uppsala, the strategy not only adopts careful means testing but also aims at shortening the benefit period by imposing stricter requirements

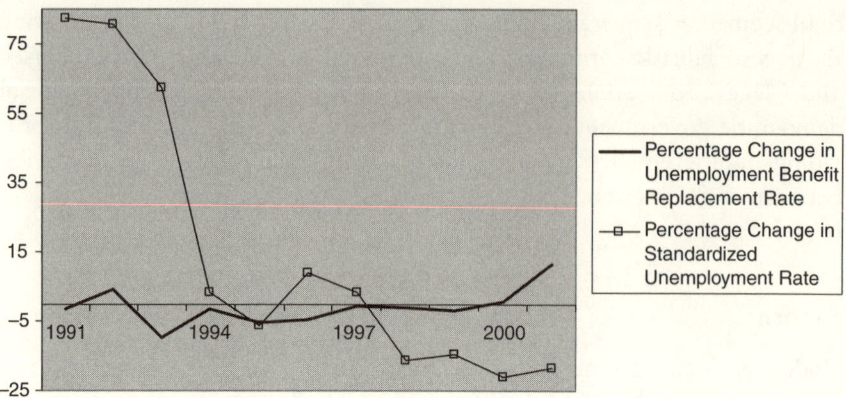

FIGURE 6.4. Change in Unemployment Rate and Replacement in Sweden 1991–
2001 (*Source:* OECD 2007a [unemployment]; Scruggs 2004 [replacement rate]).

on the unemployed to make full-time efforts to look for jobs (Hort 2001:
256). The Uppsala model reflects a more general pattern of change in social
assistance since the 1990s. After the Social Service Act of 1998, the social
democrats had made it explicit that social assistance recipients would have
the obligation to participate in municipal work or training programs, and
refusal to do so would lead to reduction or withdrawal of benefits (Kildal
2001: 10).

Compared with the government's record in reforming social assistance,
there had been less progress in reforming unemployment benefits. An
important reason for the greater difficulty in restructuring unemployment
insurance is that benefits are restricted to members of insurance funds.
Based on the Ghent system, the funds are voluntary, but the insurance
schemes are affiliated with unions. As other case studies in this book have
shown, when the capacity for cooperation between social partners is in
decline, reforms often cannot go ahead, due to resistance from unions.
(Chapter 7 on corporatism explains in greater detail the process of decline
in Swedish wage coordination.) Given the union connection, both the level
and duration of unemployment insurance is a politically sensitive issue for
the Swedish social democrats. Therefore, right after returning to power
in 1994, they rescinded the bourgeois government's cut of unemployment
insurance duration to 60 weeks.

The government established an Official Commission of Inquiry (the
ABROM commission) to examine policy options for reforming unemployment

benefits. The commission reported in October 1996, but its recommendations were opposed by the labor movement. The LO was against the limitation of benefits to 600 days, and the white-collar union TCO was opposed to tighter restrictions on both the benefit amount and the qualifying conditions for university students. The government, therefore, had to organize a second commission, which offered a compromise, postponing the introduction of a time limitation until further study by yet another commission (Jochem 2003: 128–129; Hort 2002: 141; Bjorklund 2000: 156; K. Anderson 2002: 18–19). This new commission also retracted the issue of benefit level. When the social democrats reduced the replacement rate for unemployment insurance from 80% to 75% in the 1995 budget, this deal was made more attractive with a 12% reduction in the value added tax (VAT) on food. However, unions strongly opposed, and in response, the commission revised upward the replacement rate back to 80% of qualifying income. Later, the social democrats actually further improved the package's generosity by raising the benefit level for the first 100 days of unemployment (Benner and Vad 2000: 430–432; K. Anderson 2002: 18–19; Olofsson 2001: 20).

Besides the level and duration of unemployment insurance, unions take even more seriously their privilege in the administration of these benefits. Early in its term, the social democratic government was quick to reverse legislation by the bourgeois parties to make unemployment insurance compulsory and to remove unions from unemployment insurance administration. The social democrats made the overturning of these policies a big issue in their 1994 election campaign, and they duly carried out these changes right after coming back to power. As a result, unemployment insurance became voluntary again, and managed by unions through the insurance funds (Boesby, Dahl, and Ploug 2002: 22).

Compared with the limited changes to unemployment insurance, there were deeper cuts and tighter eligibility conditions for sickness insurance and work injury insurance. The social democratic reforms in sickness cash benefits were a component of their activation strategies. Employers were forced to pay for sickness benefits for a limited period, and this created strong incentives for businesses to improve working conditions and prevent too many workers from exiting the labor market to collect sickness benefits. There was more decisive action by the government in these policy areas, partly because unions mounted only symbolic resistance, as these benefits were not as vital for the labor movement as the core schemes of unemployment insurance and pensions. In addition, the social democrats also used retrenchments in these benefits as a trade-off in negotiations with the bourgeois parties, so that areas of social security deemed most fundamental by both the party and the labor movement were spared from major retrenchment (K. Anderson 2002: 20).

In the domain of social services, the main trends after the early 1990s had been a growing element of user financing, emphasis on the market, and decentralization of service administration to the regional and local levels (Hort 2003: 264; Palme et al. 2002: 341). During the bourgeois incumbency between 1991 and 1994, there was growing emphasis on introducing market competition to social service delivery. The center-right parties, for example, introduced vouchers equivalent to 85% of the cost of education in a public school in order to allow families to choose between public and private schools. In health, a "house doctor" system was established to allow individuals to choose their own doctor, and the state also started financing private day care under the same condition as public providers. After the social democrats returned to power, they rescinded some of the center-right measures aimed at bringing more private providers into social security, and they also extended social rights services for the handicapped, elderly, and children. Nevertheless, the party has come to accept the option of private providers based on state regulation and financing (Swank 2002: 139; Huber and Stephens 2001: 247–248; Dios 2002: 11). In the administrative aspect of social security benefit delivery, there was a general consensus among major Swedish parties that the integration of unemployment insurance and social assistance would be beneficial, and the social democratic government went on to combine the administration of the two systems (Boesby, Dahl, and Ploug 2002: 29–42).

On the whole, given a combination of unemployment and deficit problems in the early 1990s, a limited tightening in the Swedish social security system became necessary. As the government's fiscal situation deteriorated, cost control temporarily became the preoccupying issue. Therefore, the general approach to the social security system during the bourgeois incumbency was to cut benefits as well as raise the share of employees in social security contributions. However, the mere shifting of social contributions from employers to employees, without reducing the overall level of contribution, had made little impact in reducing non-wage labor costs. As seen in Figure 6.5, after returning to power, the social democratic party maintained some of the bourgeois cuts, for example, in unemployment and pension benefits. However, later they increased unemployment benefits again, after having improved the macroeconomic situation significantly (more details on macroeconomic adjustments in Chapter 7). Furthermore, throughout the entire period of incumbency, the social democrats increased public expenditures on active labor market measures almost persistently.

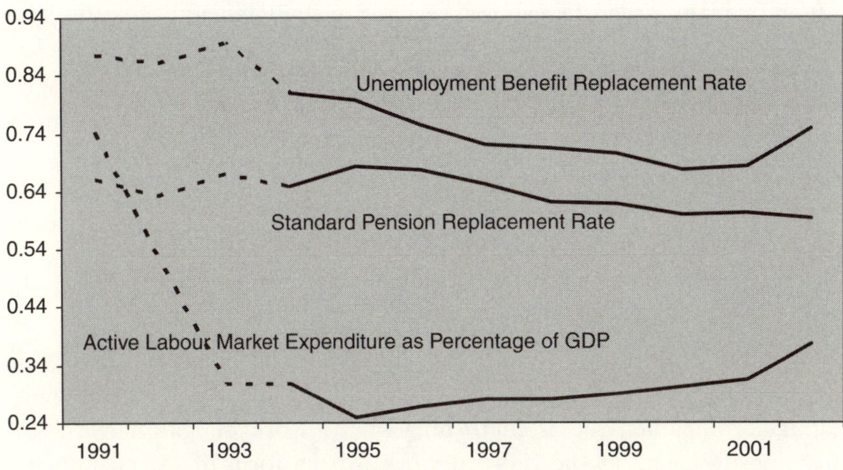

FIGURE 6.5. Passive and Active Benefits in Sweden 1991–2002 (*Source:* OECD 2006a [expenditure]; Scruggs 2004 [replacement rate]).

Norway

When the Norwegian economy entered a period of recession during the early 1990s, the Labor government did not introduce any major welfare cutbacks. Instead, between May 1992 and 1993, the party further extended the duration of unemployment benefits to a maximum of 186 weeks, due to pressure from unions concerned with long-term unemployment. Unemployment benefits for a supported child were doubled in 1992, and the government also increased resources for social assistance to families, especially families with children. While it continued to increase benefits generously, Labor also imposed stronger obligations to work on the unemployed, by tightening the entitlement to social security benefits. The government brought stricter qualifying conditions for unemployment insurance, so that recipients were now required to accept offers of activation programs or jobs. Meanwhile, Labor also toughened the requirement on both geographical and vocational mobility in job searches, and benefit recipients were expected to move to relatively distant areas if jobs were available. These requirements were later further strengthened with regard to the young. Entitlement rules for disability pensions were also changed so that only medical conditions, rather than the more general social and financial problems, could be considered in assessing eligibility. The government further restricted qualifying conditions for minimum unemployment benefits in 1998, after doubling the minimum income requirement for receiving unemployment benefits in 1997 (Kildal 2001: 12; Kuhnle 2000a: 214; Dahl and Drøpping 2001: 282; Solem and Overbye 2004). In social services, Labor allowed for a greater role for private providers in health, education, and social work, but the activities of the private providers were regulated by the state, with both subsidies and sanctions (Swank 2002: 152).

Under Labor, the major reform package targeted at recipients of social assistance was the Social Services Act of 1991. With this act, recipients of means-tested social assistance became obliged to take suitable work for the municipality, for benefits in the minimum safety net on terms inferior to comparable work in the regular labor market. This obligation to work on less favorable terms was targeted specifically at the young. Meanwhile, Labor accompanied the strengthening of the work obligation with further improvements in the right to work, in the form of offers individually tailored to the personal circumstances of social assistance recipients. The Social Services Act represented the first time in sixty years that local authorities were empowered to enforce the obligation to work on social assistance beneficiaries, and with this act the *arbeidslinje* principle was for the first time extended to the domain of social assistance. Given the greater autonomy granted to local authorities in enforcing work obligations, the government merely set out broad policy guidelines in the Social Services Act. Both actual policy design and implementation were devolved to municipalities (Halvorsen 2002: 167–173; Dahl and Drøpping 2001: 279; Kildal 2001: 12).

On a local level, the municipalities were expected to offer individually tailored packages that were limited in time and duration to the young on social assistance. However, the central government had provided neither the necessary financial resources nor detailed guidelines to accompany the devolution of policy design and implementation. As a consequence, on the local level a process of goal substitution had apparently taken place. Local authorities simply designed their measures with the purpose of increasing municipal savings, instead of changing the behavior for young recipients of social assistance. Cost-conscious local authorities chose to structure their measures with less attention to individual circumstances and fewer resources for training and education than the national government desired. About 59% of the local authorities implemented the Social Services Act in conflict with national guidelines, and the majority of municipalities exploited the *arbeidslinje* principle to install a much harsher and narrowly focused program on quickly moving the young unemployed away from social assistance. This strong compulsion to work had drawn attention to the similarities between Labor's efforts to reform the social assistance system and American workfare programs (Lødemel 2001a: 143–155; Kildal 2001: 12).

The analogy to coercive and cost-cutting U.S. workfare is uncharacteristic for Scandinavian activation, which is generally well known for its enabling and public-investment priorities. As echoed in Chapter 2, this Norwegian peculiarity illustrates, from the opposite side, the logic of positive externalities from organization. Young social-assistance beneficiaries are politically weak, new social risk groups, and intrinsically there is little electoral pressure for governments to activate them by pouring public resources into human capital investment, rather than simply cutting benefits. However, if the unemployed in general are organizationally integrated in the labor movement, social democratic governments have a stronger preference for enabling than for coercive activation measures, and these enabling resources will spill over to the politically cloutless young recipients of social assistance. Without the Ghent system, the unemployed are thinly organized in Norway relative to other Scandinavian cases. As noted in Chapter 5, for the 1998/2002 time frame, the unemployed/employed union density ratio was 0.27 in Norway, but for Sweden and Denmark it was, respectively, 0.84 and 0.93 (Ebbinghaus 2006: 128). Without strong organizational integration of the unemployed, the young social-assistance beneficiaries had few benefit spillovers to receive, and their activation also relied more on coercion and cost cutting than on public investments in training and education.

Despite harsher methods for the one specific category of youths on social assistance, evaluated as a whole, Labor's reform in passive protection was mild. The party responded to the unemployment crisis by implementing active measures, and it left the core unemployment benefit system largely intact in its generosity (Karlsen 1997: 151). The first sign of disruption to this general stability in social security did not appear until Labor was near the end of its government tenure, when the party passed a bill in 1996 to limit the combined duration of unemployment benefits and ALMPs. In the 1996 legislation, Labor raised the income threshold for unemployment benefits to 49,000 kroner and shortened the maximum duration from 186 to 150 weeks. However, at the same time, there was also a guarantee from employment placement services that placement in jobs or activation programs would occur before the benefits ran out (Dolvik et al. 1997: 76). Figure 6.6 shows an overall pattern similar to that in Sweden: While the social democrats made some limited reductions to passive benefits, these were coupled with a corresponding increase in active labor market expenditure.

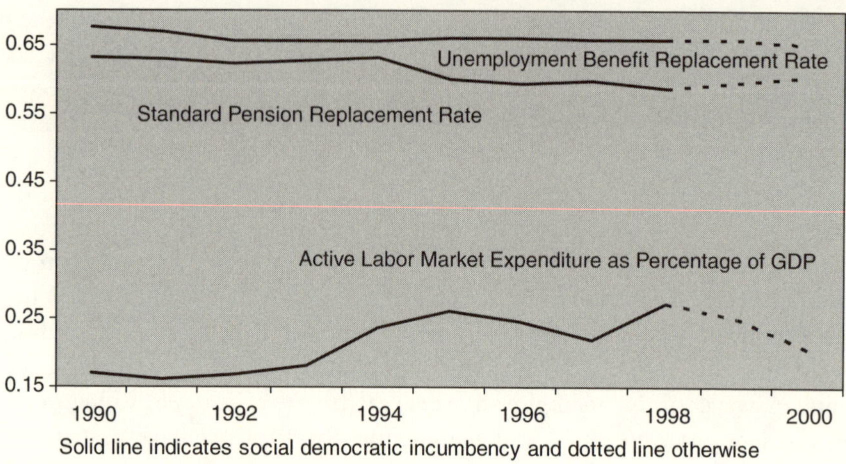

FIGURE 6.6. Passive and Active Benefits in Norway 1990–2000 (*Source:* OECD 2006a [expenditure]; Scruggs 2004 [replacement rate]).

Though not a dramatic example of benefit rollback, the 1996 legislation was indeed the first time the Norwegian government decided to put a formal limit on the existing passive benefits. After the 1996 reforms, the Labor government had further strengthened the work test and tightened qualifying conditions for unemployment, disability, and insurance benefits, but at the same time, benefit levels were left intact. For example, among Scandinavian countries, Norway is the only case where the sickness insurance replacement rate was kept stable at one to six times the basic amount, while all other Northern European countries reduced sickness insurance benefits considerably. At the same time, Labor shortened the benefit eligibility period for lone parents from ten to three years in order to increase job-search incentives. Apart from making welfare benefits less attractive, the government also reinforced the positive side of *arbeidslinje* by expanding active labor market measures for skill rehabilitation and workers' requalification, especially for the long-term unemployed. The rationale was to reintegrate the long-term unemployed by training them for ordinary jobs. This way, their skill mismatches can be overcome, and the danger of permanent labor exclusion can be reduced for them (Ploug 1999: 100; Halvorsen 2002: 171; Kosonen 2001: 167; Kuhnle 2000a: 214).

Although the emphasis on obligation became stronger, in general Labor's approach was still characterized by its moderation and reluctance to coerce. For example, the obligation to accept offers of activation was enforced by the threat of benefit loss in case of refusal, but the unemployed were still permitted to refuse up to three offers without any impact on their benefits (Jochem 2000: 132). In addition, unlike other Nordic countries in the 1990s, measures to make passive social security more active largely bypassed any cuts in benefit level or increases in waiting period. Instead, Labor attempted to scale back passive measures primarily by tightening either eligibility or benefit duration (Stephens 1996: 52). The limited extent of change in passive protection is even more conspicuous if one takes into consideration the fact that unemployment benefits in Norway are non Ghent, noncontributory, and tax-funded. Such financing structure already makes it easier for the government to bring changes to the system, since benefits are not claimed by employees as delayed wages, and it is less likely for collective action failure among unions to be an issue in impeding reforms (Karlsen 1997: 152). At the same time, strengthening the obligation to work went hand in hand with increasing the financial resources for enabling to work.

During the unemployment crisis of the 1990s, Norway had largely avoided welfare retrenchment. There was no fundamental change to any aspect of social security, and it certainly had not moved toward a more residualist direction. Rather than retrenching social security, the booming oil economy gave Labor the opportunities and resources to further maintain or increase welfare benefits. In addition, the party also strengthened the work orientation of welfare programs and increasingly utilized targeting to direct benefits to the most needy. All these reforms took place in the context of preserving the basic structure of the Norwegian welfare. In macroeconomic performance, state revenues from oil production led to a budget surplus, and unemployment did not resurge, and so there was little economic or fiscal pressure on the government to further fine-tune, let alone retrench, the existing social security system. Norway, in other words, seems to have had the best of all worlds, and its welfare state appears to be the one under least pressure in the Nordic world. However, this situation is unlikely to remain unchallenged, in the event of a consistent drop in oil prices (Freeman 1997: 18; Eitrheim and Kuhnle 2000: 53–54; Halvorsen 2002: 172–177; Clasen and van Oorschot 2002a: 241).

The Netherlands

Before the PvdA came to power in 1989, the center-right coalition adopted an overall approach to reforming the welfare state, with emphases on cost control and expenditure restraint. For social security expenditure, the

Lubbers I and II administrations subscribed to a "price" policy, by freezing and lowering the level of benefits and shortening benefit duration. In the short period between 1985 and 1987, the basic benefit-wage replacement ratios for unemployment, sickness, and disability were all lowered from 80% to 70%. The link between flat-rate benefits and the minimum wage was suspended, and the government temporarily stopped adjusting the minimum wage to the cost of living. After Lubbers's reforms in 1987, the safety net function of Dutch social security became more prominent at the expense of wage replacement. The share of above-minimum benefit recipients in social insurance programs diminished considerably. However, since these austerity reforms relied mainly on spending cuts, they did not alter the passive nature of the social security system. Such measures also proved ineffective in bringing down the actual costs of passive welfare, especially in the most abused part of the social security system: disability benefits. By 1990, the number of disability benefit recipients stood at 894,000, while the benefit scheme itself was designed only for a maximum capacity of 200,000 recipients. Despite persistent efforts by the center-right coalition to retrench the income replacement programs, the social partners further extended their industry-wide collective schemes to finance early retirement through these benefits (Hartog 2000: 35; Stigter 1997: 13–19; Hassel and Ebbinghaus 2000: 76–77; Hemerijck, Manow, and van Kersbergen 2000: 220).

After the PvdA joined the coalition, the government's emphasis started to shift from "price" to "volume." As a non-negotiable condition for joining the coalition, the PvdA secured a guarantee from the Christian Democrats that the level and duration of social benefits would not be tampered with. Now, in the volume framework, the priority of social security reform turned to reducing benefit enrollment, rather than simply cutting benefit levels or duration. On the one hand, program entitlement was tightened; on the other hand, the government undertook a major institutional overhaul in program administration for social security. For the PvdA, what retrenchment there was to social security was justified as a response to economic necessity rather than as an ideological attack on the social democratic principle of solidarity (Green-Pedersen 2002: 98). This task was made easier by the growing economic and welfare fiscal crisis, and a decade of ambiguous outcomes from the center-right's cost-control campaigns further highlighted the urgency to find a different solution to the problem of labor market exclusion.

Unlike the PvdA's wage moderation/flexicurity policies, which relied heavily on the corporatist Wassenaar framework, the strategy it adopted in dealing with the labor movement in passive-income replacement reforms was very different. The party played an instrumental role in totally eliminating the administrative privilege of unions and employers in passive benefits and in making their opposition immaterial in actual impact. The party, in other words, was able to create policy changes by rejecting corporatism, but this was at considerable political cost, with a serious setback for both coalition partners in the 1994 election, fought primarily over welfare reform issues. With the Christian democrats now in opposition and the Liberal Party (VVD) as a junior coalition partner, the PvdA assumed overall policy leadership from this point on, and it continued with these reforms undeterred. The government went on to dismantle existing corporatist benefit-administration institutions and separate social partners from social security management. At the same time, it increased the role of legal regulation and direct supervision by the state, and also expanded financial incentives for employers to provide better working conditions and improve workplace environment (van der Veen and Trommel 1999; Hemerijck and Manow 2001: 227–228; Snels 1999: 133).

After the PvdA joined the government, changes to the unemployment benefit system had gradually moved it away from a demand-driven system. Instead, through decentralization of administrative tasks, local authorities were given increasing autonomy to develop their own initiatives in restructuring unemployment compensation for the purpose of enabling the unemployed to return to work (Schmidt 2000: 286–288; Anderson 2002: 7). With the introduction of New Public Management practices, deregulation and competition have become the key characteristics of social security administration. The Central Board of Employment Services now receives funding allocated on the basis of its performance. By emphasizing both responsibility delegation and the state's ultimate steering function, the government has attempted to transform passive benefit administration into a public service directed toward clients but with a strong input from political guidance (Hemerijck and Visser 2000: 241–242; Cox 1998: 12–14).

As a whole, the restructuring of passive social benefits under the PvdA can be characterized as a process of "managed liberalization." On the one hand, social risks increasingly became the responsibility of individual firms; on the other hand, coordination and supervision by the state in benefit administration intensified. The primary losers in this process were unions, and, to a lesser extent, employers (van der Veen and Trommel 1999: 290; Hemerijck and Manow 2001: 227–228). Typical for Christian democratic welfare regimes, unions and employers had long been externalizing the cost of economic adjustment through social insurance benefits. However, by

1999, a new round of fundamental institutional redesign in passive benefits had further reduced the possibility for continued cost externalization, as social security, social assistance, and job-search support now became integrated into one administrative regime through central coordination. The expected result was that all persons of working age willing to work would fall under the responsibility of various components within this one integrated mechanism (Keizer 2003: 296).

The PvdA's social security reform also extended into social assistance benefits. In 1995, the government introduced the New Public Assistance Act, the first major change in the social assistance system since 1963. This act introduced explicit principles of activation and emphasized the duties associated with the right to assistance. The act also allowed for decentralization of social assistance administration, so that municipalities achieved greater discretion in setting benefit levels. To activate the unemployed, municipalities could now raise basic allowance by up to 20% as a positive incentive, or reduce benefits by up to 15% as a negative one (Cox 1998: 14–15). Overall, the government's strategy in social assistance was a combination of cuts to the level of benefits, and extra allowance for disadvantaged groups, plus central guidance and information on employment and training opportunities for job searchers. Social-assistance recipients were now generally expected to actively look for employment and accept a job offer. Nevertheless, despite tightened eligibility, more mandatory participation, and further sanction warnings, the government did not resort to the extensive imposition of penalties. Although activation contracts were now drawn, in most cases public-assistance recipients who failed to fulfill their side of the contract were not punished with direct cuts to benefits (Gilbert 2002: 85; Keizer 2001: 121; Handler 2002: 30). Similar to organizational changes in social insurance, the government also applied the principal-agent model in managing social-assistance benefits. By devolving both administrative responsibility and a portion of the social assistance budget to municipalities, the PvdA tried to increase the efficiency and flexibility of reforms being implemented at the local level (van der Veen and Trommel 1999: 305–307).

Overall, the PvdA managed to achieve some savings in social expenditure without drastically cutting benefits. Figures 6.7 and 6.8 show that since the start of its incumbency in 1989, the PvdA had steadily reduced the steepness of (or simply reversed) cuts to unemployment, pension, and sickness benefits, as well as further expanding the duration of unemployment benefits. At the same time, however, qualifying conditions were drastically tightened for the now more generous unemployment benefits. Furthermore,

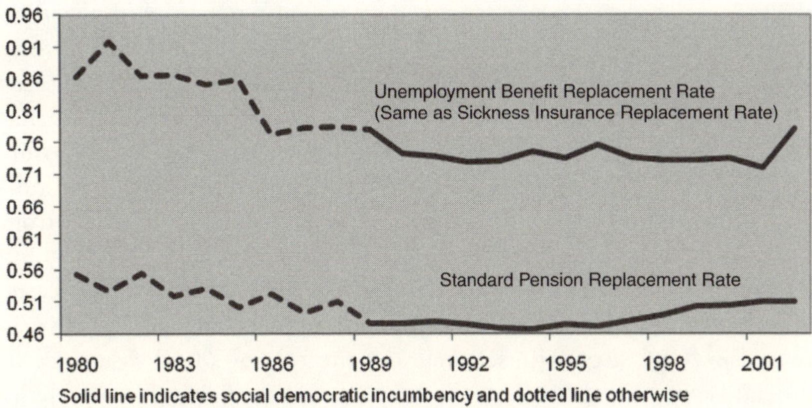

FIGURE 6.7. Passive Benefits Replacement Rates in the Netherlands 1980–2002 (*Source:* Scruggs 2004).

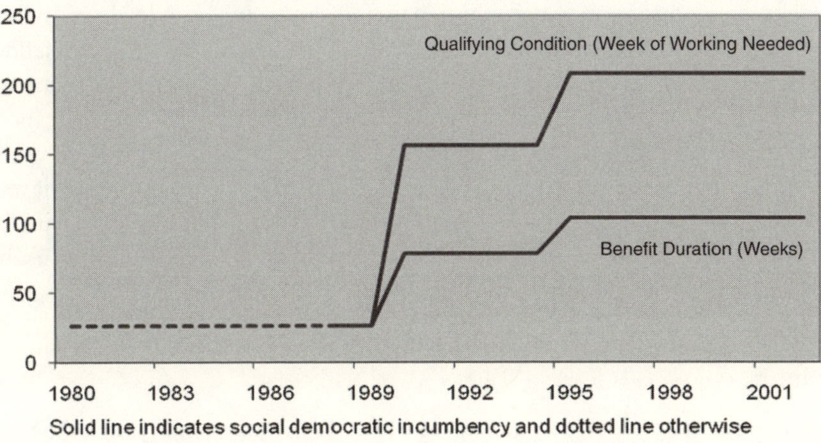

FIGURE 6.8. Unemployment Benefit Duration and Qualifying Conditions in the Netherlands 1980–2002 (*Source:* Scruggs 2004).

Figure 5.12 from Chapter 5 has shown that these savings from tighter benefit restrictions helped the government to fund a clear parallel expansion of active labor market measures. While trying to suppress wage demand, the government also funded compensatory targeted tax breaks for low-wage workers, and it also upgraded hourly wages and benefits of part-time and temporary workers. While the PvdA continued with efforts from previous governments to reduce budget deficits, the party also put more emphasis on maintaining basic social protection and avoiding social exclusion or poverty in work (Schmidt 2000: 286–288; Braun and Giraud 2004: 49). Whereas the Lubbers administrations of the mid-1980s prioritized expenditure and benefit cuts, under the PvdA company- or sector-wide supplementary insurance delivered through collective bargaining continued to grow. These individual compensation schemes, to a great extent, cushioned the effect from earlier cuts in social programs (Trommel and de Vroom 2002: 93).

As a result of the PvdA's reforms, the Dutch social security system became more selective, partly due to the introduction of means testing in the basic state pension and survivors' scheme, and the role of social assistance in the social security system gradually increased. New Beveridge-type basic benefits were introduced for vulnerable social groups with a nonexistent or insufficient contribution record. The expansion of means testing served mainly younger and marginal workers, but for older and core workers the government left the overall system intact. It retained the principles of reciprocity contribution and the maintenance of adequate standards of living for core workers (van Oorschot 1998: 14–15; Clasen and van Oorschot 2002b: 102). This, similar to what occurred in both Germany and France, led to increasing dualism in the Dutch welfare state, with the insurance layer catering generously for insiders, and the assistance layer targeted with minimum benefits to outsiders. The addition of the social-assistance layer does deliver social protection to the marginal groups, but the increasingly differentiated social security arrangement it helps to perpetuate is itself unlikely to fundamentally reduce the insider–outsider divide.

France

Although the 1983 U-turn meant that the Socialists formally switched to macroeconomic orthodoxy, the party believed that this change in economic policy should have no impact on its traditional goals of social justice and egalitarianism. The government continued to regard combating social exclusion as one of its key objectives, and it further expanded French social security during the 1980s, despite a tighter budgetary and interest rate framework, constrained by the policy of *franc fort* (Levy 2000: 329). As Figure 6.9 indicates, well into the early 1990s the Socialists kept steady or continued to increase the generosity of all key passive benefits. After the conservative Balludar and Juppé cabinets implemented sharper retrenchment reforms, the returning Jospin government did not reverse this trend. However, these savings in passive benefits helped the Socialists

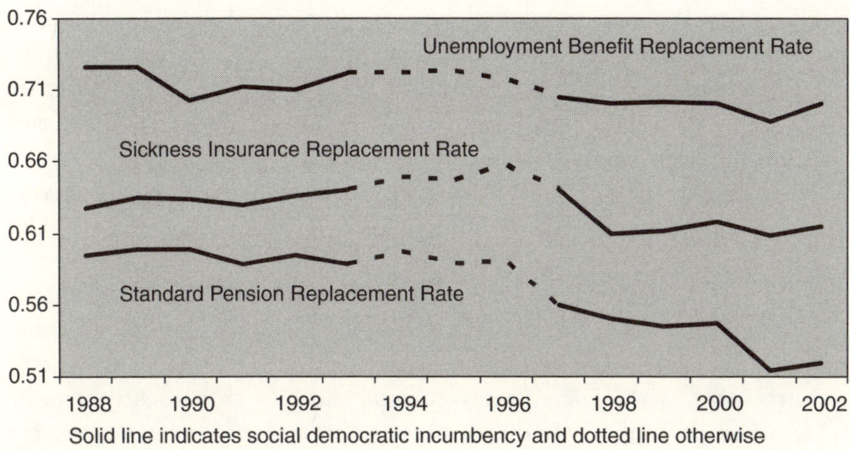

FIGURE 6.9. Passive Benefits Replacement Rates in France 1988–2002 (*Source:* Scruggs 2004).

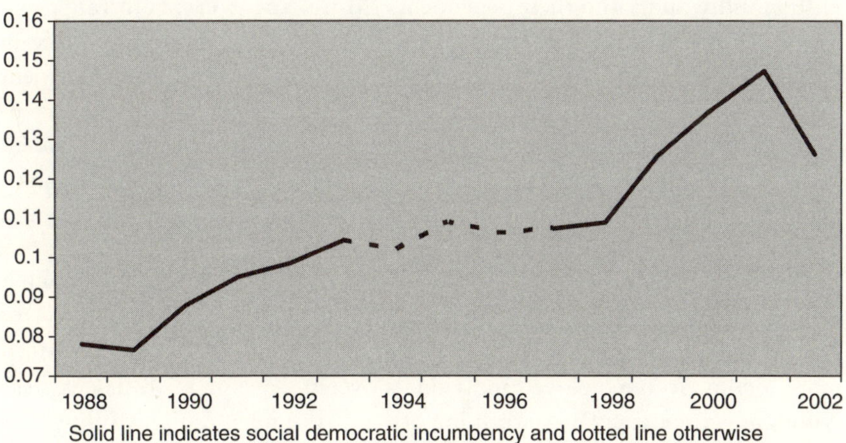

FIGURE 6.10. Active Labor Market Expenditure as Percentage of GDP in France 1988–2002 (*Source:* OECD 2006a).

to significantly increase expenditure in active labor market programs. Figure 6.10 shows that since the late 1980s these labor market measures had undergone clear expansion under the Socialists, while they remained stagnant when the center Right was in power.

The Socialist government's activism in social and labor market policies is path dependent, shaped by the historical legacy of statism in French public policy. Problems of unemployment, poverty, and social exclusion are regarded not as issues of individual responsibility but as matters requiring collective response from the social security system (Enjolras et al. 2001: 66). Given the rising social costs of economic liberalization during the 1980s, the Socialists attempted to compensate through welfare as well as labor market measures, and the most crucial policy instrument serving this social purpose was the Minimum Income of Insertion (RMI). This scheme is unique in its dual nature as both the primary locus for French ALMPs and the only major social assistance benefit in France. In Chapter 5 I focused on the active side of RMI, and in this chapter I give greater attention to its passive, social assistance, aspect.

Introduced by the Socialist government under Michel Rocard in 1988, RMI offers not only a guarantee of means-tested minimum income but also access to basic social rights like health care, housing, and work-injury insurance. In addition, it offers the right to reintegration into the labor market (insertion). By the end of 1991, RMI had been paid to almost two million individuals and their dependents (Morel 2004: 115; Hantrais 1996: 65). Since its introduction, the package has gradually secured its place in French social security as the primary substitution for both unemployment insurance and the main minimum income. Ninety percent of the unemployed who receive RMI do not receive any other form of unemployment benefits, and for this reason RMI has gradually become the "third component" of the unemployment compensation system in France (Barbier and Théret 2003: 149; Ughetto and Bouget 2002: 103).

Given the labor market insertion requirements of RMI, its growing weight in the social security system facilitated the Socialists' efforts to combat unemployment with more active protection. RMI offers a minimum income to unemployed individuals over the age of 25 if they express willingness to participate in training programs or jobs. A highly innovative feature of the scheme is its universalistic reach. All French citizens over 25 can claim the benefits on work or training conditions. A decade after the scheme's introduction, the Jospin government further extended its universalistic principle by giving all long-term unemployed a right to income support based on citizenship. For the young, income support is combined with a training program of 18 months that includes internships or education leading to a professional qualification; for adults, the content of original insertion-based contracts has been further expanded (Béland and Hansen 2000: 57–58).

Another peculiar feature of RMI is that it is financed out of general taxation, which is clearly incongruent with the predominantly Bismarckian nature of French social security. In 1991, the Socialist government introduced the General Social Contribution (CSG), which started off as a 1.1% tax levied on all incomes. The introduction of CSG and its financing of RMI signaled the first genuine change from contributions to general taxation as the funding mechanism for French social security. CSG's levy rate was raised steadily by governments left and right, reaching 7.5% by 1998. As CSG became an increasingly important source of welfare financing, the government was able to expand the range of programs subjected to this gradual transition from contributions to tax-based financing (Béland and Hansen 2000: 57–58). On the basis of this process, the Jospin government established a universal health-care cover, one of its biggest social policy achievements. This overhaul of health-care benefits transformed a scheme traditionally funded disproportionately by employees' contributions into one increasingly funded by general taxation. CSG replaced most of the health-care contributions from employees, and by 1999 more than 20% of all social protection resources, and 35% in the health-care system, in particular, came from CSG. Leading a gradual shift away from contribution financing, CSG helped to suppress non-wage costs in the economy by reducing payroll taxes. The scheme is designed as revenue neutral in the long run, so that it can increase competitive efficiency in economic production at no extra cost (Clift 2001: 174–175; Palier 2000: 130–131; Ferrera and Hemerijck 2003: 113).

For the Socialists, growing reliance on CSG has another long-term advantage. As welfare financing becomes increasingly tax-funded, union leverage and their proprietary claim on social security benefits also weakens. This can reduce potential union resistance to future social reforms, which is likely to be strong due to their insufficient organizational capacity to achieve collective action. In other words, influence from the French state over social spending and welfare standards has strengthened at the expense of bipartite committees that manage social insurance (Taylor-Gooby 2004: 16–17; Palier 2002: 19).

After the 1980s, the Socialists intensified the prioritarian emphasis in their approach to passive income benefits. The government introduced in-work incentives for those most affected by economic restructuring, and it called for greater efficiency in redistributive policies. The party advocated redistribution of added value in favor of salaried workers in general and low-income earners in particular. Shortly after coming to power, it implemented a three-year plan aimed specifically at preventing social exclusion for young people with some social difficulties. Called "The Road to Employment" (TRACE), the program offered individual case management for the least employable young people. TRACE functioned as a coordinating mechanism, by strengthening linkages between various regular youth-activation programs and the passive social security system (Schmidt 2000: 294; Schmidt 2001: 254; Enjolras et al. 2001: 64).

In 1998, the Jospin government introduced the Law of Orientation for the Fight against Exclusion (LOLE). LOLE was an integrated approach to the promotion of fundamental social rights. It contained an ambitious set of new schemes aimed at combating exclusion in all its possible aspects, such as employment, education, health, housing, debt, and culture. Meanwhile, LOLE also carried further the reinsertion emphasis of RMI and continued to promote employment-centered social solidarity. Measures in LOLE included not only new job creation schemes for those under 26 but also an updated employment service program tailored to the specific needs of unemployed individuals (Morel 2004: 93–94, 115–120). In order to strengthen income support in favor of the poor, the government reorganized the tax system for the 2000–2003 period, reducing the tax burden in the lower brackets and making taxes more progressive. It raised the minimum wage by 4%, increased the basic benefit level in RMI, and also made two other minimum income guarantees in passive social security more generous. The Socialists proposed extended coverage for both health insurance and collective benefits (the latter to 100%), and they also abolished health insurance charges for low-wage earners (Clift 2004: 3; Hemerijck and Schludi 2000: 170; Wren 2001: 262; Clift 2001: 174–175).

RMI and other similar means-tested tax-funded benefits were an important new addition to the contribution-based French social security system. While the social insurance component of the welfare state continues to serve the core purpose of maintaining living standards and cementing solidarity among the primary workforce, the means-tested benefits have been crucial in responding to the new social risks of outsiders, such as the young, unskilled, and part-time workers, who were excluded from social insurance due to inability to establish a stable working career. The activation and training components of RMI make a further contribution to helping these high-risk groups returning to the labor market. While the means-tested benefits do reach previously excluded outsiders, it is important to recognize that these schemes are not ideal long-term solutions to insider–outsider problems. As in the Netherlands (and Germany, to be discussed next), the growing dualism in the social security system actually further intensifies a two-tier structure for social protection. By contrast, in Scandinavian welfare states, unemployment insurance has been both highly encompassing and undifferentiated (Palier and Mandin 2004: 128–129; Clasen and Clegg 2006: 201).

Although there was growing pressure from the center-right parties for more privatization or individualization of rights in such areas as health care and pensions, under the Jospin government there was no major attempt to privatize social security arrangements. Throughout its tenure, the government maintained public ownership of all basic welfare services and introduced positive discrimination in their financing and pricing. A growing number of services were restructured to be more universally accessible, and even if privatization was carried out, it was done under close state supervision (Sferza 2002: 137–139; Théret and Barbier 2002: 16). The Socialists stuck to three principles over the social security implications of economic liberalization. First of all, if government spending must be reduced, cuts should be targeted at the affluent. Secondly, high-income earners should bear the primary cost of structural reforms in the social security system. Thirdly, even when the government was pursuing genuine economic austerity, the process should occur with progressive redistributive consequences to the maximum extent possible. The 1983 U-turn indeed led to a retreat from *dirigisme* in economic policy, but this did not end state activism in passive income support (Levy 2000: 340–345). On the contrary, partly to offset the costs of economic liberalization and partly to activate the labor market, the Socialists further intensified state activism in restructuring social security. As an indication of the Socialists' success in combating social exclusion, in 2001 the French programs aimed at combating exclusion were selected, together with the Dutch and Danish cases, as good examples of a strategic approach to promote social cohesion by the European Commission (Morel 2004: 130).

Germany

When the SPD returned to power after sixteen years in opposition, it was in firm agreement with the center-right parties on macroeconomic principles, such as anti-inflationary prudence and fiscal austerity. In order to reinforce its image as a party with fiscal responsibility, the SPD government attempted to put some restrictions on the existing social security system. The Ministry of Labor alone was asked to contribute almost half of the 30 billion deutsche marks in total savings that the federal government was hoping to achieve in the 2000 budget. However, fearing a potential electoral backlash against retrenchment policies, the government attempted to make cuts to passive benefits by stealth or at least indirectly. In pensions, for example, they bypassed direct reduction in benefit levels and chose instead to alter the indexation rules for benefit calculation (Hering 2004: 102; Busch and Manow 2001: 185; Leibfried and Obinger 2003: 215). The government's overall principle in reforming social security gradually shifted toward emphasizing individual responsibility, in line with its attempt to encourage labor market activation, and these activation-oriented reforms focused in particular on the unemployment benefit system.

In late 2003, the Red-Green coalition introduced a comprehensive proposal for restructuring the unemployment compensation system. Named Hartz I-IV after the head of the commission on labor market reform, the new proposal recommended significant cuts in benefits for the long term unemployed by the year 2005. According to Hartz I-IV, the regular unemployment insurance payment, called Unemployment Benefit I, would be limited to 12 months, and a second tier of flat-rate and fully means-tested basic income would be instituted for workers who have exhausted their unemployment insurance payment. As a whole, this reform reduced benefit levels in the insurance tier and tightened eligibility rules in the assistance tier (Seeleib-Kaiser 2004a: 16). On the basis of the Hartz-IV recommendations, in early 2005 the government also transformed unemployment assistance and general assistance into an integrated means-tested benefit called Unemployment Benefit II, paid at the level of the lower benefit. This way, minimum social assistance becomes the only benefit available for the long-term unemployed. These reforms in unemployment benefits continued to rely primarily on the manipulation of incentives for individuals, and only secondly did the government consider broader issues of integration and human capital as activation strategies (Hanesch 2003a: 160–161; Hanesch 2003b: 215; Dingeldey and Linke-Sonderegger 2004: 27).

While it imposed stricter limits on the unemployment compensation system as a whole, the Schröder government also tried to increase protection for those who really couldn't work. The Red-Green coalition reversed a number of marginal cost-saving measures and deregulatory reforms in the labor market introduced by the previous center-right government. In 1998, it lowered the copayment for prescription drugs and waived copayments for transportation, drugs, and other associated treatment costs for those chronically ill. In 2001, the SPD balanced cuts in old-age pensions with the introduction of new state-subsidized, partially private pension arrangements. The government also reinstated full statutory sick-pay benefits and restored the replacement rate to 100%. Meanwhile, statutory rules for lay-offs in small enterprises were also tightened again (Schröter 2004: 24; Leibfried and Obinger 2003: 212–216; Seeleib-Kaiser 2002: 32). Despite

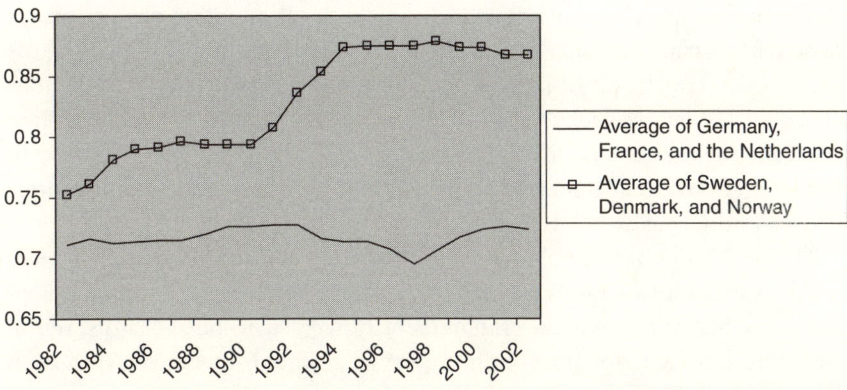

FIGURE 6.11. Percentage of Labor Force Covered by Unemployment Insurance 1982–2002 (*Source:* Scruggs 2004).

tightening the welfare budget, the social democrats nevertheless established a separate social insurance scheme for long-term care. This scheme meant not only a substantial expansion of resources devoted to people needing long-term care but also a reinforcement of the contribution-based German social security system. To protect the elderly living below the poverty line within the existing pension system, the government also introduced a complementary public assistance scheme that offers flat-rate benefits financed through taxation (Leitner and Lessenich 2003: 333–339).

However, not all social categories benefited directly from the government's reforms. On the whole, the SPD's measures had largely failed to deal with the emergence of new social risks. The tightening of eligibility conditions and relaxation of the unemployment protection occurred primarily for those outside the core labor force (such as those on social assistance), but benefits and employment protection for those enjoying social insurance were left intact during most of the SPD incumbency. It was not until the 2005 Hartz-IV reforms that the party started to reduce the segmentation in social protection between the core and outsiders, and this was seven years after it came to power and one year before leaving office. As Figure 6.11 indicates, the proportion of the labor force covered by the core social insurance system for this book's three continental cases was lower than in Scandinavia, leaving more people excluded as outsiders, and this gap had worsened significantly after the 1990s. In Germany, the insiders, who are the dominant and export-oriented high-skill sector unions, insisted on maintaining a clear differentiation in the level of social protection for those with social insurance versus those on social assistance. Reflecting the institutional constraint of path dependency, a key reason why these unions were able to exercise such overwhelming influence was the historic coupling between unemployment insurance and wage bargaining in Germany, so that changes to the former had to be negotiated in the process of the latter (Clasen and Clegg 2006: 202–210).

The SPD had not been able to introduce any effective mandatory activation measures into the social security system. With regard to unemployment benefits, it is the local employment officers who have the discretion over sanctions when work conditionality is violated. By contrast, in both the Dutch and Danish cases, participation in activation is compulsory, setting in automatically after some time in unemployment. The SPD's reforms in unemployment compensation were characterized by selective restrictions that actually tend to hit particularly hard those who are already less attached to the labor market. The government decreased the level of unemployment benefits with greater length of unemployment, and it also restricted suitability criteria for benefit claims. However, it had made only limited efforts to go beyond these simple measures to make work more attractive (Hering 2004: 104; Seeleib-Kaiser 2004b: 133; Clasen 2000: 90–103).

The Schröder government's social security reforms represented a gradual process of "dual transformation." On the one hand, the preservation of status and the guarantee of living standards are gradually declining in their importance in social security. On the other hand, policies toward the family are being increasingly taken up by public welfare. The growing liberal as well as social democratic element in German social security was connected through the participation-based communitarian principle (Seeleib-Kaiser 2004a: 20). In the long run, this development in passive protection was in alignment with the party's expansion in active protection. However, most of these changes were moderate alterations at the margins, and in social security the contribution-based mechanism favoring the core workforce had not been changed (Lawson 1996: 47). The general trend in the German welfare state is toward some cost containment and a slightly more streamlined social insurance state, in the overall context of very high stability. Figure 6.12 shows that for much of the crisis-laden 1990s and early 2000s, there was no major decline in either benefit expenditure or generosity. The key potential problem in this kind of stability is the government's continuing inability to deal with persistent high unemployment (Seeleib-Kaiser 2004b: 134; Leibfried and Obinger 2003: 214–216).

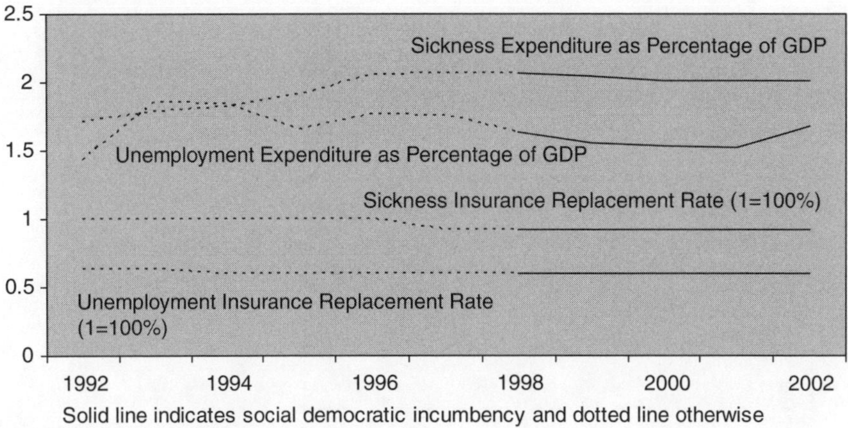

FIGURE 6.12. Unemployment and Sickness Insurance in Germany 1992–2002 (*Source:* OECD 2006a [expenditure]; Scruggs 2004 [replacement rate]).

United Kingdom

Compared with continental welfare regimes, the fiscal pressure for controlling social expenditure and reducing benefits was not as strong in the UK. This enabled New Labour to preserve the overall contour of the existing means-tested income-replacement system, and instead devote the bulk of its attention to labor market measures such as the New Deal. Apart from active labor market policies, there was no major change in formal social security under New Labour. Nevertheless, the government did manage to intensify social protection for the worst-off by making some functional adjustments on the basis of existing benefits. The Treasury, under the leadership of Gordon Brown, was particularly active in introducing some redistribution of income, not only through increased means testing of passive benefits but also through innovative fiscal welfare measures such as the Working Families' Tax Credit and the minimum wage. In addition, there is also a massive increase in child benefits. However, it is important to point out that expansion in these areas of social security was funded more by stealth and windfall taxes than by a direct increase in income tax, which the party pledged not to raise. In the 2002 spending review, the chancellor of the Exchequer committed the government to continued increase in social expenditure, until at least 2006 (Pierson and Ellison 2003: 349–350; Mullard 2000: 4–8). With a strategy characterized by M. Ferrera and A. Hemerijck (2003: 103) as "functional recalibration," New Labor

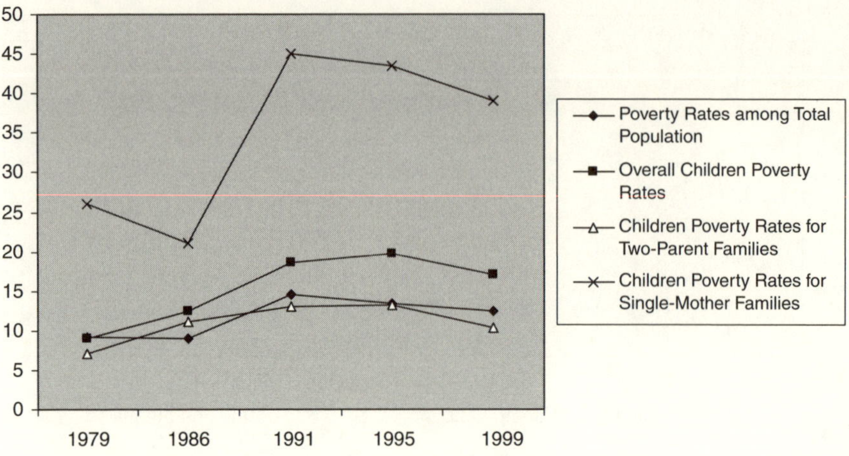

FIGURE 6.13. Poverty (50% Median) Rates in the UK 1979–1999 (*Source:* Luxemburg Income Study).

tried to bring structural changes to social security and eliminate welfare traps through means testing and changes to benefit rules. At the same time, the party also tried to combat poverty and social exclusion by introducing income guarantees, new targeted programs in social security, and fiscal redistribution such as generous tax credits. As a result of these changes, the worst-off quintile of the population became better-off, whereas the best-off quintile changed their position very little (Jessop 2003).

Based on data from the Luxemburg Income Study (LIS), Figure 6.13 reflects the social impact of New Labour's welfare policies. Because LIS relies on country-specific surveys, the range of time points with available data is limited, with just one observation (1999) for the New Labour period. With such limitation, one can still see how the government oversaw a reduction in poverty rates for various social categories. The reduction of child poverty is especially successful for single-mother families, a classic new social risk group with weak political power. This, as alluded to in Chapter 5's discussion of tax-credit benefits for families, is in no small measure related to the advocacy by female MPs inside the parliamentary party, and this again illustrates the logic of positive externalities from organization in protecting politically weak outsiders.

In its efforts to restructure the distribution of welfare benefits, New Labour continues to encourage the trend, started under the Conservatives, toward increasing utilization of the needs principle at the expense of the contribution principle. The government ushered in a gradual transformation of the British welfare state, toward a hybrid system combining employment, private occupational insurance (for the elderly), and fiscal welfare (tax credits for the low-paid) (Adler 2004: 88, 94; Clasen and van Oorschot 2002b: 107). In their approach to targeting, New Labour differentiated itself from classic Poor Law by its emphasis on inclusion rather than exclusion. Despite increased targeting, there is yet little sign of systematic change toward American minimalism. While the government carried forward the Conservative emphasis on tightening benefit eligibility, it also renewed the emphasis on including the out-of-work population and on investing in human resources and training (Trickey and Walker 2001: 181; Johnson 2001: 74; Hewitt 1999: 169–170). Similar to the ALP's asset-based egalitarianism in the Australian context, New Labour encouraged a kind of asset-based welfare, where individuals are encouraged to save for themselves and pursue asset accumulation as a way to fund their own future retirement. As an incentive for individual saving, the government introduced state bequests for children and donations for adults that match the amount saved. In addition to means-tested cash assistance and services in kind, the government is now trying to promote asset-based social protection as a third pillar of welfare financing (Hewitt 2002: 189).

Australia

After coming to power in 1984, the Hawke government was keen to control the rising cost of social security and reduce the large budget deficit left by the Fraser coalition, and the party publicly committed itself not to further increase social expenditure. As Figure 6.14 indicates, although there was some modest rise in spending between 1983 and 1985, this was followed by clear restraint until the end of the decade. Over the Hawke period as a whole, social spending did not significantly increase as a percentage of GDP. The ALP was able to achieve major cost efficiencies in Medicare, Superannuation, higher-education funding, and care for the elderly, and the government's asset test for pensions for the aged had massively reduced the number of aged pensioners. Most of the net expenditure increase in social security took place later, after Paul Keating became prime minister in 1991 (Graycar and Jamrozik 1993: 121; Watts 1989: 117–118; Gibson 1990: 184–186).

Despite the pressure to limit social expenditure, the ALP was simultaneously able to implement some social amelioration policies. With Medicare, child care, family income supplements, and various other schemes, it focused income redistribution on the worst-off. Figure 6.15 shows that over its period

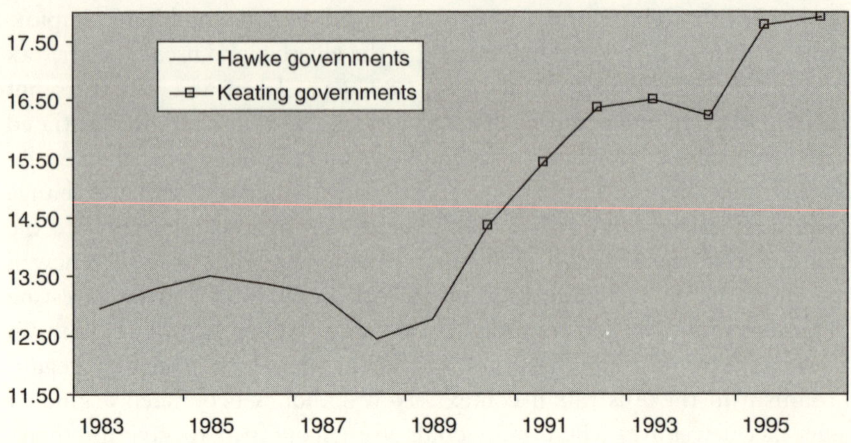

FIGURE 6.14. Social Expenditure as Percentage of GDP under the ALP
(*Source:* OECD 2006a).

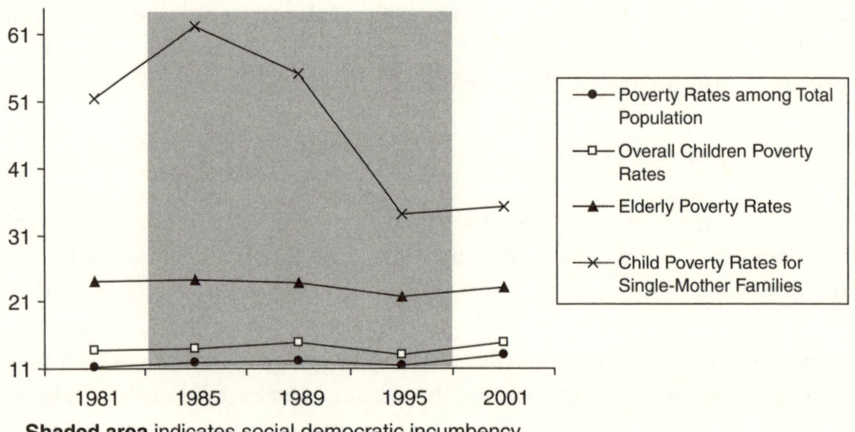

FIGURE 6.15. Poverty (50% Median) Rates in Australia 1981–2001
(*Source:* Luxemburg Income Study).

in office, the party was able to reduce poverty rates, especially for the new
social risk group of single-mother families. Since the overall level of passive-
benefits spending did not increase, the party's success in delivering these
social justice objectives relied almost totally on redistribution of resources
within the existing social security system. Much of this redistribution
occurred as a result of readjusting means testing under the Labor government. At the same time, the repeated increase of social wages to compensate

for a decline in nominal wages, as part of the Accord arrangements, also greatly facilitated the general improvement in welfare provision.

The concept of social wage was one of the most important incentives for the labor movement to sign up to the Accord. The social wage and an adequate benchmark for social provision helped prevent inequality from rising as a result of economic liberalization. Based on the social security system, the social wage encompasses a wide variety of benefits, ranging from basic retirement-income support (single-age pension), rent assistance, and working-family support to the reinstitution of Medicare. Under the Accord, the social wage, along with tax cuts, became the primary compensation for the decline in real wages for the labor movement. During the initial period between 1983 and 1985, increases in the social wage came mostly from the reinstitution of Medicare, but later its expansion came from further means testing at the top and the raising of benefits from the bottom, especially for family benefits (Swank 2002: 240; Schwartz 1998: 269; Watts 1989: 117–118; Whiteford 1994: 242–243). As an addition to the Accord's social wage component, the ALP also encouraged the extension of community services on a means-tested basis. The reduction of social expenditures during the earlier years of ALP incumbency went hand in hand with further development of community care, so that those benefiting could receive a subsidized service (Carter 1993: 264–277).

The reliance on means testing from the top as the principal method of expenditure control and redistributive justice was a key feature that distinguished the ALP from its center-right predecessor. The previous coalition government under Fraser attempted to control costs by directly letting the level of benefits fall across the board. By contrast, Labor achieved most of its cost efficiencies not through direct cuts to benefits but through adjustments to means-testing rules. In principle, the government had three options in restraining social expenditure: cutting benefits, tightening means testing, and redefining the categories of means-tested recipients in order to reduce the number of claimants. While it made use of all three methods, Labor relied most heavily on the third one. The previous coalition government removed the indexation of unemployment benefits in an attempt to save costs, but after the Hawke government came to power, it not only restored indexation but also prioritized increases in nonindexed benefits. Figure 6.16 shows that the level of unemployment benefits actually rose further under the ALP (Saunders 2002: 226; Cass and Whiteford 1989: 285–295; Gibson 1990: 195).

Means testing under the ALP did not imply always restricting benefits to the worst-off. On the contrary, targeting often involved both selective

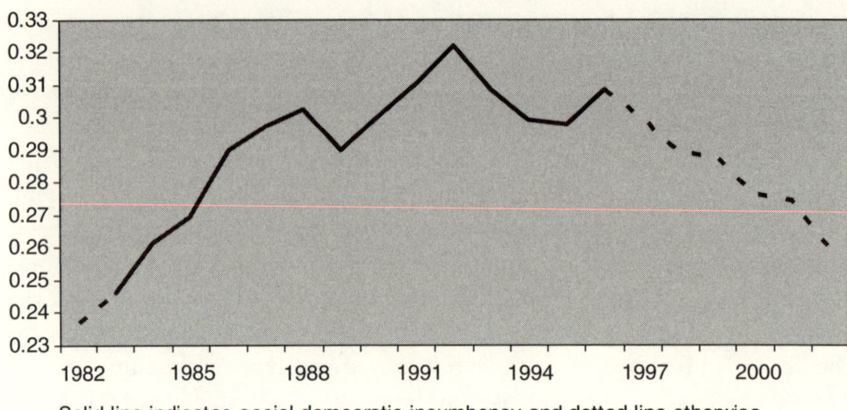

FIGURE 6.16. Unemployment Benefit Replacement Rate in Australia 1982–2002 (*Source:* Scruggs 2004).

cuts and increases, accompanied by the development of new programs and expenditures. The main focus of targeting was the middle- and higher-income earners. While reducing its financial support for broadly targeted programs, the government concentrated its resources on those most in need. It was precisely on this basis that Labor started to means test the child allowance, up until then the only universal cash-benefit program in the country. Similarly, given the very high (80%) level of home ownership in Australia, the criteria in asset tests for pensions for the aged excluded ownership of a family home from the test. Although a vast range of means testing was introduced, the cut-off point for targeting remained generous. Greater targeting in unemployment benefits and assistance for low-income families all followed this logic (Beilharz, Considine and Watts 1992: 123; Gibson 1990: 195; Castles and Pierson 1996: 239–240).

Under Labor, tightened benefit eligibility was compensated with improvements in the actual level of income support. This process of trade-off was made easier by the corporatist Accord framework. In order to improve the provision of social security, the government met its commitment to raise the single-age pension to 25% of the total average weekly earnings of males and substantially increased the maximum level of rent assistance. Between 1983 and 1986, it achieved no noticeable outcome in combating child poverty, but after 1987, the government made significant policy changes to tackle poverty, especially by reforming the Family Allowance. This universal program was transformed into the means-tested Family

Allowance Supplement (FAS), which involved both higher levels of payment and eligibility requirements. The government later improved the real value and relaxed the means testing of FAS, and indexed child payments against inflation. Hawke increased payments to single parents substantially and introduced the Child Support Scheme. Under the previous coalition government, the real value of payments to low-income families with children had declined. By contrast, Labor gave its highest priority to reversing this trend, and as a result of its targeted measures, the party oversaw substantial increases in benefit payments for families with children (Castles and Pierson 1996; 239–240; Whiteford 1994: 244–245; Gibson 1990: 193–195; Castles 1994: 133–134; Cass and Whiteford 1989: 286–290).

As long as economic (and employment) growth was not compromised, the ALP tried actively to remove the poverty trap, with the major beneficiary being families with children in poverty. At the same time, tightened eligibility requirements were imposed on many other social groups. Compared with the fourth Labour government in New Zealand, the ALP both used tighter targeting and offered greater compensation for the worst-off groups (Hemerijck and Schludi 2000: 195–199; Beilharz, Considine, and Watts 1992: 91–94).

In welfare financing, Hawke tried to rely less on income tax and more on increasing the relative weight of the sales tax, the rationalization of tax rates, and the widening of the tax base to cover both capital gains and fringe benefits, against opposition from the coalition parties. The impact from Labor's tax reforms was greatest for those at the top and bottom of the income ladder, while most of the cost was borne by those in the middle (K. Davis 1989: 100–103; Pierson and Castles 2001: 9–10). While changes in marginal tax rates mostly benefited higher earners, and social expenditure in general was successfully curtailed (which the Fraser coalition failed to do), the ALP also introduced measures to reduce fiscal advantages for higher-income earners, such as taxation on lump-sum Superannuation payments and asset tests on pensions. From this perspective, Labor made a more effective commitment than the center-right coalition to both market efficiency and social redistribution (Graycar and Jamrozik 1993: 121).

During ALP's tenure, inequality increased among full-time employees, but the position of the worst-off was not adversely affected. By the end of the 1980s, poverty had fallen substantially and living standards had increased. Labor's restructuring of social security was based on the principle of "asset-based egalitarianism," which was very compatible with the means-tested and small formal Australian welfare state, where the level of homeownership is very high by international standards. Following this guideline, the government tackled inequality not just through fiscal redistribution of income support but also through the accumulation of human/social capital assets for those excluded from the labor market, so that their return to employment could become easier (Castles and Pierson 1996: 240; Pierson and Castles 2001: 13; Whiteford 1994: 251). The transition from strict redistributive egalitarianism to prioritarian egalitarianism focused on activating the most excluded is a common ideological thread running through other third way cases as well.

New Zealand

Compared with other countries' reforms, those under the fourth Labour government had unique characteristics. Here, both the labor market and social security domains were subordinate to the deregulatory reforms in the macroeconomy. As Figure 6.17 shows, despite the intensity and scope of neoliberal economic reforms, cuts to various aspects of social security were not steep, and there was no large difference in benefit generosity between the beginning and end of Labour's tenure. This helped dampen the immediate social impact from economic liberalization, as well as preempt any backlash from Labour's core constituencies. Members inside the parliamentary Labour Party who were concerned with the deregulatory reforms mobilized to explicitly fence off social security from the Treasury's influence, by commissioning a series of reviews devoted to social issues (O'Brien and Wilkes 1993: 35). Changes to passive income support during this period occurred

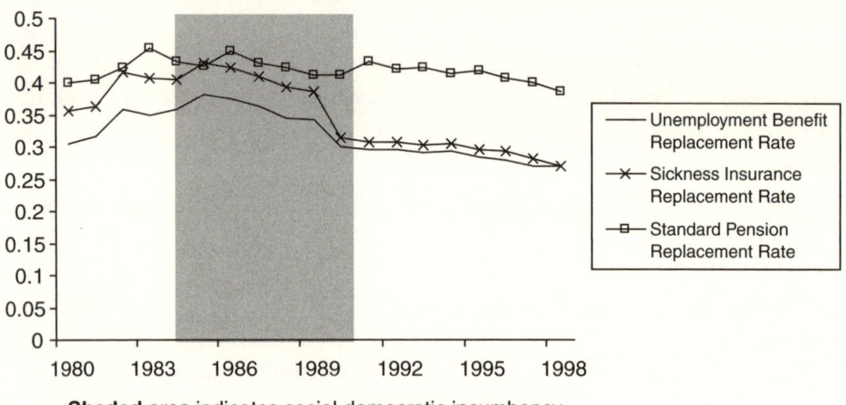

FIGURE 6.17. Passive Benefits Replacement Rates in New Zealand 1980–2002 (*Source:* Scruggs 2004).

mostly as a by-product of economic liberalization, that is, through a series of changes in fiscal welfare.

Because of smaller ambitions in this area, Labour's only clearly specified objective for social security was cost control. However, due to pressure from within the party, it avoided a full-scale reduction in benefits. The guideline was instead to "do more with less," with greater targeting as the main principle in achieving cost control. Under Labour, changes in social expenditures were soon superseded by changes to the title and structure of benefits. During the 1980s, there were significant changes in the functional categories to which public spending was directed. The proportion devoted to welfare benefits increased, primarily at the expense of spending on industrial or producer assistance, in line with Labour's deregulation and privatization reforms in the economy (O'Brien 1993: 14–27; Castles and Pierson 1996: 241; Rudd 1990: 87–88). As a result, as seen in Figure 6.18, aggregate social spending actually increased during the Labour period.

In addition to greater targeting and decreasing generosity for state pensions, the value of universal child benefits was allowed to decline, but increasing family poverty also led to new targeted benefits for families. After 1987, the government also substantially increased the levy for insurance-based accident compensation. The area experiencing the most significant move from universal to targeting was family assistance. Between 1984

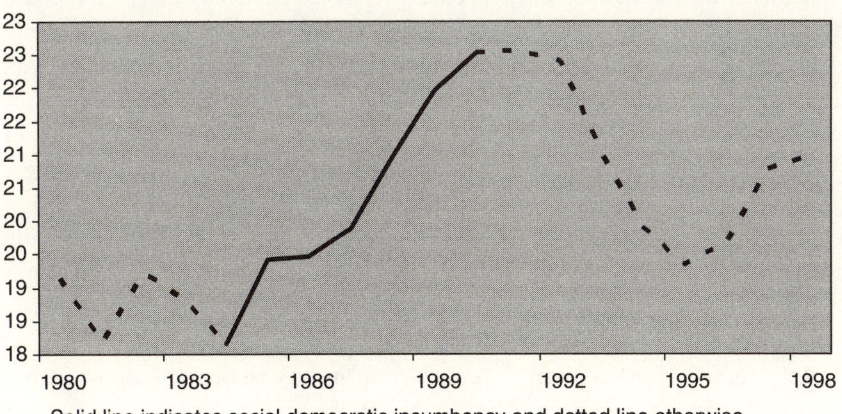

FIGURE 6.18. Total Social Expenditure as Percentage of GDP in New Zealand 1980–1998 (*Source:* OECD 2006a).

and 1991, New Zealand moved from a fully universal to a fully targeted system with the introduction of Family Support and Guaranteed Minimum Family Income (McClure 1998: 216–218; Mackay 2001: 81–83). Labour went into the 1990 election proposing a single basic rate for all benefits except superannuation. Had this new basic rate been implemented, it would have meant substantial reduction in benefits for many types of recipients. Alongside greater targeting and reduction in replacement rates, there was an expansion in second-tier supplementary assistance programs, which grew almost eight times between 1985 and 1990 (Castles and Pierson 1996: 241; O'Brien 1992: 159; Mackay 2003: 81–83).

Overall, Labour reformed passive income support not by directly cutting social expenditure but by indirectly widening the tax base. The introduction of a consumption tax helped increase government revenues despite lower taxes on income. The indirect fine-tuning of social security by fiscal manipulation accelerated after Labour was reelected in 1987. The government formally shifted the focus of its reforms from economic deregulation to an overhaul of the tax system. It attempted to integrate the tax and benefit systems, and changed the adjustment of benefit rates from every six months to an annual basis (O'Brien and Wilkes 1993: 67, 77). In its second term, Labour introduced a comprehensive goods and services tax (GST) of 10%, sharply reduced marginal personal taxes, flattened the tax scale, and introduced a taxation surcharge on superannuation. Traditionally, New Zealand combined internationally low levels of overall taxation with high rates of a personal tax, but since the 1986 tax reforms, the system had been radically transformed. The tax scale was reduced from a five-step scale to a two-step scale. The progressiveness of the income tax was sharply reduced, with cuts to marginal tax rates in 1988. Meanwhile, the GST was increased to 12.5% by 1987. The regressive nature of these reforms meant that those in the top income quintile received a much greater increase in their fiscal resources than did those at the lowest quintile, and the biggest improvement in financial position occurred in the top quintile (O'Brien 1992: 152–154; Shannon 1991: 12–18; Castles 1994: 134). Unfortunately, unlike in Australia and the UK, there are no comparable data tracking social indicators such as poverty across time, because New Zealand was not included in the Luxemburg Income Study.

As a remedy for the regressive nature of its tax reforms, Labour introduced increased targeting and other minor changes in income supports to ameliorate the impact on low-income earners. Increased targeting, meanwhile, also served as a way to control costs. Traditionally, social expenditures in New Zealand were heavily dominated by payments to universal

Superannuation, which was funded by general taxation. By the early 1990s, however, the fiscal weight of Superannuation had diminished significantly due to sharp reductions in tax rates and the introduction of a superannuation surcharge. Also important was the introduction of Family Support, an income-tested refundable tax credit, which replaced both child-supplement and family-care benefits. Labour's strategy of restructuring passive benefits by fiscal manipulation clearly influenced the later trajectory of social security reform under the National government in the 1990s. Since welfare financing relied increasingly on regressive indirect taxes (such as the GST), plus a flattened direct-tax scale, it became easier for the Nationals to defend their own policy of further intensifying targeting in the social security system (Boston 1999: 9; Hawke 1992: 442–443; Rice 1992: 485–486).

In contrast to Labour's balancing act between economic rationalism and social amelioration, the Nationals were less dependent on retaining core working-class votes. The center-right government extended neoliberal reforms firmly into both social security and industrial relations. Breaking with Labour's incremental approach to social security, there was now rapid retrenchment. The government's first priority was budget consolidation. It implemented sharp cuts in cash benefits, which forced people into employment, and it also introduced market principles into the provision of social services (Hemerijck and Schludi 2000: 193–195; Schwartz 2000: 88). While there was some income redistribution to poorer individuals, actual spending per recipient declined for most categories. Because the Nationals' core constituency was increasingly rural and older, the government's targeting prioritized the elderly and non-earners, and only secondly did the resources reach low-income earners. The group particularly left out was low-income households (Shannon 1991: 17).

The neglect and then rapid decline of social security under the fourth Labour government and its center-right successor is closely related to the general absence in New Zealand of the social wage mechanism. In Australia, the social wage was used as a powerful instrument to compensate for the impact of economic liberalization throughout the social security system. The absence of a social wage in New Zealand can be accounted for by problems in the industrial relations system. The Nationals, in a clear contrast to the Australian Accord, retreated from wage-fixing procedures. The 1991 Employment Contracts Act terminated arbitration, and the country's wage earners' welfare state in effect came to an end. With any connection between income support and wage negotiation severed, there was no longer any reference to the social wage. Wage fixing now strictly reflected market realities, and the informal, but historically important, part of social security in New Zealand no longer existed. Social protection was now delivered through either formal welfare or, increasingly, fiscal welfare, in the form of tax credits for low-income workers. Fiscal and occupational/private welfare added considerably to the overall system of social protection in New Zealand (Mackay 2003: 108; Shannon 1991: 13).

After Labour returned to power in 1999, it faced a very different political landscape, with governments by coalition, a new electoral system, and strong popular resentment against the neoliberal reformers. The fifth Labour government continued to rely heavily on fiscal welfare. However, in contrast with the past, its policies became more redistributive, especially for the least-advantaged groups and offered more positive incentives for working. For example, Labour relaxed means testing for both Domestic Purposes Benefit recipients (single parent, caregiver for someone infirm, or single woman 50 years or older) and widows for weekly incomes between $80 and $180 (NZ) (St. John and Rankin 2002: 7).

On a broader level, the Working for Families package introduced in the 2004 budget sharply removed the benefit clawback based on earned incomes, and this represented the first major resource redistribution toward lower-income earners in New Zealand in 30 years. Projections in the budget indicated that Working for Families could reduce child poverty by at least 30% by 2008. Starting from April 2005, there was an increase of $25 per week in Family Support for the first child and $15 for each additional child for all low-income families, even if the families do not work. By 2007, there was a further increase of $10 each child. The government promised to index these family benefits from 2008 and make adjustments when the consumer price index shows a cumulative increase of 5%. Reflecting the redistributive impact of these income-support schemes, once the reforms were to be fully implemented by March 2008, there would be a substantial increase in family support for various groups at or below the average wage level. The biggest beneficiary will be the one-child family, projected to see a 59% increase in benefits when the family is at the 75% of the average wage-earner level. For this group, the reform package will restore their family support benefit to the level of 1986 (St. John 2004; St. John and Craig 2004). In benefit administration, Labour also reduced the reliance on contractors and merged various stand-alone delivery agencies under a single Ministry of Social Development. The government attempted to establish a partnership between the state and voluntary or community sectors. This community-partnership approach has focused especially on the agenda of combating child poverty (Porter and Craig 2004).

Analysis of Reactionary Compensation

Policy changes in reactionary income compensation lend some support to the power-resources logic of welfare-state changes. Social democratic governments distinguished themselves from Christian Democrats in taking greater initiatives to reduce the passivity in the social security system. They also differed from their secular-right counterparts by focusing on restructuring and further redistribution, rather than on straightforward dismantling.

In this book, none of the successful labor market activation cases involved wholesale retrenchment in passive protection. On the contrary, some, such as in the Netherlands and Denmark, still have a social security system highly generous in delivering de-commodifying benefits. Others, such as in Australia and France, further increased income support in the process of third way reforms. In Nordic countries in the 1990s, the social democrats tried to restrain passivity by tightening eligibility and limiting benefit duration, while at the same time keeping replacement rates high. In Sweden and Norway, the governments continued to expand social security entitlement into the late 1980s. The pure extent of social security retrenchment appears to have little association with the effectiveness of third way activation. Instead, social democratic retrenchment has been more directly related to the rapid rise in unemployment. After the late 1980s, unemployment increase was far more serious in Sweden than in Denmark and Norway. Correspondingly, larger cutbacks occurred in Sweden. However, as the country's fiscal and macroeconomic situation started to improve, the social democrats went on to reverse the cuts (Lødemel 2001b: 299; Huber and Stephens 2001: 301; Scharpf and Schmidt 2000: 335; Kuhnle 2000a: 211–213).

No countries that witnessed a substantial increase in active labor market expenditure had a substantial decrease in passive expenditures, and for the two top-performing cases of Denmark and the Netherlands, the pattern was simultaneous expansion in active and passive measures. Actually, from the mid-1980s to the mid-1990s, both countries saw the largest spending on passive measures internationally. Only in Sweden do active measures stably dominate passive ones. Today, Sweden remains not only the country with the highest active-to-passive expenditure ratio but also the EU country with the largest spending on active programs, a fact remarkable in itself because the country also has one of the most generous passive social security systems (Hvinden 2003: 277; Hauser et al. 2000: 27–28; Daguerre 2004: 43–44; Ferrera and Hemerijck 2003: 94).

Across country cases, social democratic governments were reluctant to radically reduce the generosity of social security. While they now share with the secular Right the belief in moving people from welfare to work, the two partisan governments take different approaches in achieving this objective. Social democratic parties prefer activation through the expansion of active labor market measures funded by the state. Secular-right parties, by comparison, focus more on dismantling passive income compensation, while keeping a minimum state presence in the active side. The Christian Democrats, on the other hand, mostly maintained the status quo. Across different welfare regimes, countries such as Britain, Norway, Sweden, and France all experienced a decline in unemployment compensation generosity during center-right incumbencies, and then significant rebound after social democrats took power (Wren 2001: 254).

Governments of different partisan persuasion adopted contrasting paradigms in reforming passive protection, but even the same paradigm led to different implementation strategies and outcomes, reflecting path dependency on traditional welfare state institutional settings. For example, increased targeting is a widely used policy instrument by third way social democrats to reduce the passive influence of income support. In some cases, they applied this instrument from the top to exclude the best-off, as in Australia. In other instances, it is applied from the bottom to retain the worst-off, as in Britain under New Labour. The ideological justification for targeting is its prioritarian effect, in focusing the protection on the worst-off. Some of the measures involving increased targeting started off by introducing means testing to formerly universal benefits. In continental countries, by contrast, the introduction of targeting into the existing social security system was less feasible, due to the institutional legacy of social insurance and contribution as the fiscal basis for this system. The core social insurance component of passive protection was therefore left largely intact. The main change, instead, was to establish a separate, tax-funded minimum tier, means tested from the bottom, in order to protect the worst-off who are already excluded from social insurance benefits. This strategy, however, has led to further segmentation between social protection for insiders and outsiders.

Given their initial design as the last line of defense in minimum income provision, social assistance programs become subject to work conditionality relatively late, and the incorporation of activation principles into social assistance benefits has come to represent the cutting edge of third way reforms in passive protection (Trickey 2001: 258; Handler 2002: 25). The exception to this is, of course, the French RMI, which was introduced as early as 1988 and was, in theory, the first major attempt to combine social assistance and activation, through the principle of insertion. However, as I discussed in Chapter 5, with lax enforcement RMI served only half of its original purpose (that of a basic income guarantee, which did not exist in France before 1988). As a functioning active labor market package, by contrast, RMI had little substance. For continental European cases saddled with large tax wedges, governments gradually moved the fiscal burden away from employers to both the state and employees, by means of social contribution reductions for the former and corresponding increases from the latter two groups. However, although smaller fiscal obligations for businesses do encourage employers to hire, the shuffling of contributions between employers and employees without reducing their total levels cannot reduce the non-wage labor cost effectively. Furthermore, these changes have taken place in the (as yet unchanged) overall context of highly generous public welfare (Daly 2001: 94; Kautto 2001: 252–259; Kautto et al. 1999: 28).

2. ANTICIPATORY COMPENSATION

Passive income compensation can be reactionary, occurring after employment is terminated. It can also be anticipatory, occurring before a genuine loss of employment. In this case, the benefit schemes in question are usually referred to as early exit pathways or labor-market-clearing measures. These measures directly reduce the supply of the labor force and can therefore be utilized as an expedited instrument to reduce the unemployment rate in the short term. Commonly used early exit pathways include age-related schemes that facilitate early retirement and health-related benefits such as disability and sickness insurance. Other typical early exit mechanisms include a wide range of leave arrangements that serve purposes ranging from child rearing to education. The fundamental difference between reactionary and anticipatory compensation is that the former primarily targets persons *outside* the labor market or the unemployed, but early exit pathways target persons who are *still in* the labor market.

Reactionary income replacement, such as unemployment benefits, sometimes leads to work disincentives and creates obstacles for reentry into the labor market. Anticipatory compensation goes one step further by actually moving those who are still inside the labor market out of it, and early exit pathways are therefore especially problematic for labor market activation. In anticipatory compensation, the partisan difference in reform strategies is noticeably smaller than in active social protection. For different ideological reasons, both social democrats and secular-right parties favor the removal of such measures. Christian democratic parties are ideologically sympathetic to labor saving. However, they are also aware that insufficient employment is the fundamental problem behind the severe fiscal crisis of Christian democratic welfare states. Therefore, parties across the ideological spectrum have attempted to roll back anticipatory compensation. However, there is still some evidence for partisan differences in the reform process. Social democratic dismantling of anticipatory schemes have focused on reducing enrolment and promoting employment with further public investment in enabling measures. From the center Right, the response has ranged from inaction to directly cutting benefits to save costs.

Since removing early exit pathways is tantamount to directly taking away (rather than just restructuring) benefits often jointly administered by social partners, a corporatist breakdown and collective action failure among interested actors is an important contributing factor to path dependency in these reforms. This is especially so in continental European countries, where unions and employers have the strongest vested interest in perpetuating the old system. Attempts to push forward any reforms without union cooperation has led to serious electoral backlash, as the Dutch case will show. Also reflecting path dependency is the fact that there was very little anticipatory compensation in Anglo-Saxon countries to start with. The level of means-tested benefits in liberal welfare states has generally been too low to attract voluntary withdrawal from employment. Due to this institutional setting, there were no retrenchment reforms in these countries. For this reason, neither Australia nor New Zealand feature in the analysis. As a road map for the analysis, Table 6.2 shows key policy developments in this area across countries.

Denmark

Initially, the expansion of various leave schemes and other early retirement measures was a crucial, and arguably most innovative, part of the paradigm-shifting 1994 labor market reform by the Danish social democrats. Targeted primarily at the retention of unskilled workers, these schemes reflected the party's human capital emphasis and its concern with the risk of social exclusion for people with disadvantaged conditions in the labor market. During the 1994 reform, the government significantly improved educational and parental leave schemes, and it also introduced a wholly new sabbatical leave. The maximum leave period was increased to 52 weeks, and more controversially, eligibility for leave schemes was extended to include both the self-employed and the unemployed, as long

TABLE 6.2. *Key Reforms in Anticipatory Income Compensation, by Country and Theoretical Implications*

Key policies in order of appearance in the chapter	Theoretical Implications ⇒	Power Resources	Path Dependency
	Denmark	Various leave schemes reduced or canceled	
	Sweden	Early retirement restricted	• Reforms depend on corporatist cooperation from social partners, especially in continental Europe.
	Norway	Early retirement, disability, and sickness leave schemes restricted	
	Netherlands	Fundamental reform of disability benefits	
	France	Late retirement encouraged (limited effect)	• In Nordic countries, some of the leave measures have enabling (human capital) effects in addition to labor saving.
	Germany	Age of eligibility for pension raised (limited effect)	
	United Kingdom	New Deal for the Disabled New Deal 50+	
	Australia	No significant anticipatory income compensation preexisted	
	New Zealand		

Note: Countries in shaded areas have no major policy innovation during period under examination and do not feature in the analysis.

as an unemployed person could be hired as a replacement during the leave period. Meanwhile, compensation worth 80% of full unemployment insurance benefits was available for the duration of the leave schemes. The social democrats also removed obligations on the firms to take in substitutes, and they established a formal right for employees to take parental leave. These changes further increased incentives for both individuals and firms to utilize the leave schemes. The initial opposition from employers, in particular, was defused by the government's guarantee of full discretion over whether employees should be allowed to go on leave (Ploug 1999: 97; Bjorklund 2000: 155–156; Loftager and Madsen 1997: 133; Compston 1997: 200; Compston and Madsen 2001: 121).

The premise for these leave schemes was the concept of "comprehensive approach," introduced during the 1994 labor market reform. This concept dictates that activation of the unemployed should be combined with efforts to upgrade skills for the workforce in general. The most explicit representation of this principle is job rotation, which is the key underlying mechanism for all the leave schemes. By linking shorter working time with expansion in vocational training, job rotation represents a radically innovative and productive way of reducing working time (Seifert: 1998: 636; Madsen 1998: 712). In a job rotation scheme, persons going on leave will be replaced by the unemployed, who therefore get an opportunity to be reintegrated into the labor market, although employers are not obliged to hire a substitute except in the case of sabbatical leave. These schemes are labeled as "pull-strategies" because they create job vacancies for the unemployed instead of improving qualifications for them, as the traditional "push-strategies" would do. Meanwhile, these leave schemes purposely use public expenditures to fund the temporary withdrawal from the labor market. In this sense, the programs reflect a notion of citizens' income, an idea slowly being replaced by the principle of participation-based communitarianism in third way reforms. In addition to changes in leave schemes, the social democratic government also extended the transitional allowance to those 50 to 54 years old (Etherington 1998: 148; Goul Andersen 2002a: 152; Loftager and Madsen 1997: 123; Madsen 1999: 66).

However, although originally part of the social democratic reforms, over time the three core schemes of parental, educational, and sabbatical leaves all came under questioning over their status and role in labor market activation. The newly introduced sabbatical leave received the greatest criticism, not only because of the extremely generous support it offered (up to 70% of normal benefits for one year) for the leave takers, but also for the very lax interpretation of what sabbatical activities should involve. Comparatively, the parental leave scheme was more popular with the public and the educational scheme more popular with the government given its potential to increase labor market flexibility (Lind 1999: 197). Nevertheless, despite their forward-looking orientation, all three leave schemes, plus other early retirement measures, did have the inevitable effect of further reducing the labor force and clearing the labor market. Partly spurred on by a positive experience with pilot schemes under the previous bourgeois government, the social democrats rushed in the three leave schemes in reaction against the unprecedented rise in unemployment in 1993. And the direct impact of the schemes was indeed quick: By 1995 the paid-leave policy had reduced registered unemployment by approximately 2% of the workforce (Loftager and Madsen 1997: 135; Clasen 2000: 102–103; Compston and Madsen 2001: 118).

Despite the immediate effect in reducing unemployment, in the long run these leave schemes shrank the size of the labor force. These negative long-term job consequences became clear after unemployment declined rapidly and the Danish economy went into a boom by the mid-1990s. The schemes' labor-market-clearing mechanism now became out of sync with the dynamics of employment. Famously declared as instruments to "break the curve of unemployment" by the social democratic prime minister, Poul Rasmussen, in a period of falling unemployment the leave policies had the opposite effect by producing bottlenecks. The bottleneck problem was made worse by frequent abuse of the leave schemes, given their generosity and lax interpretation. In response, starting from 1995 the social democrats began a U-turn on these policies. The government canceled sabbatical leaves, cut benefits for parental leave, and also imposed a more stringent requirement to replace workers who take leaves. By 2002, many new leave schemes were either terminated or marked for phasing out (Cox 1998: 9; Goul Andersen 2002b: 66–69; Goul Andersen 2002c: 6; Green-Pedersen, van Kersbergen, and Hemerijck 2001: 317).

In addition to leave schemes, another major focus for the government was to stamp out various early retirement pathways. In 1999, the social democrats merged two existing early retirement schemes into one, so that exit from the labor market could be better tailored to individual needs. They abolished the previous rule, which excluded the unemployed above 60 years of age from early retirement benefits if they were to become sick. This way, the elderly would not have to leave early for fear of losing the right to early retirement in the event of illness. Meanwhile, the early retirement benefit level was cut to 91% of the full amount for those who leave before the age of 62, in order to create disincentives for prematurely leaving the labor force. The decision to scale down early retirement benefits proved politically difficult for the social democrats, because unions have historically claimed ownership of this issue. Union opposition was somewhat softened after it emerged that white-collar retirees were also exploiting this scheme. For this reason, by 1999 the labor movement had agreed to accept stricter criteria for early retirement (Jensen 2004: 44–54; Goul Andersen 2002b: 69; Hansen 2002: 180–181). Still, reforms in early retirement benefits were often regarded as a key reason for the electoral rout of the social democrats in the 2001 general election. This is because the party made an "early retirement guarantee" back in the 1998 election campaign, to the effect that it would not touch the existing early retirement scheme. In this context, once it was in office, the party's decision to drastically restructure the policy in 1999 was not only resented for insufficient consultation with unions but also widely regarded as a direct breach of an election promise (Lind 2000: 149–150).

In order to make them correspond with changes in early retirement, the social democrats made minor adjustments to the part-time pension scheme and phased out the transitional allowance for those 50 to 54 years old in the 1996 budget. The number of disability pension recipients was also declining after the late 1990s, for two possible reasons. Firstly, flex jobs for people with permanently reduced working capacity helped in moving them from disability pensions into employment. Secondly, with the devolution of disability pension financing to the regions after 1999, local authorities became more reluctant to grant disability pension entitlements (Jensen 2004: 58).

Most of the policies aimed at stopping early retirement targeted employees, but the social democrats also brought in measures making it more difficult for employers to fire older employees with long seniority. The government also made it easier for the elderly to transit to employment, through a wide variety of job schemes targeted specifically at them. For example, it introduced both Job Offices and a Senior Fund to help coordinate and support projects aimed at integrating the elderly into the labor market. Firms were also offered consultations with a maximum of five hours on how to design senior policies. After 1999, the government had experimented with service jobs, which are ordinary jobs in the public-service sector requiring a minimal level of education and training. This fits the circumstance of many elderly unemployed who are in danger of permanent exclusion from the labor market. Employers are subsidized by the state in channeling these elderly people into service jobs (Larsen and Bredgaard 2004: 10–16; Lind 1999: 192; Hansen 2002: 192–194; Foden and Jepsen 2002: 451). Figure 6.19 indicates that by the end of its tenure, the social

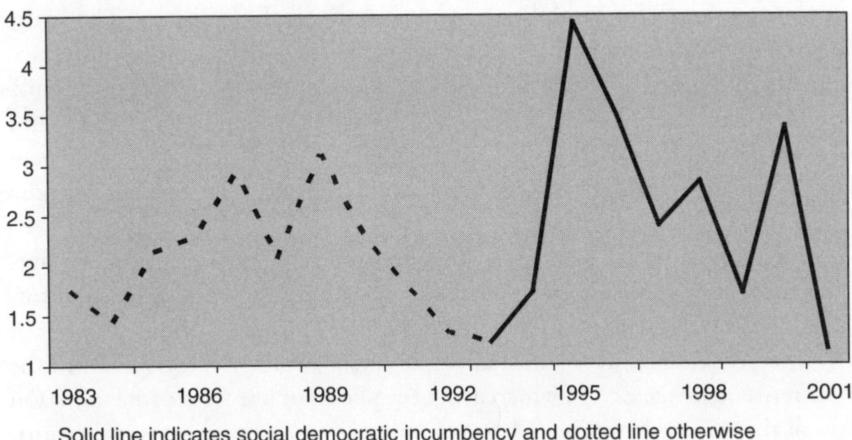

FIGURE 6.19. Share of Total Unemployment for 60–64 Years of Age in Denmark 1983–2001 (*Source:* OECD 2007a).

democratic government was able to wrench down elderly unemployment, from its historical peak in 1995 back to the level of the early 1980s.

Sweden

Given the traditional dominance of active over passive measures in Swedish social policy, early exit pathways had seldom been a significant part of the Swedish employment policy apparatus. Instead, a high proportion of older workers are placed in active labor market programs (Wadensjo 2002: 381). This situation, however, was briefly interrupted in the early 1990s by a rapid rise in unemployment. Similar to the case in Denmark, the Swedish bourgeois government resorted to clearing the labor market and reducing the labor force by means of early exit schemes, as a short-term but quick solution to growing unemployment.

After the social democrats returned to power in 1994, there was a renewed emphasis on active labor market measures, and more specifically, on requalifying the labor force rather than further shrinking its size. The government restricted pathways of invalidity and long-term sickness benefits to only medical criteria, excluding labor market factors from the eligibility assessment. The party's separate pension reform in 1998 also indirectly provided incentives for remaining in the labor market longer. Part-time pensions were abolished, and similar to sickness benefits, the party narrowed eligibility criteria for disability pensions to medical conditions. The really important change, however, was the shift in ATP calculation from defined benefits to defined contribution, which significantly strengthened the linkage between benefit levels and length of contribution, and served as a major incentive for elderly workers to remain in employment. Changes in the pension system also brought greater flexibility to the age of retirement (Mandin 2004: 10; Olofsson 2001: 19).

In 2001, the social democrats introduced a new law on retirement age. This made it possible for an employee to work until 67 years of age, and forbade collective agreements from including rules forcing workers to retire at 65. The government also adjusted employment-protection legislation to the new retirement age of 67 by increasing the age span of career protection. On top of these measures targeted specifically at early exit schemes, other programs originally designed for general labor market activation also proved helpful in reintegrating the older unemployed. For example, the 2000 program Activity Guarantee intended to cover anyone over 20 in danger of long-term unemployment, but it has benefited the over 55s most significantly, as a third of the participants in this program are within the 55–64 age band. The measures taken by Swedish social democrats to close early exit pathways might appear limited relative to the major reforms in the Netherlands or Denmark. However, the main reason for this relative inactivity is that, as is true for several other aspects of Swedish labor market policy, the country already had a participation rate among the elderly that is close to the general participation rate. The dominant tradition in Swedish employment policy, furthermore, has always been to include rather than exclude the elderly from the labor market (Foden and Jepsen 2002: 450).

Norway

In line with its traditionally strong emphasis on activation and, in particular, on the work line, Labour deliberately shunned instruments of labor force reduction or labor-market-clearing as a short-term response to high unemployment. Not only did the party fear that a planned reduction in the labor supply would increase the non-wage labor cost and hurt competitiveness, but the party also actively promoted the retention of elderly workers to help ease the excessive financial burden on the pension system. For this reason, Labour has generally taken a proactive attitude toward avoiding early exit pathways. It rejected work sharing, reduction in overtime, or reduction in standard working hours as strategies to reduce unemployment. Instead of reducing the pension age through early retirement, it proposed to increase the de facto pension age of 60 by three years in the next fifteen years. Starting from 2002, payroll taxes were also reduced for workers over 62 years of age to increase the financial incentive for employers to retain older workers (Halvorsen 2002: 170–172).

For the various health-related exit pathways such as disability pensions or sickness benefits, Labour adopted a combination of tighter eligibility and intensified follow-ups. In 1991, the government tightened claims to occupational and geographical mobility for claimants of disability pensions. Geographical disability was discounted substantially, whereas more stringent criteria were used to assess the direct causal relationship between medical condition and vocational disability. The government also increased the referral trend to better utilize residual work capacity and raised the lowest age for disability pension eligibility. With regard to employers, Labour proposed to double the employer-financed sick-pay period, from two to four weeks, in an attempt to encourage employers to take more preventive methods and improve the workplace environment. This proposal was rejected by parliament, but Labour succeeded in extending the sick-pay period to three weeks (Halvorsen 2002: 170–172; Solem and Overbye 2004: 30; Drøpping, Hvinden, and van Oorschot 2000: 50; Dahl and Drøpping 2001: 274).

In an effort to further close various exit pathways, the government introduced a new program in 2000 based on the committee report "An Inclusive Working Life." With this new proposal, Labour hoped to reduce absence due to sickness by 20% by the end of 2005 and further enhance the labor market participation of older workers and those on disability pensions. The program's focus was on rehabilitation and retraining, rather than compulsion. The government's decision to improve conditions in work, rather than cutting benefits, played an important role in securing support from unions for the reform. In the package, much attention was placed on policy implementation on the company level, through the establishment of 19 Regional Centers for Inclusive Working Life at a cost of 27 million euros for 2002. Companies were encouraged to engage in active dialogue not only with individuals on sickness or disability benefits but also with the local security offices, in order to design more flexible arrangements for labor market integration on the company level. To encourage the hiring of disabled persons, Labour offered salary subsidies of up to 50% for three years for companies that adjust tasks so that they can be performed by persons with reduced capacities. On the whole, as seen in Figure 6.20, the government oversaw a sharp increase in public expenditures on employment measures for the disabled. Similarly, in order to encourage older workers to remain employed,

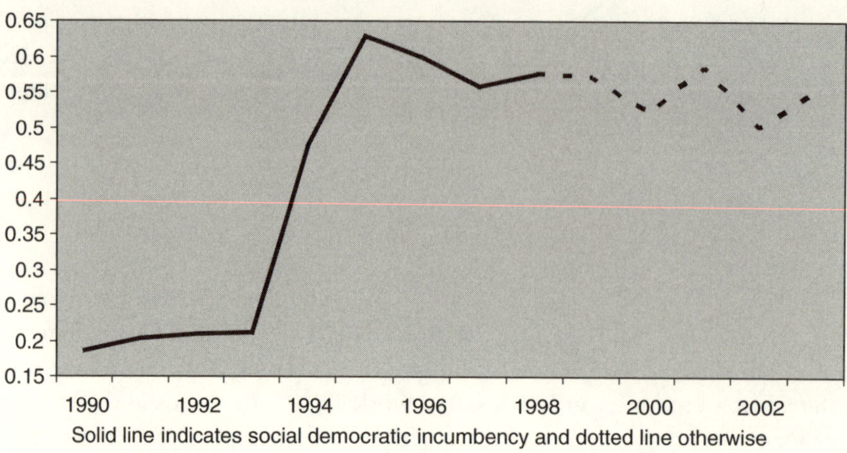

FIGURE 6.20. Expenditure on Employment Measures for the Disabled as Percentage of GDP in Norway 1990–2003 (*Source:* OECD 2006a).

the government also encouraged the growing use of time accounts (Solem and Overbye 2004: 34–37).

The Netherlands

By the early 1980s, sickness and disability schemes had become the most inefficient and abused parts of the Dutch social security system. A broad definition of disability, the inclusion of labor market chances in benefit calculation, and the close relation between sickness pay and extended benefits had all contributed to the system's vulnerability to excessively exploitation. Employers, unions, and the social policy administration were in de facto collusion by externalizing the costs of economic slack onto the social security system. As a result, a severe welfare trap was created for the disabled (Hemerijck and Visser 2000: 239; Visser and Hemerjick 1997: 139).

In 1987, the Dutch government formally started to tackle the disability crisis. However, initial measures under the Lubbers administration were modest in financial resources, with the primary concern being the level rather than the structure of benefits. The government reduced both the duration and level of benefits and froze social assistance and state pensions. By 1991, the central plank of the Christian Democrats' disability policy platform was still a proposal to cut benefits for all recipients under 50 years of age. These strategies, however, could not stem the continuously

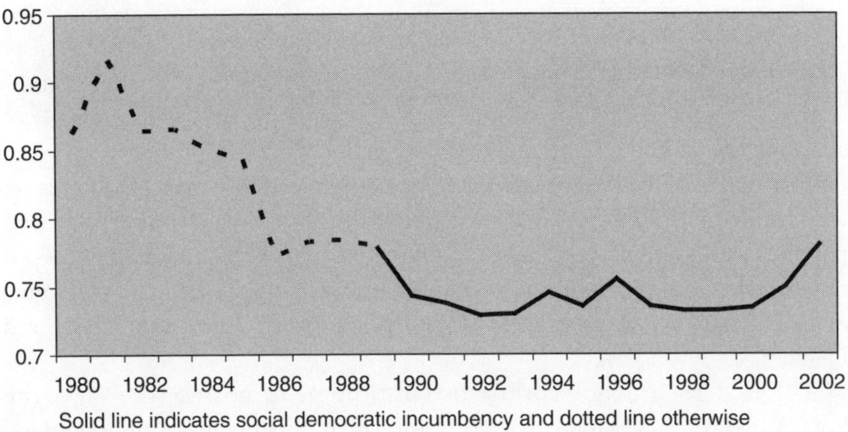

FIGURE 6.21. Sickness Insurance Replacement Rate in the Netherlands 1980–2002 (*Source:* Scruggs 2004).

rising number of benefit claimants. After the PvdA came to power, the government gradually shifted its focus from cutting benefits to changing the structure of benefit entitlement, distribution, and payment administration. As seen in Figure 6.21, after the PvdA joined the coalition, not only did sickness benefit retrenchment slow down significantly, but some cuts were actually restored by the end of this period (Trommel and de Vroom 2002: 93; Aarts and de Jong 1996: 66; Lamping and Vergunst 2004: 19; van Oorschot 2002a: 110).

The PvdA spearheaded key elements of the disability reforms, including the removal of social partners from benefit administration, which struck at the heart of union interests. As a result, the government, and the PvdA in particular, suffered the largest postwar demonstration and the most significant vote losses in the ensuing 1994 election. However, the social democrats weathered the storm from the unions and returned to power as the dominant coalition partner with the VVD. The shift to the Purple Coalition gave the party increased control over policy direction, and the two Purple Coalitions after 1994 oversaw most of the radical reforms in Dutch sickness and disability benefits.

Traditionally, the daily administration and implementation of workers' compensation schemes were managed jointly by unions and employers' organizations. However, this arrangement was questioned by the 1993 Parliamentary Inquiry and the Buurmeijer Committee investigating the functioning and administration of social security. The investigations exposed gross inefficiency, and abuse, in these compensation schemes, and the Buurmeijer Committee recommended that the bipartite social security administration be halted. The committee also suggested that benefit administration be monitored by a government agency operating fully independently of social partners. The government endorsed most of the Buurmeijer recommendations and amended the Social Insurance Organization Act in 1994. This set in motion an institutional breakthrough, as the discretionary powers of social partners were completely removed, with the progressive dismantling of corporatist institutions previously responsible for managing the benefits (Trommel and de Vroom 2002: 93; Hemerijck and Manow 2001: 227–228; Visser and Hemerijck 1997: 148–151).

The first such major corporatist institution to go was the tripartite Social Insurance Council (SVR), whose membership was dominated by unions and employers' associations. Traditionally, the council controlled and monitored the implementation of social security legislation, but in 1994, these responsibilities were divided up and transferred to an independent organization responsible for supervision and implementation (Ctsv). The Ctsv was an attempt to restore the primacy of politics at the expense of social partnership in benefit administration. In 1997, the temporary Ctsv was replaced by the permanent independent organization, LISV, which sets the yearly premium for different social security schemes. During the same year, market incentives were formally introduced into benefit management, all local industrial insurance boards were dismantled, and policy administration was devolved to private operators. On the basis of independent monitoring, the Purple Coalition introduced significant financial incentives into the management of disability and sickness funds. Firms were required to cover sick pay during the first week of an employee's absence. A "bonus malus" system was introduced, under which employers were entitled to a subsidy if they employed a disabled worker for at least a year. Businesses would either pay wages for sick employees directly or reinsure the risk through private insurance, an option most employers ended up taking. It is now in employers' interest to actively reduce absenteeism due to sickness (van Oorschot 2002a: 117; Trommel and de Vroom 2002: 93; Visser and Hemerjick 1997: 150; Ebbinghaus and Hassel 1999: 17).

By forcefully removing both unions and employers from the administration of social transfers, the government weakened their ability to resist further changes to these exit schemes. This was a nonconsensual approach that bypassed corporatist institutions, and it led to enormous electoral costs. For this reason, both the French and German social democrats avoided such a strategy in their own attempts to stamp out early exit. Nevertheless,

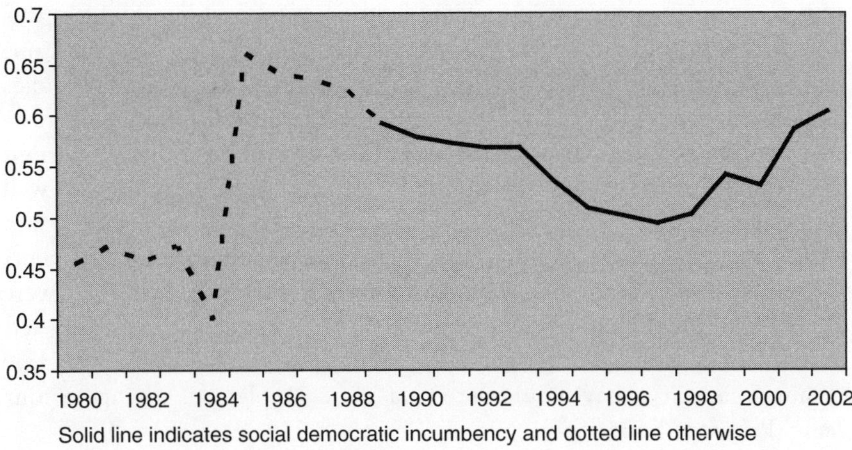

FIGURE 6.22. Employment Measures for the Disabled as Percentage of GDP in the Netherlands 1980–2002 (*Source:* OECD 2006a).

regardless of the political cost, the increased policy leverage for the Dutch state at the expense of unions and businesses had made the reforms easier and more radical (Levy 1999b: 260–261).

Besides expanding the state's supervisory role and the weight of legal ruling, another major aspect of the reforms was to bring significant financial incentives and encourage retention in employment. Figure 6.22 shows that while public expenditure on employment measures for the disabled continued to decline after the PvdA came to power, during the government's third term it sharply increased again, back to the level of the early 1980s. In 1998, financing mechanisms for the Disability Benefits Act were completely revised. The government imposed greater responsibility on employers to take up the cost of disability benefits. This created incentives for firms to adopt a preemptive attitude toward early exit and develop better workplace safety or sick leave policies (van der Veen and Trommel 1999: 299; Pennings 2002: 298).

In additional to redistributing financial responsibilities, the fiscal incentives for employers also came as direct cash subsidies. The general principle of the Wim Kok government was to encourage businesses to hire older workers through favorable tax instruments. Tax credits and reductions in social security contributions were granted to employers for hiring the long-term unemployed over 50 years of age and earning up to 150% of the minimum wage, and progressively higher credits were available for the over 58s and over 65s. In 1998, a Replacement Subsidy of up to 8,000 guilders was introduced for employers who retained disabled employees with at least one year of work history within the enterprise. Another separate set of subsidies was offered to employers who were willing to recruit disabled workers as new employees for at least six months. The government further revised the disability schemes and introduced differentiation on premiums, as well as the possibilities for employers to opt out (Snels 1999: 133; Foden and Jepsen 2002: 153). Besides employers, there were also financial supplements to encourage employees to stay on. Disabled individuals, for example, were offered additional income support under the Reintegration Promotion Act, so that if they were willing to accept a job with wages below their healthy earnings capacity, they would receive a wage supplement for up to four years (Pennings 2002: 297).

Along with carrots as subsidies, the government directly imposed some sticks, by increasing the financial costs of employee disability. In 1996, for example, the compulsory wage payment by firms for disabled workers was extended to 52 weeks. The PvdA also toughened requirements on benefit recipients. The government decided to medically reexamine all disability scheme beneficiaries, training and retraining for the disabled became more important, and the fiscal attractiveness and accessibility of disability benefits were reduced (Keizer 2003: 294–295; van der Veen and Trommel 1999: 302).

After the PvdA came to power in 1989, reforms in health-related early exits had left a clear impact. Compared with the failure of the 1987 reforms to contain disability claims, after 1992 the number of disability beneficiaries started to decrease. It became much more difficult for older workers to receive a 100% disability claim, and the number of new entrants aged between 55 and 64 decreased from 14,300 in 1993 to 10,000 in 1995. During the same period, the total number of benefit recipients dropped from 894,000 to 862,000, the very first time in history that the growth trend had been reversed. However, by the end of the 1990s, enrollment was still high by international standards (8.6% of the total labor force in 1998). More seriously, after 1995, enrollment started to climb again, and absences due to sickness also rose (Stigter 1997: 18–19; de Vroom 2004: 139; van der Veen and Trommel 1999: 308).

In addition to the health-related early exit pathways, the Dutch social democrats also attempted to reduce age-related exits, such as early retirement benefits collectively agreed to at the sectoral level and financed as a top-up to unemployment benefits (Auer 2002: 91). After 1995, a number of policy initiatives were developed by the Dutch government to raise the awareness of age discrimination. After 1996, the Purple Coalition had attempted to restrict voluntary unemployment through legislation on administrative penalties. In 1999, a bill was introduced to regulate the prohibition of age discrimination, which covers not only work-related recruitment and selection but also work-related training, education, and promotion (de Vroom 2004: 136; Auer 2002: 91). In addition to tackling age discrimination, the government also took direct measures to close age-related early exits, by restructuring or simply dismantling existing programs. The Early Retirement Scheme (VUT), for example, was gradually phased out, and tax support for the scheme was abolished in July 2002. The collective pay-as-you-go VUT premiums were gradually replaced with individualized savings schemes, so that younger workers have greater incentives to save for their own early retirement. In many collective agreements, VUT packages were replaced by pension schemes with a flexible retirement date, and the pension base was changed from final pay to average pay. By 1998, nearly half of the collective agreements had already replaced the early retirement benefits with flexible pension schemes (de Vroom 2004: 139–147; Delsen 2002a: 307–320).

The government also took a critical look at two exceptional clauses in the general unemployment benefit system. One was the "elderly guideline," which legitimized the selection of older workers as the first target group in mass dismissal. The other was the "57.5 age rule," which released the older unemployed over 57.5 years of age from the obligation to find work. Taking advantage of these two exceptional clauses, almost as many workers slipped out of the labor market via general unemployment compensation as they did through VUT. In response, the government in 1994 replaced the elderly guideline with the rule that mass dismissal should reflect the overall age profile of the company. It introduced an element of partial risk for employers themselves who dismiss elderly workers 57.5 years of age or older, by requiring them to finance part of the unemployment benefits for the dismissed. After 1994, selective dismissal and compulsory dismissal of older workers was no longer allowed, and in 1995 the tripartite Board of Public Employment Service removed the age criteria from all of its training and placement measures. Replacing these early exit pathways, the government introduced new programs such as "flexible retirement," "pre-retirement," and "demotion," so that there is more flexibility in choosing between work and non work. The government also used direct financial incentives to attract those who retired early back to employment. For example, workers who return from early retirement to difficult posts to fill in the Dutch Railways or the education sector are entitled to a penalty reduction in VUT.

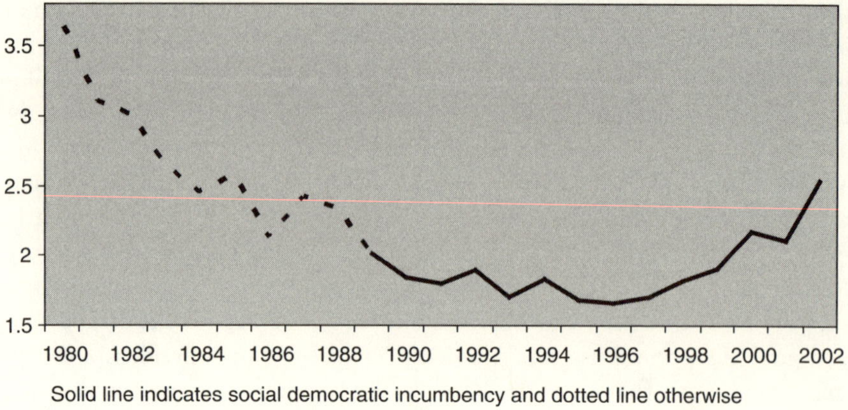

FIGURE 6.23. Share of Total Employment for 60–64 Years of Age in the Netherlands 1980–2002 (*Source:* OECD 2007a).

Since 2001, those returning to the health-care sector can work without incurring any reduction in either their VUT or pensions (de Vroom 2004: 139–147; Delsen 2002a: 307, 319–320; Foden and Jepsen 2002: 446, 453).

With these diverse strategies to stop early exit, the PvdA had brought a fundamental change to the basic principles underlying early retirement policies. The theoretical framework for these policies shifted from social rights and compensation entitlement to a system focused on incentives to remain in work. The government expanded the coverage of ALMPs to cover unemployed workers aged 45 and over who were excluded from the active labor market measures before 1995. On the basis of this new active aging principle, the second Kok government explicitly targeted a permanent increase in elderly employment, and as Figure 6.23 shows, by its third term the PvdA had achieved tangible results in meeting this objective (Foden and Jepsen 2002: 446; Guillemard 2001: 10; Delsen 2002a: 310–311).

France and Germany

In continental welfare states, reforms to remove early exit benefits showed strong signs of path dependency, and collective action failure among social partners was an especially important contributing factor to such path dependency. The major success of the Dutch social democrats in pushing through reforms was due to a combination of specific factors, such as the dramatic extent of the disability crisis and the government's unusual decision to bypass corporatist institutions in benefit administration (which itself was a politically costly strategy). By contrast, the French and German social democrats displayed a more expected pattern, with many of their reforms in early exits unsuccessful due at least partly to their inability to bring unions on board.

Before the early 1990s, policies adopted in France to combat early exits had focused primarily on restricting the pension benefit level or entitlement. However, these were merely changes in policy settings and instruments. Without a fundamental revision of policy objectives to focus more on enabling activation, these measures did not succeed in reversing the rising early exit trend (Guillemard 2001: 9). After that, governments responded with additional strategies. French state intervention over this issue has developed through three methods: (1) closure of pathways to early exit, (2) measures to facilitate the retention of older workers, and (3) adjustments in the pension system to postpone retirement, such as raising the statutory retirement age by lengthening the contribution period. In order to close early retirement pathways, the Socialist government tightened control over the Special Pre-Retirement Allocation program and made it more expensive for firms to dismiss wage earners older than 50 years of age. The Jospin government restricted access to the Special National Employment Fund, and contributions to the fund paid by firms was raised in June 2001 to increase the direct cost of early exits. The Socialists also offered employers financial aid for recruitment in order to lower their labor costs. In addition, they also financed training programs aimed at requalifying older workers with inadequate skills (de Vroom and Guillemard 2002: 194–197; Guillemard and Argoud 2004: 169, 174; Mandin 2004: 18). Efforts to reduce working time, such as the 35-hour week, were also expected by the government to help in retaining some older workers.

However, most schemes introduced at that time showed limited results. First of all, proposals to discourage early retirement involving changes to the pension system were either watered down (the Balladur reforms in 1993) or completely defeated (the Juppé reforms in 1995) because of union opposition, and after the Juppé debacle, the incoming Socialist government decided to postpone all pension reforms. Secondly, the Socialists provided insufficient public resources for reforming these schemes. The party's attempt to combat early exit was characterized by a proliferation of individual programs but a lack of coherence and financial backing. This trend has more or less been followed by the center-right government since 2002. The center-right cabinets went on to close more early exit pathways but, reflecting their even greater concern with cost restraint, have so far

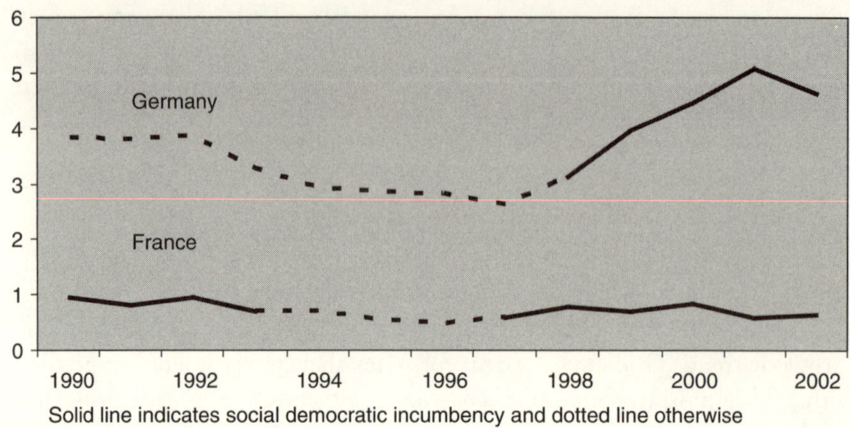

FIGURE 6.24. Share of Total Unemployment for 60–64 Years of Age in France and Germany 1990–2002 (*Source:* OECD 2007a).

failed to come up with any measure that actually helps the elderly return to employment. So the paradoxical situation in France today is that while the state progressively makes it more difficult to retire early, it does not offer corresponding public resources to enable older workers to work longer (de Vroom and Guillemard 2002: 194–197; Guillemard and Argoud 2004: 169–174; Mandin 2004: 18; Jolivet 2002: 245–270). For policy outcomes, Figure 6.24 shows clearly that the Socialists were unable to reduce elderly unemployment throughout their periods in power.

Well into the mid-1990s, the German government continued to use early exit as a short-term strategy for reducing the labor supply and, hence, the unemployment rate (Leibfried and Obinger 2003: 215; Teipen and Kohli 2004: 100). After 1992, however, the government attempted to raise the age limit for pension access. In order to avoid a severe impact on the immediately eligible age groups, the reforms were planned to be phased in very gradually. With the Pension Reform Act of 1999, the Red-Green coalition considerably shortened the transition period to a higher age limit for pension benefits. Through a series of steps, it raised the eligibility age from 63 to 65 and the retirement age from 60 to 65 on the grounds of unemployment. Early retirement can still occur but will incur considerable financial loss. In 2000, the government also further extended a part-time retirement law introduced by the previous center-right coalition, offering older workers the possibility of reducing working time without incurring excessive income loss. The social democrats made increasing use of both part-time employment and time accounts to encourage the retention of elderly workers. On the one hand, they reached agreements with social partners over the explicit purpose of encouraging lifelong learning and work-time accounts. On the other hand, they also introduced legislation not only allowing full-time workers to migrate to part-time work but also protecting part-time workers from discrimination. However, the government's measures in part-time employment have not achieved the intended outcomes, as workers continue to prioritize saving for full-time retirement (Foden and Jepsen 2002: 447–452).

Beyond these measures, the SPD had no labor market policies designed with the explicit objective of activating the elderly. This situation only began to change with a new law on the reintegration of older workers in 2003. This new proposal, however, was severely weakened by the fact that it combined two policy designs serving opposite purposes. On the one hand, it contained measures to make work pay for the elderly, such as subsidies from the labor office for old job seekers who accept a job with lower wages than their previous one, or subsidies for employers willing to hire an older job seeker. Based on negotiations in the Alliance for Jobs, the qualifying age for reintegration subsidies for the elderly was lowered to 50. On the other hand, the new law also proposed a bridging system to make it easier for older workers over 55, especially white-collar employees, to leave the labor market. Facing heavy criticism over the conflicting logic in the proposal, the government was forced to withdraw the bridging system. As a whole, as Figure 6.24 shows, the Red-Green coalition actually oversaw a further sharp increase in elderly unemployment. A crucial factor behind the SPD's indecisive policies was the metalworkers' union IG Metall. As by far the most dominant component within the German labor movement, IG Metall continued to prioritize early retirement as the primary strategy in reducing unemployment. Union resistance was fundamental in affecting the government's reform strategies because, in contrast to the PvdA, the Schröder government preferred to navigate changes in a highly consensual manner, as clearly demonstrated in the pension reform process (Anderson and Meyer 2003; Lehmbruch 2003: 153; Mandin 2004: 16).

United Kingdom

In continental welfare regimes, passive income-replacement benefits are primarily funded out of social contributions, and are therefore liable to being exploited as an outlet for externalizing the cost of economic adjustment. On the contrary, tax-funded benefits common in liberal welfare regimes have generally prevented the emergence of age-related early exits. Instead, New Labour turned its attention to health-related benefits, especially disability schemes. To discourage enrollment, the government tightened work conditionality for the benefit, and in 2002 it unified the individual gateway services of the six New Deal programs. By merging services for employment (Employment Service) and benefits (Benefits Agency), New Labour created a mega-gateway organization, Jobcenter Plus, for all benefit recipients of working age. With Jobcentre Plus, benefits become conditional upon a compulsory work-focused interview, for healthy as well as disabled beneficiaries (Wright, Kopac, and Slater 2004: 18).

In order to increase the financial return from work for the disabled, the government relaxed means testing, so that earned income is disregarded in assessing the financial contribution a disabled person has to make toward personal assistance. In 1999, New Labour introduced the National Strategy for Carers, which provided funding to local authorities over a three-year period to establish services for community care. The Carers and Disabled Children Act of 2000 made it easier to assess the needs of community caregivers and offer them financial compensation. Meanwhile, the government also promoted a style of social work that focused more on the activation potential than on the incapacities of the disabled (Morris 2003: 220–222; Jordan and Jordan 2000: 106–107).

One of the six major New Deals was devoted to the specific purpose of combating health-related early exit, in the form of the New Deal for Disabled People. And in order to encourage older workers to remain longer in employment, New Labour brought in the New Deal for 50 years and older (ND50+). The Gateway service of ND50+ assigns a personal advisor to each elderly participant, and offers advice and information about job searching in individually tailored counseling sessions. For those who remain excluded from work after the Gateway period, ND50+ provides a range of follow-up measures. These include possible job or training placements and financial help, such as training grants. Through ND50+, the government also offers an employment credit of 60 pounds per week, as a form of guaranteed minimum income for those unemployed for more than 6 months. Since 2003, this tax credit has been incorporated into the new Employment Tax Credit and used as a bonus for returning to work for those over 50. Promoting the idea of active aging, the government campaigned to raise awareness about age discrimination within firms. It also raised the age threshold for occupational pensions and consulted widely about bringing further flexibility into the pension system. The main flexibility problem here is the use of full retirement as the primary condition for claiming any benefits. Therefore, a change of status from full- to part-time work for the elderly will not count as retirement. This arrangement creates a barrier to work, as it makes it more difficult for the elderly to remain in employment while drawing a partial pension (Mandin 2004: 13–14; Walker 2002: 421–424; Foden and Jepsen 2002: 450). After its reelection in 2001, New Labour further intensified its active aging measures. The ND50+ was expanded in the scope of its services, and the government introduced the Third Age Apprenticeships in order to retain elderly workers in sectors with skill shortages (Walker 2002: 425).

Analysis of Anticipatory Compensation

Anticipatory compensation measures remove people from the labor market before compensation. Social democratic governments have tried to restrict such labor-market-clearing measures by reducing enrollment and enabling reintegration. By contrast, the center Right response has varied. Some were instrumental in the establishment of these very schemes and continued to perpetuate their existence (such as in Germany), while others (such as in the Netherlands) attempted to save costs by directly cutting benefit levels. Nevertheless, as a whole, the partisan difference here pales beside the cross-country path-dependent diversities, in both policy implementation and outcomes.

The initial response to sharply rising unemployment after the early 1980s often relied on these early exit schemes to reduce the labor supply (and therefore the unemployment rate). Given their quick effects, these measures of temporary market clearing tended to become permanent and remain in the system. This problem is most severe in continental welfare regimes, given the contributory nature of social security and the deep involvement of social partners. Into the 1990s, these policies not only failed to further reduce unemployment but also hurt labor force participation by creating bottlenecks. Though generally ineffective in the long run, the Danish versions of the leave scheme with an enabling bent, such as sabbatical, educational, and parent leave programs, were more employment friendly than the Dutch and German practice of permanent labor shedding (Green-Pedersen, van Kersbergen and Hemerijck 2001: 314; Hemerijck and Schludi 2000: 214). Nevertheless, after the early 1990s, all social democratic governments made some attempts to close off these early exit channels.

Despite the strong similarity in overall policy paradigms, the reform's outcomes varied, not only across but also within traditional welfare state regimes. The Scandinavian and British reforms were generally more successful than their continental counterparts. Nevertheless, the PvdA was able to implement some drastic changes, while the German SPD made little headway in reducing early retirement. Where reforms stalled, the inability to secure cooperation from social partners in a corporatist framework was often an important reason. In fact, even when the primary early exit routes were blocked, unions and employers colluded in perpetuating these practices in domains beyond immediate state control, such as supplementary schemes. For early retirement benefits, government intervention to remove them was neutralized as collectively negotiated early retirement schemes on the company level rapidly filled in the void. The same is true for disability benefits, because private employer insurance still leaves the option open for removing redundant workers on the pretense of disability (Ebbinghaus 2000: 536–547; Hassel and Ebbinghaus 2000: 80–81).

These secondary routes to early exit weaken the overall effect of social democratic reforms in anticipatory passive benefits. In these instances of collusion and cost externalization, the corporatist concertation between unions and employers was more an obstacle than conduit toward third way reforms. This puts in perspective the dramatic policy success of the PvdA, which made the point of totally destroying the traditional corporatist institutions of benefit administration (albeit at high electoral costs). These highly diverse empirical cases highlight the context-specific role of corporatism in third way reforms, already echoed in the theoretical Chapter 2: Institutional changes do not necessarily occur when corporatism is strong, or necessarily stop when corporatism is weak. Whether, and to what extent, the logic of collective action explains institutional self-reinforcement depends on the nature of the reforms in question.

3. ANALYSIS OF PASSIVE PROTECTION

Compared with the role of parties in active protection, the difference between social democrats and the center-right parties in passive protection reforms is noticeably smaller. In the context of permanent austerity, parties left and right have attempted to control social expenditures, retrench elements of income support (especially early exit pathways), and remove potential work disincentives in income-replacement programs. Passive-protection reforms involve direct changes to the social security system. For this reason, policy implementation in passive reforms strongly reflects path dependency on existing welfare state regimes and other institutional settings.

Despite the clear evidence for path dependency, these institutional constraints still leave some room for partisan differentiation in policy paradigms and for a power resources account of the reform process. Passive protection can be reactionary or anticipatory. For reactionary compensation, the status of loss in earning power is sustained through income replacement (such as unemployment benefits). For these measures, social democrats have focused on restructuring rather than blanket retrenchment. In the restructuring process, benefits were tightened for those truly able to work but increased for the least advantaged. By reducing work disincentives in these income-replacement programs, the social democrats aligned passive-protection reforms with a corresponding expansion in active protection. The reduction of benefit generosity relaxed the traditional egalitarian principle of approximating income parity between the working and nonworking by means of social security. At the same time, resources were increased for helping the worst off, including both those at the bottom of income distribution and those who can't find employment. This policy paradigm in passive protection reflects the work-based notion of solidarity and the growing prioritarian emphasis in egalitarianism, in other words, the two core components of third way ideology.

For Christian democratic parties, a strong attachment to Bismarckian de-commodification and labor-market clearing has reduced their incentives for changing the status quo. For the secular Right, there is no clear normative justification for intensifying either social redistribution or active labor market expenditure as a counterbalance against cuts to passive benefits. In other words, the center-right response to passive protection shows a division between inaction and radical retrenchment, albeit united by the common opposition to further increase in state involvement in resource redistribution. Where both the Left and Right were engaged in restructuring social security, the former integrated passive reforms with further intensification in active protection. For the latter, by contrast, passive changes were detached from active ones, simply because they had presided over little expansion (if not occasional rollback) in public resources for active protection.

This Left and Right difference in reforming reactionary compensation can be seen, for example, in changes to unemployment benefits. The Christian Democrats were both unwilling and unable to significantly reduce benefit generosity or remove work disincentives, for a combination of ideological and institutional reasons. The secular Right was much more enthusiastic ideologically, but often held back by the popularity of these programs. This was a particular dilemma facing the bourgeois parties in Northern Europe, and instead it was the Anglo-Saxon secular Right that implemented significant cuts. Where retrenchment did occur, the focus of the (secular) center

Right was on cost saving, and for this reason, the cuts were drastic and typically fell directly on the level of benefits. By contrast, when social democratic governments restricted income replacement, they preferred to avoid sharp cuts in benefit levels, and instead focused on tightening work conditions or shortening benefit duration. In fact, *short but generous* benefits provide incentives rather than disincentives for adequate job searching, and this helps to reduce the long-term potential for structural unemployment.

While the mainstream economics literature emphasizes the potential reservation-wage effect and work disincentives in generous unemployment replacement, stratification research in institutional mobility regimes, such as education or the welfare state (Gangl 2004; DiPrete and McManus 2000; DiPrete 2002), highlights the "scar effects" of unemployment spells on individual life courses. A trigger event, such as loss of a job, can lead to accumulated deterioration in economic status and a decline in capacity to recover from career interruptions. The institutional mobility regime of welfare state transfers can reduce such scar effects, not only through short-term income compensation. More importantly, it also contributes to long-term employment recovery by serving as an incentive for private risk taking. If there is sufficient benefit support, during brief unemployment spells individuals are more likely to conduct adequate job searches and locate the jobs that match their skills. In general, unemployment replacement is an important form of social insurance for long-term investment, especially in asset-specific high skills (Iversen 2005). Generous unemployment replacement can encourage labor market participation, and it is primarily the persistence in such cash transfers that has the opposite effect.

Compared with reactionary compensation, partisan difference is even more limited in reforming anticipatory compensation. Both social democratic and secular Right parties are opposed to these early exit pathways. For the former, these measures worsen labor market and social exclusion. For the latter, they contribute to welfare waste and economic inefficiency. Christian Democrats are ideologically more sympathetic toward these measures, but their social security systems have been under the greatest fiscal burden due to these very programs. Labor force decline is a particularly serious problem for continental Europe, and this is where the main (limited) action has to be in rolling back anticipatory compensation.

For ideological as well as policy reasons, retrenchment was more or less the uniform response from the Left and Right for early exit pathways. However, in continental Europe, the distance between efforts and outcomes can be significant in this policy area. Where such reforms are most needed, path dependency exercises the greatest constraining effect.

The contribution-based continental benefit structure and the historical entrenchment of social partners in benefit administration has played an important role in thwarting reforms. In Scandinavia, the early exit pathways took a less malignant form, as the various leave schemes were both temporary in duration and human capital friendly in function. These leave schemes were also less entrenched into social security contributions, and the logic of corporatist collective action (failure) was a less relevant factor in the Northern European experience. The Scandinavian social democrats were largely successful in reversing the temporary leave programs, and they also made greater headway in stemming early retirement than in the German and French cases.

7

Economic and Corporatist Contexts
for the Third Way

The third way is premised on labor market activation. Aside from subsidizing new jobs financially, few third way policies directly create jobs from the demand side. Ultimately, the effectiveness of labor market measures depends on an economy with a persistent capacity for job creation. Therefore, in addition to the core strategies of active and passive social protection, effective third way reforms also require an economic context of growth and investment, sufficient enough to sustain and increase employment opportunities in the labor market. Across OECD countries, due to a highly different economic context than in the Golden Age era, economic prudence is more than ever an important condition for sustainable job creation. Since the early 1980s, advanced industrialized economies have intensified the transition to a postindustrial service structure, and concomitantly there has been a further decline in the core manufacturing industries. At the same time, gradual economic internalization, especially in finance, has increased the cost of high budget deficits, and made devaluation or interest-rate manipulation unfeasible. This pressure toward low inflation and small budget deficits was especially strong for countries constrained by the Stability and Growth Pact and the conservative monetarist policy of the European Central Bank (ECB). It is important to emphasize that the key factor behind the pressure toward austerity is the internationalization of finance, rather than production or trade, which has historically been highly integrated internationally, especially for the Northern European economies (Huber and Stephens 2001).

Due to these constraints on government options in stimulating the economy, the extent of partisan differentiation is minimized in economic policy. Nevertheless, there is still some limited evidence for ideological preferences.

In some cases, policies from different partisan governments do demonstrate contrasting intellectual interpretations of the purpose of economic prudence. While neoliberal reformers implement economic austerity for ideological reasons, for social democrats this approach has a more instrumental purpose: creating employment. This implies that within the context of prudent economy, social democratic governments are willing to undertake some expansionary measures. Where austerity and employment really became conflicting objectives (for example, in France, Germany, and New Zealand in the late 1990s), social democratic parties preferred to maximize the latter at the cost of the former. More generally, even where continued prudence is justified for employment purposes, the increased revenues are essentially resources for later expansion in social programs and other public spending. Clearly, the partisan difference in this case is nuanced, rather than categorical. Governments left and right cut taxes, because proper tax reductions do indeed stimulate stronger investment and employment growth. Furthermore, social expenditures can continue to climb simply on the basis of growing unemployment, regardless of the parties in power. Therefore, it is infeasible to use one indicator (for example, whether there is a budget surplus or its size) to differentiate left from right parties. Instead, evidence for ideological principles is more likely to be found in the greater extent to which social democrats are willing to balance one strategy (for example, hard currency) with another (for example, some fiscal expansion).

While fiscal caution and tax reforms are primarily macroeconomic strategies, continuous investment and employment growth also relies on microeconomic conditions, especially wage restraint. On a micro level, keeping wage increase below the increase in productivity is crucial for protecting the profit margins of businesses. Regardless of firm size, retained earnings are far more important than external channels, such as banking or equity, as the primary source of finance for investment and R&D. Where firms anticipate excessive wage demands from unions, they are willing to substitute physical investment for R&D because the former is more price-elastic, and is less likely to be passed on to unions as rents. Of course, the long-term consequence of this "satisficing" strategy is that technological innovation and employment prospects will decline (Simon 1955; Allen and Gale 2000; Menezes-Filho and van Reenen 2003). On a macro level, wage moderation increases the room for lowering interest rates while maintaining noninflationary increase in employment. There are exceptional cases where serious union weakness alone is sufficient to prevent wage inflation (such as post-Thatcher Britain), but in general, corporatism remains an important institutional condition for delivering wage restraint.

For this reason, the external context for the third way naturally extends from the economy to corporatist concertation, and both factors are discussed together for each country in this chapter. In the previous two chapters on core active- and passive-protection strategies, corporatism was an important theoretical variable for its role in preventing collective action failure, and corporatist failure is often (though not always) a contributing factor to path-dependent institutional self-reinforcement. This chapter highlights that corporatism is also important substantively, as a constituent component of the third way paradigm through its connection to wage moderation and job growth. Rather than duplicating the path-dependency arguments in the previous two chapters, here I focus more specifically on the empirical connection between developments in corporatist institutions and job creation (predominantly through wage moderation, but in France, through the 35-hour week as well). In addition, for both the UK and New Zealand in the late 1990s, radical success in weakening unions under previous neoliberal governments had made wage moderation through corporatist concertation a largely irrelevant issue. Nevertheless, to preserve consistency, I also briefly discuss industrial-relations developments in these two countries, especially for New Zealand, since here the industrial-relations arena was the most important target for radical government reforms over a two-decade period. The organization of this chapter is based on the two major third way contexts of economy and corporatism, and each country's key developments on these two dimensions are summarized in Table 7.1.

Denmark

While the bourgeois government had only very limited success in reforming the Danish welfare state, it did score a major victory in shifting Danish economic policy from the demand-side management of the 1970s to predominantly supply-side measures. After the early 1980s, the bourgeois parties had followed a "norm-based" economic strategy, involving a hard currency, low inflation, and a strict fiscal balance sheet (Jochem 2003: 131; Goul Andersen 2000: 73; Torfing 2001: 299). After returning to power in 1993, the social democrats continued to work within this primarily cautious policy framework. While the fiscal stance became slightly expansive, supply-side measures were largely deployed in preference to demand-side ones. While formally outside the EMU, in practice the social democrats continued with nominal convergence to the euro and the fiscal caution it requires: reduction in debts, fixed exchange rate, low interest rate, and stable price and wages (Torfing 1998: 252). As shown in Figure 7.1, for

TABLE 7.1. *Key Developments in Economic and Corporatist Contexts, by Country*

Key policies in order of appearance in the chapter	Conditions for Job Growth ⇒	Economic Prudence	Corporatism	Theoretical Implications
	Denmark	• "Norm-based" economic policy • Tax Reform	• "Centralized decentralization"	Strong convergence to economic prudence, but under social democracy it is instrumental in employment creation.
	Sweden	• "Third road" • Tax reforms	• Sector bargaining with coordination	
	Norway	• Target inflation • Credit liberalization	• Bargaining recentralization	
	Netherlands	• Continued with center-right austerity policy	• Wassenaar legacy	Corporatism an important contributor to wage moderation
	France	• Expansionary reaction to competitive disinflation past	• Consensual approach to unions	
	Germany	• Schröder softened Stability and Growth Pact	• Alliance for Jobs ineffective	
	United Kingdom	• Strict spending limit • Pledged no direct tax rise	• Industrial relations increasingly legalistic	Corporatist failure is a contributor to path dependency in reforming welfare state institutions (see Chapters 5 and 6).
	Australia	• Deregulation • Turned to monetary policy	• The Accord	
	New Zealand	• Clark government reversed radical liberalization	• 1999 Employment Relations Act	

much of their period in power, the social democrats were able to both keep inflation below 3% and significantly increase the budget surplus.

However, compared with that of their bourgeois predecessors, the social democratic strategy was toward a slightly more Keynesian direction. The growth of employment was now promoted not only through sound budgeting but also through a series of active labor market measures that involved

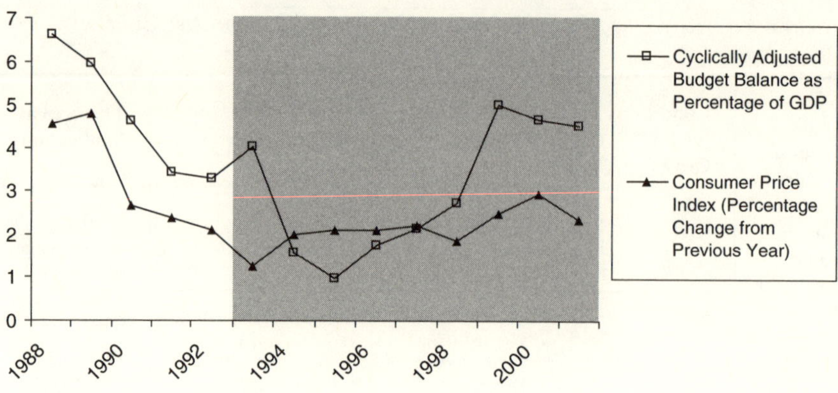

FIGURE 7.1. Budget Balance and Inflation in Denmark 1988–2001
(*Source:* OECD 2005c [budget balance]; Huber et al. 2004a [consumer price index]).

demand-side job creation and other employment subsidies (Hemerijck and Schludi 2000: 182–183). While they continued to pursue fiscal consolidation as a first priority, they also more actively used fiscal policy, especially tax changes, to smooth the economic cycle. Started in 1994, the reforms in the tax system were designed to be expansionary during the first year and revenue neutral afterwards. Faced with rapidly rising unemployment, the social democrats tried to kick start the economy in 1993 with a lowering of the marginal tax, as well as taxes on corporate and capital income. The tax reduction was largely financed through the broadening and greening of the tax base. On this basis, the economic upswing in 1993 was a typical demand-driven growth. Later, the government also used fiscal policy to perform a successful soft landing of the Danish economy in 1998. This was achieved through a lower personal income tax, plus the scaling back of interest deductions on loans and mortgages from tax income. In addition to stimulating the economy, the tax reforms also worked together with an expansion in private and public labor market pensions to boost savings incentives, which further contributed to moderation on the wage front (Green-Pedersen 2001: 9; Green-Pedersen 2002: 124; Benner and Vad 2000: 447; Madsen 2004: 200).

On the whole, the 1993 tax changes can be seen as a combination of labor tax reforms and capital tax reforms. The former contributed to a 1.5% increase in employment over the phase-in period, due largely to the wage-moderating effect of the fall in the average labor income tax rate. The latter stimulated demand and job growth over a longer period by increasing savings and generating an aggregate efficiency gain. In short, though based primarily on tax cuts of various types, the social democratic tax reforms were more instrumental in employment creation than ideologically driven by a desire to downsize the state (Lange, Pedersen, and Sørensen 1999: 146–157).

In a break with the traditional Danish model of tax-based welfare financing, the social democrats introduced a new social security contribution. This fund was earmarked to finance active labor market programs, unemployment insurance, and sickness benefits. Collected as a proportional tax on gross income from work, the new social contribution was imposed on both employees and employers. Designing the scheme to increase business cost efficiency, the government targeted the levy overwhelmingly at employees. The starting contribution rate for employees was 5% and by 1997 increased to 8%, whereas for employers the rate was merely 0.6% of the gross wage by 1998 (Benner and Vad 2000: 447).

While the tax reforms stimulated employment growth through their wage-moderating effect, corporatist cooperation from unions was another important contributing factor to wage restraint. Here, it is important to outline the bargaining developments in some detail, because Danish corporatism is a good example of how bargaining decentralization remains largely effective in delivering wage restraint. Labor market policy in Denmark had a long tradition of "free collective bargaining": The process is carried out with the strong involvement of unions and employers' organizations. Social partners in Denmark have autonomy in negotiating a number of issues that in other countries would have been dealt with by national legislation, such as pensions, working time, and holiday entitlements. Both at national and regional levels, labor market councils, dominated by representatives from both sides of the social partnership, play an influential role in the formulation of labor market policies (Madsen 1999: 55; Lind 1999: 192; Larsen and Bredgaard 2004: 12).

Since the 1980s, the Danish collective bargaining system has been gradually restructured. This development was partly in response to the norm-based economic framework adopted by Danish governments during the 1980s. The government used tight fiscal policy and low inflation to strive toward a competitive growth regime, which depended on the continuation of wage moderation. The changes in the bargaining arrangement were also accelerated by organizational developments within the Confederation of Danish Employers, which was being increasingly restructured into five components on sectoral lines. Another contributing factor was that collective agreements at the industry level had gradually become framework agreements, where the details were actually worked out at the company level. Accordingly, local actors and tripartite regional councils saw their role increase (Lind 1999: 192; Wilthagen and Tros 2003: 17).

Although there was gradual decentralization in the collective bargaining system, the extent of decentralization was moderate because the main areas of labor market policy, and the collective agreements in particular, were still bargained at the national level (Lind 2000: 139; Wilthagen and Tros 2003: 17). What is more important, this decentralization in wage bargaining was at the same time coupled with a growing degree of national coordination by peak organizations for both unions and employers. In the late 1980s and early 1990s, there was major organizational restructuring among unions. After the amalgamation and reorganization of bargaining units, union bargaining was consolidated into five major cartels. This development further helped peak union coordination in spite of decentralization in wage bargaining. In other words, decentralization in the Danish context was primarily the shift from bargaining within peak associations to bargaining within the five cartels, each of which were coordinated to an extent sufficient to enforce wage agreement on subordinate unions (Cox 2004; Jochem 2003: 134). A similar trend of better coordination at the peak level was also evident among employers' organizations. Therefore, decentralization of the Danish bargaining system was combined with internal centralization, which helped both sides of the social partnership to bind their individual members to the negotiated agreement. Throughout this book, I adopt Kenworthy's Wage Coordination Score (coded between 1 and 5) as the quantitative overall indicator of wage bargaining coordination.[1] Figure 7.2 indicates that bargaining decentralization had indeed not led to overall decline in wage coordination, which instead remained stable since the early 1980s.

The pattern of "centralized decentralization" characterized the development of industrial relations in both Denmark and the Netherlands, and it has helped in minimizing wage drift and securing slower wage growth. As

---

[1] For the Kenworthy score, 1 = fragmented wage bargaining, confined largely to individual firms or plants; 2 = bargaining mainly at industry level with little or no pattern setting; 3 = industry-level bargaining with reasonably strong pattern setting but only moderate union concentration; 4 = centralized bargaining by confederation(s) or government imposition of wage schedule/freeze – without a peace obligation, high degree of union concentration, and extensive, regularized pattern setting, tacit coordination of bargaining by employer organizations with extensive pattern setting; 5 = centralized bargaining by confederation(s) or government imposition of wage schedule/freeze – with a peace obligation, extremely high degree of union concentration and coordination of industry bargaining by confederation, extensive coordination of bargaining by employer organizations with extensive pattern setting. For greater details, see Kenworthy (2001). Data for the Kenworthy scores were taken from Huber et al. (2004a).

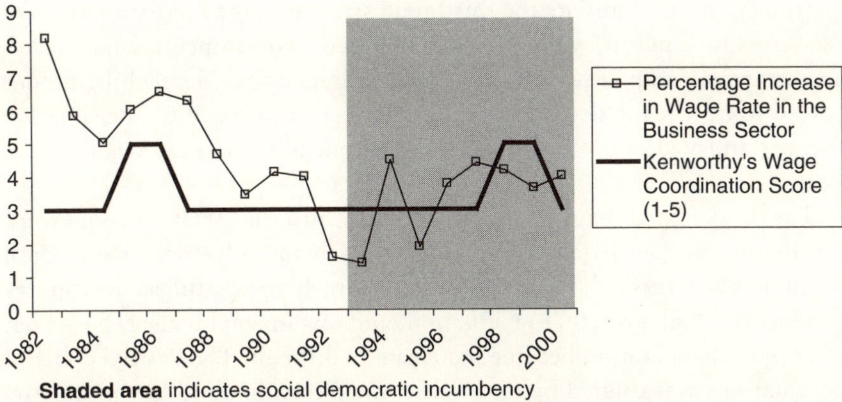

FIGURE 7.2. Wage Coordination and Wage Moderation in Denmark 1982–2000 (*Source:* OECD 2006b [wage rate]; Huber et al. 2004a [wage coordination]).

seen in Figure 7.2, although the wage increase did not become slower during social democratic incumbency, the increase was still considerably more moderate than in the early 1980s. By the end of the 1990s, both sides of the Danish social partnership were still committed to this pattern of centralized decentralization in wage bargaining (Benner and Vad 2000: 440; Jochem 2003: 129–132). Fundamentally, the crucial condition for maintaining such a social pact in Denmark was the unions' continuing acceptance of the terms and conditions in the competitive-growth economic regime (Lind 2000: 155). In this respect, the active labor market reforms under the social democrats had been helpful in consolidating the social pact. Unions regarded wage moderation as a necessary evil, which was expected to lead ultimately to more jobs being created. By massively reducing unemployment and increasing employment, the Danish ALMPs had made it easier for the unions to remain committed to wage moderation.

Sweden

The concept of mixed economy, or socially regulated market economy, is a long-established principle in Swedish economic policy (Lindgren 1999: 48). By the early 1980s, the Swedish social democrats had adopted a "third road" approach to economic policy, by which the party hoped to draw some distance from both Keynesian reflation and monetarist austerity. The key components of the third road approach included wage restraint, curbs on public-sector spending, and incentives for corporate investments. The instrument used to initiate the third road strategy was two devaluations of the krona (one put in by the previous bourgeois government), which led to a substantial competitive edge for Swedish industries. Meanwhile, unions agreed to accept the decline in real incomes as a result of the devaluation (Benner and Vad 2000: 422; Huber and Stephens 2001: 242; Swank 2002: 134–135).

The party hoped that various pieces of the third road strategy could work together to produce balanced economic growth and full employment. Until the mid-1980s, this policy package seemed largely successful, as the country experienced high growth, low inflation, and low unemployment. However, after that, its operation became increasingly difficult. The desired effect of devaluations was diluted by insufficient wage restraint and low productivity growth in the economy. Meanwhile, slow economic growth also limited the government's ability to offer compensations on the social policy front in exchange for union cooperation in continuing wage moderation. Behind the growing economic problems lay the deregulation of capital market and the ensuing boom and crash in the real estate sector. In addition, it became more difficult for the government to simultaneously use trade regulations and capital control to keep the budget in shape (Stephens 1996: 46–47; Huber and Stephens 2001: 250; Benner and Vad 2000: 419). The government's monetary policy was largely ineffective in stimulating employment, but it tried to do so by means of fiscal policy changes, especially reforms to the tax system, which helped to increase investments and business efficiency, and in the long run create more job opportunities. Keeping intact the financial foundation of the welfare state, the social democrats continued the secular shift from an income tax to an indirect tax. Marginal taxes were lowered, deductions reduced, and the tax base broadened (Hort 2002: 142; Hort 2003: 246–247). Nevertheless, the tax measures were insufficient in averting the major economic downturn caused by the collapse of credit markets, and after the early 1990s, Sweden entered a deep economic recession, signaling the end of the third road strategy.

When the social democrats returned to power in 1994, the economic situation had worsened significantly during three years of bourgeois administration, which saw further increases in both unemployment and the budget deficit. This economic context tied the government's hands and shaped its macroeconomic response. The party essentially adopted a strategy of intertemporal pooling in its policy objectives, with the first administration (1994–1998) focusing specifically on restoring fiscal soundness and later administrations devoting more attention to the expansion of social and labor market measures, which utilized resources saved during the belt-tightening

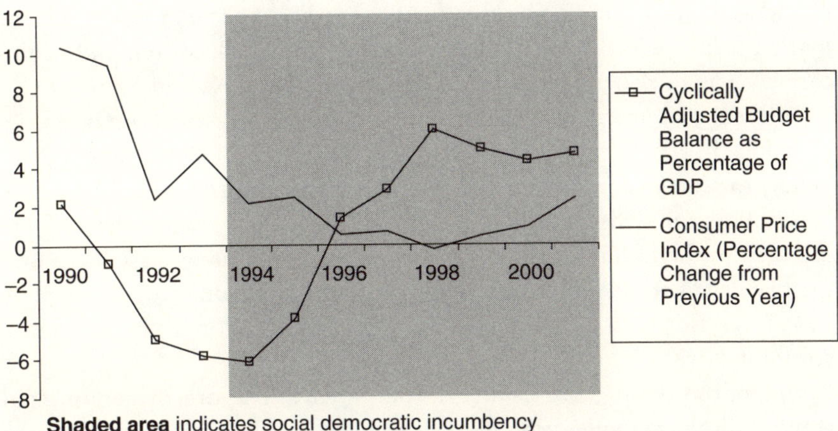

FIGURE 7.3. Budget Balance and Inflation in Sweden 1990–2001
(*Source:* OECD 2005c [budget balance]; Huber et al. 2004a [consumer price index]).

early period. In other words, this is another good demonstration of the instrumental nature of social democratic economic prudence: It has a clear social and employment purpose in the long run. The government's first term prioritized low inflation over full employment, and made a modest pledge of reducing unemployment to 4% by the end of the 1990s. Converging with the previous bourgeois parties' austerity policies, the social democrats maintained a tight fiscal limit (medium-term target set at 2% budget surplus) and the central bank kept interest rates high. Nevertheless, the government managed to avoid further depressing the economy. Instead, there was a rapid recovery on most fronts, with economic growth at 2.5% and the budget deficit eliminated (Whyman 2003). As Figure 7.3 shows, the party was able not only to transform the budget deficit into a large surplus but also to keep inflation below 3%, which was about a fourth of the inflation when the previous bourgeois parties came to power.

In its ability to restart economic growth, the government was helped significantly by the forced floating of the krona in 1992. Trade-weighted exchange rates remained more than 20% lower than the pre-float value and remained so until 1995. The maintenance of a competitive exchange rate stimulated export sectors and resulted in large surpluses in the balance of payments, and it became a primary source of expansion within an overall context of austerity. By the early 2000s, the increased revenues through budget surpluses enabled automatic stabilizers to operate very effectively. The government restored full employment as one of its primary objectives, and it used the budget surpluses to finance further expansion in active labor market measures, child allowances, student grants, education, and health care (Whyman 2003: 195–197; A. Gould 1996: 89; A. Gould 2001: 48).

While the competitive exchange rate and later fiscal expansion measures all helped in generating more employment during social democratic incumbency, the incomes policy had an ambiguous role in these economic successes. Bargaining decentralization and the consequent wage inflation were the keys to the failure of the third road economic strategy based on competitive devaluation, which ushered in the steep recession through the early 1990s. For this reason, it is important to outline developments in Swedish corporatist wage bargaining during this period.

Unlike the situation in Denmark, the Swedish corporatist institutional context for wage moderation had been in clear decline for more than two decades. After the 1980s, the employers' organization SAF had started to question the value of centralized bargaining. SAF rejected any further centralized bargaining, partly in reaction to the radical labor support for profit redistribution in the 1970s, which hurt the international competitiveness of Swedish businesses. Then, in 1983 the Swedish Engineering Employers' Association took the first step toward abandoning centralized bargaining and concluded a separate agreement with the metalworkers' union. Throughout the 1980s, collective bargaining oscillated between central and sectoral levels (Schmidt 2000: 262; Lodovici 2000: 50; Bjorklund 2000: 158; Swank 2002: 136). The stability of wage bargaining was declining, and the increasing use of legislation instead of voluntary agreements further strained the relationship between social partners. Increasing state intervention also indicated that the corporatist framework was no longer functioning properly (Benner and Vad 2000: 416).

After the 1990s, a series of further changes made by both employers and the bourgeois government contributed definitively to the decline of Swedish corporatism. In 1990, SAF decided to terminate centralized bargaining, and in 1991, it withdrew representatives from the boards of all state agencies, especially AMS. This was in protest of what it believed to be the excessive domination of these institutions by union interests. In 1993, the bourgeois government formally marginalized the AMS committee members by giving them only a narrow supervisory role. It also removed LO from the administration of unemployment insurance. This decision had the potential to vastly reduce the influence of the labor movement over Swedish social security. During the period of a decade, centralized bargaining had declined significantly, and the current situation was one of predominantly sectoral bargaining, with coordination among sectoral organizations of employers

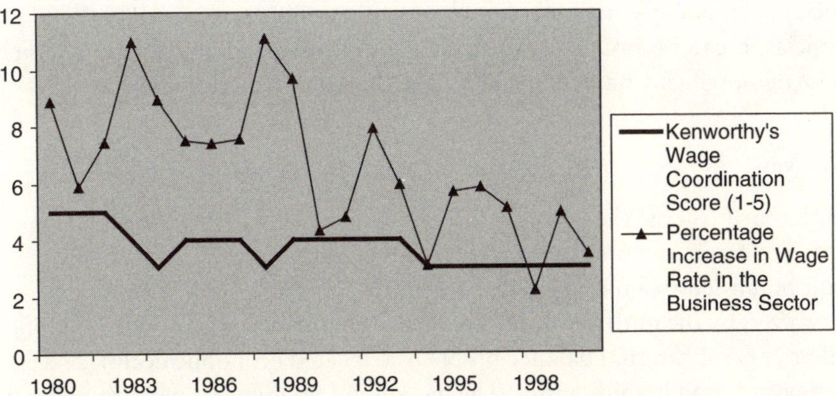

FIGURE 7.4. Wage Coordination and Wage Moderation in Sweden 1980–2000 (*Source:* OECD 2006b [wage rate]; Huber et al. 2004a [wage coordination]).

and unions, and this trajectory of decline is reflected in Figure 7.4 (Dios 2002: 11; A. Gould 2001: 142; Lodovici 2000: 50).

Segmentation of the labor market during the transition to a postindustrial economy weakened the capacity of unions to coordinate their strategy. Meanwhile, the dominance of LO in the unions, as well as the weight of Metall-led private-sector unions relative to public-sector ones, was also declining (Huber and Stephens 2001: 251–254). These factors, working together, weakened the peak organization's authority to enforce agreements. In the long run, it prevented the design of a concerted strategy to deal with increasing bargaining decentralization. This development on the union side, of course, was in parallel to a growing willingness to mount challenges from the employers' side. Consequently, labor market issues between social partners were increasingly dealt with in a confrontational manner, overshadowed by direct state intervention. In 1994, the bourgeois government sided with employers in reforming the "last in, first out" (LIFO) principle regulating redundancy, so that employers could exempt two employees from the rule. Unions also saw their right of veto under the Co-determination Act and their right to blockade small firms removed. These changes brought 30,000 workers onto the streets in protest, and the cooperative relationship between unions and employers further declined (A. Gould 2001: 149).

Despite efforts by the social democratic government to reverse this situation, no new corporatist institutions emerged in Sweden to replace the collapsed system of centralized bargaining after the late 1980s. However, as Figure 7.4 demonstrates, the current sectoral bargaining arrangement is still somewhat effective in delivering wage restraint. Nevertheless, the lack of social-partnership cooperation implies that in welfare state and labor market policies, it can become more difficult to put through some reforms (Merkel 2001: 66), which Chapters 5 and 6 have shown to be indeed the case.

Norway

In the early 1980s, the conservative government pursued extensive deregulation of credit and housing markets. This credit-financed private consumption boom led to rapid growth both in the economy and in employment. However, by the mid-1980s, the credit-driven prosperity had ended. Falling oil prices and external balance problems triggered economic decline, excessive wages, and high inflation. The incoming Labor government responded with monetarist austerity, by embracing a hard-currency strategy of fixed exchange rates, while continuing with the conservatives' liberalization measures in the credit market. The monetarist adaptation was ill-timed, as it went on to further dampen demand, decrease competitiveness, and drive up unemployment. Whereas unemployment was slowly rising in the early 1980s, after the economic hard landing around 1988 unemployment skyrocketed to 8% (Huber and Stephens 2001: 258; Dolvik et al. 1997: 55). On the whole, it is clear that Labor's macroeconomic policy had not been employment friendly. The fixed exchange-rate regime made it impossible to stimulate demand with interest-rate and credit-policy changes, and so the burden of economic adjustment was increasingly passed on to fiscal policies. However, monetarist discipline also made it impossible to implement fiscal expansion. The government kept a tight budget even while the country was experiencing the peak of its unemployment crisis, and the budget did not go into deficit until 1991–1992 (Moses 2000: 170–171). In other words, economic austerity had become counterproductive in its employment effect. As we will see later, this was a situation also faced by the German, French, and New Zealand social democrats in the late 1990s.

However, in Norway the direct impact on employment was relatively mild. The unemployment problem after the late 1980s turned out to be temporary, as unemployment started to decline again after the mid-1990s. Besides all of the government's labor market measures discussed in Chapter 5, it is important to highlight the role of the oil sector in contributing to the rapid disappearance of the unemployment problem. With exports worth 16% of GDP, the oil industries provided a unique mechanism of demand-side stimulation in the economy, and this has helped Norway avoid a severe job crisis of the Swedish or Danish type. This in turn helped prevent a more significant welfare retrenchment (Huber and Stephens 2001: 257). With oil revenue expansion after the early 1990s helping the economy withstand major external demand slacks, the small chunk of unemployment remaining in the Norwegian system was now primarily of the structural kind. The government was able to deal with this structural problem through disability benefits, early retirement, and various other early exit pathways, albeit only temporarily (Halvorsen 2002: 177).

To the extent that traditionally strong labor market measures plus oil revenues helped to quickly alleviate the unemployment crisis, Labor was under less pressure to break from macroeconomic austerity and resort to demand simulation. For other countries faced with a similar situation but without the benefit of either natural resources or an activation tradition, the governments indeed chose fiscal expansion rather than further austerity (more details in the French, German, and New Zealand analysis), thus demonstrating the fundamentally instrumental nature of economic prudence under social democracy. For Norway, the inability of both fiscal and monetary policies to stimulate demand further passed the burden of job creation onto wage moderation. For this reason, incomes policy in a corporatist framework became the most important strategy in contributing to the good employment performance after the early 1990s (Moses 2000: 187–189).

In Norway in the late 1970s, developments in incomes policy mirrored those of many other Western countries, as local wage drift gradually eroded central negotiations. However, after further industry-level negotiations in 1982 and 1984, collective bargaining was recentralized in 1987. In 1993, further legislation was introduced, allowing for the extension of collective agreements on an area- or industry-wide basis. The unions were strong supporters of the further generalization of collective agreements because they were concerned about the possible social implications from the European Economic Area agreement and the internal market. By the end of the 1990s, the Norwegian bargaining system had come to be regarded as the most centralized in the OECD area. Meanwhile, union density in Norway, remarkably, continued to rise in the 1980s and early 1990s (Halvorsen 2002: 171; Freeman 1997: 21; Dolvik et al. 1997: 85).

In addition to growing density, a high degree of coordination persists among the unions, which are organized largely on sectoral and industrial rather than occupational lines, and the peak association LO enjoys substantial central authority in enforcing bargaining agreements. The LO's authority is also boosted by its extensive networks of interest representation inside the Labor Party, such as membership on the party executive and joint committees, as well as weekly consultations between party leaders and union

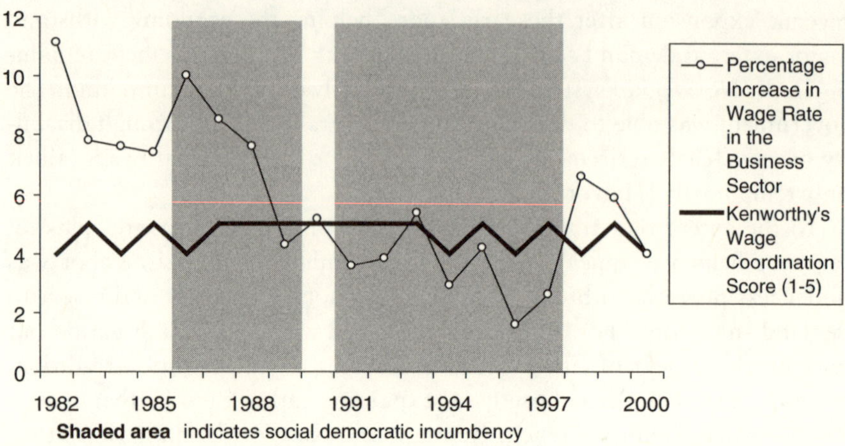

FIGURE 7.5. Wage Coordination and Wage Moderation in Norway 1982–2000 (*Source:* OECD 2006b [wage rate]; Huber et al. 2004a [wage coordination]).

leadership. Alongside continuing union strength, Norwegian employers' organizations have also remained stable in their centralized organizational structure. Based on a combination of strength and coordination, a high level of mutual trust exists between the peak associations from both sides of the social partnership. This corporatist framework has more or less persistently delivered wage moderation through a series of pay rounds since the late 1980s (Dolvik et al. 1997: 53, 82–85). Figure 7.5 demonstrates that during the 1990s, not only did bargaining coordination remain at a very high level (4 and 5 on the Kenworthy score), but there was also significant wage restraint during Labor's incumbency.

At the time of the bargaining recentralization in 1987, an interim pay round was negotiated with a "no wage increase" agreement between LO and the peak employer association NAF. Multitier bargaining was reintroduced in the 1990 pay round, with strict control at the center and limited decentralization at the industry level. Then, in 1991, a major breakthrough in Norwegian incomes policy took place, as the social partners signed up to a five-year pact called the "Solidarity Alternative" (also known as Solidarity 2000, as discussed in Chapter 5) under the auspices of the Labor government. With the explicit purpose of bringing unemployment down to 3%–3.5%, the key instrument of the pact was an incomes policy capable of improving cost competitiveness by 10% from 1993 to 1997. Based on this premise of wage moderation, the pact also asked for public expenditure efficiency, structural change to the labor market, low-inflation economic prudence, and, crucially, active labor market policies to enhance skill formation. In a pattern similar to the Australian Accord operating contemporaneously, the Solidarity Alternative made it possible for Norwegian unions to consistently give up rises in nominal wages in exchange for the social wage, in the form of a government guarantee to save major welfare schemes from retrenchment. In addition, the Labor government also contributed to the bargaining process by cofinancing early retirement, increasing parental leave, and introducing time accounts for parents. Backed up by this whole set of instruments, the Solidarity Alternative delivered satisfactory results. The pay rounds from 1991 to 1996 all maintained low wage increases, even though the 1994 round was the first one conducted at the industry level since 1986. By 1996, the Solidarity Alternative had significantly overachieved its initial target in reducing unemployment (Dolvik et al. 1997: 92–93).

Over the past two decades, Norwegian developments in almost every key aspect of the corporatist framework, including union strength, bargaining coordination, and incomes policy, have followed a direction opposite the Swedish case (Dolvik and Martin 2000: 279; 314–316). Together with expanding oil revenues, this contrast in industrial relations helps explain the better economic performance of Norway than Sweden (and all other Nordic countries) during the 1990s. The uniquely high degree of central coordination in incomes policy in the Norwegian labor movement not only paved the way for high employment but also made it possible to sustain close to full employment without inflationary wage demands. Wage moderation has also helped in canceling out the potentially inflationary or anti-employment impact of any possible inflexibility in the Norwegian labor market. Wage moderation and, in turn, full employment were particularly easy to accomplish with Labor in government, because the close connection between unions and the party made concessions from both sides easier. This pattern is also evident in the successful record of the Australian Accord, between the ALP and the Australian Council of Trade Unions (ACTU) (Solem and Overbye 2004: 35–36; Dolvik et al. 1997: 95; Rodseth 1997: 182).

The Netherlands

The PvdA continued the economic austerity and efficiency policies of the previous center-right Lubbers administrations. During its first term alone, the government was able to reduce the public deficit by 2.9% and the tax burden by 0.7%. However, this fiscal tightening did not come at the cost

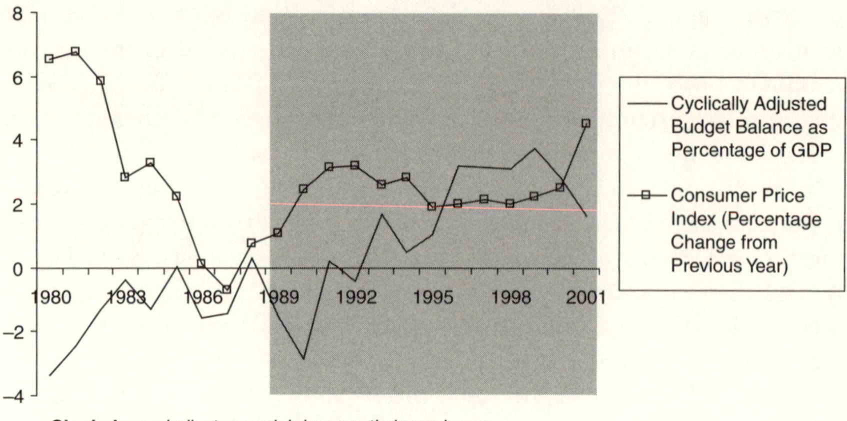

FIGURE 7.6. Budget Balance and Inflation in the Netherlands 1980–2001 (*Source:* OECD 2005c [budget balance]; Huber et al. 2004a [consumer price index]).

of social programs, as social spending increased by 1.4% during the same period. As Figure 7.6 indicates, starting from 1993, the budget was kept at a surplus. By 1998, the tax wedge was reduced to 41% on the average-income level and 16% on the minimum-wage level, and by 1996 the average wedge on labor income in the Netherlands was lower than in Belgium, Germany, Italy, and France (Delsen 2002b: 26–27; Snels 1999: 130). On the other hand, Figure 7.6 shows that the PvdA was less successful in controlling inflation, which by the end of its term in power returned to the level of the early 1980s. Overall, the government's austerity measures had no negative impact on job creation, as unemployment started to fall after the PvdA's first term.

Besides the labor market measures discussed in previous chapters, there are two other interrelated factors that enabled the "Dutch miracle" in employment creation to occur in a context of tight fiscal prudence: tax reforms and wage restraint. Firstly, the government's tax reforms in 1990 (The Oort Operation), the largest change since the Second World War, provided major incentives for business investment and led to the aforementioned reduction in tax-wedge and labor costs. The government simplified nine rates (with the top rate at 72%) into three rates of 36%, 50%, and 60%, and the latter two rates were subsequently reduced to 42% and 52%, respectively. More generally, the tax base was shifted from income to a combination of VAT and environmental levies. The tax reforms also targeted the bottom of the income scale, and in this process contributed to employment by directly offering incentives for transferring from welfare to

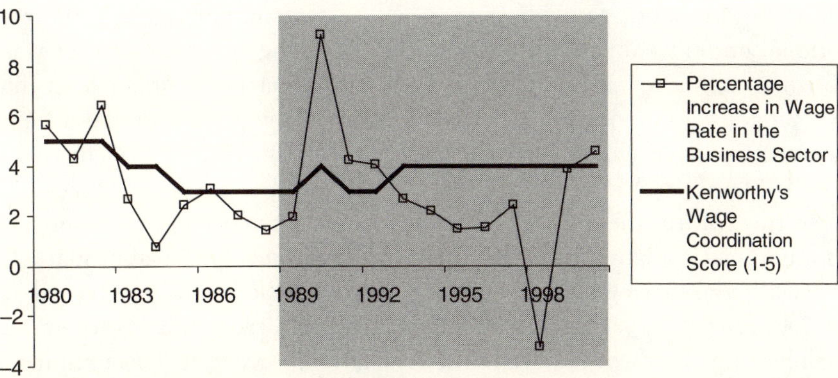

FIGURE 7.7. Wage Coordination and Wage Moderation in the Netherlands 1980–2001 (*Source:* OECD 2006b [wage rate]; Huber et al. 2004a [wage coordination]).

work. For example, there are tax subsidies for employers willing to hire the long-term unemployed or part-time workers. A uniform tax credit calculated on the basis of individuals rather than couples increased the incentives for married women to reenter employment (Delsen 2002b: 24, 45; Merkel 2001: 63).

The tax reductions also made it easier for the government to secure union cooperation in wage restraint. As Figure 7.7 shows, during its first two terms, the PvdA was extremely successful in achieving wage moderation. The government also oversaw a stable pattern of bargaining centralization, which largely remained at a high level (4 on the Kenworthy score) by the end of the 1990s. Given the heavily part-time and service-sector nature of jobs created in this period, wage restraint was arguably the most important reason behind the macroeconomic miracle of job creation. It not only provided opportunities for consensual negotiations over labor market flexibility reforms (see Chapter 5), but its cost-efficiency effect also boosted business competitiveness and job-creation capacity. The corporatist framework set out in the Wassenaar agreement during the early 1980s was a key contributor to the Dutch success in wage moderation.

Union weakness, employers' strength, and the moral suasion of economic necessity all contributed to the social partners' quick acceptance of Wassenaar (Negrelli 2000: 104). On the one hand, persistent crisis in the Dutch economy by the early 1980s had led to a growing consensus to accept the supply-side diagnosis for the nature of these economic problems.

On the other hand, partly because of job losses and partly based on traditional union weakness, throughout the 1980s the balance of power was shifting further toward employers. The union capacity to organize in the Netherlands was moderate, relative to Dutch employers, who had a high degree of peak-level coordination among their organizations (Hemerijck, van de Meer, and Visser 2000: 259).

In this regard, the unions' acceptance of Wassenaar can be interpreted as a pragmatic adaptation to shifting power relations in the labor market, especially the soaring unemployment that had reached a postwar record of 12% by the early 1980s. Steep unemployment led directly to a loss of union membership and the rapid decline of associational strength. This imminent question of survival narrowed union options in dealing with the crisis. The threat of state intervention in incomes policies by the Lubbers administration in the early 1980s further increased incentives for both sides of the social partnership to preempt government intervention. The nearest shortcut to achieving that was to accept the offer of Wassenaar. For these reasons, the social partners, especially unions, signed onto Wassenaar without any serious hesitation. Three years after the agreement came into effect, the practice of cost-of-living clauses in wage claims had largely been stopped (Becker 2003; Hemerijck, Manow, and van Kersbergen 2000: 116–117; den Butter and Mosch 2001: 22–24; Rhodes 1998: 237). The decline of union strength triggered by unemployment also paved the way for the relatively consensual and smooth path toward flexicurity reforms in the next decade. As their core membership was being chipped away by falling employment, unions tried to sustain their strength by diverting attention to the more peripheral and precarious segments of their constituency, and they willingly took on board some issues of concern for people in atypical jobs (Rhodes 1998: 196).

In the Wassenaar agreement, the central unions and employers' organizations agreed to give priority to the recovery of profits as a condition for investment and jobs. Long-term wage restraint and cuts in public expenditures were exchanged for a stronger employment commitment from employers' organizations. Under Wassenaar, the employers' job-creation efforts would focus in particular on labor time reduction and, less importantly, the creation of part-time jobs. Unions, meanwhile, agreed to keep wage increases below productivity growth in exchange for a modest reduction in annual and weekly working hours. In 1993, social partners signed a major follow-up to Wassenaar, in the form of the agreement "A New Course." This new document carried further the decentralization of bargaining to the company level, and the mode of voluntary bilateral collective bargaining became more or less consolidated. An innovative development in the New Course was greater involvement by social partners at the local level. As a quid pro quo for further decentralization, employers agreed to give up blanket resistance to a reduction in working hours, and the creation of jobs, especially part-time jobs, remained the first priority for both sides of the social partnership (Visser and Hemerjick 1997: 60, 103; Hemerijck and Visser 2000: 240; Keizer 2001: 114–115; Hemerijck and Schludi 2000: 159; Negrelli 2000: 104–105). This Wassenaar strategy of wage restraint in exchange for employment or social compensation has entrenched itself as the key principle in all of the following bipartite negotiations in the Dutch labor market.

After Wassenaar, the Netherlands witnessed largely uninterrupted wage restraint for almost a decade, which helped the country to avoid any major job consequences from the government's harsh noninflationary macroeconomic policies. Consistent wage moderation improved the competitiveness of the export sectors, and over 40% of the new jobs created in the 1990s can be attributed to such prolonged wage moderation (Hemerijck and Manow 2001: 224–225; den Butter and Mosch 2001: 4–5; Huber and Stephens 2001: 281). More significantly in the long run, the range of potential offers from employers in exchange for wage moderation has expanded in recent years. By the 1990s, unions had gradually changed their emphasis in negotiations with employers. Besides working-time changes, wage moderation was now compensated also with tax- and social-contribution reductions or investment increases in industrial reconstruction. In this process, the tax reform of 1990 partially integrated social security charges and income taxes, broadened the tax base, and lowered tax rates. A tripartite Common Policy Framework was signed between the government and social partners on the exchange of wage moderation for economic growth, more jobs, and tax relief. In a new round of agreements signed in 1997, unions accepted wage moderation in return for employers' responsibility to organize and finance school activities, and to introduce flexible wages. The growing attention to labor market flexibility as a bargaining condition has the potential to set the trend for future negotiations (Gorter 2000: 205; Hemerijck, Manow, and van Kersbergen 2000: 116–117; Hemerijck, Unger, and Visser 2000: 263; Salverda 2000).

In its impact on bargaining organization, Wassenaar led Dutch corporatism into a new era of resurgence, characterized by union acceptance of "centralized decentralization" and the principle that more business profit is both necessary and desirable (Schmidt 2000: 286–288). In 1994, tripartite consultation led to an agreement among social partners to focus wage negotiation on the lowest wage scales allowable legally, since the lowest negotiated wages were still much higher than the legal minimum, creating a barrier for low-skilled workers to find a job (Keizer 2001: 122). Over the long term, Wassenaar set in motion a decentralizing trend in collective bargaining, with growing numbers of sector- or firm-level agreements. At the same time, these growing firm-level negotiations have been accompanied by greater central coordination in the wage-formation process. The nature of wage bargaining has shifted, from central tripartite negotiations with direct state intervention to highly coordinated bipartite agreements. In the 1970s, the state had to frequently intervene in order to break the stalemate in wage negations, but after Wassenaar, the government retreated from incomes policies. Since 1982, there has been no political intervention in wage setting. The peak organizations have assumed responsibility for directing negotiating parties on the sectoral level (Gorter 2000: 190; Hemerijck and Manow 2001: 224–225; Levy 1999b: 259; Hemerijck 2003: 65–66).

The government exercised its influence in incomes policy in a more indirect manner. Through the "shadow of hierarchy," it tacitly encouraged social partners to reach bipartite and voluntary agreements without state interference. The social democrats regard such strategies as components of a more general proposal to strengthen "cultural democracy," to reinforce the role of civil society and grant it more autonomy from the still-prominent influence of the state (Braun and Giraud 2004: 53; Hemerijck, Manow, and van Kersbergen 2000: 117). Another effect of the corporatist resurgence was that company- or sector-wide negotiations led to supplementary insurance measures, which neutralized the direct impact of what limited retrenchment there had been in the social security system (Trommel and de Vroom 2002: 94).

France

The 1983 Socialist U-turn ushered in a period of relatively coherent austerity and deregulation policies. Compared with what the party espoused in the 1970s, these changes did mark a significant break from past practices. In monetary policy, after the mid-1980s the Socialist government became firmly committed to the principle of *franc fort* and competitive disinflation, within the constraint of the European Monetary System. Economic growth was encouraged with tax and social security contribution reductions, in order to assist employment creation and boost purchasing power (Clift 2003: 158–161; Levy 2000: 340–342; Barbier and Théret 2003: 122–123).

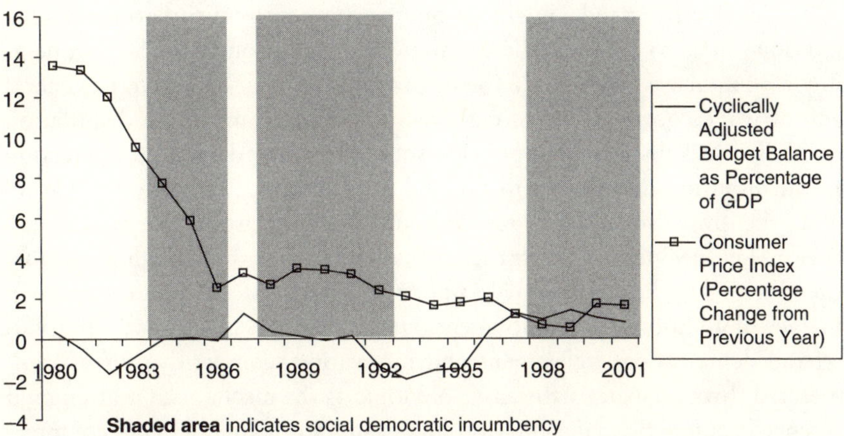

FIGURE 7.8. Budget Balance and Inflation in France 1980–2001
(*Source:* OECD 2005c [budget balance]; Huber et al. 2004a [consumer price index]).

The performance-based New Public Management principle was gradually introduced into the administration of the public sector, which in turn paved the way for later privatization attempts under the Gaullist government. Capital controls were lifted, and the Socialists also reduced the scale of assistance offered to national industries and relaxed rules for competition. After 1983, the principle of budget discipline and deregulation was rarely interrupted by changes of government. Figure 7.8 shows that all of the three Socialist governments since the early 1980s were largely successful in keeping inflation low and the budget in balance or surplus.

The Jospin government also continued with and expanded the industry privatization measures of the previous Gaullist administration. Ignoring its 1997 election promise to roll back the center-right privatization reforms, the Socialists in government sold off more national companies than its predecessors. In 1998, liberalization was introduced into the telecommunications sector, and in 1999 full privatization took place for Crédit Lyonnais. The government also deregulated the electricity sector, ending the monopoly of Electricite de France. Alongside privatization and deregulation in selected sectors of national industries, the Jospin government also encouraged the formation of public–private partnerships. In addition, the Socialists became increasingly selective in policies over aid to industries, shifting government help from ailing industries to growth sectors. Direct subsidies to industries were gradually replaced with tax credits for research and development (Levy 2000: 324–326, 340–342; Bouvet and Michel 1999: 43–44).

While effective in reducing inflation, the competitive disinflation strategy had done little to increase the economy's job-creation capacity, as unemployment increased from 8.3% in 1983 to 12.6% by 1997. Given the general lack of wage coordination across French unions, competitive disinflation operates as a substitute, supply-side source of wage discipline. Reflecting that disinflation had gone too far and hurt demand, capacity utilization fell to the lowest since the 1970s, although business profitability continued to rise. The pegging of the franc to the deutsch mark through *franc fort* forced a pro-cyclical monetarist policy: repeated rise of interest rates in the face of additional unemployment. Fundamentally, due to its inability to expand demands for investment and innovation, competitive disinflation operated through exactly the same old logic as the mechanism it attempted to replace: competitive devaluation (increasing the competitiveness of interest rates rather than industries). The French experience is one clear example where norm-based economic austerity had become counterproductive to employment. In response, the Jospin government adopted some measures of fiscal expansion to stimulate the economy, such as redistribution from profit to wages and a reduction in working hours. More crucially, the Socialists were prepared to reject the Stability and Growth Pact as a constraint on economic policy, and in this process directly confront Germany (Lordon 2001: 123–137). Nevertheless, it turned out that the Schröder government faced similar problems due to excessive monetarist austerity, and in the end the French and German social democrats worked in concert to water down the Stability and Growth Pact.

Instead of major retrenchments to social security, the Socialists actually expanded benefits for those most affected by economic liberalization. Using fiscal as well as social policies to reduce the impact of economic reforms, they let the welfare state play a critical cushioning role in the process of the economic U-turn. The government's 1998 budget redesigned income testing to exclude the affluent in social programs such as family allowance, and its cuts in income tax disproportionately favored low-income earners and those with no income. A new and progressive Solidarity Tax on Wealth was introduced and then strengthened in 1998, along with increases in company taxes and special taxes on income from financial investments. In addition, the government raised the rate of the uniform levy, CSG, to finance both health-care coverage and the country's main minimum-income guarantee RMI. As a result, income-related contributions to health insurance were almost entirely abolished (Levy 1999b: 247; Clift 2003: 158–161; Merkel 2001: 69–70). The Socialists managed to carry out most of these left progressive and demand-side reforms while remaining within the overall framework of economic prudence. Much of the redistributive reform was based on fiscal "cost shuffling," from lower to higher income groups without any net increase in the state's financial burden (Clift 2003: 160). Therefore, although the government continued to dismantle macroeconomic *dirigisme*, there was no shrinking of the welfare state but a redeployment of state resources. The government's focus shifted away from economic demand management and industrial regulation to issues such as social protection and the labor market. Between continuously expanding versus downsizing the French state, the Socialists chose a third option of replacing old forms of state intervention with new ones (Levy 2000: 340–345; Levy 2002: 4–7, 36).

As noted earlier, it was the nonaccommodating stance of competitive disinflation that contributed to wage discipline, rather than voluntary or centralized coordination from social partners. In the French wage bargaining process, negotiations and decisions are traditionally made between employers and employees with little interference from the government (Spicker 2002: 120–121). However, the discourse and practice of these negotiations are adversarial in nature, given the unions' weak and particularistic organizational patterns. Through time, the French system of wage determination has followed a gradual trend toward decentralization within the framework of collective bargaining, and intervention from the state has further weakened. In this process, one major change of note was the Aurox Law, which assigned a more significant role to plant-level collective agreements and sought to strengthen both union organization at the plant level and collective bargaining. However, overall there were no fundamental changes to the structure of this relatively weak system of collective bargaining (Malo, Toharia, and Gautié 2000: 247–253; Wren 2001: 260). As Figure 7.9 indicates, French bargaining coordination remained stable at a very low level, not only far below the Scandinavian average but also clearly below the average for the three continental European countries included in the book.

Partly due to the clear failure of the Gaullist government to push ahead social reforms against widespread union opposition, the Socialists under Jospin adopted a more consensual and accommodating attitude toward the labor movement. For example, the government extended the rights for union representatives in codetermination procedures in wage bargaining (Schröter 2004: 25). This consensual approach was crucial in securing support from social partners for the Jospin government's one key instrument of job creation: the 35-hour week. As a labor market strategy, the working time reforms were discussed in greater detail in Chapter 5 on labor market

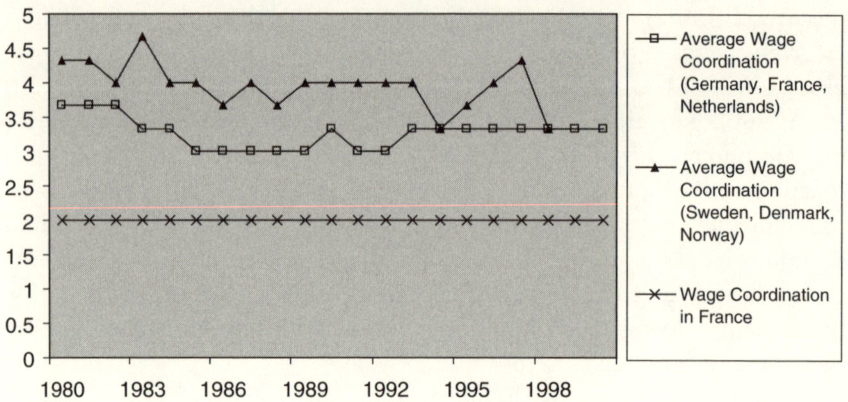

FIGURE 7.9. Kenworthy's Wage Coordination Score France in Comparison 1980–2001 (*Source:* Huber et al. 2004a]).

flexibility, but here it is important to highlight again the connection from social-partner cooperation to job creation in the economy.

Germany

Throughout its first term in power, the Red-Green coalition stuck to a policy of fiscal prudence and economic efficiency. The social democrats kept to their promise that no deficit would be created to finance fiscal expansion programs, and they adopted a pro-cyclical policy strictly within the limits of the Stability and Growth Pact. The Finance Ministry put forward a series of tax reforms, starting with the ecology tax in April 1999, followed by a major change of income and corporate taxes. The government increased the basic personal allowance from about DM 12,300 to 14,000 in 2001, and to 15,000 by 2005. The basic tax rate was cut from 25.9% to 19.9%, and the top rate was reduced from 53% in 1998 to 15% in 2005. To provide businesses with greater incentives for investment, the government lowered the corporate tax to a uniform rate of 25% in 2001. This was the most significant component of the entire tax reform, as it replaced a 40% rate on retained profits, as well as a 30% rate on distributed profits. These changes enabled firms to shift retained profits intertemporally in order to minimize their actual tax payments, causing a significant increase in government net expenditure. This directly contributed to persistent deficit problems, which later forced the social democrats to renege on the Stability and Growth Pact. For the tax reforms, the government also exempted dividends as well as the capital gains of shareholding sales from taxation. Employers, in other words, were the primary beneficiaries of the Schröder government's tax reforms (Hübner 2004: 113–114; Bispinck and Schulten 2000: 207–208; Seeleib-Kaiser 2004b: 127).

The government's fiscal austerity and business incentive measures were aimed at reducing budget deficits as well as creating economic and job growth. However, none of these objectives were reached. During its first term in office, average GDP growth per year stood at 1.5% (lowest in the euro area), below the minimum threshold that could trigger an employment increase. Since 2002, the government had been persistently unable to meet the 3% deficit target of the Stability and Growth Pact, and the public debt ratio increased by 5.8% from 1998 to 2004. Apart from reunification discussed in Chapter 3, another key reason for the inability to generate growth and employment was the harsh interest rate policy of the European Central Bank, which uses a very narrow definition of price stability (annual increase below 2% in harmonized consumer price index) and reacts to inflation asymmetrically (raising rates for rising inflationary expectations but *not* lowering rates for declining inflationary expectations) (Hein and Truger 2007: 154; Feldmann 2007: 116–131).

As the government's second term went on, it became clear that EMU-enforced fiscal and monetary austerity packages had further reduced, rather than enhanced, the ability of the German economy to generate more employment. As noted in the French case study, the Jospin government was suffering from the same problem due to years of competitive disinflation. In response, the German and French governments exercised their influence within the European Council and Commission, and lobbied other member states for a revision of the Stability and Growth Pact. Due to pressure from the German government, the European Council refrained from issuing a warning for breaching the pact in 2002, and by the end of 2004, when both France and Germany breached the pact for the third consecutive year, the European Commission interpreted the measures taken by the two countries so far as "adequate," rather than urging them to reduce deficits. Finally, in 2005 the Council of Ministers and Heads of State and Government of the EU adopted a new version of the pact, replacing the medium-term objective of "surplus or almost balanced budget" with country-specific objectives, which are as soft as 1% deficit (Feldmann 2007: 134–136). Given the importance that the French and German social democrats attach to fiscal responsibility, their resistance to the pact was a very clear demonstration of the instrumental nature of their economic prudence: It is only permissible to the extent that it actually contributes to employment growth.

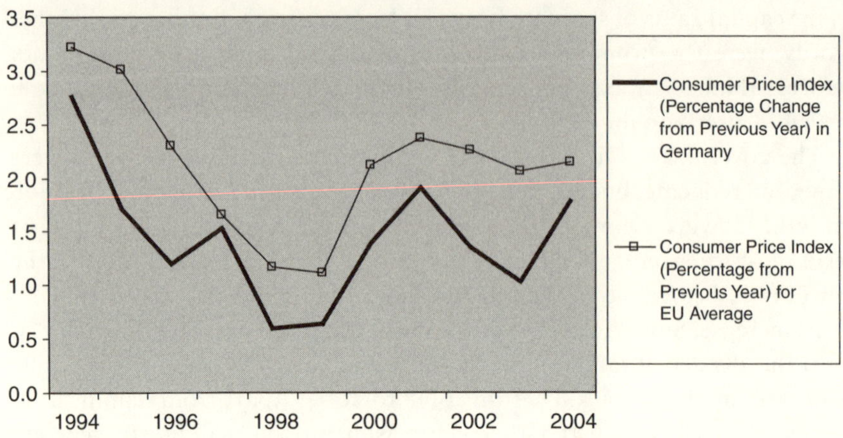

FIGURE 7.10. Inflation in Germany and the EU Compared 1994–2004 (*Source:* OECD 2007b).

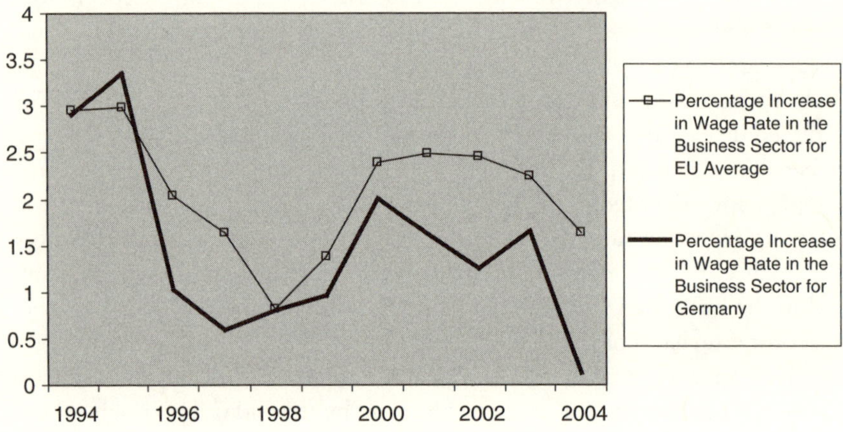

FIGURE 7.11. Wage Moderation in Germany and the EU Compared 1994–2004 (*Source:* OECD 2007b).

It is helpful to further reflect on how the European Central Bank's (ECB's) harsh interest rate policy contributed to German unemployment. As Figures 7.10 and 7.11 show, after 1996 Germany had consistently below-EU average inflation and wage increase. By 2004 there had been a decline in the growth of the nominal labor unit cost, implying a risk of deflation. This implies that Germany was suffering from a real interest rate higher than the EMU average (Hein and Truger 2007: 157–158). As P. Hall and R. J. Franzese (1998) argue, with coordinated bargaining it is typically sufficient for the central bank to deter wage inflation by signaling its intention, without actually using interest rates to reduce employment. In Germany, the extreme employment consequences of low inflation imply that the effectiveness of corporatist bargaining in delivering wage restraint has declined, relative to the effectiveness of harsh interest rates in achieving the same purpose.

An important feature of German industrial relations is the principle of *Tarifautonomie*, which grants autonomy to employers and unions from state intervention in collective bargaining. Here, the metals union IG Metall often takes the lead. The German (later European) Central Bank exercises indirect constraint on bargaining autonomy by punishing inflationary wage settlements with retaliatory interest rate increases. While German unions had not been aggressive in wage demands, they were not able to commit themselves to long-term wage moderation. At the insistence of employers, this issue of long-run wage restraint entered the agenda for the corporatist agreement Alliance for Jobs (BA). However, unions had been reluctant to discuss wage developments directly with either the government or their social partners (Bispinck and Schulten 2000: 198; Negrelli 2000: 102).

The pivotal position of IG Metall within the labor movement was an important reason for the difficulty in reaching wage compromises. Given its dominance among unions, IG Metall alone is sufficient to block reforms it doesn't like. As the Dutch Wassenaar process showed, corporatist concertation can become less difficult if negotiating parties can expand the range of issues subject to trade-offs and compromises. The ambition of Schröder's BA proposal was indeed to integrate a wide range of social and labor market policies into tripartite negotiations, including unemployment insurance, pensions, taxes, and health care. However, the institutional preconditions for cross-domain negotiations were insufficient, given the sectorally segmented structure of the unions and their large self-regulatory competence in key policy areas. There is, therefore, incompatibility between macroconcertation on the federal level and institutional segmentation in meso corporatist partnership on the level of social partners. Overall, the unions had not refrained from lifting wages above the market-clearing level (Hemerijck and Schludi 2000: 152–153; Hemerijck, Manow, and van Kersbergen 2000: 120–122; Lamping Thnd Vergunst 2004: 25–36).

The Schröder government did attempt to play a more active role, for example by taking over employment policy funding and design responsibilities from BA. However, both unions and employers' confederations were unwilling to negotiate in a tripartite setting, and the government remained excluded from much of the process. On the whole, BA negotiations achieved little substantive results. IG Metall as the dominant player proved crucial in BA's failure. It not only insisted on the continued use of early retirement, but it also opposed the inclusion of wage moderation in the negotiation agenda. Unlike the Swedish LO prior to bargaining decentralization, the German Confederation of Labor does not have coordinating power over collective bargaining, and the primary players are individual sectoral unions. The lack of peak authority in coordination led to persistent disagreements among unions over a strategic response to the need for reform, with the chemical and mining unions more receptive toward changes than the metals union. The same problem also confronted employers' organizations. Not only was their authority over individual member firms declining, but the disaccord between functionally distinct peak authorities such as the BDA (Confederation of German Employers' Associations) and BDI (Federation of German Industry) further reduced the possibility for strategic coordination. The heightened uncertainty over strategic action fed back onto the unions, which became increasingly skeptical about the sincerity of the promises by business to reward wage moderation with high employment (Lehmbruch 2003: 153–154; Hassel and Ebbinghaus 2000: 79–80).

United Kingdom

New Labour acknowledged that the competitiveness of the British economy was compromised by the lack of policy commitment to long-term economic stability. In response, the government recalibrated its macroeconomic objectives to focus specifically on stability, with low inflation as the key. For the management of the short-term economy, it abandoned fiscal policy and relied chiefly on monetary adjustment. The chancellor of the Exchequer assumed overall responsibility in setting the inflation target, and the Bank of England, through the Monetary Policy Committee, became the primary target enforcer. In order to reduce government intervention in monetary policy, New Labour committed itself to a high level of transparency by transferring interest rate decision making completely to the Bank of England. To keep expenditures under control, the government stuck to its golden rule on public finance: It would borrow only for investment, not for funding current expenditures, and even borrowing for investment would only occur if there were demonstrable returns over the economic cycle. Given that the early net investment forecast was set at 1% of GDP per year, the golden rule essentially constrained the net public debt from falling

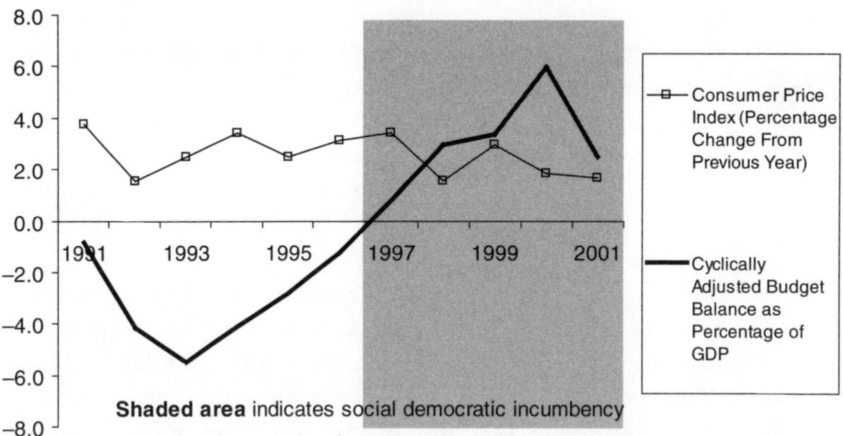

FIGURE 7.12. Budget Balance and Inflation in the UK 1991–2001
(*Source:* OECD 2005c [budget balance]; Huber et al. 2004a [consumer price index]).

below 40% of GDP (Mullard 2000: 122; Glyn and Wood 2001: 202; Lund 2002: 189). New Labour, as shown in Figure 7.12, was not only extremely successful in achieving a budget surplus but was also capable of keeping inflation at a moderate level.

However, rather than ideologically driven, these fiscal-tightening measures are largely instrumental, for the purpose of creating employment in the long run. As evidence for this pragmatism, although the Monetary Policy Committee is responsible for meeting the inflation target, it has no mandate for driving inflation below the target, and this is to prevent the negative consequences of excessively high interest rates on job creation. If inflation indeed falls below the target while unemployment is rising, there is the expectation that the Bank should cut interest rates and the government should utilize both automatic stabilizers and fiscal expansion to reduce unemployment. During its first term, New Labour was effective in reducing both unemployment and the public deficit, but this was a process already started under the previous Conservative government. Similar to the situation in Sweden, the forced floating of the pound in 1992 delivered a relatively competitive exchange rate, which, by increasing export-sector revenues, provided more job opportunities as well as a better balance of payments. On this basis, the Bank's conservative high interest rate policy prevented serious inflationary consequences from the fall in unemployment (Glyn and Wood 2001: 202).

Reflecting the instrumental purpose of its economic prudence, New Labour changed policy priorities after improving the government's fiscal situation during the first term. While it stuck to the Conservative spending limit for the first four years, after reelection in 2001 there was a significant increase in expenditures on the welfare state, public services, and active labor market measures. Spending on welfare programs grew almost at the same rate as the economy, and even faster after the 2002 budget. In this budget, the government legislated for increases in national insurance contribution by employers, employees, and the self-employed on all earnings above the threshold. This de facto increase in indirect tax provided the public resources the government needed for its programs, while at the same time keeping its election promise of no increase in direct taxes. With its attention increasingly focused on labor market activation and the resources needed to fund activation, New Labour became more flexible in its budgetary stance, while working within the general framework of economic prudence (Regan 2003: 271–275; Bauld, Judge, and Paterson 2003: 170).

The previous Conservative government used tax revenues almost exclusively to fund the reduction of public debts. By contrast, New Labour channeled increasing portions of tax revenues, especially those from windfall taxes, levies on private utilities, and capital receipt releases from council house sales, into its active labor market programs, including the New Deal and other public services such as health and education in particular. The utilization of tax funds for public services intensified in each round of New Labour's Comprehensive Spending Reviews, especially after the party was reelected in 2001 (Burchardt and Hills 1999: 46–47; Lund 2002: 190). New Labour proposed a raise in health spending in Britain to the level of the European average, and as mentioned earlier, it increased national insurance contributions instead of general taxes in order to fund the growing healthcare expenditures. This way, the link between benefits and the contribution in national insurance is broken on an increasingly frequent basis. National insurance comes to be regarded more and more by the public as a form of general taxation (Regan 2003: 278–279).

Figure 7.13 shows that although total social expenditures declined during the initial period of New Labour's incumbency, this was followed by significant and relatively consistent increases well into its second term in office. Similarly, in Figure 7.14, while the government started by lowering taxes, after reelection in 2001 it raised taxes again, to finance the increased public investments in labor market and social programs. As detailed in Chapter 5, New Labour also used the fruits of early economic austerity to tackle poverty and social exclusion, through the introduction of a series of negative

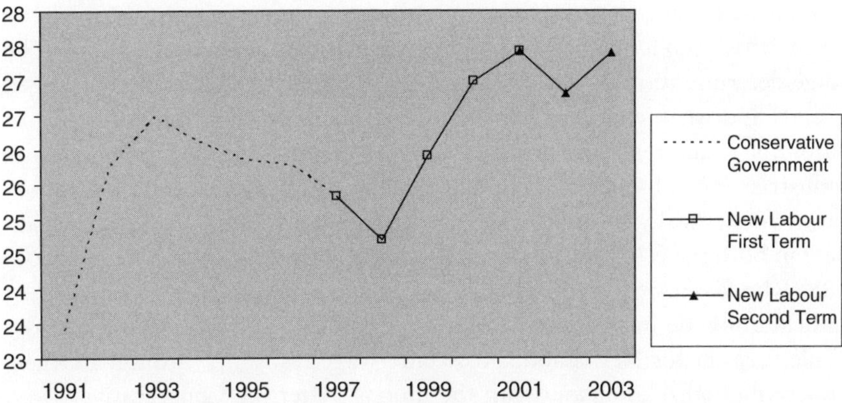

FIGURE 7.13. Total Social Expenditure as Percentage of GDP in the UK 1991–2003 (*Source:* OECD 2006a).

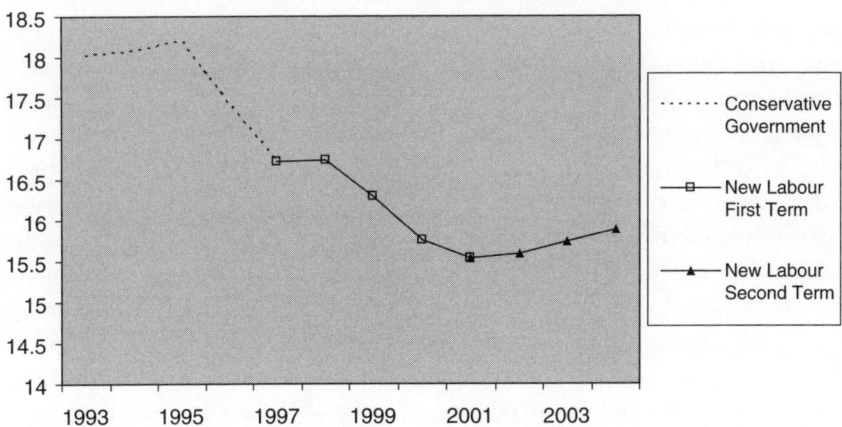

FIGURE 7.14. Effective Tax Rate on the Average Production Worker (APW) in the UK 1993–2004 (*Source:* OECD 2005a).

income taxes (Ferrera and Hemerijck 2003: 103–107; Merkel 2001: 58). The government pledged itself to the halving of child poverty by 2010 and its eradication in twenty years, and after the Comprehensive Spending Review for the 2001–2004 round, New Labour further increased its spending to achieve these objectives (Bauld, Judge, and Paterson 2003: 215).

Excessive wage claims and union militancy were problems that used to beset British economic and employment growth throughout the 1970s. The wage determination system was historically characterized by decentralized unions and weak employer organizations. Such a system was incapable of enforcing wage restraint or an effective voluntary incomes policy across industries. The absence of the social wage mechanism as a welfare compensation for centrally enforced wage moderation contributed to chronic weakness in both the economy and social security (Hemerijck and Schludi 2000: 188; Rhodes 2000a: 162; Rhodes 2000b: 54). However, two decades of radical union de-institutionalization by Conservative governments actually made it easier for New Labour to secure wage restraint, through a largely nonconflictual relationship with the unions. After the Conservative years, unions were already significantly weakened, and they were both unable and unwilling to mount coordinated resistance against government reforms. In addition, as a party linked to the labor movement, New Labour did make notable efforts in reversing the Conservative de-unionization campaigns.

New Labour adopted a more conciliatory attitude toward unions. The government set up several reviews and proposed a partnership between the party and union organizations, as well as between public and private sectors (Hewitt 1999: 167). The 1999 Employment Relations Act reintroduced a statutory recognition procedure for unions, and as part of its general strategy to facilitate labor market participation, the government also provided unions with public resources for skill upgrading, such as the Union Learning Fund (Rhodes 2000b: 60–61). Meanwhile, however, Blair continued to keep state intervention in incomes policy at a minimum, and generally shied away from formal corporatist interaction with unions. The party made little attempt to rescind the Conservative measures aimed at deregulating workplace relations or curbing union rights. Similarly, it retained the restrictions on the right to strike and on trade union governance. Although the government re-institutionalized union recognition, this was limited to the workplace or company level. It did not reinstate multiemployer bargaining, and there was no attempt to introduce industrial democracy. Unions simply became part of a supply-side partnership with the government. The partnership's primary objective was productivity, wage restraint, and labor market activation (Ewing 2003: 148).

The government encouraged the expansion in the coverage of legislation for individual rights, so that working conditions and wages for most workers are now regulated by laws, rather than by collective bargaining. The framework of labor law in Britain became much more legalistic under New Labour. The center of gravity in industrial relations shifted to a primary concern with employment and labor market activation, away from such goals as union empowerment. A comprehensive labor code gradually took shape under New Labour. Although industrial relations became more legalistic, the government made efforts to ensure that these regulatory acts cover some issues crucial to union interests and to the integration of the disadvantaged in the labor market. For example, the new labour code includes clauses on equality of opportunity and rights at the workplace. It also covers areas previously considered external to industrial relations, such as the balance between work and family and greater transparency by employers over the terms and conditions of employment (Deakin and Reed 2000: 125; Ewing 2003: 147–151; Ferrera and Hemerijck 2003: 103–107; Cressey 1999: 171).

Australia

Australia and New Zealand shared common characteristics in their pursuit of macroeconomic job growth. For both countries, a unique but fundamental condition for sustainable employment was to liberalize the protected and unproductive manufacturing industries, because the resources-based primary sector had lost its traditional export markets. Labor's removal of industrial protection was a significant policy departure from the previous coalition government. However, with the Accord framework, Labor's deregulatory reforms were more incremental than in neighbouring New Zealand. The Hawke government started with two drastic changes: floating the Australian dollar and freeing the banking and financial sectors; after that, strategies became more mixed. Labor reduced the number of producers and slashed industrial assistance, but it delayed direct cuts to existing protectionist mechanisms or barriers to trade until the tariff reductions in 1988. Rather than a genuine decline in industrial intervention, the ALP simply recalibrated the target of intervention in order to focus on more competitive industries. Nevertheless, as international competition intensified throughout the 1980s, the competitive disadvantage of manufacturing contributed directly to an escalation of foreign debt and to balance-of-payment problems, which came to dominate the government's agenda (Warhurst and Stewart 1989: 160–175; Stutchbury 1990: 58–60; K. Davis 1989: 105–106; Beilharz, Considine, and Watts 1992: 117–119).

After late 1985, Labor shifted from fiscal to monetary adjustment in order to support the currency and constrain domestic demand. It publicly committed itself to a "trilogy of no increases," in taxes, expenditures, or borrowing, as a percentage of GDP. The government was able to deliver four successive budget surpluses, from 1985/86 to 1988/89. Nevertheless, Labor pursued austerity instrumentally, for the purpose of maintaining employment and social expenditure, rather than for ideological reasons. Between 1983 and 1992, the government achieved budget consolidation largely by cutting revenue transfers to state governments and defense, and it then used the surpluses to finance expansion in labor market programs, social security, health, and education (Easton and Gerritsen 1996: 30; Wanna 1994: 239). Due to union opposition to the regressive nature of the GST, Labor's attempt to push it through failed, and the government instead balanced income tax cuts with the introduction of fringe benefits and capital gains taxes. A parallel process of economic reform took place in New Zealand, at a much faster pace, but the results were very different. During the 1980s and early 1990s, the ALP presided over increases in economic growth and employment, whereas New Zealand suffered continuous net economic contraction and high unemployment. A key reason for the better outcomes of fiscal conservatism in Australia was that wage increases were kept below price increases, leading to a fall in real exchange rate and a rise in the world market share of export industries. The extent of import infiltration due to liberalization was therefore milder than in New Zealand (Easton and Garritsen 1996: 45). The wage-restraint success, so crucial to Labor's achievement in macroeconomic and job growth, was made possible by the corporatist Accord framework.

During Labor's incumbency, the Accord was periodically renegotiated and updated through two basic phases. The first phase focused on varying degrees of centralization in wage bargaining within the framework of wage decline. The second phase turned to bargaining decentralization, including the formal introduction of enterprise bargaining through the Australian Industrial Relations Commission. In both phases, the Accord helped encourage consultation among the labor movement, the party, and businesses. Labor established the tripartite Economic Planning Advisory Council and convened the National Economic Summit in 1983. The summit brought the three sides together for extensive discussions over both economic and labor market reforms, and it helped secure the support of business for centralized wage fixing (Boreham 1990: 45–51; Stutchbury 1990: 54–55). Meticulous consultation, plus the explicit promise of a better social wage, laid a solid ground of public support for the Accord, which helped preserve both the Industrial Relations Commission and the arbitration system, despite extensive economic liberalization.

Although its mechanisms were consensual and mostly tripartite, the Accord considerably strengthened the labor movement vis-à-vis business.

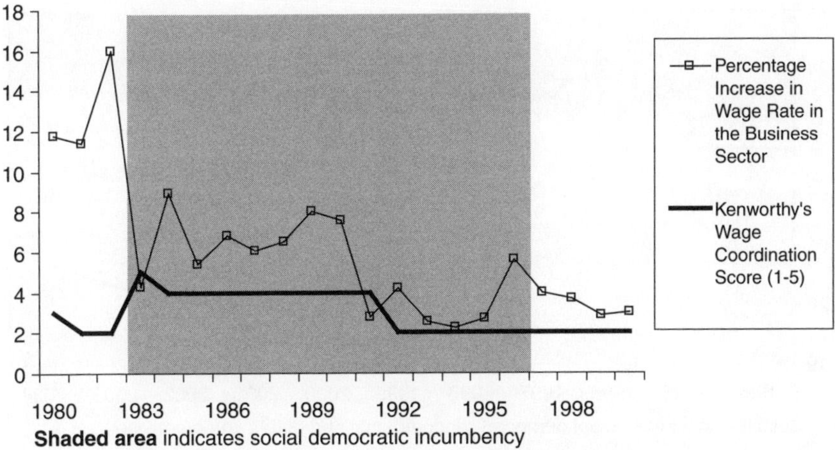

FIGURE 7.15. Wage Coordination and Wage Moderation in Australia 1980–2000 (*Source:* OECD 2006b [wage rate]; Huber et al. 2004a [wage coordination]).

Given their traditional suspicion of unions, employers were by comparison more reluctant to participate in the negotiations, and consequently it was the Labor government and unions that specified the roles and objectives for businesses in the Accord framework. In other words, incomes policy through the Accord was essentially based on a single-issue coalition between only two partners, unions and the ALP (Gardner 1990: 82–93). The Accord became the conduit through which unions gained direct access to macroeconomic policymaking. The prospect of wider influence over policy direction was a major incentive for the labor movement, whose objectives used to be confined to wages and working conditions (Peetz 1998: 161–163; Gardner 1990: 85–93; E. Davis 1986: 133). There was also asymmetry between businesses and labor in their ability to enforce the Accord agreements. Given their relatively fragmented organizational structure, businesses found it difficult to work consistently within the Accord framework, and their weakness constrained their capacity to extensively pursue labor market deregulation (Buchanan and Nicholls 2003: 47–48).

Over time, the Accord gave the ALP a number of advantages. Besides strengthening both the party and the movement, it created a stable environment for collective action, increasing the possibilities for union cooperation in government reforms. The Accord also allowed decentralization of bargaining while preserving basic social protection. Most importantly, as Figure 7.15 shows, it was largely effective in delivering wage restraint, the key to long-term economic and job growth in Australia. The Accord

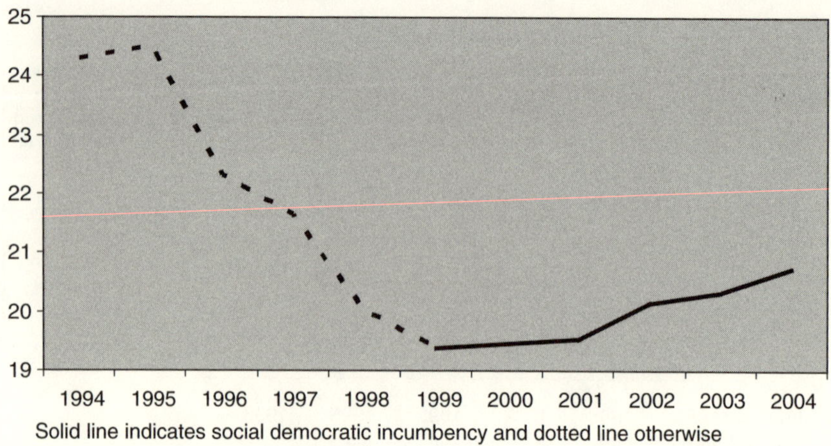

FIGURE 7.16. Effective Tax Rate on the Average Production Worker (APW) in New Zealand 1994–2004 (*Source:* OECD 2005a).

framework enabled the Labor government to make a relatively costless exit from the wage-freeze mechanism, imposed by the previous center-right coalition after it failed to achieve a voluntary incomes policy. In neighboring New Zealand, the Lange government's dismantling of a similar wage-freeze system led to an explosion of inflationary wage claims, but Australia had a very different experience. Accord Mark I oversaw wage moderation in exchange for controls on prices and non-wage incomes. Later phases of the Accord then aligned wage rises with increases in productivity. Although the ALP promised to fully index wages to the consumer price index, unions did not pursue "catch-up" claims from the wage freeze, and Accord Mark II managed to deliver a significant fall in real wages. Unions also agreed that the introduction of Medicare would lead to lower private health-care costs, which in turn slashed the consumer price index by more than 2%. Consequently, no indexation was awarded for the second half of 1984. Labor's wage-moderation policy did not aim at altering the wage/profit share, and the burden of adjustment was thinly spread (Stutchbury 1990: 55–58; Davis 1989: 94–97; Buchanan and Nicholls 2003: 50, 53).

The Accord also contributed to further centralization in Australian union coordination. In the Accord negotiation process, unions were represented by one peak authority, the ACTU. During each of the eight Accord updates, as the difficulty of negotiation increased, so did ACTU's authority and influence over local branches. This centralized authority made the enforcement of wage restraint much easier. Reflecting Mancur Olson's logic, the centralization of coordination was a crucial reason why the Accord process helped solve the collective action problem within the Australian labor movement. And the arbitration mechanism acted as an additional institutional enforcer, constraining and stabilizing individual unions' bargaining behavior (Gardner 1990: 96–99).

Finally, the Accord also made it easier for unions to accept the gradual emergence of bargaining decentralization. Enterprise bargaining became a key issue after the Accord Mark III negotiations, and the government slowly integrated it into the industrial relations system, first through the 1988 Industrial Relations Act and later the 1993 Industrial Relations Reform Act. The latter act formally introduced pattern bargaining and imposed clearer limits on strike activities, and Accord Mark VI also extensively promoted enterprise bargaining as an alternative to central awards. As Figure 7.15 shows, after the early 1990s there was indeed a clear decentralization in wage bargaining, reversing the centralization achieved during the preparation for Accord Mark I in 1983. However, Labor consistently balanced enterprise bargaining with policies to maintain basic social security and labor market standards. With the Arbitration Commission now safely entrenched in the Accord framework, the growing decentralization did not fundamentally undermine existing institutional settings (Schwartz 2000: 112–114; Buchanan and Nicholls 2003: 30–45; Castles 1994: 137). Although there was extensive deregulation in the economy, the Treasury accepted wage restraint within the Accord as its main instrument for controlling labor costs, and it abandoned labor market deregulation as an alternative strategy. Actually, on most issues, the two unlikely partners of the Treasury and ACTU maintained a strong alliance (Stutchbury 1990: 66–67).

After the coalition government returned to power in 1996, the industrial relations system became massively deregulated. Following the example of New Zealand's Employment Contracts Act, the coalition government passed the Workplace Relations Act in 1996, giving employers the option of avoiding negotiations over collective employment contracts. Instead, employers could now negotiate wage awards with unions on an individual basis. Although awards through the arbitration system still existed, they were now regarded as a safety net of minimum standards (Lansbury and Michelson 2003: 227–231; Buchanan and Nicholls 2003: 30–45; Harbridge and Bagley 2002: 186–189).

New Zealand

Under the fourth Labour government, economic reforms focused on deregulation. Labour removed exchange rate control and credit guidelines, freed the banking system, and dismantled industry assistance, especially producer subsidies. Contrary to the Keynesian tradition, Labour's fiscal policy was strictly subordinate to monetary policy (Whitwell 1990: 105; Hawke 1992: 441). The party transformed New Zealand's financial sector from the most to the least regulated among OECD countries. Refusing to supply additional money, the government insisted on fully funding any deficit, and its principle of industrial intervention shifted from structural (restrictions on firms and individuals entering particular markets) to conduct (measures affecting how firms and individuals behave in their chosen market) regulations (Rudd 1990: 92–93; Hawke 1992: 441). However, these radical reforms accelerated, rather than slowing down, an economic decline. Unemployment persisted and then worsened rapidly through the 1980s. Between 1987 and 1994, the country's GDP performed about 30% below the trend line, and GDP shrank between 1985 and 1992, in contrast to continued expansion in most other OECD countries. Aggregate productivity declined, and when it started to recover after 1995, it ironically returned only to the level of the pre-reform Muldoon era, which was itself characterized by excessive state intervention (Dalziel 1999: 62–70; Kelsey 1995: 9–10).

After Labour returned to power again in 1999, it became clear that the previous fifteen years of fiscal austerity had been excessive, and had further impeded, rather than helped, macroeconomic job creation. As noted earlier, both the French and German social democrats faced a similar problem (in somewhat different contexts). Demonstrating its instrumental approach to economic prudence, the fifth Labour government fought back against the fiscal restrictions, rather than further persisting with them. While Labour did not abandon monetary policy as a tool for inflation control, it started a series of fiscal expansion. Figure 7.16 shows that after drastic tax cuts during the Nationals' neoliberal reforms, the fifth Labour government broke with this trend, by gradually raising taxes again. The government argued that high-income households had already benefited the most from past economic reforms and that economic policy should now serve social redistributive purposes, by asking the well-off to contribute more to funding for social services. Labour took a radical step of directly increasing the top marginal income tax from 33% to 39%. By contrast, at the time of the 1999 election, the Nationals were offering to further cut the top personal and company income tax from 33% to 30%, and a similar pledge was reaffirmed when the Nationals elected Don Brash as their new leader in 2003 (Dalziel and Lattimore 2004: 83; Hazledine and Quiggin 2006: 148).

The government also expanded financial resources for industrial and regional assistance, abandoning the liberalization drive started in the early

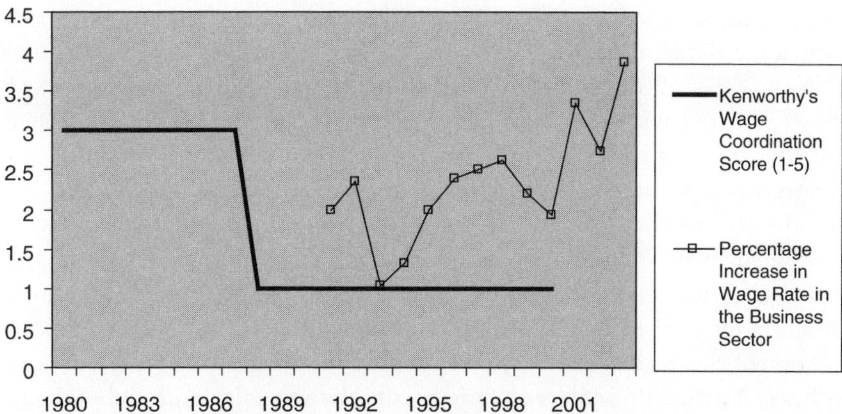

FIGURE 7.17. Wage Coordination and Wage Moderation in New Zealand 1980–2003 (*Source:* OECD 2007b [wage rate]; Huber et al. 2004a [wage moderation]).

1980s. It adopted a "picking winners" strategy, targeting particularly those high-tech industries with strong potential for innovation and job growth. Labour established separate task forces for four seed sectors, including biotechnology, information and communication technology (ICT), screen production, and screen design. In the 2003 budget, $110 million (NZ) was allocated over a four-year period to assist these industries. By the 2004 budget, the government had consolidated its industrial assistance policy into the Growth and Innovation Framework, backed up by $500 million in public funding. For the first time since the onset of neoliberal reforms, the government was reversing the trend toward further privatization. Labour approved the state-owned savings bank Kiwibank in 2001, and pumped spending into the unraveling rail networks and Air New Zealand. There was also greater tolerance for price regulation in the electricity and telecommunications network industries (Goldfinch 2004; Dalziel and Lattimore 2004: 96).

Besides radical deregulatory and austerity fiscal experiments by both major parties, another important factor behind New Zealand's abysmal job performance since the 1980s was the failure in voluntary incomes policy. Frequent bouts of wage explosion, seen in Figure 7.17,[2] led to excessive labor costs and further increased the pressure on monetary policy through interest rate hikes. The consequent economic decline, on top of large public-

---

[2] Data on wage rates and bargaining centralization are relatively incomplete for New Zealand, and this is reflected in the uneven lengths of the two time series in Figure 7.17.

sector redundancies, significantly contributed to growing unemployment. The wage-moderation meltdown took place amid the total dissolution of New Zealand's corporatist bargaining system, which, as Figure 7.17 shows, started with the 1987 Labour Relations Act. This act weakened the coordination of collective bargaining but did not totally abandon the arbitration system. While encouraging more enterprise bargaining, the act also included awards for weaker groups, and the legislation's premise continued to be industry-based rather than enterprise-based (Walsh and Brosnan 1999: 117–119). While Labour argued that enterprise bargaining should grow at the expense of employment awards, the act allowed unions to control the pace of change, by retaining their right to choose between industry awards or enterprise agreements. Labour also restored compulsory unionism, which was abolished by the previous National government. As a compensation for union consent to enterprise bargaining in the act, the government promised to expand the formal welfare state (Harbridge and Walsh 2002: 200–201; Huber and Stephens 2001: 294; Hemerijck and Schludi 2000: 193–195). Backed by the Labor Ministry (which itself made skillful use of its union connection), the government tried to retain the existing framework of union rights and successfully resisted the pressure to end blanket coverage of wage awards. In the struggles within the party leading up to the act, the Treasury's attempt to radically deregulate the labor market was completely rejected (Walsh and Brosnan 1999: 117; Walsh 1989: 167–168).

However, despite all these measures, Labour was unsuccessful in securing either wage moderation or a functioning corporatist relationship with unions. The labor movement continued to be relatively weak, segmented, and unable to coordinate or enforce bargaining agreements. Historically, the political insertion of the labor movement in New Zealand has been less successful than in Australia. By the late nineteenth century Australia had already developed a substantial mining sector, whereas New Zealand continued to be dominated by agriculture. For this reason, unlike their Australian counterparts, New Zealand unions were more dominated by craft- or guild-level organizations in limited sectors. The Industrial Conciliation and Arbitration Act of 1894 required that unions be formed along occupational lines, and this requirement was interpreted very strictly. Highly decentralized in organization and geographically dispersed, unions in New Zealand lacked serious political representation (Kelsey 1995: 73; Buchanan and Nicholls 2003: 92–96).

Given their decentralized structure, peak organizations of labor and capital were not as effective as their Australian counterparts in enforcing wage restraint. After Robert Muldoon's comprehensive wage and price controls were removed in 1984, wages were primarily determined by direct employer–union bargaining, in the absence of a voluntary incomes policy. Unable to intervene formally in incomes policy, the government was forced to fight inflation (unsuccessfully) through monetarist and fiscal policies. There was a major escalation in industrial disputes in the 1985/1986 wage round over wage relativities. This ultimately triggered a further decline in the economy and growing unemployment (Boston 1987: 151–154, 165–180; Oliver 1989: 40–41). In order to break wage relativity, Labour actually did propose, similarly to their Australian counterpart, social wage increases in return for tight fiscal and monetary policies. However, unions and employers' organizations all remained divided and unable to formulate a coherent response to the government's proposal. The collective action failure among social partners made it impossible to pursue employment growth, a social wage, or wage moderation through corporatist institutions. This formed a clear contrast with the experience of the Dutch Wassenaar, Norwegian Solidarity Alternative, or Australian Accord (Boston 1993: 124; Schwartz 2000: 88–93, 98–99).

As the foundation for New Zealand's wage earners' welfare state, the collective bargaining and arbitration system was completely destroyed by the following National government, through the 1991 Employment Contracts Act. With the act, the Nationals replaced arbitration with purely private contracts between individuals and firms. In a decisive break with a century of industrial relations policy, the government for the first time used the market as the primary wage-fixing instrument. After dismantling arbitration in 1991, the Nationals went on to replace unemployment benefits with a workfare scheme called community wage. This narrowly targeted scheme replaced the social wage, the last remnant of the wage earners' welfare state, and on this basis, New Zealand's informal welfare state became history (Mackay 2003: 100–107; Harbridge and Walsh 2002: 202).

By the time a Labour-led coalition returned to power in 1999, deregulation had become as discredited as state intervention was in the early 1980s. The fifth Labour government made a series of attempts to reverse the neoliberal legacy in industrial relations. The paradigm-shifting 1991 Employment Contracts Act was replaced by the Employment Relations Act, which restored legal recognition for trade unions and extended union access. Although the act shied away from a direct return to centralized or sectoral bargaining, collective bargaining at the shop level and multiemployer bargaining were again encouraged. In addition, the act provided an automatic extension of the terms of agreements to all new employees.

The government renewed provisions for industrial action and removed the Nationals' community wage program. Some rights were also extended to unions that should genuinely assist them in their organizational revival. After the Employment Relations Act of 2000, union membership in New Zealand rose each year, and over a four-year period between 1999 and 2003 there was a total increase of 13%. Two major peak union bodies, formerly rivals, merged in 2000, strengthening the informal power of the newly formed peak authority Council of Trade Unions, which is now restored to a partnership relationship with the fifth Labour government. After bearing the brunt of neoliberal deregulation for almost a decade, unions wholeheartedly threw their support behind Labour's ameliorative measures (Boxall 2001; Harbridge and Walsh 2002: 211–215; Harbridge, Walsh, and Wilkinson 2002: 74–75; Buchanan and Nicholls 2003: 105–106; Cooper and May 2005: 2–3; de Bruin 2002: 222–223).

Analysis of Economic and Corporatist Contexts

Due to the external constraint of permanent austerity, all social democratic cases, to different extents, converged to the center-right position on economic policy. Governments cut corporate taxes to increase business efficiency and encourage investment, and they simplified or reduced income taxes to stimulate purchasing power. In monetary policy, social democratic governments that inherited a hard currency and a tight interest-rate legacy from center-right predecessors (Scandinavia, Germany, France under Jospin, the Netherlands, and the UK) did little to abandon this framework, and those without this legacy (France under François Mitterand, the Antipodes) took an active initiative in creating such monetary constraint. All social democratic governments attempted, many successfully, to reduce public deficits, and where there used to be tight protection for industries (the Antipodes), they implemented extensive deregulatory and liberalization reforms. Between 1981 and 2001, the average cyclically adjusted budget balance for the nine cases under social democratic incumbency was a surplus of 0.28% of GDP, while during the same period, the center-right incumbency average was 0.04% (OECD 2005c). In other words, the social democrats were doing at least as well as their center-right counterparts in protecting fiscal soundness, if not better. In terms of institutional evolution, the bipartisan policy convergence to economic prudence indicates a clear departure from the Keynesian institutions that had permeated all these countries for decades after the Second World War. In terms of intellectual outlook, these policy changes also signal a significant change of direction for social democratic parties. On this basis, the macroeconomic pressure of permanent austerity has overcome both institutional and ideological constraints, and has led to path-breaking, rather than path-dependent, changes.

After acknowledging the overarching influence of external economic circumstances, one can still find some social democratic philosophical rationale behind these economic reforms. While the social democrats tightened public expenditure, cut taxes, kept the hard currency, and reduced deficits, there is little evidence that these changes were implemented and left there just for their intrinsic normative values (in other words, ideologically driven). Instead, economic prudence in the third way was largely instrumental, to the ultimate purpose of creating more employment opportunities and, therefore, making active labor market measures more effective. Austerity was simply a means, made necessary by the economic context of the retrenchment era, to serve the end of job creation. Where the means no longer served the end, the governments readily ditched the means. There are some rather dramatic examples of this instrumentality in third way economic prudence. France and Germany, arguably the two most important actors behind Europe's turn to hard-currency economic union, both revolted against the very framework they helped create. The Schröder and Jospin governments made successful lobbying efforts to water down the Stability and Growth Pact, which then allowed them to use larger deficits to combat worsening employment. For similar purposes, Labour in New Zealand also turned its back on neoliberal reforms that it had started fifteen years earlier. Clearly, these governments did not totally abandon economic prudence, but where the objectives of job creation and prudence conflicted, they adjusted the latter to fit the former.

Besides these direct attempts to reverse austerity, there are also instances of employment-oriented pragmatism even during the very process of exercising austerity. For example, governments in Sweden and the UK adopted a strategy of intertemporal pooling of objectives, with fiscal tightening concentrated in the early term and fiscal expansion in later terms, relying on revenues saved during the budget consolidation period. For Australia, expenditure control was achieved by focusing cuts on defense and federal redistribution, and the additional revenues were pumped right back into labor market and social programs. In the Netherlands and New Zealand, reforms in the tax system focused specifically on increasing financial incentives for the marginal labor force to rejoin the ranks of the employed.

However, not all of these policies of instrumental prudence were ultimately effective in their employment objectives. Comparing the well-performing cases (Norway, Denmark, the Netherlands, and Australia) with borderline or failed ones (Germany, France, Sweden during the collapse of the "third road," and New Zealand under the fourth Labour government), it is clear that in the former group, corporatist bargaining institutions remained highly effective. By contrast, for the latter group, there was either interest rate intervention (with unemployment costs), which enforced wage constraints, or simply genuine wage inflation, all in the process of corporatist decline, to various extents. For this reason, in general, the corporatist context is an important component in the third way policy paradigm, through its connection to wage moderation and job creation. Job creation, in turn, directly contributes to labor market activation as the core of third way strategies. Looking across cases, New Zealand's pattern of direct decline in bargaining coordination was more the exception than the norm. Britain's comprehensive bargaining deregulation, of course, had been completed before New Labour came to power. For most other cases, the general pattern was limited decline, in the context of overall stability during social democratic incumbency. The primary reason behind this centrifugal pressure on collective bargaining was increasing skill and wage differentiation at the firm level (Huber and Stephens 2001: 225). To some extent, most social democratic governments oversaw increasing "centralized decentralization," which led to a decentralized wage setting coupled with peak-level coordination. The Dutch, Danish, and Australian social democrats in particular implemented a thorough process of centralized decentralization, and this pattern also reflects the current bargaining arrangement in Sweden (Lodovici 2000: 50–51; Ferrera et al. 2001: 132).

The advantage of coordinated decentralization is that it combines macroeconomic priorities (on the coordinated macro level) and firm-level objectives (on the decentralized micro level), which are closer to the concerns of individual employers and employees. The three exemplar cases of centralized decentralization (the Netherlands, Denmark, and Australia) all benefited from such two-level bargaining by achieving both economic competitiveness and wage solidarity to some extent. Also called "competitive corporatism," these productivity-oriented social pacts have so far proved to be highly effective (Hemerijck and Schludi 2000: 207–212; Scharpf and Schmidt 2000: 318–323; Green-Pedersen, van Kersbergen, and Hemerijck 2001: 318–319; Rhodes 1998: 200).

In the context of open capital markets, there are few other sustainable ways of directly stimulating macroeconomic growth beyond the continuing pursuit of wage restraint. However, the presence of ongoing wage moderation alongside a coordinated bargaining decline indicates that wage restraint has over time become more robust, surviving under less friendly institutional settings than in the Golden Age. Nevertheless, organized wage restraint is still harder to achieve where the capacity for collective action is weaker, for example, when unions are too fragmented (as in France) or too dominated by a single body resistant to reform (as in Germany). Finally, for the *fin-de-siècle* Labour governments in New Zealand and the UK, previous neoliberal reforms have already removed wage inflation, simply by fundamentally weakening the unions. For these two cases, the role of corporatist institutions in macroeconomic and job growth is relatively marginal.

8

Conclusion

Theories of Possibilities

Based on the experience of nine countries, this book has proposed several theories about various aspects of the third way. Among these theoretical propositions, the most important for the book's purpose is the possibility for conflicting ideologies to create incentives for making costly changes to institutions. This is the main focus of the book. As a general thesis potentially speaking to all patterns of institutional evolution, I used it to evaluate two well-known competing theories of welfare state changes: power resources and path dependency. The book's main task has been to demonstrate the possible circumstances under which ideological beliefs can create sufficient incentives for absorbing the cost of unmaking old rules and making new ones. On this basis, the book contributes to the welfare state literature, in outlining the possibilities for power resources to create path-breaking, rather than path-dependent, welfare reforms after the Golden Age.

In the process of establishing this argument, I have also proposed several other related theories. These include a thesis on contemporary social democratic ideological transformation, a thesis on the way in which positive externalities that result from being organized can spill benefits over to unorganized outsiders, and a thesis about the components and structure of the third way as a policy paradigm. None of these theories is deterministic about the outcomes. They merely identify the often (though not always) necessary, rather than sufficient, conditions for these outcomes to eventuate. The book, for example, does not lend strong support to those who believe that ideology *is* more powerful than institutional legacy, or that social democracy *will* reduce the insider–outsider divide. But the book does make clear that, given the right conditions, it can happen.

THE POSSIBILITIES FOR CONTINUING SOCIAL DEMOCRATIC ADAPTATION

Rather than occurring in the abstract, ideological evolution takes place in reaction to changing empirical circumstances (Freeden 1996). For this reason, with all its normative faith and prescriptive outlook, ideology has a pragmatic side, which enables it to adapt and survive as a system of relevant beliefs about a changing world. Two such important changes in the empirical world created the necessity for notions of solidarity and egalitarianism to evolve: the growing heterogeneity of the social democratic electorate and increasing unemployment.

When social democrats split with communists to enter the electoral field, they also broadened solidarity among workers into solidarity among wage earners. It is probably inaccurate to suggest that the purpose of this ideological adaptation was to increase the diversity of the social democratic electoral base. The purpose was more likely to reduce the electoral cost from such diversity. As A. Przeworski and J. Sprague (1986) made clear, because there are not enough blue-collar workers, the voting constituency for social democracy has always been heterogeneous and increasingly so. The real problem is how steep a trade-off such heterogeneity creates, when an appeal to non working-class votes dilutes working-class ones. An ideological notion of solidarity across the class line provides a possible solution to this electoral problem, but it generates an intellectual problem of its own. While solidarity *among* the poor can rely on shared experiences and common consciousness, solidarity *with* the poor by definition cannot. Instead, it has to be more instrumental and rely on reciprocity: The rich agree to help the poor so that the latter become a more productive investment in the economy. Without reciprocity, solidarity cannot be clearly differentiated from charity. In short, the need to appeal to a heterogeneous voter base increases the need for an employment-based productivist emphasis in social democratic ideology.

Electoral heterogeneity alone is not enough. Enabling to work as a doctrine resonates with difficulty when almost everyone already has work. In such a scenario, inclusive solidarity often has to be expressed through some other unifying themes. The radicalization of social democratic politics over social protest issues during the 1960s reflects this process. Therefore, a serious increase in unemployment provided another major necessary condition for the ideology of activation to emerge. The empirical problem of unemployment after the 1970s threatened both wage compression and highly de-commodifying income replacement as traditional instruments of social democratic egalitarianism. In response, egalitarianism as an ideological principle also had to adapt, shifting resources from equality in outcome to equality in opportunity. The relaxation of existing equality becomes justifiable as along as it is compensated with increased protection for the worst-off. The growing prioritarian emphasis in egalitarianism implies that preventing poverty in work is now prioritized over pay equity in work, and enabling to work is now prioritized over maintaining income parity through social security.

Productivist solidarity and prioritarian egalitarianism differ not only from the traditional Left. These ideas also make contemporary social democracy distinct from the center Right. Christian democracy has its own interpretation of solidarity, based on God's natural communities. When employment conflicts with these communities, the latter are preferred over the former (as seen in family and work). Reducing inequality, furthermore, is not a Christian democratic priority. Laissez-faire libertarians emphasize work, but they reject both solidarity and egalitarianism, given their belief in the natural right to, and the welfare-maximizing potential of, individual liberty.

As I said at the beginning of this chapter, the theory of third way ideology is about possibilities rather than outcomes. There is nothing inevitable about the ideological transformation toward enabling to work. This is unlikely to happen when either of the two necessary conditions (electoral and economic) identified in this book is not present. When both conditions are present (as is increasingly the case after the Golden Age), they expand the possibility for ideological transformation toward enabling to work. For nine countries, Chapter 3 documented this very process of philosophical rethinking toward activation. However, this is still different from predicting certainty. The 1984 neoliberal hijack of the fourth Labour government in New Zealand showed that while electoral and unemployment conditions increase the possibility for third way ideological adaptation, the ultimate outcome, inevitably, depends on other factors as well.

Ideological principles can be reflected in both discourse and policies. Examination of the former can only reveal a somewhat partial picture. Partly a tool of public rhetoric, discourse understandably emphasizes the appealing over the unappealing components within the very same set of beliefs. While there are plenty of partisan statements highlighting the need to increase protection for the worst-off, few readily comment on the corresponding decline in traditional equality. Similarly, depending on the country, solidarity often appears in different guises in public discourse, such as citizenship, social inclusion, or community. To get a more complete picture of third way ideology, it is important to examine not only discourse but also policy behavior, and the bulk of this book is devoted to third way reforms in social and labor market policies.

THE POSSIBILITIES FOR COSTLY INNOVATION

Policy changes are attempts to change institutions, which are "rules of the game." Institutional innovation is difficult because institutions both persist through time and affect a large number of players. The accumulation of time steadily increases the information and sunk costs of devising new institutions, and so old ones self-reinforce through path dependency. The large number of individuals affected by institutions imply that if the above-mentioned costs of creating new rules are widely diffused (this does not always happen), then the incentive to shirk increases for each individual. Collective action failure can result, and there is no change in institution. This process further contributes to path dependency, but since its mechanism is cross-sectional cost diffusion, I have highlighted it as a *sometimes important contributing factor* to path dependency, rather than simply equating it with path dependency.

These informational and sunk costs will constitute formidable obstacles toward breaking path dependency, if the rules of the game are the only constraints on human behavior. However, they are not. Ideologies also limit the options for individual action. *Rules of the game cannot be mutually conflicting, and they affect all players. On the contrary, there are conflicting ideologies, and each only constrains some individuals but not others. This difference in how ideologies versus institutions constrain human action is the fundamental reason why "rules of the game" can become "public evils."* People agree to disagree but, regardless, have to live with the same rules. For the (often many) unhappy individuals, these rules become public evils rather than goods. The evils are public because, as Hirschman (1970) pointed out, exit is usually not an option for consumers in the political market. The elimination of exit increases the incentives for voice: absorbing the cost of changing the rules. Such incentives are further strengthened when the direct ability to change the rules is contestable, through consistent, stable, and predictable procedures safeguarded by democratic political institutions.

Again, this is a theory of possibilities rather than outcomes. I have proposed that institutional innovation is more likely when the rules are ideologically contested. However, whether innovation *will* occur is a contingent question. On this basis, the stronger the conflicting ideological preferences, the more likely the change. The more indifferent the preferences, the more likely is path dependency. To test this theory of possibilities, one has to compare the two scenarios of strong preference versus indifference, and in this book I have done so, by comparing policy paradigms with policy implementation in third way reforms. Both paradigms and implementation are ways of describing policy changes. Paradigms can be regarded as *a summary representation* (Aoki 2001) of policy tools that reflect the fundamental ideological principles, and implementation is the selection of specific policies fitting the given summary representation. To the extent that specific policies fit the same summary representation, parties are indifferent about their selection. In other words, policy paradigms are more ideologically contested than policy implementation. On this basis, the logic of public evils suggests that the partisan color of government is more likely to be dominant in policy paradigms, but specific policy implementation is more likely to be path dependent. Furthermore, while ideological contestation provides an important condition for institutional change, this is not invariably the case. A major crisis in the economy can provide equally strong incentives for change, across the ideological divide, as shown in the macroeconomic convergence to monetarism across the OECD world. The empirical chapters lent support to these theoretical arguments about institutional innovation, across the major components of the third way paradigm: expanding active protection, restructuring reactionary passive protection, retrenching anticipatory passive protection, and economic contexts.

In active protection, its expansion strongly followed the initiation of social democratic incumbency. Not only did social democratic governments take the initiative in introducing new labor market measures, but these new programs also emphasized education, training, and in-work incentives as opposed to cuts in benefit levels. By contrast, center-right governments were much less enthusiastic about introducing new ALMPs. Furthermore, in cases of secular-Right incumbency, there were attempts to replace expensive labor market programs with harsh workfare measures premised on coercive reduction in benefits. At the same time, within the active paradigm, the policy implementation process offered strong evidence for path dependency. For example, ALMPs were training focused in Denmark, funded through unemployment insurance in Germany, lax in enforcement in France, but relatively coercive in the UK. All these patterns in today's implementation directly reflect the policy institutions established in these countries many decades ago. Based on the same logic, in-work incentives focused on expanding child care in Scandinavia, on reducing payroll taxes on the continent, and on negative income taxes in Anglo-Saxon countries.

In passive protection, the partisan difference was noticeably smaller. Passive income compensation can be reactionary, occurring after the loss of employment. It can also be anticipatory, as early exit pathways clear people from the labor market. The common problem of passive protection is the potential work disincentives. Therefore, for all governments, the main reform agenda is a combination of restructuring and retrenchment. Nevertheless, one can still perceive partisan differences in passive reform paradigms. The social democratic reforms *did not* involve blanket retrenchments in reactionary benefits. Cuts were often unemployment driven, and restored when the employment situation improved. Restrictions were imposed on existing welfare programs, more often by shortening the duration than by cutting benefit levels. In addition, these changes went together with further increases in benefits for the least advantaged. For early exit pathways, social democrats cut more, but not for cost saving, because at the same time they also increased public resources devoted to enabling the early-leaving population to rejoin the ranks of the employed.

For the center Right, the pattern was different. Rather than limiting early exits, Christian Democrats presided over the most expansive era of these very measures. For the secular Right, there were attempts to implement large cuts on all dimensions of passive benefits, reactionary as well as anticipatory. Cost saving appeared to be a much more important objective in this case, as beneficiaries were threatened with reduced social security but received little additional public resources in returning to work. When it comes to policy implementation, there is again clear evidence for path dependency. Again, benefit restructuring followed distinct patterns across three types of welfare regimes. Scandinavian social democrats favored tying benefits to enabling job offers, while Anglo-Saxon governments tightened or relaxed means testing. On the other hand, their continental counterparts largely kept the insider-biased social insurance system intact, while supplementing it with a tax-funded minimum tier. Furthermore, in some cases, the lack of corporatist cooperation further reduced the room for reform and contributed to the reinforcement of traditional policy patterns, especially when it came to early exits.

Moving from core third way strategies to the external context of macroeconomy, both partisan differentiation and path dependency became barely noticeable. The effect of permanent austerity was strong across countries and the partisan divide. Unless austerity became excessive and hurt employment, there was genuine social democratic convergence toward the center-right austerity approach to economic policy. Over issues such as wage moderation, low budget deficit, national debts, or inflation, partisan ideological differentiation was significantly diminished. Compared with the macroeconomic practice during the Golden Age, this was a genuinely path-breaking reform, but it also broke the traditional constraints of ideology, especially for the center Left. Nevertheless, within this overall context of partisan consensus, in a few cases one can still find evidence for contrasting intellectual approaches to economic prudence. The center-right strategy treated prudence as a normative end in itself, whereas for the social democrats, it was prudence with a (social) purpose, that of increasing job growth and providing revenues for social spending in the long run. Where budgetary discipline was excessive and reduced employment, the government became more tolerant of budget deficits and increased public borrowing (as the Jospin and Schröder cases showed). More generally, after some period of prudence, the social democrats channeled the increased revenues back to the public sector, through expansion of active labor market measures and social policies combating exclusion. There were attempts either to raise taxes directly or to do so stealthily. By contrast, the fruits of austerity were more often directly released as tax cuts across the board by center-right governments.

Overall, across different domains of the third way paradigm, there was strong evidence for the influence of partisan ideology. Partisan differentiation was especially clear in the core component of the third way: active protection through ALMPs. The fundamental shift in policy paradigm from income replacement to enabling employment almost always followed the shift in power from right to left. This suggests a fundamental logic of power resources behind the third way reforms. The primary effort in this book has been to use the third way reforms to demonstrate the logic of public evils: the potential that ideological contestation can create for costly institutional changes. In Chapter 2, the public evils thesis was developed from a combination of Hirschman's and Olson's well-known general arguments. This expands the potential external validity of the public evils thesis. Its mechanisms should be general and abstract enough to speak to institutional changes broadly defined, not just for welfare state and employment policies. For this reason, I hope that this book will also be of some interest to scholars whose theoretical pursuits include institutions and ideologies, but whose substantive focus is in other areas. This logic of public evils has already received some theoretical and empirical support from studies of related but nonidentical policy domains, such as training (Thelen 2004), investment (Boix 1998), and retrenchment of income replacement (Korpi and Palme 2003). Clearly, there are many other dimensions of institutional change where this thesis can be put to the test.

THE POSSIBILITIES FOR BRIDGING THE DIVIDE

The externalities of organization describe the process whereby benefits generated from organization can spill over to individuals who cannot organize. To the extent that the weakly and strongly organized have some overlapping preferences, the former will obtain access to a level of preference maximization that they cannot achieve on the basis of their own strength. This theory is important because of the possibilities it creates for reducing the division between insiders and outsiders in third way reforms. For a long time, the core blue-collar workers embraced the notion of solidarity from a (socioeconomic) position of weakness. They tended to be the worst-off relative to all other social categories: white-collar workers, farmers, and employers. However, economic and demographic transitions have generated new social risk groups, suffering from greater vulnerabilities than the core working class: single mothers, the disabled, the unskilled, and so on. The ideological difficulty of appealing to the better-off during the 1920s reenacts itself today, with a switch of actors. The blue-collar enthusiasm for solidarity with the worst-off inevitably dampened, as they gradually vacated the social category of the worst-off and consequently no longer on the receiving end of solidarity. To the extent that the third way ideology is premised on prioritarianism and solidarity, the greater exclusion of outsiders reflected the greater limitation and failure for third way reforms.

The externalities of organizations increase the possibilities for bridging this insider–outsider divide. Single-parent families and part-time workers are undoubtedly weakly organized outsiders with little political muscle, but their new social risk preferences overlap significantly with females, who, in some cases, are much more entrenched inside the labor movement or its party (such as in Scandinavia, the Netherlands, and the UK under New Labour). The organizational integration of women generated goods, such as flexible labor markets, a large public sector, and public child care, which benefited not only women but also these weaker groups. These policy legacies in turn created more stable preferences for other policies targeted specifically at outsiders (Armingeon 2006). The same logic applies to the training resources bundled into ALMPs. While the unskilled and the young are powerless, the unemployed are by comparison more strongly organized inside the labor movement, especially in Scandinavia. This organizational integration delivers such goods as ALMPs focused on deepening human capital. The benefit of these goods reaches not only the unemployed but also spills over to the unskilled and the young. Again, this is a theory of possibilities, not certain outcomes, and one should use the former rather than the latter as the criteria in evaluating the theory. Organizational externalities increase the likelihood of indirectly protecting outsiders, but the weaker the organization, the smaller the externalities, and the more serious the insider–outsider divide. In continental Europe, the growing dualism in social security and the persistent difficulty in activating marginal groups have been closely related to unions' limited capacity to organize beyond core workers.

I agree with the well-known Rueda (2007) thesis that blue-collar workers, as the core organizational basis for social democracy, can be identified as a key culprit when this situation of insider–outsider divide occurs. However, it is crucial to bear in mind that the insider–outsider divide tends to be more severe in cases of weaker social democracy (in terms of organizational strength, where insiders are not powerful enough to integrate borderline constituencies, such as women and the unemployed). The larger implication of this pattern should not be missed: *In effect it turns the association between social democracy and the insider–outsider divide on its head: Social democracy, when fully specified (considering both incumbency and organizational capacity), bridges rather than worsens the insider–outsider divide.* The Scandinavian cases in this book highlighted the social mechanism behind this assertion particularly clearly. On a broader level, since ALMPs play a crucial role in incorporating labor market outsiders, the central association among these policies, the third way, and social democracy identified in this book points toward the same conclusion: To bridge the divide, social democracy has to increase its strength, by expanding its organizational resources.

The classics of power resources theory (Stephens 1979; Korpi 1983) paid careful attention to both the power (incumbency) and resources (organizational) dimension of working-class movements. However, over time, the organizational aspect has somewhat fallen by the wayside in the literature, as attention has turned to the implications of center-left incumbency. The third way reforms in this book have shown that organizational resources directly affect the exercise of power. Institutions affect a large number of actors, and when costs are widely diffused, shirking can be too tempting for costly changes to occur. The capacity to organize more members, and even more crucially, the ability to centrally coordinate their actions through corporatist institutions, is crucial for preventing collective action failure in reforms. Where these coordinational resources were insufficient or in decline, not only did social democratic incumbents achieve limited outcomes in protecting outsiders, but they were also more generally thwarted, in reforms involving widely diffused sunk costs. Where businesses needed to contribute to the reforms (for example, in implementing ALMP train-ing measures), this logic of corporatist coordination extends directly to the employer side of the social partnership. For this book, corporatist institu-tions are important in an abstract sense, in the theoretical role they play for solving the collective action problem and for initiating costly but path-breaking changes. As Chapter 7 showed, corporatist institutions are also important in a substantive sense, as they directly affect wage moderation, which is itself a component in the third way policy paradigm in the real world.

In general, the impact of organizational capacity was not wholly system-atic. Due to various country-specific factors, coordinational resources both rebounded (Norway, Australia, and the Netherlands) and declined (Sweden, New Zealand, and Germany), cutting across different welfare state and production regime types. In addition, the role of organizations was more relevant in reforms involving widely diffused costs (abolishing early exits, relaxing employment protection) than those from which few suffered direct costs (in-work incentives). Nevertheless, to the extent that the "effect of large numbers" constitutes a genuine obstacle to institutional change, it is important to study both the power and resource aspects of social democ-racy, in evaluating its contribution to institutional innovation.

References

Aarts, L. J., and P. de Jong. 1996. "Evaluating the 1987 and 1993 Social Welfare Reforms: From Disappointment to Potential Success," in Aarts, Burkhauser, and de Jong (eds.).

Aarts, L. J., R. Burkhauser, and P. de Jong (eds.). 1996. *Curing the Dutch Disease: An International Perspective on Disability Policy Reform.* Brookfield, VT: Avebury.

Abrahamson, P., and W. van Oorschot. 2002. "The Dutch and Danish Miracles Revisited: Comparing the Role of Activation Policies within the Two Different Welfare Regimes." Paper presented at the COST A15 Conference, Oslo.

Achen, C. 2000. "Why Lagged Dependent Variables Can Suppress the Explanatory Power of Other Independent Variables." Paper delivered at the Annual Meeting of the Political Methodology Section of the American Political Science Association, University of California, Los Angeles.

Ackers, P., and A. Wilkinson (eds.). 2003. *Understanding Work and Employment: Industrial Relations in Transition.* Oxford: Oxford University Press.

Addison, J. T., and C. Schnabel (eds.). 2003. *International Handbook of Trade Unions.* Northhampton, MA: Edward Elgar.

Adler, M. 2004. "Combining Welfare-to-Work Measures with Tax Credits: A New Hybrid Approach to Social Security in the United Kingdom." *International Social Security Review* 57: 87–106.

Aldrich, J. 1995. *Why Parties? The Origin and Transformation of Political Parties in America.* Chicago: University of Chicago Press.

Allen, F., and D. Gale. 2000. *Comparing Financial Systems.* Cambridge, MA: MIT Press.

Andersen, T. M., S. E. H. Jensen, and O. Risager (eds.). 1999. *Macroeconomic Perspectives on the Danish Economy.* London: Macmillan.

Anderson, K. 2002. "Welfare State Adjustment in Sweden and the Netherlands." Paper presented at the Conference of Europeanists, Chicago.

Anderson, K., and T. Meyer. 2003. "Social Democracy, Unions and Pension Politics in Germany and Sweden." *Journal of Public Policy* 23: 23–54.

Aoki, M. 2001. *Towards a Comparative Institutional Analysis*. Cambridge, MA: MIT Press.

Armingeon, K. 2006. "Reconciling Competing Claims of the Welfare State Clientele: The Politics of Old and New Social Risk Coverage in Comparative Perspective," in Armingeon and Bonoli (eds.).

Armingeon, K., and G. Bonoli (eds.). 2006. *The Politics of Post-Industrial Welfare States: Adapting Postwar Social Policies to New Social Risks*. New Work: Routledge.

Arneson, R.J., 1989. "Equality and Equal Opportunity for Welfare." *Philosophical Studies* 56: 77–93.

Auer, P. 2002. "Flexibility and Security: Labour Market Policy in Austria, Denmark, Ireland and the Netherlands," in Schmid and Gazier (eds.).

Auer, P., and S. Cazes (eds.). 2003. *Employment Stability in an Age of Flexibility: Evidence from Industrialized Countries*. Geneva: ILO.

Aust, A., and F. Bönker. 2004. "New Social Risks in a Conservative Welfare State: The Case of Germany," in Taylor-Gooby (ed.).

Bäcker, G. 2003. "Child and Family Poverty in Germany," in Krause, Bäcker, and Hanesch (eds.).

Barbier, J. 2001. "Welfare to Work Policies in Europe: The Current Challenges of Activation Policies." Centre d'etudes de l'emploi working paper, Noisy-le-Grand.

Barbier J., and B. Théret. 2001. "Welfare-to-Work or Work-to-Welfare: The French Case," in Gilbert and van Voorhis (eds.).

2003. "The French System of Social Protection: Path Dependence and Societal Coherence," in Gilbert and van Voorhis (eds.).

Bartolini, S. 2000. *The Political Mobilization of the European Left, 1860–1980*. New York: Cambridge University Press.

Bassett, M. 1998. *The State in New Zealand, 1840–1984: Socialism without Doctrines?* Auckland: Auckland University Press.

Bastow, S., and J. Martin. 2003. *Third Way Discourse: European Ideologies in the Twentieth Century*. Edinburgh: Edinburgh University Press.

Bauld, L., K. Judge, and I. Paterson. 2003. "New Directions for the British Welfare State," in Gilbert and van Voorhis (eds.).

Baumol, W. 1967. "Macroeconomics of Unbalanced Growth: The Anatomy of Urban Crisis." *American Economic Review* 57: 415–426.

Beck, N., and J.N. Katz. 1995. "What to Do (and Not to Do) with Time-Series Cross-Sectional Data." *American Political Science Review* 89: 634–647.

1996. "Nuisance versus Substance: Specifying and Estimating Time-Series Cross-Sectional Models." *Political Analysis* 6: 1–36.

2004. "Time-Series Cross-Section Issues: Dynamics 2004." Paper delivered at the annual meeting of the Society for Political Methodology, Stanford University.

Becker, U. 2000. "Welfare State Development and Employment in the Netherlands in Comparative Perspective." *Journal of European Social Policy* 10: 219–239.

2003. "Competitive Corporatism? National and Transnational Elements in the Dutch Employment Miracle," in Overbeek (ed.).

Beech, M. 2006. *The Political Philosophy of New Labour*. London: Tauris Academic Studies.

Beilharz, P., M. Considine, and R. Watts. 1992. *Arguing about the Welfare State: The Australian Experience*. Sydney: Allen & Unwin.

Béland, D. 2007. "The Social Exclusion Discourse: Ideas and Policy Change." *Policy & Politics* 35: 123–139.

Béland, D., and R. Hansen. 2000. "Reforming the French Welfare State: Solidarity, Social Exclusion and the Three Crises of Citizenship." *West European Politics* 23: 47–64.

Bell, S., and B. Head (eds.). 1994. *State, Economy and Public Policy in Australia*. Melbourne: Oxford University Press.

Benner, M., and T. B. Vad. 2000. "Sweden and Denmark: Defending the Welfare State," in Scharpf and Schmidt (eds.).

Bennett, B., and K. Cole. 1989. "Industrial Relations," in Head and Allan (eds.).

Berlin, I. 1969. *Four Essays on Liberty*. New York: Oxford University Press.

Beukema, L., and B. Valkenburg. 1999. "Atypical Employment in the Netherlands," in Lind and Møller (eds.).

Bispinck, R., and T. Schulten. 2000. "Alliance for Jobs: Is Germany Following the Path of Competitive Corporatism?" in Fajerta and Pochet (eds.).

Bjorklund, A. 2000. "Going Different Ways: Labour Market Policy in Denmark and Sweden," in Esping-Andersen and Regini (eds.).

Bleses, P., and M. Seeleib-Kaiser. 2004. *The Dual Transformation of the German Welfare State*. New York: Palgrave Macmillan.

Boesby, D., K. Dahl, and N. Ploug. 2002. "Welfare Systems and the Management of the Economic Risk of Unemployment: Sweden." Danish National Institute of Social Research working paper, Copenhagen.

Boix, C. 1998. *Political Parties, Growth and Equality: Conservative and Social Democratic Economic Strategies in the World Economy*. New York: Cambridge University Press.

Bonoli, G. 2004. "Social Democratic Party Policies in Europe: Towards a Third Way?" in Bonoli and Powell (eds.).

Bonoli, G., and M. Powell (eds.). 2004. *Social Democratic Party Policies in Contemporary Europe*. London: Routledge.

Bonoli, G., and H. Sarfati. 2002. "Conclusions: The Policy Implications of a Changing Labour Market-Social Protection Relationship," in Sarfati and Bonoli (eds.).

Boreham, P. 1990. "Corporatism," in Jennett and Stewart (*eds.*).

Boston, J. 1987. "Wages Policy and Industrial Relations Reform," in Holland and Boston (eds.).

   1999. "New Zealand's Welfare State in Transition," in Boston, Dalziel, and St. John (eds.).

Boston, J., and M. Holland. 1987. "The Fourth Labour Government: Transforming the Political Agenda," in Holland and Boston (eds.).

Boston, J., P. Dalziel, and S. St. John (eds.). 1999. *Redesigning the Welfare State in New Zealand: Problems, Policies, Prospects*. Oxford: Oxford University Press.

Bouvet, L., and F. Michel. 1999. "Pluralism and the Future of the French Left," in Kelly (ed.).

Boxall, P., 2001. "Evaluating Continuity and Change in the Employment Relations Act 2000." *New Zealand Journal of Industrial Relations* 26: 27–44.

Braun, D., and O. Giraud. 2004. "Models of Citizenship and Social Democratic Policies." in Bonoli and Powell (eds.).

Brunsdon, E., and M. May. 2002. "Evaluating New Labour's Approach to Independent Welfare Provision," in Powell (ed.).

Buchanan, P. G., and K. Nicholls. 2003. *Labour Politics in Small Open Democracies.* New York: Palgrave Macmillan.

Burchardt, T., and J. Hills. 1999. "Public Expenditure and the Public/Private Mix," in Powell (ed.).

Busch, A., and P. Manow. 2001. "The SPD and the Neue Mitte in Germany," in White (ed.).

Bussemaker, J. 1998a. "Gender and the Separation of Spheres in Twentieth Century Dutch Society: Pillarization, Welfare State Formation and Individualization," in Bussemaker and Voet (eds.).

1998b. "Vocabularies of Citizenship and Gender: The Netherlands." *Critical Social Policy* 18: 333–354.

Bussemaker, J., and R. Voet (eds.). 1998. *Gender, Participation and Citizenship in the Netherlands.* Brookfield, VT: Ashgate.

Carter, J. 1993. "Dealing with Policy Failure: A Social Policy Perspective," in Marsh (ed.).

Cass, B., and P. Whiteford. 1989. "Social Policies," in Head and Patience (eds.).

Castles, F. G. 1982. *The Impact of Parties: Politics and Policies in Democratic Capitalist States.* London: Sage.

1988. *Australian Public Policy and Economic Vulnerability: A Comparative and Historical Perspective.* Sydney, NSW: Allen & Unwin.

1994. "The Wage Earners' Welfare State Revisited: Refurbishing the Established Model of Australian Social Protection: 1983–93." *Australian Journal of Social Issues* 29: 120–145.

Castles, F. G., and C. Pierson. 1996. "A New Convergence: Recent Policy Developments in the United Kingdom, Australia and New Zealand." *Policy and Politics* 24: 233–244.

Castles, F. G., R. Garritsen, and J. Vowles (eds.). 1996. *The Great Experiment: Labour Parties and Public Policy Transformation in Australia and New Zealand.* St. Leonards, NSW: Allen & Unwin.

Chandler, A. 1990. *Scale and Scope: The Dynamics of Industrial Capitalism.* Cambridge, MA: Belknap Press of Harvard University Press.

Cheyne C., and M. Belgrave. 1997. *Social Policy in Aotearoa/New Zealand: A Critical Introduction.* Oxford: Oxford University Press.

Clasen, J. 2000. "Motives, Means and Opportunities: Reforming Unemployment Compensation in the 1990s," in Ferrera and Rhodes (eds.).

Clasen, J., and D. Clegg. 2003. "Unemployment Protection and Labour Market Reform in France and Great Britain in the 1990s: Solidarity versus Activation?" *Journal of Social Policy* 32: 361–381.

2006. "New Labour Market Risks and the Revision of Unemployment Protection Systems in Europe," in Armingeon and Bonoli (eds.).

Clasen, J., and W. van Oorschot. 2002a. "Work, Welfare and Citizenship: Diversity and Variation within European (Un)employment Policy," in Goul Andersen et al. (eds.).

Clasen, J., and W. van Oorschot. 2002b. "Changing Principles in European Social Security." *European Journal of Social Security* 4: 89–115.

Clegg, D. 2002. "The Political Status of Social Assistance Benefits in European Welfare States." *European Journal of Social Security* 4: 201–226.

Clift, B. 2001. "The Jospin Way." *Political Quarterly* 72: 170–179.

2003. *French Socialism in a Global Era*. New York: Continuum.

2004. "The Social and Employment Policies of the Jospin Government," in Bonoli and Powell (eds.).

Cohen, G. A. 1989. "On the Currency of Egalitarian Justice." *Ethics* 113: 745–763.

Compston, H. 1997. "Comparisons and Conclusions," in Compston (ed.).

Compston, H. (ed.). 1997. *The New Politics of Unemployment: Radical Policy Initiatives in Western Europe*. London: Routledge.

Compston, H., and P. K. Madsen. 2001. "Conceptual Innovation and Public Policy: Unemployment and Paid Leave Schemes in Denmark." *Journal of European Social Policy* 11: 117–132.

Comte, A. [1852] 1973. *System of Positive Polity*. New York: Burt Franklin.

Cooper, R., and R. May. 2005. "Union Revitalization in Australia and New Zealand, 1995–2005." *New Zealand Journal of Employment Relations* 30: 1–17.

Cox, R. H. 1998. "From Safety Net to Trampoline: Labour Market Activation in the Netherlands and Denmark." WIP Occasional Paper, University of Tübingen.

2004. "The Path-Dependency of an Idea: Why Scandinavian Welfare States Remain Distinct." *Social Policy and Administration* 38: 204–219.

Cressey, P. 1999. "New Labour and Employment, Training and Employee Relations." in Powell (ed.).

Cressey, P. 2002. "Women and Atypical Working in the United Kingdom: The Prospects for Positive Flexibility," in Sarfati and Bonoli (eds.).

Culpepper, P. 2003. *Creating Cooperation: How States Develop Human Capital in Europe*. Ithaca, NY: Cornell University Press.

Curtin, J., and H. Devere. 2006. "Global Rankings and Domestic Realities: Women, Work and Policy in Australia and New Zealand." *Australian Journal of Political Science* 41: 193–207.

Daguerre, A. 2004. "Importing Workfare: Policy Transfer of Social and Labour Market Policies from the USA to Britain under New Labour." *Social Policy & Administration* 38: 41–56.

2006. "Childcare Policies in Diverse European Welfare States: Switzerland, Sweden, France and Britain." in Armingeon and Bonoli (eds.).

Daguerre, A., and P. Taylor-Gooby. 2003. "Adaptation to Labour Market Change in France and the UK." *Social Policy & Administration* 37: 625–638.

Dahl, E., and J. A. Drøpping. 2001. "The Norwegian Work Approach in the 1990s: Rhetoric and Reform," in Gilbert and van Voorhis (eds.).

Dahl, K., et al. 2002. "Welfare Systems and the Management of the Economic Risk of Unemployment: Denmark." The Danish National Institute of Social Research working paper, Copenhagen.

Daly, M. 2000. "A Fine Balance: Women's Labour Market Participation in International Comparison," in Scharpf and Schmidt (eds.).

2001. "Globalization and the Bismarckian Welfare States," in Sykes, Palier, and Prior (eds.).

Dalziel, P. 1999. "Macroeconomic Constraints," in Boston, Dalziel, and St. John (eds.).

Dalziel, P., and R. Lattimore. 2004. *The New Zealand Macroeconomy: Striving for Sustainable Growth with Equity*. Melbourne: Oxford University Press.

Davis, E. 1986. "Unions and Industrial Democracy," in Davis and Lansbury (eds.).

Davis, E., and R. Lansbury (eds.). 1986. *Democracy and Control in the Workplace*. Melbourne: Longman Cheshire.

Davis, K. 1989. "Managing the Economy," in Head and Patience (eds.).

Deacon, A. 2003. "Social Security Policy," in Ellison and Pierson (eds.).

Deakin, S., and H. Reed. 2000. "River Crossing or Cold Fish? Deregulation and Employment in Britain in the 1980s and 1990s," in Esping-Andersen and Regini (eds.).

Dean, H. 2002. "Business versus Families: Whose Side is New Labour On?" *Social Policy and Society* 1: 3–10.

de Bruin, A. 2002. "The New Zealand Reforms: Outcomes and New Directions," in Sarfati and Bonoli (eds.).

Delsen, L. 2002a. "Active Strategies for Older Workers in the Netherlands," in Jepsen, Foden, and Hutsebaut (eds.).

2002b. *Exit Polder Model? Socioeconomic Changes in the Netherlands*. Westport, CT: Praeger.

den Butter, F., and R. Mosch. 2001. "The Dutch Miracle: Institutions, Networks, and Trust." Research Memorandum 2001–18, ALERT, Vrije Universiteit Amsterdam.

de Schampheleire, J., and R. van Berkel. 2001. "Subsidized Labour in Belgium and the Netherlands." *TRANSFER* 1: 41–53.

de Vroom, B. 2004. "Age-Arrangements, Age-Culture and Social Citizenship: A Conceptual Framework for an Institutional and Social Analysis," in Maltby et al. (eds.).

de Vroom, B., and A. Guillemard. 2002. "From Externalization to Integration of Older Workers: Institutional Changes at the End of the Worklife," in Goul Andersen and Jensen (eds.).

Dingeldey, I., and M. Linke-Sonderegger. 2004. "Welfare State Transformation between 'Workfare' and an 'Enabling' State." Paper presented at the ESPAnet Conference, Oxford.

Dios, M. 2002. "Understanding the Relationship between Welfare State and Social Forces in Sweden, Spain, and the USA." Paper presented at the ECPR Joint Sessions, Torino.

DiPrete, T.A. 2002. "Life Course Risks, Mobility Regimes, and Mobility Consequences: A Comparison of Sweden, Germany, and the United States." *American Journal of Sociology* 108: 267–309.

DiPrete, T.A., and P.A. McManus. 2000. "Family Change, Employment Transitions, and the Welfare State Household Income Dynamics in the United States and West Germany." *American Sociological Review* 65: 343–370.

Dixon, J., and R.P. Scheurell (eds.). 2002. *The State of Social Welfare: The Twentieth Century in Cross-National Perspective*. Westport, CT: Praeger.

Dolvik, J., and A. Martin. 2000. "A Spanner in the Works and Oil on Troubled Waters: The Divergent Fates of Social Pacts in Sweden and Norway," in Fajertag and Pochet (eds.).

Dolvik, J., and A. Steen (eds.). 1997. *Making Solidarity Work? The Norwegian Labour Market in Transition.* Oslo: Scandinavian University Press.

Dolvik, J., et al. 1997. "Norwegian Labour Market Institutions and Regulations," in Dolvik and Steen (eds.).

Downing, B.M. 1992. *The Military Revolution and Political Change: Origins of Democracy and Autocracy in Early Modern Europe.* Princeton, NJ: Princeton University Press.

Downs, A. 1957. *An Economic Theory of Democracy.* New York: Harper and Brothers.

Drøpping, J.A., B. Hvinden, and K. Vik. 1999. "Activation Policies in the Nordic Countries," in Kautto et al. (eds.).

Drøpping, J.A., B. Hvinden, and W. van Oorschot. 2000. "Reconstruction and Reorientation: Changing Disability Polices in the Netherlands and Norway." *European Journal of Social Security* 2: 35–68.

Durkheim, E. [1893] 1984. *The Division of Labour in Society.* London: Macmillan.

Dworkin, R. 1981a. "What is Equality? Part 1: Equality of Welfare." *Philosophy and Public Affairs* 10: 185–246.

1981b. "What is Equality? Part 2: Equality of Resources." *Philosophy and Public Affairs* 10: 283–345.

1985. *A Matter of Principle.* Oxford: Oxford University Press.

Easton, B. (ed.). 1989. *The Making of Rogernomics.* Auckland: Auckland University Press.

Easton, B., and R. Gerritsen. 1996. "Economic Reform: Parallels and Divergences," in Castles, Gerritsen, and Vowles (eds.).

Ebbingaus, B. 2000. "Another Way Out of 'Exit from Work'? Reversing the Entrenched Pathways of Early Retirement," in Scharpf and Schmidt (eds.).

2006. "Trade Union Movements in Postindustrial Welfare States: Opening up to New Social Interests?" in Armingeon and Bonoli (eds.).

Ebbinghaus, B., and A. Hassel. 1999. "Striking Deals: Concertation in the Reform of Continental European Welfare States." MPIFG working paper, Cologne.

Ebbinghaus, B., and P. Manow (eds.). 2001. *Comparing Welfare Capitalism: Social Policy and Political Economy in Europe, Japan and the USA.* London: Routledge.

Eichbaum, C., and R. Shaw. 2006. "Labour in Government, Social Democracy and the Third Way: The New Zealand Experience." Paper for the British Political Studies Association annual conference, Reading University.

Eichbaum, C., et al. (eds.). 1999. *The New Politics: The Third Way for New Zealand.* Palmerston North: Dunmore Press.

Eitrheim, P., and S. Kuhnle. 2000. "Nordic Welfare States in the 1990s: Institutional Stability, Signs of Divergence," in Kuhnle (ed.).

Ellison, N., and C. Pierson (eds.). 2003. *Developments in British Social Policy.* New York: Palgrave Macmillan.

Enjolras, B., et al. 2001. "Between Subsidiarity and Social Assistance: The French Republic Route to Activation," in Lødemel and Trickey (eds.).

Esping-Andersen, G. 1980. *Social Class, Social Democracy and State Policy: Party Policy and Party Decomposition in Denmark and Sweden*. Copenhagen: New Science Monographs.

1990. *Three Worlds of Welfare Capitalism*. Princeton, NJ: Princeton University Press.

Esping-Andersen, G. (ed.). 1996. *Welfare States in Transition: National Adaptations in Global Economies*. London: Sage.

Esping-Andersen, G., and M. Regini (eds.). 2000. *Why Deregulate Labour Markets?* Oxford: Oxford University Press.

Esping-Andersen, G., and M. Regini. 2000a. "Introduction," in Esping-Andersen and Regini (eds.).

2000b. "Conclusions," in Esping-Andersen and Regini (eds.).

Etherington, D., 1998. "From Welfare to Work in Denmark: An Alternative to Free Market Policies?" *Policy & Politics* 26: 147–158.

Etzioni, A. 1993. *The Spirit of Community: Rights, Responsibilities and the Communitarian Agenda*. New York: Crown.

2000. *The Third Way to a Good Society*. London: Demos.

Evans, M., and P. Cerny. 2003. "Globalization and Social Policy," in Ellison and Pierson (eds.).

Ewing, K. 2003. "Labour Law and Industrial Relations," in Ackers and Wilkinson (eds.).

Fajertag, G., and P. Pochet (eds.). 2000. *Social Pacts in Europe: New Dynamics*. Brussels: ETUI.

Fargion, V. 2000. "Timing and the Development of Social Care Services in Europe," in Ferrera and Rhodes (eds.).

Farvaque, N. 2002. "The French 'Rights and Responsibility' System for Young People in a European Perspective." Paper presented at the COST A15 Conference, Oslo.

Feldmann, H. 2007. "From Initiating to Breaching to Diluting the Stability and Growth Pact," in Hölscher (ed.).

Ferrera, M., and A. Hemerijck. 2003. "Recalibrating Europe's Welfare Regimes," in Zeitlin and Trubek (eds.).

Fererra M., and M. Rhodes (eds.). 2000. *Recasting European Welfare States*. London: Frank Cass.

Fererra M., et al. (2001). "The Future of Social Europe: Recasting Work, and Welfare in the New Economy," in Giddens (eds.).

Finn, D. 1999. "Job Guarantees for the Unemployed: Lessons from Australian Welfare Reform." *Journal of Social Policy* 28: 53–71.

2003. "Employment Policy," in Ellison and Pierson (eds.).

Foden, D., and M. Jepsen. 2002. "Active Strategies for Older Workers in the European Union: A Comparative Analysis of Recent Experiences," in Jepsen, Foden, and Hutsebaut (eds.).

Foray, D. 2004. *Economics of Knowledge*. Cambridge, MA: MIT Press.

Freeden, M. 1996. *Ideologies and Political Theory: A Conceptual Approach*. Oxford: Oxford University Press.

Freeman, R. 1997. "Are Norway's Solidaristic and Welfare State Policies Viable in the Modern Global Economy?" in Dolvik and Steen (eds.).

Freyssinet, J. 1998. "France: A Recurrent Aim, Repeated Near-Failures and a New Law." *TRANSFER* 4: 641–656.

Furåker, B. 2002. "Is High Unemployment Due to Welfare State Protection? Lessons from the Swedish Experience," in Goul Andersen et al. (eds.).

Gallie, D. (ed.). 2004. *Resisting Marginalization: Unemployment Experience and Social Policy in the European Union*. New York: Oxford University Press.

Gallie, D., and S. Paugam (eds.). 2000. *Welfare Regimes and the Experience of Unemployment in Europe*. Oxford: Oxford University Press.

Galston, W. 1991. *Liberal Purposes: Goods, Virtues, and Diversity in the Liberal State*. New York: Cambridge University Press.

Gangl, M. 2004. "Welfare States and the Scar Effects of Unemployment: A Comparative Analysis of the United States and West Germany." *American Journal of Sociology* 109: 1319–1364.

Gardner, M. 1990. "Wage Policy," in Jennett and Stewart (eds.).

Garrett, G. 1998. *Partisan Politics in the Global Economy*. New York: Cambridge University Press.

Gauthier, A.H., and A. Bortnik. 2001. *Comparative Maternity, Parental, and Childcare Database (Version 2)*, University of Calgary.

George, V., and P. Taylor-Gooby (eds.). 1996. *European Welfare Policy: Squaring the Welfare Circle*. New York: St. Martin's.

Gibson, D. 1990. "Social Policy," in Jennett and Stewart (eds.).

Giddens, A. 2000. *The Third Way and Its Critics*. Cambridge: Polity Press.

Giddens, A. (ed.). 2001. *The Global Third Way Debate*. Cambridge: Polity Press.

Gilbert, N. 2002. *Transformation of the Welfare State: The Silent Surrender of Public Responsibility*. Oxford: Oxford University Press.

Gilbert, N., and A. Parent (eds.). 2004. *Welfare Reform: A Comparative Assessment of the French and U.S. Experiences*. London: Transaction.

Gilbert, N., and R. van Voorhis (eds.). 2001. *Activating the Unemployed: A Comparative Appraisal of Work-Oriented Policies*. London: Transaction.

2003. *Changing Patterns of Social Protection*. London: Transaction.

Glyn, A. (ed.). 2001. *Social Democracy in Neoliberal Times: The Left and Economic Policy since 1980*. New York: Oxford University Press.

Glyn, A., and S. Wood. 2001. "New Labour's Economic Policy," in Glyn (ed.).

Goes, E. 2004. "The Third Way and the Politics of Community," in Hale, Leggett, and Martell (eds.).

Goldberg G.S., and M.G. Rosenthal (eds.). 2002. *Diminishing Welfare: A Cross-National Study of Social Provision*. London: Auburn House.

Goldfinch, S. 2004. "Economic Reform in New Zealand: Radical Liberalization in a Small Economy." *Otemon Journal of Australian Studies* 30: 75–98.

Goldstone, J. 1991. *Revolution and Rebellion in the Early Modern World*. Berkeley and Los Angeles: University of California Press.

Gorter, C. 2000. "The Dutch Miracle?" in Esping-Andersen and Regini (eds.).

Goul Andersen, J. 2000. "Welfare Crisis and Beyond: Danish Welfare Policies in the 1980s and 1990s," in Kuhnle (ed.).

2002a. "Denmark: From the Edge of the Abyss to a Sustainable Welfare State," in Goul Andersen et al. (eds.).

2002b. "Work and Citizenship: Unemployment and Unemployment Policies in Denmark, 1980–2000," in Goul Andersen and Jensen (eds.).

2002c. "A Note on the Termination of the Danish Job Leave Programmes." Paper presented at the COST A13 Conference, Oslo.

Goul Andersen, J., and J. Jensen. 2002a. "Employment and Unemployment in Europe: Overview and New Trends," in Goul Andersen et al. (eds.).

2002b. "Different Routes to Improved Employment in Europe," in Sarfati and Bonoli (eds.).

Goul Andersen, J., and P.H. Jensen (eds.). 2002. *Changing Labour Markets, Welfare Policies and Citizenship*. Bristol: Policy Press.

Goul Andersen, J., et al. (eds.). 2002. *Europe's New State of Welfare: Unemployment, Employment Policies and Citizenship*. Bristol: Policy Press.

Gould, J. 1982. *The Rake's Progress? The New Zealand Economy since 1945*. Auckland: Hodder and Stoughton.

Gould, A. 1996. "Sweden: The Last Bastion of Social Democracy," in George and Taylor-Gooby (eds.).

2001. *Developments in Swedish Social Policy: Resisting Dionysus*. New York: Palgrave Macmillan.

Graycar, A., and A. Jamrozik. 1993. *How Australians Live: Social Policy in Theory and Practice*. Melbourne: The Macmillan Company of Australia.

Green-Pedersen, C. 2001. "Minority Governments and Party Politics." MPIFG working paper, Cologne.

2002. *Politics of Justification: Party Competition and Welfare State Retrenchment in Denmark and the Netherlands from 1982 to 1998*. Amsterdam: Amsterdam University Press.

Green-Pedersen, C., K. van Kersbergen, and A. Hemerijck. 2001. "Neo-liberalism, the 'Third Way' or What? Recent Social Democratic Policies in Denmark and the Netherlands." *Journal of European Public Policy* 8: 307–325.

Grover, C., and J. Stewart. 2000. "Modernizing Social Security? Labour and Its Welfare-to-Work Strategy." *Social Policy & Administration* 34: 235–252.

Guillemard, A. 2001. "Continental Welfare States in Europe Confronted with the End-of-Career Inactivity Trap: A Major Challenge to Social Protection in an Ageing Society." Paper for the conference "Rethinking Social Protection: Citizenship and Social Policy in the Global Age," Harvard University.

Guillemard, A., and D. Argoud. 2004. "France: A Country with a Deep Early Exit Culture," in Maltby et al. (eds.).

Hale, S. 2004. "The Communitarian Philosophy of New Labour," in Hale, Leggett, and Martell (eds.).

Hale, S., W. Leggett, and L. Martell (eds.). 2004. *The Third Way and Beyond: Criticisms, Futures, Alternatives*. Manchester: Manchester University Press.

Hall, P. 2002. "The Comparative Political Economy of the Third Way," in Schmidtke (ed.).

Hall, P., and R.J. Franzese. 1998. "Mixed Signals: Central Bank Independence, Coordinated Wage-Bargaining and European Monetary Union." *International Organization* 52: 506–536.

Hall, P., and D. Soskice (eds.). 2001. *Varieties of Capitalism: The Institutional Foundations of Comparative Advantage*. New York: Oxford University Press.

Halvorsen, K. 2002. "Unemployment and (Un)employment Policies in Norway: The Case of an Affluent but Oil-dependent Economy: The Paradox of Plenty?" in Goul Andersen et al. (eds.).

Handler, J. 2002. "Social Citizenship and Workfare in the United States and Western Europe: From Status to Contract." Paper presented at the BIEN 9th International Conference, Geneva.

Hanesch, W. 1999. "The Debate on Reforms of Social Assistance in Western Europe," in *Linking Welfare and Work*, publication of the European Foundation for the Improvement of Living and Working Conditions, Dublin.

2003a. "Social Assistance between Social Protection and Activation in Germany," in Krause, Bäcker, and Hanesch (eds.).

2003b. "Labour Market Related Poverty in Germany," in Krause, Bäcker, and Hanesch (eds.).

Hansen, H. 2002. "Active Strategies for Older Workers in Denmark," in Jensen, Foden, and Hutsebaut (eds.).

Hantrais, L. 1996. "France: Squaring the Welfare Triangle," in George and Taylor-Gooby (eds.).

Harbridge, R., and P. Bagley. 2002. "Social Protection and Labour Market Outcomes in Australia," in Sarfati and Bonoli (eds.).

Harbridge, R., and P. Walsh. 2002. "Labour Market Reform in New Zealand," in Sarfati and Bonoli (eds.).

Harbridge, P., P. Walsh, and D. Wilkinson. 2002. "Re-regulation and Union Decline in New Zealand: Likely Effects." *New Zealand Journal of Industrial Relations* 27: 65–77.

Harris, P. 1999. "Rogernomics, the Washington Consensus and New Zealand Economic Policy," in Eichbaum et al. (eds.).

Hartog, J. 2000. "So What's So Special about the Dutch Model?" ILO working paper, Geneva.

Hassel, A., and B. Ebbinghaus. 2000. "From Means to Ends: Linking Wage Moderation and Social Policy Reform," in Fajertag and Pochet (eds.).

Hauser, R., et al. 2000. "Unemployment and Poverty: Change Over Time," in Gallie and Paugam (eds.).

Hawke, G. 1992. "Economic Trends and Economic Policy, 1938–1992," in Rice (ed.).

Hazledine, T., and J. Quiggin, 2006. "No More Free Beer Tomorrow? Economic Policy and Outcomes in Australia and New Zealand since 1984." *Australian Journal of Political Science* 41: 145–159.

Head, B., and A. Patience (eds.). 1989. *From Fraser to Hawke*. Melbourne: Longman Cheshire.

Hedström, P., and R. Swedberg. 1998. "Social Mechanisms." *Acta Sociologica* 39: 281–308.

Hein, E., and A. Truger. 2007. "Macroeconomic Policies, Wage Developments and Germany's Stagnation," in Hölscher (ed.).

Hemerijck, A. 2003. "The Resurgence of Dutch Corporatist Policy Coordination in an Age of Globalization," in van Waarden and Lehmbruch (eds.).

Hemerijck, A., and P. Manow. 2001. "The Experience of Negotiated Reforms in the Dutch and German Welfare States," in Ebbinghaus and Manow (eds.).

Hemerijck, A., and M. Schludi. 2000. "Sequences of Policy Failures and Effective Policy Responses," in Scharpf and Schmidt (eds.).

Hemerijck, A., and J. Visser. 2000. "Change and Immobility: Three Decades of Policy Adjustment in the Netherlands and Belgium," in Ferrera and Rhodes (eds.).

  2001. "Dutch Lessons in Social Pragmatism," in White (ed.).

Hemerijck, A., P. Manow, and K. van Kersbergen. 2000. "Welfare without Work? Divergent Experiences of Reform in Germany and the Netherlands," in Kuhnle (ed.).

Hemerijck, A., B. Unger, and J. Visser. 2000. "How Small Countries Negotiate Change: Twenty-Five Years of Policy Adjustment in Austria, the Netherlands, and Belgium," Scharpf and Schmidt (eds.).

Hemerijck, A., M. van de Meer, and J. Visser. 2000. "Innovation Through Coordination: Two Decades of Social Pacts in the Netherlands," in Fajertag and Pochet (eds.).

Hering, M. 2004. "Turning Ideas into Policies: Implementing Modern Social Democratic Thinking in Germany's Pension Policy," in Bonoli and Powell (eds.).

Hespanha, P., and I. Møller. 2001. "Activation Policies and Social Inclusion in Denmark and Portugal." *TRANSFER* 1: 54–73.

Hewitt, M. 1999. "New Labour and Social Security," in Powell (ed.).

  2002. "New Labour and The Redefinition of Social Security," in Powell (ed.).

Hicks. A. 1994. "Introduction to Pooling," in Janowski and Hicks (eds.).

  1999. *Social Democracy and Welfare Capitalism.* Ithaca, NY: Cornell University Press.

Hicks, A., and D. Swank, 1984. "Redistribution in Rich Capitalist Democracies." *Policy Studies Journal* 13: 265–286.

Higgins, J. 1999. "From Welfare to Workfare," in Boston, Dalziel, and St. John (eds.).

Hirschman, A. 1970. *Exit, Voice and Loyalty: Responses to Decline in Firms, Organizations and States.* Cambridge, MA: Harvard University Press.

Holland, M., and J. Boston (eds.). 1987. *The Fourth Labour Government: Radical Politics in New Zealand.* Oxford: Oxford University Press.

  1990. *The Fourth Labour Government: Politics and Policy in New Zealand.* Auckland: Auckland University Press.

Hölscher, J. (ed.). 2007. *Germany's Economic Performance: From Unification to Euroization.* New York: Palgrave Macmillan.

Holtug, N., and K. Lippert-Rasmussen (eds.). 2007a. *Egalitarianism: New Essays on the Nature and Value of Equality.* Oxford: Clarendon Press.

  2007b. "An Introduction to Contemporary Egalitarianism," in Holtug and Lippert-Rasmussen (eds.).

Hoop, R. 2004. "Social Policy in Belgium and the Netherlands: Third Way or Not?" in Bonoli and Powell (eds.).

Hort, S. 2001. "Sweden: Still a Civilized Version of Workfare?" in Gilbert and van Voorhis (eds.).

2002. "Sweden," in Dixon and Scheurell (eds.).

2003. "Back on Track to the Future? The Making and Remaking of the Swedish Welfare State in the 1990s," in Gilbert and van Voorhis (eds.).

2005. "After Equality? Normative Innovations from Lindbeck to Svegfors: Towards a Dynamic Conservatism?" in Kildal and Kuhnle (eds.).

Huber, E., and J.D. Stephens. 2000. "Partisan Governance, Women's Employment and the Social Democratic Service State." *American Sociological Review* 45: 323–342.

2001. *Development and Crisis of the Welfare State: Parties and Policies in Global Markets*. Chicago: University of Chicago Press.

Huber, E., and J.D. Stephens. 2006. "Combating Old and New Social Risks," in Armingeon and Bonoli (eds.).

Huber, E., *et al*. 2004a. *Comparative Welfare States Data Set*, Northwestern University, University of North Carolina, Duke University, and Indiana University.

2004b. "The Welfare State and Gender Equality." Luxemburg Income Study Working Paper No. 279, Luxemburg.

2006. "Politics and Inequality in Latin America and the Caribbean." *American Sociological Review* 71: 943–963.

Hübner, K. 2004. "Policy Failure: The Economic Record of the Red-Green Coalition in Germany, 1998–2002," in Reutter (ed.).

Huo, J., M. Nelson, and J.D. Stephens. 2008. "Decommodification and Activation in Social Democracy: Resolving the Paradox." *Journal of European Social Policy* 18: 5–20.

Hvid, H. 1999. "Development of Work and Social (Ex)Inclusion," in Lind and Møller (eds.).

Hvinden, B. 2003. "Activation in the Western Europe of the 1990s: Did It Make a Difference?" in Krause, Bäcker, and Hanesch (eds.).

Innis, H. 1940. *The Cod Fisheries: The History of an International Economy*. New Haven: Yale University Press.

Iversen, T. 2005. *Capitalism, Democracy and Welfare*. New York: Cambridge University Press.

Iversen, T., and A. Wren. 1998. "Equality, Employment, and Budgetary Restraint: The Trilemma of the Service Economy." *World Politics* 50: 507–546.

Janowski, T., and A. Hicks (eds.). 1994. *The Comparative Political Economy of the Welfare State*. New York: Cambridge University Press.

Jennett, C., and R. Stewart (eds.). 1990. *Hawke and Australian Public Policy: Consensus and Restructuring*. Melbourne: The Macmillan Company of Australia.

Jensen, P. 1999. "Activation of the Unemployed in Denmark since the Early 1990s." CCWS (Centre for Comparative Welfare Studies) working paper, University of Aarhus.

Jensen, P. 2004. "Ageing and Work: From Early Exit to Late Exit in Denmark," in Maltby et al. (eds.).

Jepsen, M., D. Foden, and M. Hutsebaut (eds.). 2002. *Active Strategies for Older Workers in the European Union*. Brussels: ETUI.

Jespersen, S.P., and S.L. Rasmussen. 1998. *Fra Velfærdsstat til Velfærdssamfund-en Analyse af 90'ernes Velfærdsdebat, Specialeopgave*. Institut for Statskundskab, Aarhus University.

Jessop, B. 2003. "From Thatcherism to New Labour: Neo-Liberalism, Workfarism and Labour-Market Regulation," in Overbeek (ed.).

Jochem, S. 2000. "Nordic Labour Market Policies in Transition." *West European Politics* 23: 115–138.

2003. "Nordic Corporatism and Welfare State Reforms: Denmark and Sweden Compared," in van Waarden and Lehmbruch (eds.).

Johnson, N. 2001. "New Labour: A Distinctive Vision of Welfare Policy?" in White (ed.).

Jolivet, A. 2002. "Active Strategies for Older Workers in France," in Jespen, Foden, and Hutsebaut (eds.).

Jones, M. 2002. "Australia," in Dixon and Scheurell (eds.).

Jones, T. 1996. *Remaking the Labour Party: From Gaitskell to Blair.* London: Routledge.

Jordan, B. 1998. *The New Politics of Welfare: Social Justice in a Global Context.* London: Sage.

Jordan, B., and C. Jordan. 2000. *Social Work and the Third Way: Tough Love as Social Policy.* London: Sage.

Junankar, R., and C. Kapuscinski. 1997. "Was Working Nation Working?" Technical Report Discussion Paper no. 54, Graduate Program in Public Policy, Australian National University.

Karlsen, T. 1997. "Norway," in Compston (ed.).

Kautto, M. 2001. "Moving Closer? Diversity and Convergence in Financing of Welfare States," in Kautto et al. (eds.).

Kautto, M., et al. (eds.). 1999. *Nordic Social Policy: Changing Welfare States.* London: Routledge.

1999. "Introduction: The Nordic Welfare States in the 1990s," in Kautto et al. (eds.).

Kautto, M., et al. (eds.). 2001. *Nordic Welfare States in the European Context.* London: Routledge.

Keizer, P. 2001. "From Welfare to Workfare: Dutch Policies in the Nineties," in Gilbert and van Voorhis (eds.).

2003. "Social Security and Welfare in the Netherlands Before and After the Year 2000," in Gilbert and van Voorhis (eds.).

Kelly, G. (ed.) 1999. *The New European Left.* London: Fabian Society.

Kelsey, J. 1995. *Economic Fundamentalism.* London: Pluto.

Keman, H. 2003. "Explaining Miracles: Third Ways and Work and Welfare." *West European Politics* 26: 115–135.

Kennedy, R. (ed.). 1989. *Australian Welfare: Historical Sociology.* Melbourne: The Macmillan Company of Australia.

Kenworthy, L. 2001. "Wage-Setting Measures: A Survey and Assessment." *World Politics* 54: 57–98.

Kildal, N. 1999. "Justification of Workfare: The Norwegian Case." *Critical Social Policy* 19: 353–370.

2001. "Workfare Tendencies in Scandinavian Welfare Policies." ILO working paper, Geneva.

Kildal, N., and S. Kuhnle (eds.). 2005. *Normative Foundations of the Welfare State: The Nordic Experience.* London: Routledge.

Kitschelt, H. 1994. *The Transformation of European Social Democracy.* New York: Cambridge University Press.

2001. "Partisan Competition and Welfare State Retrenchment: When Do Politicians Choose Unpopular Policies?" in Pierson (ed.).

Knutsen, O. 2006. *Class Voting in Western Europe: A Comparative Longitudinal Study.* Lanham, MD: Lexington Books.

Koopman-Boyden, P. 1990. "Social Policy: Has There Been One?" in Holland and Boston (eds.).

Korpi, W. 1983. *The Democratic Class Struggle.* London: Routledge and Kegan Paul.

Korpi, W., and J. Palme. 1998. "The Paradox of Redistribution and Strategies of Equality: Welfare State Institutions, Inequality and Poverty in Western Countries." *American Sociological Review* 63: 661–687.

2003. "New Politics and Class Politics in the Context of Permanent Austerity and Globalization: Welfare State Regress in 18 Countries, 1975–95." *American Political Science Review* 97: 425–446.

Kosonen, P. 2001. "Globalization and the Nordic Welfare States," in Sykes, Palier, and Prior (eds.).

Krause, P., G. Bäcker, and W. Hanesch (eds.). 2003. *Combating Poverty in Europe: The German Welfare Regime in Practice.* Burlington, VT: Ashgate.

Kuhnle, S. 2000a. "The Scandinavian Welfare State in the 1990s: Challenged but Viable," in Ferrera and Rhodes (eds.).

Kuhnle, S. (ed.) 2000b. *Survival of the European Welfare State.* London: Routledge.

Kvist, J. 2000. "Activating Welfare States: Scandinavian Experiences in the 1990s." The Danish National Institute of Social Research working paper, Copenhagen.

2002. "Nordic Activation in the 1990s." The Danish National Institute of Social Research working paper, Copenhagen.

Lamping, W., and N. Vergunst. 2004. "Organized Interests, Institutional Veto Points and Welfare State Reform in Germany and the Netherlands." Paper presented at the ECPR Joint Sessions, Uppsala.

Lange, K., L. H. Pedersen, and P. B. Sørensen. 1999. "The Danish Tax Reform Act of 1993: Effects on the Macroeconomy and on Intergenerational Welfare," in Andersen, Jensen, and Risager (eds.).

Lansbury, R., and G. Michelson. 2003. "Industrial Relations in Australia," in Ackers and Wilkinson (eds.).

Larsen, C. 2004. "The Importance of Institutional Regimes for Active Labour Market Policies: The Case of Denmark." Danish National Centre for Labour Market Research (CARMA) working paper, Aarhus.

Larsen, F., and T. Bredgaard. 2004. "Flexicurity and Older Workers on the Danish Labour Market." Background paper for the Flexicurity Research Program at Aalborg University.

Lawson, R. 1996. "Germany: Maintaining the Middle Way," in George and Taylor-Gooby (eds.).

Lehmbruch, G. 2003. "Welfare State Adjustment between Consensual and Adversarial Politics: The Institutional Context of Reform in Germany," in van Waarden and Lehmbruch (eds.).

Leibfried, S., and H. Obinger. 2003. "The State of the Welfare State: German Social Policy between Macroeconomic Retrenchment and Microeconomic Recalibration." *West European Politics* 26: 199–243.

Leitner, S., and S. Lessenich. 2003. "Assessing Welfare State Change: The German Social Insurance State between Reciprocity and Solidarity." *Journal of Public Policy* 23: 325–347.

Levitas, R. 1998. *The Inclusive Society? Social Exclusion and New Labour.* London: Macmillan.

Levy, J. 1999a. *Tocqueville's Revenge: State, Society and Economy in Contemporary France.* Cambridge, MA: Harvard University Press.

1999b. "Vice into Virtue? Progressive Politics and Welfare Reform in Continental Europe." *Politics & Society* 27: 239–273.

2000. "France: Directing Adjustment?" in Scharpf and Schmidt (eds.).

2002. "The State after Statism: French Economic and Social Policy in the Age of Globalization." Paper presented at the Conference of Europeanists, Chicago.

2003. "Responsibilities and Rights: Changing the Balance," in Ellison and Pierson (eds.).

2005. "Redeploying the State: Liberalization and Social Policy in France," in Streeck and Thelen (eds.).

Lind, J. 1999. "Labour Market Flexibility and Regulation," in Lind and Møller (eds.).

2000. "Recent Issue on the Social Pact in Denmark," in Fajertag and Pochet (eds.).

Lind, J., and I.H. Møller (eds.). 1999. *Inclusion and Exclusion: Unemployment and Non-standard Employment in Europe.* Brookfield, VT: Ashgate.

Lindgren, A. 1999. "Swedish Social Democracy in Transition," in Kelly (ed.).

Lødemel, I. 2001a. "National Objectives and Local Implementation of Workfare in Norway," in Lødemel and Trickey (eds.).

2001b. "Discussion: Workfare in the Welfare State," in Lødemel and Trickey (eds.).

2004. "The Development of Workfare within Social Activation Policies," in Gallie (ed.).

Lødemel, I., and H. Trickey (eds.). 2001. *An offer You Can't Refuse: Workfare in International Perspective.* Bristol: Policy Press.

Lodovici, M.S. 2000. "The Dynamics of Labour Market Reform in European Countries," in Esping-Andersen and Regini (eds.).

Loftager, J. 1998. "Solidarity and Universality in the Danish Welfare State." Paper presented at the 7th BIEN International Congress, Amsterdam.

Loftager, J., and P. Madsen. 1997. "Denmark," in Compston (ed.).

Lordon, F. 2001. "The Logic and Limits of *Désinflation Compétitive*," in Glyn (ed.).

Lund, B. 2002. *Understanding State Welfare: Social Justice or Social Exclusion?* London: Sage.

Lunt, N., P. Spoonley and P. Mataira. 2002. "Past and Present: Reflections on Citizenship within New Zealand," *Social Policy & Administration* 36: 346–362.

MacIntyre, A. 1981. *After Virtue: A Study in Moral Theory*. Notre Dame, IN: Notre Dame University Press.

Mackay, R. 2001. "Work-Oriented Reforms: New Directions in New Zealand," in Gilbert and van Voorhis (eds.).

2003. "Remaking the Welfare State in New Zealand," in Gilbert and van Voorhis (eds.).

Madsen, P. 1998. "Working Time Policy and Paid Leave Arrangements: The Danish Experience in the 1990s." *TRANSFER* 4: 692–713.

1999. "Flexibility, Security and Labour Market Success." ILO working paper.

2002. "The Danish Model of Flexicurity: A Paradise with Some Snakes," in Sarfati and Bonoli (eds.).

2003. "Flexicurity through Labour Market Policies and Institutions in Denmark," in Auer and Cazes (eds.).

2004. "The Danish Model of 'Flexicurity': Experiences and Lessons." *TRANSFER* 2: 187–207.

Mahoney, J. 1999. "Nominal, Ordinal, and Narrative Appraisal in Macrocausal Analysis." *American Journal of Sociology* 104: 1154–1196.

2000. "Path Dependency in Historical Sociology." *Theory and Society* 29: 507–548.

Mahoney, J., and G. Goertz. 2006. "A Tale of Two Cultures: Contrasting Quantitative and Qualitative Research." *Political Analysis* 14: 227–249.

Malo, M., L. Toharia, and J. Gautié. 2000. "France: The Deregulation That Never Existed," in Esping-Andersen and Regini (eds.).

Maltby T., et al. (eds.). 2004. *Ageing and the Transition to Retirement: A Comparative Analysis of European Welfare States*. Aldershot, England: Ashgate.

Mandin, L. 2004. "Active Ageing in Europe." Paper presented at the 2nd ESPAnet Conference, Oxford.

Manow, P., and E. Seils. 2000a. "The Employment Crisis of the German Welfare State," in Ferrera and Rhodes (eds.).

Manow, P., and E. Seils. 2000b. "Adjusting Badly: The German Welfare State, Structural Change, and the Open Economy," in Scharpf and Schmidt (eds.).

Mantzavinos, C. 2001. *Individuals, Institutions and Markets*. New York: Cambridge University Press.

Marsh, I. (ed.). 1993. *Governing in the 1990s: An Agenda for the Decade*. Melbourne: Longman Cheshire.

Marston, C., J. E. Larsen, and C. McDonald. 2004. "The Active Subjects of Welfare Reform: A Comparative Study of Employment Services in Australia and Denmark." Paper presented at the RC19 Annual Conference, Paris.

Martin, C. J. 2004. "Reinventing Welfare Regimes: Employers and the Implementation of Active Social Policy." *World Politics* 57: 39–69.

Martin, C. J., and D. Swank. 2004. "Does the Organization of Capital Matter? Employers and Active Labour Market Policy at the National and Firm Levels." *American Political Science Review* 98: 593–612.

McClelland, A., and S. St. John. 2006. "Social Policy Responses to Globalization in Australia and New Zealand, 1980–2005." *Australian Journal of Political Science* 41: 177–194.

McClure, M. 1998. *A Civilized Community: A History of Social Security in New Zealand 1898–1998*. Auckland: Auckland University Press.

McCullen, P., and C. Harris. 2004. "Generative Equality, Work and the Third Way: A Managerial Perspective," in Sale, Leggett, and Martell (eds.).

Menezes-Filho, N., and J. van Reneen. 2003. "Unions and Innovation: A Survey of the Theory and Evidence," in Addison and Schnabel (eds.).

Merkel, W. 2001. "The Third Ways of Social Democracy," in Giddens (ed.).

Meyer, T. 2005. "Laggard Germany: The Missing Discourse on Welfare Recalibration," in Schmidt et al. (eds.).

Millar, J. 2000. "Lone Parents and the New Deal." *Policy Studies* 21: 333–345.

2002a. "Diminishing Welfare: The Case of the United Kingdom," in Goldberg and Rosenthal (eds.).

2002b. "Adjusting Welfare Policies to Stimulate Job Entry: The Example of the United Kingdom," in Sarfati and Bonoli (eds.).

2003. "Squaring the Circle? Means Testing and Individualization in the UK and Australia." *Social Policy and Society* 3: 67–74.

Møller, I. H. 1999. "Trends in the Danish Social Mode of Economic Regulation," in Lind and Møller (eds.).

Morel, S. 2004. "Workfare and Insertion: How the U.S. and French Models of Social Assistance Have Been Transformed," in Gilbert and Parent (eds.).

Morris, J. 2003. "Community Care or Independent Living?" in Ellison and Pierson (eds.).

Moschonas, G. 2002. *In the Name of Social Democracy: The Great Transformation, from 1945 to Present*. London: Verso.

Moses, J. W. 2000. *Open States in the Global Economy: The Political Economy of Small-State Macroeconomic Management*. New York: St. Martin's.

Mullard, M. 2000. *New Labour, New Thinking: The Politics, Economics and Social Policy of the Blair Government*. Huntington, NY: Nova Science.

Myles, J., and J. Quadagno, 2002. "Political Theories of the Welfare State." *Social Service Review* 76: 34–59.

Negrelli, S. 2000. "Social Pacts in Italy and Europe: Similar Strategies and Structures; Different Models and National Stories," in Fajertag and Pochet (eds.).

Nolan, P. 2004. "When Work Does Not Pay: Family Structures and Poverty Traps in New Zealand's Social Security System." Paper presented at the 45th Conference of the New Zealand Association of Economists, Wellington.

Nordlund, A. 2005. "Nordic Social Politics in the Late Twentieth Century: An Analysis of the Political Reform Agenda," in Kildal and Kuhnle (eds.).

North, D. C. 1990. *Institutions, Institutional Change and Economic Performance*. New York: Cambridge University Press.

Nozick, R. 1974. *Anarchy, State, and Utopia*. New York: Basic Books.

O'Brien, M. 1992. "Recent Developments in Social Security in New Zealand: Old Times Revisited," in *Social Policy in Australia: Options for the 1990s (proceedings of the National Social Policy Conference)*. Kensington, New South Wales: University of New South Wales Press.

1993. "New Wine in Old Bottles: Social Security in New Zealand 1984–1990." Social Policy Research Centre (SPRC) research paper, University of New South Wales.

O'Brien, M., and C. Wilkes. 1993. *Tragedy of the Market: A Social Experiment in New Zealand*. Palmerston North: Dummore.

OECD (Organization for Economic Cooperation and Development). 2004. *Employment Outlook*. Paris: OECD.

OECD (Organization for Economic Cooperation and Development). 2005a. *Taxing Wages*. Paris: OECD.

OECD (Organization for Economic Cooperation and Development). 2005b. *OECD Statistical Compendium*. Paris: OECD.

OECD (Organization for Economic Cooperation and Development). 2005c. OECD *General Economic Problems Database*. Paris: OECD

OECD (Organization for Economic Cooperation and Development). 2006a. *Social Expenditure Database (SOCX)*. Paris: OECD.

OECD (Organization for Economic Cooperation and Development). 2006b. *Economic Outlook Database*. Paris: OECD.

OECD (Organization for Economic Cooperation and Development). 2007a. Labour *Market Database (OECD Member Countries)*. Paris: OECD.

OECD (Organization for Economic Cooperation and Development). 2007b. *OECD Main Economic Indicators Database*. Paris: OECD.

Oliver, H. 1989. "The Labour Caucus and Economic Policy Formation, 1981–1984," in Easton (ed.).

Olofsson, G. 2001. "Age, Work, and Retirement in Sweden." Paper presented at the conference "Millennium Project," Tokyo.

Olson, M. 1965. *The Logic of Collective Action: Public Goods and the Theory of Groups*. Cambridge, MA: Harvard University Press.

   1982. *The Rise and Decline of Nations*. New Haven: Yale University Press.

Oppenheim, C. 2001. "Enabling Participation? New Labour's Welfare-to-Work Policies," in White (ed.).

Orloff, A.S. 1993. *The Politics of Pensions: A Comparative Analysis of Britain, Canada, and the United States, 1880–1940*. Madison: University of Wisconsin Press.

Outshoorn, J. 1998. "Furthering the Cause: Democrat Strategies in National Government," in Bussemaker and Voet (eds.).

Overbeek, H. (ed.) 2003. *The Political Economy of European Employment: European Integration and the Transnationalization of the (Un)employment Question*. London: Routledge.

Page, R. 2002. "The United Kingdom," in Dixon and Scheurell (eds.).

Palier, B. 2000. "Defrosting the French Welfare State," in Ferrera and Rhodes (eds.).

   2002. "How Can We Analyze the Process of Welfare State Reforms in Continental Europe?" Paper presented at the COST A15 Conference, Oslo.

Palier, B., and C. Mandin. 2004. "France: A New World of Welfare for New Social Risks?" in Taylor-Gooby (ed.).

Palme, J., et al. 2002. "Welfare Trends in Sweden: Balancing the Books for the 1990s." *Journal of European Social Policy* 12: 329–346.

Parfit, D. 1984. *Reasons and Persons*. Oxford: Clarendon Press.

   1991. *Equality or Priority? The Lindley Lecture*. Lawrence: University of Kansas Press.

Parry, R. 2000. "Exploring the Sustainable Limits of Public Expenditure in the British Welfare State," in Kuhnle (ed.).

Peck, J. 2001. *Workfare States.* New York: Guilford Press.

Peetz, D. 1998. *Unions in a Contrary World: The Future of the Australian Trade Union Movement.* Cambridge: Cambridge University Press.

Pennings, F. 2002. "A Critical View of Incentives to Help Benefit Recipients into Work in the Netherlands," in Sarfati and Bonoli (eds.).

Perry, B. 2004. "Working for Families: The Impact on Child Poverty." *Social Policy Journal of New Zealand* 22: 19–54.

Peters, M., and J. Marshall. 1996. *Individualism and Community: Education and Social Policy in the Postmodern Condition.* London: The Falmer Press.

Pierson, C., 2001. "Learning from Labor? Welfare Policy Transfer between Australia and Britain." Graduate Program in Public Policy discussion paper, Australian National University.

Pierson, C. and F.G. Castles. 2001. "Australian Antecedents of the Third Way." Paper presented at the ECPR Joint Sessions, Grenoble.

Pierson, C., and N. Ellison. 2003. "Conclusion: New Labour, New Welfare State?" in Ellison and Pierson (eds.).

Pierson, P. (ed.). 2001a. *The New Politics of the Welfare State.* New York: Oxford University Press.

2001b. "Coping with Permanent Austerity: Welfare State Restructuring in Affluent Democracies," in Pierson (ed.).

2004. *Politics in Time: History, Institutions and Social Analysis.* Princeton, NJ: Princeton University Press.

Plantenga, J. 1998. "Double Lives: Labour Market Participation, Citizenship and Gender," in Bussemaker and Voet (eds.).

Plantenga, J., and R. Dur. 1998. "Working Time Reduction in the Netherlands: Past Developments and Future Prospects." *TRANSFER* 4: 678–691.

Ploug, N. 1999. "Cuts in and Reform of the Nordic Cash Benefit System," in Kautto et al. (eds.).

2000. "The Scandinavian Experience: Trajectories of Adjustment." Danish National Institute of Social Research working paper, Copenhagen.

Plümper, T., V. Troeger and P. Manow. 2005. "Panel Data Analysis in Comparative Politics: Linking Method to Theory." *European Journal of Political Research* 44: 327–354.

Pontusson, J. 2005. *Inequality and Prosperity: Social Europe vs. Liberal America.* Ithaca, NY: Cornell University Press.

Porter, D., and D. Craig. 2004. "Third Way for the Third World: Poverty Reduction, Social Inclusion and the Rise of 'Inclusive' Liberalism." Paper presented at the RC19 Annual Conference, Paris.

Powell, M. (ed.) 1999. *New Labour, New Welfare State?* Bristol: Policy Press.

Powell, M. 2002. *Evaluating New Labour's Welfare Reforms.* Bristol: Policy Press.

Przeworski, A., and J. Sprague. 1986. *Paper Stones: A History of Electoral Socialism.* Chicago: University of Chicago Press.

Przeworski, A., and H. Tenue. 1970. *The Logic of Comparative Social Inquiry.* New York: John Wiley.

Ragin, C. 1987. *The Comparative Method: Moving beyond Qualitative and Quantitative Strategies*. Berkeley: University of California Press.

Rawls, J. 1971. *A Theory of Justice*. Cambridge, MA: Belknap Press of Harvard University Press.

Regan, S. 2003. "Paying for Welfare in the 21st Century," in Ellison and Pierson (eds.).

Regini, M. 2000. "The Dilemmas of Labour Market Regulation," in Esping-Andersen and Regini (eds.).

Reutter, W. (ed.). 2004. *Germany on the Road to "Normalcy": Policies and Politics of the Red-Green Federal Government (1998–2002)*. London: Palgrave Macmillan.

Rhodes, M. 1998. "Globalization, Labour Markets and Welfare States: A Future of Competitive Corporatism?" in Rhodes and Mény (eds.).

    2000a. "Restructuring the British Welfare State: Between Domestic Constraints and Global Imperatives," in Scharpf and Schmidt (eds.).

    2000b. "Desperately Seeking a Solution: Social Democracy, Thatcherism and the 'Third Way' in British Welfare," in Ferrera and Rhodes (eds.).

Rhodes, M., and Y. Mény (eds.). 1998. *The Future of European Welfare: A New Social Contract?* New York: St. Martin's Press.

Rice, G. W. 1992. "A Revolution in Social Policy, 1981–1991," in Rice (ed.).

Rice, G.W. (ed.). 1992. *The Oxford History of New Zealand*. Oxford: Oxford University Press.

Roder, K. 2003. *Social Democracy and Labour Market Policy: Developments in Britain and Germany*. London: Routledge.

Rodseth, A. 1997. "Why Has Unemployment Been so Low in Norway?" in Dolvik and Steen (eds.).

Roemer, J.E. 1996. *Theories of Distributive Justice*. Cambridge, MA: Harvard University Press.

Rogers, W.H. 1993. "sg17: Regression Standard Errors in Clustered Samples." *Stata Technical Bulletin* 13: 19–23.

Rosdahl, A., and H. Weise. 2001. "When All Must be Active: Workfare in Denmark," in Lødemel and Trickey (eds.).

Rudd, C. 1990. "Politics and Markets: The Role of the State in the New Zealand Economy," in Holland and Boston (eds.).

Rueda, D. 2005. "Insider–Outsider Politics in Industrialized Democracies: The Challenge to Social Democratic Parties." *American Political Science Review* 99: 61–74.

Rueda, D. 2007. *Social Democracy Inside Out: Partisanship and Labour Market Policy in Industrialized Democracies*. New York: Oxford University Press.

Rueschemeyer, D., E.H. Stephens and J.D. Stephens. 1992. *Capitalist Development and Democracy*. Chicago: University of Chicago Press.

Ryner, J.M. 2002. *Capitalist Restructuring, Globalization and the Third Way: Lessons from the Swedish Model*. London: Routledge.

Salverda, W. 2000. "Is There More to the Dutch Miracle Than a Lot of Part-Time Jobs?" in Schupp and Solga (eds.).

Sandel, M. 1982. *Liberalism and the Limits of Justice*. New York: Cambridge University Press.

1996. *Democracy's Discontent: America in Search of a Public Philosophy.* Cambridge, MA: Belknap Press of Harvard University Press.

Sarfati, H., and G. Bonoli (eds.). 2002. *Labour Market and Social Protection Reforms in International Perspective.* Aldershot, England: Ashgate.

Saunders, P. 1995. "Improving Work Incentives in a Means-Tested Welfare System." *Fiscal Studies* 16: 45–70.

2002. *The Ends and Means of Welfare: Coping with Economic and Social Change in Australia.* Cambridge: Cambridge University Press.

Scharpf, F. W. 1991. *Crisis and Choice in European Social Democracy.* Ithaca, NY: Cornell University Press.

Scharpf, F. W., and V. Schmidt (eds.). 2000. *Welfare and Work in the Open Economy.* New York: Oxford University Press.

Schmid, G., and B. Gazier (eds.). 2002. *The Dynamics of Full Employment: Social Integration through Transitional Labour Markets.* Northampton, MA: Edward Elgar.

Schmidt, V. 2000. "Values and Discourse in the Politics of Adjustment," in Scharpf and Schmidt (eds.).

2001. "The Politics of Economic Adjustment in France and Britain." *Journal of European Public Policy* 8: 247–264.

Schmidt, V., et al. (ed.). 2005. *Public Discourse and Welfare State Reform: The Social Democratic Experience.* Amsterdam: Mets & Schilt.

Schmidtke, O. (ed.). 2002. *The Third Way Transformation of Social Democracy: Normative Claims and Policy Initiatives in the 21st Century.* Aldershot, England: Ashgate.

Schröter, E. 2004. "How Many Third Ways? Comparing the British, French and German Left in Government." Institute of European Studies working paper, University of California, Berkeley.

Schupp, J., and H. Solga (eds.). 2000. *Niedrig Entlohnt = Niedrig Qualifiziert? Chancen und Risiken eines Nniedriglohnsektors in Deutschland.* Conference proceedings, May 11–12, 2000, Max Planck Institution for Human Development Berlin (CD-ROM). Berlin, DIW.

Schwartz, H. 1998. "Social Democracy Going Down or Down Under: Institutions, Internationalized Capital, and Indebted States." *Comparative Politics* 30: 253–272.

2000. "Internationalization and Two Liberal Welfare States: Australia and New Zealand," in Scharpf and Schmidt (eds.).

Scruggs, L. 2004. Welfare State Entitlements Data Set: A Comparative Institutional Analysis of Eighteen Welfare States, Version 1.1.

Seeleib-Kaiser, M. 2002. "A Dual Transformation of the German Welfare State?" *West European Politics* 25: 25–48.

2004a. "Germany: Still a Conservative Welfare State?" Paper presented at the Conference of Europeanists, Chicago.

2004b. "Continuity or Change: Red-Green Social Policy after Sixteen Years of Christian Democratic Rule," in Reutter (ed.).

Seeleib-Kaiser, M., and T. Fleckenstein. 2007. "Discourse, Learning and Welfare State Change: The Case of German Labour Market Reforms." *Social Policy & Administration* 41: 427–448.

Seeleib-Kaiser, M., S. van Dyk, and M. Roggenhamp. 2004. "What Do Parties Want? An Analysis of Programmatic Social Policy Aims in Austria, Germany, and the Netherlands." Paper presented at the 2d annual ESPAnet Conference, Oxford.

Seifert, H. 1998. "Working Time in Germany: Searching for New Ways." *TRANSFER* 4: 621–640.

Sferza, S. 2002. "The Third Way in France: Tertium non Datur?" in Schmidtke (ed.).

Shannon, P. 1991. *Social Policy.* Auckland: Oxford University Press.

Shapiro, D. 2007. *Is the Welfare State Justified?* New York: Cambridge University Press.

Shaver, S. 2002. "Australian Welfare Reform: From Citizenship to Supervision." *Social Policy & Administration* 36: 331–345.

Shaver, S., and P. Saunders. 1995. "Two Papers on Citizenship and Basic Income." SPRC discussion paper, University of New South Wales, Sydney.

Simon, H. 1955. "A Behavioral Model of Rational Choice." *Quarterly Journal of Economics* 69: 99–118.

Sinfield, A. 2002. "Taxation and Labour Market Entry," in Sarfati and Bonoli (eds.).

Skevik, A. 2005. "Women's Citizenship in the Time of Activation: The Case of Lone Mothers in 'Needs-Based' Welfare States." *Social Politics* 12: 42–66.

Skocpol, T. 1979. *States and Social Revolutions: A Comparative Analysis of France, Russia, and China.* Cambridge: Cambridge University Press.

    1992. *Protecting Soldiers and Mothers: The Political Origins of Social Policy in the United States.* Cambridge, MA: Harvard University Press.

Smyth, P. 2002. "British and European Influence on the 'Australian Way' from the 1980s." *Social Policy & Administration* 36: 426–442.

Snels, B. 1999. *Politics in the Dutch Economy: The Economics of Institutional Interaction.* Aldershot, England: Ashgate.

Solem, P. E., and E. Overbye. 2004. "Norway: Still High Employment among Older Workers," in Maltby et al. (eds.).

Spicker, P. 2002. "France," in Dixon and Scheurell (eds.).

Spies, H., and R. van Berkel. 2001. "Workfare in the Netherlands: Young Unemployed People and the Jobseekers' Employment Act," in Lødemel and Trickey (eds.).

Spiess, C. K., and G. G. Wagner. 2003. "Why Are Day Care Vouchers an Effective and Efficient Instrument to Combat Child Poverty in Germany?" in Krause, Bäcker, and Hanesch (eds.).

Spoonley, P. 2004. "Is Non-standard Work Becoming Standard? Trends and Issues." *New Zealand Journal of Employment Relations* 29: 3–24.

Stephens, J. D. 1979. *The Transition from Capitalism to Socialism.* London: Macmillan.

    1996. "The Scandinavian Welfare States: Achievements, Crisis, and Prospects," in Esping-Andersen (ed.).

Stigter, A. I. 1997. "Dutch Experiences in Reforming Social Insurance and Implementing Active Labour Market Policy in 1987–1995." ALEERT research memoranda, Vrije Universiteit.

Stjernø, S. 2005. *Solidarity in Europe.* New York: Cambridge University Press.

St. John, S. 2004. "Family Assistance for the Young: 1980–2008." Policy discussion paper No. 25, Auckland: Department of Economics, Auckland University.

St. John, S., and D. Craig. 2004. "Cut Price Kids: Does the 2004 'Working for Families' Budget Work for Children?" Auckland: Child Poverty Action Group.

St. John, S., and K. Rankin. 2002. "Entrenching the Welfare Mess." Policy discussion paper No. 24. Auckland: Department of Economics, Auckland University.

Stokke, O. S., and O. Tunander (eds.). 1994. *The Barents Region: Cooperation in Arctic Europe.* London: Sage.

Streeck, W., and K. Thelen (eds.). 2005. *Beyond Continuity: Institutional Change in Advanced Political Economies.* Oxford: Oxford University Press.

Stutchbury, M. 1990. "Macroeconomic Policy," in Jennett and Stewart (eds.).

Swank, D. 2002. *Global Capital, Political Institutions, and Policy Change in Developed Welfare States.* New York: Cambridge University Press.

Sykes, R., B. Palier, and P. Prior (eds.). 2001. *Globalization and European Welfare States: Challenges and Change.* New York: Palgrave Macmillan.

Taylor-Gooby, P. 2002. "The Silver Age of the Welfare State: Perspectives on Resilience." *Journal of Social Policy* 31: 597–621.

Taylor-Gooby, P. (ed.). 2004. *New Risks, New Welfare: The Transformation of the European Welfare State.* New York: Oxford University Press.

Taylor-Gooby, P., and T. P. Larsen. 2004. "The UK: A Test Case for the Liberal Welfare State?" in Taylor-Gooby (ed.).

Teipen, C., and M. Kohli. 2004. "Early Retirement in Germany," in Maltby et al. (eds.).

Temkin, L. S. 1993. *Inequality.* New York: Oxford University Press.

Thelen, K. 2004. *How Institutions Evolve: The Political Economy of Skills in Germany, Britain, the United States, and Japan.* New York: Cambridge University Press.

Théret, B., and J. Barbier. 2002. "On the Endogenous Capacity of National Systems of Social Protection to Address the Globalization Challenge – the French Case." Paper presented at the COST A15 Conference, Oslo.

Thomson, S. 2000. *The Social Democratic Dilemma: Ideology, Governance, and Globalization.* New York: St. Martin's.

Timonen, V. 2003. *Restructuring the Welfare State: Globalization and Social Policy Reform in Finland and Sweden.* Northampton, MA: Edward Elgar.

  2004. "New Risks: Are They Still New for the Nordic Welfare States?" in Taylor-Gooby (ed.).

Torfing, J. 1998. *Politics, Regulation and the Modern Welfare State.* New York: St. Martin's.

  1999. "Workfare with Welfare: Recent Reforms of the Danish Welfare State." *Journal of European Social Policy* 9: 5–28.

  2001. "Path-Dependent Danish Welfare Reforms: The Contribution of the New Institutionalisms to Understanding Evolutionary Change." *Scandinavian Political Studies* 24: 277–309.

Trickey, H. 2001. "Comparing Workfare Programs: Features and Implications," in Lødemel and Trickey (eds.).

Trickey, H., and R. Walker. 2001. "Steps to Compulsion with British Labour Market Policies," in Lødemel and Trickey (eds.).

Trommel, W., and B. de Vroom. 2002. "New Institutional Forms of Welfare Production: Some Implication for Citizenship," in Goul Andersen and Jensen (eds.).

Tuck, R. 2008. *Free Riding*. Cambridge, MA: Harvard University Press.

Ughetto, P., and D. Bouget. 2002. "France: The Impossible New Social Compromise?" in Goul Andersen et al. (eds.).

Vail, M. 1999. "The Better Part of Valour: The Politics of French Welfare Reform." *Journal of European Social Policy* 9: 311–329.

2002. "Negotiating Density: The Return of the State in German Social-Protection Reform." Paper presented at the 13th International Conference of Europeanists, Chicago.

2003. "Rethinking Corporatism and Consensus: The Dilemmas of German Social-Protection Reform." *West European Politics* 26: 41–66.

Vallentyne, P. 2002. "Brute Luck, Option Luck, and Equality of Initial Opportunities." *Ethics* 112: 529–557.

van Berkel, R., and J. de Schampheleire. 2001. "The Activation Approach in Dutch and Belgian Social Policies." *Journal of European Area Studies* 9: 27–41.

van Berkel, R., H. Cohen, and A. Dekker. 1999. "Regulating the Unemployed: From Protection to Participation," in Lind and Møller (eds.).

van der Veen, R., and W. Trommel. 1999. "Managed Liberalization of the Dutch Welfare State: A Review and Analysis of the Reform of the Dutch Social Security System, 1985–1998." *Governance* 12: 289–310.

van Kersbergen, K. 1995. *Social Capitalism: A Study of Christian Democracy and the Welfare State*. London: Routledge.

van Oorschot, W. 1998. "The Reconstruction of the Dutch Social Security System." CCWS working paper, University of Aarhus.

1999. "Work, Work, Work: Labour Market Participation Policies in the Netherlands, 1970–2000." Paper presented at the conference "The Modernization of Social Protection and Employment," Florence.

2002a. "Labour Market Participation in the Netherlands: Trends, Policies and Outcomes," in Goul Andersen et al. (eds.).

2002b. "Miracle or Nightmare? A Critical Review of Dutch Activation Policies and Their Outcomes." *Journal of Social Policy* 31: 399–420.

2004. "Flexible Work and Flexicurity Policies in the Netherlands." *TRANSFER* 4: 208–225.

van Oorschot, W., and P. Abrahamson, 2003. "The Dutch and Danish Miracles Revisited: A Critical Discussion of Activation Policies in Two Small Welfare States". *Social Policy & Administration* 37: 288–304.

van Waarden, F., and G. Lehmbruch (eds.). 2003. *Renegotiating the Welfare State: Flexible Adjustment through Corporatist Concertation*. London: Routledge.

Visser, J., and A. Hemerijck. 1997. *"A Dutch Miracle": Job Growth, Welfare Reform and Corporatism in the Netherlands*. Amsterdam: Amsterdam University Press.

Visser, J. 2001. "Negotiated Flexibility in Working Time and Labour Market Transitions: The Case of the Netherlands." Amsterdam Institute for Advanced Labour Studies working paper, Amsterdam.

   2002. "The First Part-Time Economy in the World: A Model to be Followed?" *Journal of European Social Policy* 12: 23–42.

Voet, R. 1998. "Citizenship and Female Participation," in Bussemaker and Voet (eds.).

Voges, W., H. Jacobs and H. Trickey. 2001. "Uneven Development: Local Authorities and Workfare in Germany," in Lødemel and Trickey (eds.).

Wadensjo, E. 2002. "Active Strategies for Older Workers in Sweden," in Jepsen, Foden, and Hutsebaut (eds.).

Walker, A. 2002. "Active Strategies for Older Workers in the UK," in Jepsen, Foden, and Hutsebaut (eds.).

Walker, R., and M. Wiseman. 2003. "Making Welfare Work: UK Activation Policies under New Labour." *International Social Security Review* 56: 3–29.

Walsh, P. 1989. "A Family Fight? Industrial Relations Reform under the Fourth Labour Government," in Easton (ed.).

Walsh, P., and P. Brosnan. 1999. "Redesigning Industrial Relations: The Employment Contracts Act and Its Consequences," in Boston, Dalziel, and St. John (eds.).

Walzer, M. 1983. *Spheres of Justice: A Defense of Pluralism and Equality.* New York: Basic Books.

Wanna, J. 1994. "Can the State Manage the Macroeconomy?" in Bell and Head (eds.).

Warhurst, J., and J. Stewart. 1989. "Manufacturing Industry Policies," in Head and Patience (eds.).

Watts, R. 1989. "In Fractured Times: The Accord and Social Policy under Hawke, 1983–87," in Kennedy (ed.).

Weber, M. [1922]. 1978. *Economy and Society: An Outline of Interpretive Sociology.* Berkeley: University of California Press.

Weinert, P. et al. (eds.). 2001. *Employability: From Theory to Practice.* London: Transaction.

Weinkopf, C. 2003. "Social Protection and Activation for the Unemployed," in Krause, Bäcker, and Hanesch (eds.).

White, S. (ed.). 2001. *New Labour: The Progressive Future.* New York: Palgrave Macmillan.

Whiteford, P. 1994. "Income Distribution and Social Policy under a Reformist Government: The Australian Experience." *Policy & Politics* 22: 239–255.

Whitwell, J.L. 1990. "The Rogernomics Monetarist Experiment," in Holland and Boston (eds.).

Whyman, P. 2003. *Sweden and the "Third Way": A Macroeconomic Evaluation.* Burlington, VT: Ashgate.

Wickham-Crowley, T. 1992. *Guerillas and Revolutions in Latin America: A Comparative Study of Insurgents and Regimes Since 1956.* Princeton, NJ: Princeton University Press.

Wilthagen, T. 1998. "Flexicurity: A New Paradigm for Labour Market Policy Reform?" Flexicurity Research Program research paper, Tilburg University.

2003. "The Flexibility-Security Nexus: New Approaches to Regulating Employment and Labour Markets." Flexicurity Research Program research paper, Tilburg University.

2004. "Flexibility and Social Protection." Amsterdam Institute for Advanced Labour Studies working paper, University of Amsterdam.

Wilthagen, T., and F. Tros. 2003. "Dealing with the 'Flexibility-Security-Nexus': Institutions, Strategies, Opportunities and Barriers." Amsterdam Institute for Advanced Labour Studies research paper, University of Amsterdam.

Wood, S. 2001. "Education and Training: Tensions at the Heart of the British Third Way," in White (ed.).

Wren, A. 2001. "The Challenge of De-industrialization: Divergent Ideological Responses to Welfare State Reform," in Ebbinghaus and Manow (eds.).

Wright, S., A. Kopac, and G. Slater, 2004. "Continuities within Paradigmatic Change: Activation, Social Policies and Citizenship in the Context of Welfare Reform in Slovenia and the UK." *European Societies* 6: 511–534.

Zeitlin, J., and D. Trubek (eds.). 2003. *Governing Work and Welfare in a New Economy: European and American Experiments.* Oxford: Oxford University Press.

Zwinkels, W., and M. Peter. 2001. "Flexicurity in the Netherlands," in Weinert, P. et al. (eds.).

Index

active labor market policies, 37, 102–3,
  152–4
  measurement of expenditure, 6
  Nordic precedents, 12, 55, 68–9, 70,
    112
Anderton, Jim, 82
Arneson, Richard, 13, 16, 74
Australia
  Accord, 146, 233, 283, 302–5
  ACTU, 304
  asset-based welfare, 235
  Australian Social Security Review,
    80, 147
  child poverty, 234–5
  combating new social risks, 170, 232
  corporatist institutions, 145,
    302–305
  demand side job creation, 150
  economic deregulation, 301
  enterprise bargaining, 302, 305
  Family Allowance Supplement, 235
  fiscal welfare, 235
  Fraser coalition government, 97, 169,
    233, 235
  Howard coalition government, 148,
    305
  influence of liberalism, 79
  Job Compact, 147
  labor market flexibility, 147
  means-testing, 64, 169, 232–4
  measures for long term
    unemployment, 146–7
  Medicare, 169, 231–3, 304
  rising unemployment, 97–8
  social exclusion, 98
  social expenditure, 98, 231
  Superannuation, 146
  tax reform, 302
  wage moderation, 303
  Work for the Dole, 148
  work/family policies, 168–70
  Working Nation, 80, 147–50
  Workplace Relations Act, 1996,
    305

Balladur, Édouard, 93
Baumol's cost disease, 14
Berlin, Isaiah, 15, 70
Bernstein, Eduard, 8, 68
Blair, Tony, 77–9
Blewett, Neil, 81
Brown, Gordon, 77, 229
Buchanan, James, 15

Caygill, David, 81
centralized decentralization, 274,
  287–288, 312
Clark, Helen, 82, 152
Clement, Wolfgang, 75
Cohen, G. A., 13

collective action
  contribution from organization, 23
  failure, 5, 36, 244, 258, 309
  role in path dependency, 30, 188,
    317
communitarianism, 17, 71–2, 75, 78,
  80, 206, 228, 246
compensation
  anticipatory, 38, 243–4, 263–4,
    266
  reactionary, 38, 199–200, 241–3,
    265
Comte, Auguste, 7
corporatism
  contribution to collective action, 36,
    178, 259, 264, 322–3
  contribution to job creation, 269–70,
    311–13
  its contingent role, 43, 264
cost externalization of economic
  adjustment, 57, 61, 217, 252, 264
Crosland, Anthony, 77

den Uyl, Joop, 72
Denmark
  1994 labor market reform, 104–8,
    200, 244
  bourgeois parties, 88, 206, 270
  combating new social risks,
    108–10, 206
  Confederation of Danish Employers,
    273
  corporatist institutions, 111, 202,
    273–5
  early retirement, 247–9
  economic prudence, 88, 270
  fiscal welfare, 204
  free collective bargaining, 273
  golden triangle, 186
  job rotation, 246
  labor market measures, 275
  leave schemes, 244–7
  LO, 67, 248, 274
  policy decentralization, 107
  Radical Liberal Party, 68
  rising unemployment, 86–9
  sanctions, 204
  September compromise, 53
  social assistance, 203–4
  social democratic ideological
    change, 68
  structural unemployment, 67, 110
  tax reform, 271–3
  training, 106, 205
  unemployment benefits, 53, 105,
    200–3, 205–7
  wage moderation, 88, 274
  Youth Allowances Scheme, 104
Dennis, Bengt, 69
dilemma, electoral
  alliance, 69, 73, 75
  tradeoff, 11, 315
Douglas, Roger, 81, 100
Durkheim, Émile, 7
Dworkin, Ronald, 13, 15, 74, 144

early exit pathways. *See* compensation,
  reactionary
egalitarianism
  desert, 16
  equality of what?, 13, 15,
    17, 74
  its instrumental nature, 9, 13
  Leveling Down, 9, 16, 77
  prioritarianism, 16, 18, 70, 74, 76,
    77, 236, 265, 316
Erlander, Tag, 69
Esping-Andersen, Gøsta, 70
Etzioni, Amitai, 17, 78
European Central Bank, 268, 293
European Monetary Union (EMU),
  270, 293
externalities of organization, 4, 22–3,
  192, 321
  atypical workers, 23–4, 154, 175,
    230, 321
  its contingent nature, 25, 321
  low-skilled or unemployed, 24–5,
    153–4, 213, 321

Fabianism, 12, 76, 79
Feldt, Kjell-Olof, 69
flexicurity, 38, 175–6, 188–90
Foot, Michael, 76

France
  35-hour week, 182–3, 291
  Aubry Plan, 130
  combating new social risks, 128, 224
  competitive disinflation, 288, 290, 293
  corporatist institutions, 134, 183, 291–2
  early retirement, 259–60
  economic deregulation, 289
  Employment Premium, 159
  fiscal welfare, 224, 290
  Gaullist governments, 92, 220, 259
  General Social Contribution, 74, 223, 290
  hybrid welfare, 60
  labor market measures, 221
  Minimum Income of Insertion (RMI), 74, 127–9, 133, 222–3, 242, 290
  Plan to Help the Return to Employment (PARE), 134
  rising unemployment, 92–3
  Road to Employment (TRACE), 223
  social exclusion, 73, 220, 224
  social security contributions, 159
  statism, 59, 74, 131–3, 183, 221, 223, 225, 291
  training, 133, 259
  unions, 128, 134, 223, 259, 291
  U-turn, 92, 288
  wage moderation, 290
  work/family policies, 159
Friedman, Milton, 15

Galston, William, 17, 78
Germany
  1989 Berlin program, 75
  Alliance for Jobs, 136, 138, 261, 295
  Bad Godesberg, 74
  combating new social risks, 139, 163, 227
  corporatist institutions, 139, 185, 228, 261, 295–6
  counterproductive macroeconomic policy, 293
  early retirement, 260–1
  employment protection, 185–6
  Hartz Commissions, 136–7
  Hartz IV and V, 137, 226
  IG Metall, 261, 295–6
  Job-AQTIV, 137–9
  labor market measures, 94
  measures for young unemployed, 135–6
  part time employment, 184
  reunification, 94
  rising unemployment, 93–5
  social security contributions, 160
  social security measures, 226, 228
  Tarifautonomie, 60, 184, 295
  tax reform, 292
  training, 138
  wage moderation, 295
  work/family policies, 160–3
  Youth with a Perspective (JUMP), 135
Ghent system, 53–4, 57, 202, 208, 213, 215
Giddens, Anthony, 18, 67, 78
globalization, of finance, 268

Harvester Judgment, 63, 79
Hattersley, Roy, 77
Hawke, Bob, 147, 231, 233, 301
Hayek, Friedrich, 15
Higgins, Henry, 79
Hirschman, Albert, 33, 320
Hobson, J. A., 79
Howard, John, 79, 149

ideology, Christian democratic
  attitude towards egalitarianism, 9, 20
  response to economic crisis, 19–20, 192, 265
  subsidiarity, 8
ideology, social democratic, 7–8, 32–3
insider-outsider divide
  emergence, 22, 220, 224, 242
  implications for social democracy, 22, 25, 191–7, 321–2

institutions
    compared with ideologies, 32–3
    definition, 29
    negative returns, 4, 314, 317
    positive returns, 30–1
in-work incentives, 38, 155, 173–5

Jaurés, Jean, 74
Jospin, Lionel, 73, 129
Juppé, Alain, 93

Kautsky, Karl, 8
Keating, Paul, 80, 146, 231
Kenworthy's Wage Coordination
    Score, 274
Kok, Wim, 255
Korpi, Walter, 70

Lafontaine, Oscar, 75–6
lagged dependent variable, 195
Lange, David, 81
Langmore, John, 80
libertarians, 15
    negative and positive liberty, 15, 70
Lindbeck, Assar, 70
logic of public evils, 33–4, 317–18, 320
    its contingent nature, 42, 317

MacIntyre, Alasdair, 17, 77
Macmurray, John, 78
Maharey, Steve, 82
Marshall, T. H., 80
Marx, Karl, 8
method of agreement, 49
method of difference, 50
Myrdal, Gunnar, 68

Netherlands, the
    A New Course, 286
    Christian democratic welfare,
        59, 72
    combating new social risks, 124,
        126–127
    corporatist institutions, 253–5
    debate on female participation, 71–3
    disability and sickness benefits, 58,
        216, 252–6

    Early Retirement Scheme (VUT),
        257
    early retirement, 256–8
    economic prudence, 283
    family/work policies, 158
    female employment, 182
    Flex Act of 1999, 178–9, 180
    Jobseekers' Employment Act, 126
    labor market measures, 124–7, 219,
        258
    Liberal Party, 72
    Lubbers coalition governments, 91,
        123, 216, 252, 286
    measures for the young unemployed,
        124
    Melkert job schemes, 125
    part time employment, 179,
        180–2, 286
    price versus volume policy, 91
    PvdA and the feminists, 72, 158
    rising unemployment, 91, 286
    Scientific Council for Government
        Policy, 71
    social assistance, 218
    social exclusion, 91–92
    social security reform, 216–18
    tax reform, 284, 287
    tax wedge, 284
    wage moderation, 285, 287
    Wassenaar agreement, 58, 178, 216,
        285–7
New Politics of the Welfare State. *See*
welfare state: retrenchment
literature
new social risks
    emergence, 22, 321
    risk preference, 24, 321
New Zealand
    ACCESS, 151
    arbitration institutions, 64, 239,
        307–310
    child poverty, 240
    community care, 152
    economic deregulation, 236, 305
    Employment Contracts Act of 1991,
        309
    enterprise bargaining, 308

fifth Labour government policies,
  152, 170, 240, 306–7
fiscal expansion, 306–7
fiscal welfare, 237–9
fourth Labour government policies,
  150–2, 235, 305
In Work Payment, 172
Labour Relations Act of 1987,
  308
National governments, 99, 239
neoliberal hijack of Labour Party,
  81–2, 150, 316
rising unemployment, 98–100
state intervention, 81, 99–100
tax reform, 238
unions, 308
wage moderation, 307–9
work/family policies, 171–2
Workforce, 2010, 82
Working for Families, 171, 240
nominal and ordinal analysis, 50
Norway
  An Inclusive Working Life, 251
  arbeidslinje, 70, 118, 212
  bargaining institutions, 56
  bourgeois parties, 71, 123, 280
  combating new social risks, 120
  corporatist institutions, 281–2
  counterproductive macroeconomic
    policy, 280
  disability and sickness insurance,
    251
  early retirement, 250
  industrial policy, 57
  labor market flexibility, 56, 176,
    186, 190
  labor market measures, 118–22,
    283
  LO, 281
  NAF, 282
  oil sector, 215, 280
  rising unemployment, 90, 122, 215,
    280–1
  sanctions, 214
  social assistance, 120, 212–13
  Solidarity Alternative, 119, 282
  training, 119, 121, 214

unemployment benefits, 211–15
wage moderation, 90, 281–3
Nozick, Robert, 9, 15

Olson, Mancur, 23, 320
Orthodox Marxism, 12, 73

Palme, Olof, 69
panel-corrected standard errors,
  194
Parfit, Derek, 9, 77
path dependency
  in third way policies, 46–8, 101,
    153, 165, 174, 188, 242–4,
    266–7
  social mechanism, 3, 30–32, 317
Peacock, Andrew, 79
policy paradigm
  compared with policy implementa-
    tion, 34, 318
  third way paradigm, 42
Prebble, Richard, 81

Rawls, John, 9, 16, 77
Rehn-Meidner model, 12, 55, 69, 112
robust-cluster standard errors, 195
Rocard, Michel, 73, 92, 128
Roemer, John, 13

Sandel, Michael, 17, 77
satisficying, 269
Scholz, Olaf, 75
Schröder, Gerhard, 75
Selznick, Philip, 78
Smit, Joke, 72
social protection
  active, 101, 191–7, 318
  passive, 198–9, 264–7, 319
social wage, 63–4, 145, 233, 239, 300,
  309
solidaristic wage policy, 12, 55, 67, 69
solidarity
  difference from charity, 11
  difference from communitarianism,
    17
  evolution and extension, 2, 10, 12,
    18, 315

solidarity (*cont.*)
  heterogeneous background, 11–12,
      14, 315
  homogeneous background, 10, 12
  in the Antipodes, 13
  Marxist, 8, 10
  mechanical and organic, 8, 10
  social and Christian democratic
      interpretations, 7, 8
Stability and Growth Pact, 268, 290,
    292–293
staples economies, 65
Sweden
  Activity Guarantee, 114, 250
  Bank of Sweden, 70
  bourgeois parties, 89, 113, 210, 279
  combating new social risks, 115
  competitive exchange rate, 277
  corporatist institutions, 55, 187,
      278–280
  currency devaluation, 90, 276
  early retirement, 249–50
  employment protection, 187–8,
      190
  intertemporal pooling in fiscal
      policy, 276
  labor market measures, 114–18
  LO, 69–70, 208–9, 278
  measures for the young unemployed,
      118
  National Labor Market Board
      (AMS), 112, 278
  rising unemployment, 89–90
  SAF, 278
  sickness/injury insurance, 209
  social services, 210
  tax reform, 276
  third road economic policy, 70, 89,
      275–276
  unemployment benefits, 207–9,
      210
  Uppsala model, 207
  wage moderation, 279
  welfare structure, 54

Tam, Henry, 78
Tawney, R. H., 77, 79

Temkin, Larry S., 9
third way
  as an analytic construct, 18–19, 20
  core strategies, 37–40
  economic context, 40–1, 268–9,
      310–13, 319
  philosophical principles, 20
time invariant independent variables,
    195

unemployment
  causes, 14, 84
  contribution to changing solidarity,
      13, 18, 65, 69– 70, 75, 80, 315
  long term, 84, 189, 266
  scar effects, 266
United Kingdom, the
  asset-based welfare, 231
  Bank of England, 296
  Beveridge universalism, 62
  Child Tax Credit, 165
  Christian socialists, 76
  combating new social risks, 164
  compulsion, 144
  Conservative governments, 95, 165,
      230, 297
  corporatist institutions, 145,
      299–301
  deregulation, 96
  disability and sickness benefits, 262
  early retirement, 262
  economic prudence, 296
  fiscal welfare, 229–31, 298
  Gateway Period, 141, 166, 262
  Individual Action Plan, 141
  intertemporal pooling in fiscal
      policy, 297–9
  Jobcenter Plus, 262
  measures for the young unemployed,
      142
  Monetary Policy Commitee, 297
  National Childcare Strategy, 168
  National Insurance, 63, 298
  National Minimum Wage, 164
  New Deal, 140–5, 167, 262
  retrenchment, 96
  rising unemployment, 95–7

social inclusion, 77, 230
training, 145
wage moderation, 300
work/family policies, 164–8
Working Families' Tax Credit,
    165–7

Vallentyne, Peter, 13
Vogel, Jochen, 75

wage earners' welfare state, 63–5, 146,
    239, 309

Walzer, Michael, 17
Weber, Max, 8
welfare state
    economic constraint, 27
    power resources theory, 27, 43–6,
        101, 241–2, 263–6, 268,
        320
    retrenchment literature, 27–8,
        46
Wigforss, Ernst, 8, 68
Williamson, John, 81
Willis, Ralph, 80